NEW PERSPECTIVES ON
Microsoft® Excel® 2013

BRIEF

June Jamrich Parsons
Dan Oja
Roy Ageloff
Patrick Carey

Carol A. DesJardins
St. Clair County Community College

CENGAGE
Learning·

Australia · Brazil · Japan · Korea · Mexico · Singapore · Spain · United Kingdom · United States

New Perspectives on Microsoft Excel 2013, Brief

Director of Development: Marah Bellegarde

Executive Editor: Donna Gridley

Associate Acquisitions Editor: Amanda Lyons

Product Development Manager: Leigh Hefferon

Senior Product Manager: Kathy Finnegan

Product Manager: Julia Leroux-Lindsey

Developmental Editor: Robin M. Romer

Editorial Assistant: Melissa Stehler

Brand Manager: Elinor Gregory

Market Development Managers: Kristie Clark, Gretchen Swann

Senior Content Project Manager: Jennifer Goguen McGrail

Composition: GEX Publishing Services

Art Director: GEX Publishing Services

Text Designer: Althea Chen

Cover Art: © ksyutoken/Shutterstock

Copyeditor: Suzanne Huizenga

Proofreader: Lisa Weidenfeld

Indexer: Alexandra Nickerson

For product information and technology assistance, contact us at
Cengage Learning Customer & Sales Support, 1-800-354-9706

For permission to use material from this text or product, submit all requests online at **www.cengage.com/permissions**
Further permissions questions can be emailed to
permissionrequest@cengage.com

Some of the product names and company names used in this book have been used for identification purposes only and may be trademarks or registered trademarks of their respective manufacturers and sellers.

Microsoft and the Office logo are either registered trademarks or trademarks of Microsoft Corporation in the United States and/or other countries. Cengage Learning is an independent entity from the Microsoft Corporation, and not affiliated with Microsoft in any manner.

Disclaimer: Any fictional data related to persons or companies or URLs used throughout this book is intended for instructional purposes only. At the time this book was printed, any such data was fictional and not belonging to any real persons or companies.

Library of Congress Control Number: 2013936774
ISBN-13: 978-1-285-16939-2
ISBN-10: 1-285-16939-5

Cengage Learning
200 First Stamford Place, 4th Floor
Stamford, CT 06902
USA

Cengage Learning is a leading provider of customized learning solutions with office locations around the globe, including Singapore, the United Kingdom, Australia, Mexico, Brazil, and Japan. Locate your local office at: **www.cengage.com/global**

Cengage Learning products are represented in Canada by Nelson Education, Ltd.

For your course and learning solutions, visit **www.cengage.com**

Purchase any of our products at your local college store or at our preferred online store **www.cengagebrain.com**

ProSkills Icons © 2014 Cengage Learning.

Printed in the United States of America
1 2 3 4 5 6 7 19 18 17 16 15 14 13

Preface

The New Perspectives Series' critical-thinking, problem-solving approach is the ideal way to prepare students to transcend point-and-click skills and take advantage of all that Microsoft Office 2013 has to offer.

In developing the New Perspectives Series, our goal was to create books that give students the software concepts and practical skills they need to succeed beyond the classroom. We've updated our proven case-based pedagogy with more practical content to make learning skills more meaningful to students.

With the New Perspectives Series, students understand *why* they are learning *what* they are learning, and are fully prepared to apply their skills to real-life situations.

About This Book

"This text presents students with scenarios that reflect real-world Excel problems they must analyze and solve. I recommend my students keep this text to use as a reference when they attempt to solve similar problems in the future."

— Peggy Foreman
Texas State University

This book provides essential coverage of Microsoft Excel 2013, and includes the following:

- Detailed, hands-on instruction of Microsoft Excel 2013 basics, including creating and formatting a workbook; working with formulas and functions; creating charts, sparklines, and data bars; and formatting printed worksheets
- Coverage of important spreadsheet concepts, including workbook design, order of precedence in formulas, function syntax, and absolute and relative cell references
- Exploration of features new to Excel 2013, including Flash Fill, the Quick Analysis tool, and the recommended charts tool

New for this edition!

- Each tutorial has been updated with new case scenarios throughout, which provide a rich and realistic context for students to apply the concepts and skills presented.
- A new Troubleshoot type of Case Problem, in which certain steps of the exercise require students to identify and correct errors—which are intentionally placed in the files students work with—promotes problem solving and critical thinking.
- The new "Managing Your Files" tutorial at the beginning of the book provides students with a solid foundation in organizing their files and folders.

System Requirements

This book assumes a typical installation of Microsoft Excel 2013 and Microsoft Windows 8 Professional. (You can also complete the material in this text using another version of Windows 8 or using Windows 7. You may see only minor differences in how some windows look.) The browser used for any steps that require a browser is Internet Explorer 10.

The New Perspectives Approach

Context

Each tutorial begins with a problem presented in a "real-world" case that is meaningful to students. The case sets the scene to help students understand what they will do in the tutorial.

Hands-on Approach

Each tutorial is divided into manageable sessions that combine reading and hands-on, step-by-step work. Colorful screenshots help guide students through the steps. **Trouble?** tips anticipate common mistakes or problems to help students stay on track and continue with the tutorial.

VISUAL OVERVIEW

Visual Overviews

Each session begins with a Visual Overview, a two-page spread that includes colorful, enlarged screenshots with numerous callouts and key term definitions, giving students a comprehensive preview of the topics covered in the session, as well as a handy study guide.

PROSKILLS

ProSkills Boxes and Exercises

ProSkills boxes provide guidance for how to use the software in real-world, professional situations, and related ProSkills exercises integrate the technology skills students learn with one or more of the following soft skills: decision making, problem solving, teamwork, verbal communication, and written communication.

KEY STEP

Key Steps

Important steps are highlighted in yellow with attached margin notes to help students pay close attention to completing the steps correctly and avoid time-consuming rework.

INSIGHT

InSight Boxes

InSight boxes offer expert advice and best practices to help students achieve a deeper understanding of the concepts behind the software features and skills.

TIP

Margin Tips

Margin Tips provide helpful hints and shortcuts for more efficient use of the software. The Tips appear in the margin at key points throughout each tutorial, giving students extra information when and where they need it.

REVIEW

APPLY

Assessment

Retention is a key component to learning. At the end of each session, a series of Quick Check questions helps students test their understanding of the material before moving on. Engaging end-of-tutorial Review Assignments and Case Problems have always been a hallmark feature of the New Perspectives Series. Colorful bars and headings identify the type of exercise, making it easy to understand both the goal and level of challenge a particular assignment holds.

REFERENCE

TASK REFERENCE

GLOSSARY/INDEX

Reference

Within each tutorial, Reference boxes appear before a set of steps to provide a succinct summary and preview of how to perform a task. In addition, a complete Task Reference at the back of the book provides quick access to information on how to carry out common tasks. Finally, each book includes a combination Glossary/Index to promote easy reference of material.

Our Complete System of Instruction

Coverage To Meet Your Needs
Whether you're looking for just a small amount of coverage or enough to fill a semester-long class, we can provide you with a textbook that meets your needs.

- Brief books typically cover the essential skills in just 2 to 4 tutorials.
- Introductory books build and expand on those skills and contain an average of 5 to 8 tutorials.
- Comprehensive books are great for a full-semester class, and contain 9 to 12+ tutorials.

So if the book you're holding does not provide the right amount of coverage for you, there's probably another offering available. Go to our Web site or contact your Cengage Learning sales representative to find out what else we offer.

CourseCasts – Learning on the Go. Always available…always relevant.
Want to keep up with the latest technology trends relevant to you? Visit http://coursecasts.course.com to find a library of weekly updated podcasts, CourseCasts, and download them to your mp3 player.

Ken Baldauf, host of CourseCasts, is a faculty member of the Florida State University Computer Science Department where he is responsible for teaching technology classes to thousands of FSU students each year. Ken is an expert in the latest technology trends; he gathers and sorts through the most pertinent news and information for CourseCasts so your students can spend their time enjoying technology, rather than trying to figure it out. Open or close your lecture with a discussion based on the latest CourseCast.

Visit us at http://coursecasts.course.com to learn on the go!

Instructor Resources
We offer more than just a book. We have all the tools you need to enhance your lectures, check students' work, and generate exams in a new, easier-to-use and completely revised package. This book's Instructor's Manual, ExamView testbank, PowerPoint presentations, data files, solution files, figure files, and a sample syllabus are all available on a single CD-ROM or for downloading at http://www.cengage.com.

SAM: Skills Assessment Manager
Get your students workplace-ready with SAM, the premier proficiency-based assessment and training solution for Microsoft Office! SAM's active, hands-on environment helps students master computer skills and concepts that are essential to academic and career success.

Skill-based assessments, interactive trainings, business-centric projects, and comprehensive remediation engage students in mastering the latest Microsoft Office programs on their own, allowing instructors to spend class time teaching. SAM's efficient course setup and robust grading features provide faculty with consistency across sections. Fully interactive MindTap Readers integrate market-leading Cengage Learning content with SAM, creating a comprehensive online student learning environment.

Acknowledgments

We would like to thank the many people whose invaluable contributions made this book possible. First, sincere thanks go to our reviewers: Will Demeré, Michigan State University; Peggy Foreman, Texas State University; Martha Huggins, Pitt Community College; Steve Luzier, Fortis Institute; and Paul Smith, Brown Mackie College. At Cengage Learning we would like to thank Donna Gridley, Executive Editor for the New Perspectives Series; Leigh Hefferon, Product Development Manager; Amanda Lyons, Associate Acquisitions Editor; Julia Leroux-Lindsey, Product Manager; Melissa Stehler, Editorial Assistant; Jennifer Goguen McGrail, Senior Content Project Manager; Chris Scriver, Manuscript Quality Assurance (MQA) Project Leader; and John Freitas, Serge Palladino, Susan Pedicini, and Susan Whalen, MQA Testers. Special thanks to Robin Romer, Developmental Editor, for her exceptional efforts in improving this text; and to Kathy Finnegan, Senior Product Manager, for keeping us on task and focused.
– June Jamrich Parsons
– Dan Oja
– Roy Ageloff
– Patrick Carey
– Carol A. DesJardins

TABLE OF CONTENTS

Managing Your Files

Organizing Files and Folders with Windows 8

OBJECTIVES

- Explore the differences between Windows 7 and Windows 8
- Plan the organization of files and folders
- Use File Explorer to view and manage libraries, folders, and files
- Open and save files
- Create folders
- Copy and move files and folders
- Compress and extract files

Case | *Savvy Traveler*

After spending a summer traveling in Italy, Matt Marino started Savvy Traveler, a travel company that organizes small tours in Europe. To market his company, Matt created flyers, brochures, webpages, and other materials that describe the tours he offers. Matt uses the Savvy Traveler office computer to locate and store photos, illustrations, and text documents he can include in his marketing materials. He recently hired you to help manage the office. To keep Matt connected to the office while traveling, he just purchased a new laptop computer running Windows 8. He is familiar with Windows 7, so he needs an overview explaining how Windows 8 is different. Matt asks you to train him on using Windows 8 to organize his files and folders. Although he has only a few files, he knows it's a good idea to set up a logical organization now so he can find his work later as he stores more files and folders on the computer.

In this tutorial, you'll explore the differences between Windows 7 and Windows 8, especially those related to file management tools. You'll also work with Matt to devise a plan for managing his files. You'll learn how Windows 8 organizes files and folders, and then create files and folders yourself and organize them on Matt's computer. You'll also use techniques to display the information you need in folder windows, and explore options for working with compressed files.

STARTING DATA FILES

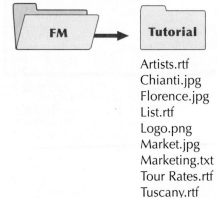

FM → Tutorial	Review	Case1	Case2
Artists.rtf	Banner.png	Fall Classes.rtf	Budget1.xlsx
Chianti.jpg	Colosseum.jpg	Instructors.txt	Budget2.xlsx
Florence.jpg	Lectures.xlsx	Kings Canyon.jpg	Report1.xlsx
List.rtf	Rome.jpg	Mojave.jpg	Report2.xlsx
Logo.png	Rome.rtf	Redwoods.jpg	Report3.xlsx
Market.jpg	Schedule.rtf	Spring Classes.rtf	Report4.xlsx
Marketing.txt	Tours.rtf	Summer Classes.rtf	Tips1.rtf
Tour Rates.rtf		Winter Classes.rtf	Tips1 – Copy.rtf
Tuscany.rtf		Workshops.rtf	Tips2.rtf
		Yosemite.jpg	Tips2 – Copy.rtf

Visual Overview:

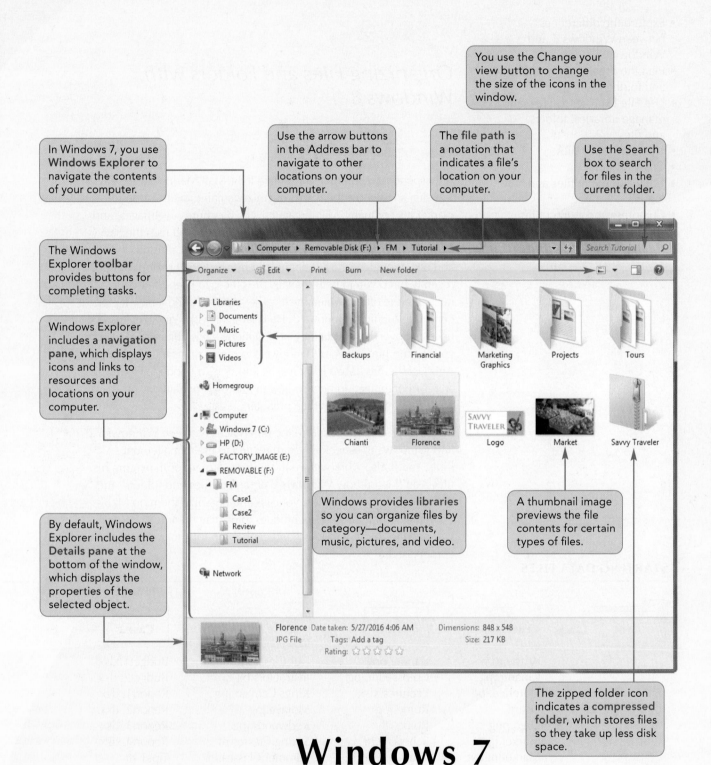

You use the Change your view button to change the size of the icons in the window.

In Windows 7, you use **Windows Explorer** to navigate the contents of your computer.

Use the arrow buttons in the Address bar to navigate to other locations on your computer.

The **file path** is a notation that indicates a file's location on your computer.

Use the Search box to search for files in the current folder.

The Windows Explorer **toolbar** provides buttons for completing tasks.

Windows Explorer includes a **navigation pane**, which displays icons and links to resources and locations on your computer.

By default, Windows Explorer includes the **Details pane** at the bottom of the window, which displays the properties of the selected object.

Windows provides **libraries** so you can organize files by category—documents, music, pictures, and video.

A thumbnail image previews the file contents for certain types of files.

The zipped folder icon indicates a **compressed folder**, which stores files so they take up less disk space.

Windows 7

Comparing Windows 7 & Windows 8

The **View tab** on the ribbon contains options for specifying how the information displays in File Explorer.

Windows provides **libraries** so you can organize files by category—documents, music, pictures, and videos.

The **Quick Access toolbar** contains buttons for viewing properties and creating a folder.

Use the arrow buttons in the Address bar to navigate to other locations on your computer.

The file **path** in the Address bar shows a file's location on your computer.

In Windows 8, you use **File Explorer** to navigate the contents of your computer.

File Explorer includes a ribbon with tools organized on tabs for working with files and folders.

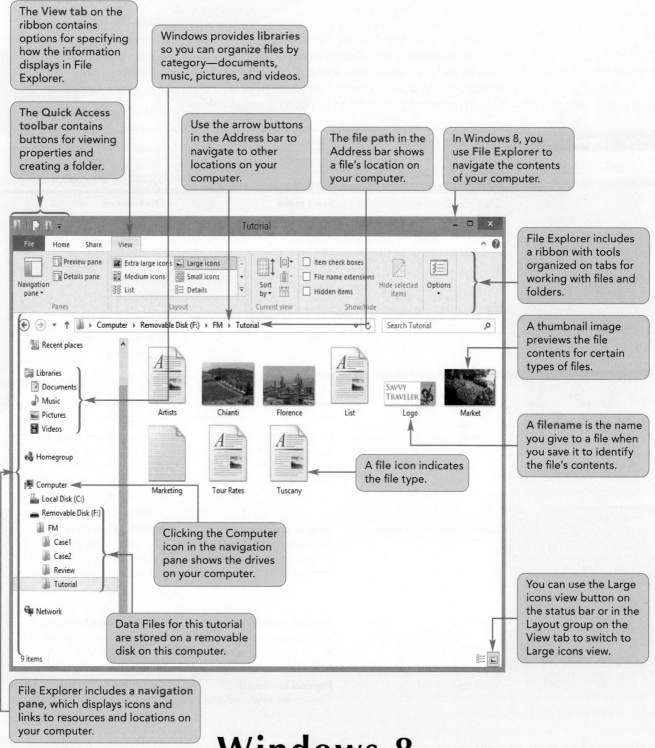

A thumbnail image previews the file contents for certain types of files.

A **filename** is the name you give to a file when you save it to identify the file's contents.

A **file icon** indicates the file type.

Clicking the Computer icon in the navigation pane shows the drives on your computer.

Data Files for this tutorial are stored on a removable disk on this computer.

File Explorer includes a **navigation pane**, which displays icons and links to resources and locations on your computer.

You can use the Large icons view button on the status bar or in the Layout group on the View tab to switch to Large icons view.

Windows 8

Exploring the Differences Between Windows 7 and Windows 8

Windows 8, the most recent version of the Microsoft operating system, is significantly different from Windows 7, the previous version. The major difference is that Windows 8 is designed for touchscreen computers such as tablets and laptops with touch-activated displays, though it runs on computers with more traditional pointing devices such as a mouse or a trackpad. This design change affects many of the fundamental Windows features you use to work on a computer. Figure 1 compares how to perform typical tasks in Windows 7 and Windows 8.

Figure 1   Comparing Windows 7 and Windows 8

Task	Windows 7 Method	Windows 8 Method
Start applications (sometimes called apps)	**Start menu** Open the Start menu by clicking the Start button.	**Start screen** The Start screen appears when you start Windows.
Access applications, documents, settings, and other resources	**Start menu** Use the Start menu, All Programs list, and Search box.	**Charms bar** The Charms bar appears when you point to the upper-right or lower-right corner of the screen, and displays buttons, called charms, for interacting with Windows 8 and accessing applications.
Select objects and commands	**Icons** Icons are small and detailed, designed for interaction with mechanical pointing devices.	**Icons and tiles** Icons and tiles are large and simplified, designed for interaction with your fingertips.
Open and work in applications	**Desktop** Applications all use a single desktop interface featuring windows and dialog boxes.	**Windows 8 and desktop** Applications use one of two interfaces: the Windows 8 interface (featuring tiles and a full-screen layout) or the desktop.
Display content out of view	**Vertical scrolling** Applications allow more vertical scrolling than horizontal scrolling.	**Horizontal scrolling** The Start screen and applications allow more horizontal scrolling than vertical scrolling to take advantage of wide-screen monitors.
Store files	**Physical storage devices** Windows primarily provides access to disks physically connected to the computer.	**Cloud storage locations** A Microsoft user account provides access to information stored online.
Enter text	**Physical keyboard** Type on the keyboard attached to the computer.	**On-screen keyboard** If your computer does not have a physical keyboard, type using the on-screen keyboard.

© 2014 Cengage Learning

Although Windows 7 introduced a few gestures for touchscreen users, Windows 8 expands the use of gestures and interactions. In Windows 8, you can use touch gestures to do nearly everything you can do with a pointing device. Figure 2 lists common Windows 8 interactions and their touch and mouse equivalents.

| Figure 2 | Windows 8 touch and mouse interactions |

Interaction	Touch Gesture	Mouse Action
Display a ScreenTip, text that identifies the name or purpose of the button	Touch and hold (or press) an object such as a button.	Point to an object such as a button.
Display an Apps bar, which displays options related to the current task and access to the Apps screen	Swipe from the top or bottom of the screen toward the center.	Right-click the bottom edge of the screen.
Display the Charms bar	Swipe from the right edge of the screen toward the center.	Point to the upper-right or lower-right corner of the screen.
Display thumbnails of open apps (the Switch List)	Swipe from the left edge of the screen toward the center.	Point to the upper-left corner of the screen, and then drag the pointer down.
Drag an object	Press and then drag.	Click, hold, and then drag.
Scroll the Start screen	Swipe from the right edge of the screen to the left.	Click the scroll arrows, or drag the scroll bar.
Select an object or perform an action such as starting an app	Tap the object.	Click the object.
Zoom	Pinch two fingers to zoom out or move the fingers apart to zoom in.	Click the Zoom button.

© 2014 Cengage Learning

Despite the substantial differences between how you interact with Windows 7 and Windows 8, the steps you follow to perform work in either operating system are the same. In a typical computer session, you start an application and open a **file**, often referred to as a document, which is a collection of data that has a name and is stored on a computer. You view, add, or change the file contents, and then save and close the file. You can complete all of these steps using Windows 7 or Windows 8. Because most of your work involves files, you need to understand how to save and organize files so you can easily find and open them when necessary.

Organizing Files and Folders

Knowing how to save, locate, and organize computer files makes you more productive when you are working with a computer. After you create a file, you can open it, edit its contents, print the file, and save it again—usually using the same application you used to create the file. You organize files by storing them in folders. A **folder** is a container for files. You need to organize files and folders so that you can find them easily and work efficiently.

A file cabinet is a common metaphor for computer file organization. As shown in Figure 3, a computer is like a file cabinet that has two or more drawers—each drawer is a storage device, or **disk**. Each disk contains folders that hold files. To make it easy to retrieve files, you arrange them logically into folders. For example, one folder might contain financial data, another might contain your creative work, and another could contain information you're gathering for an upcoming vacation.

Figure 3   **Computer as a file cabinet**

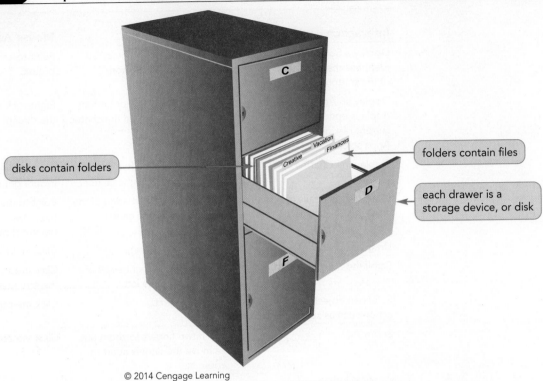

disks contain folders

folders contain files

each drawer is a storage device, or disk

© 2014 Cengage Learning

A computer can store folders and files on different types of disks, ranging from removable media—such as **USB drives** (also called USB flash drives) and digital video discs (DVDs)—to **hard disks**, or fixed disks, which are permanently housed in a computer. Hard disks are the most popular type of computer storage because they provide an economical way to store many gigabytes of data. (A **gigabyte**, or **GB**, is about 1 billion bytes, with each byte roughly equivalent to a character of data.)

To have your computer access a removable disk, you must insert the disk into a **drive**, which is a device that can retrieve and sometimes record data on a disk. A computer's hard disk is already contained in a drive inside the computer, so you don't need to insert it each time you use the computer.

A computer distinguishes one drive from another by assigning each a drive letter. The hard disk is assigned to drive C. The remaining drives can have any other letters, but are usually assigned in the order that the drives were installed on the computer—so your USB drive might be drive D or drive F.

Understanding How to Organize Files and Folders

Windows stores thousands of files in many folders on the hard disk of your computer. These are system files that Windows needs to display the Start screen and desktop, use drives, and perform other operating system tasks. To keep the system stable and to find files quickly, Windows organizes the folders and files in a hierarchy, or **file system**. At the top of the hierarchy, Windows stores folders and important files that it needs when you turn on the computer. This location is called the **root directory** and is usually drive C (the hard disk). As Figure 4 shows, the root directory contains all the other folders and files on the computer. The figure also shows that folders can contain other folders. An effectively organized computer contains a few folders in the root directory, and those folders contain other folders, also called **subfolders**.

| Figure 4 | Organizing folders and files on a hard disk |

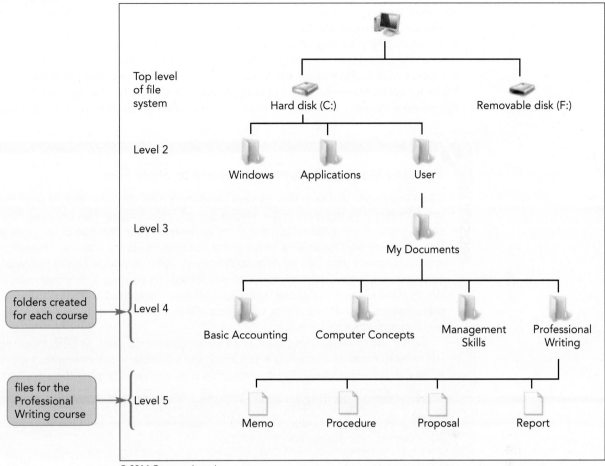

© 2014 Cengage Learning

The root directory is the top level of the hard disk and is for system files and folders only. You should not store your own work in the root directory because your files could interfere with Windows or an application. (If you are working in a computer lab, you might not be allowed to access the root directory.)

Do not delete or move any files or folders from the root directory of the hard disk; doing so could disrupt the system so that you can't start or run the computer. In fact, you should not reorganize or change any folder that contains installed software because Windows 8 expects to find the files for specific applications within certain folders. In Figure 4, folders containing software are stored at Level 2 of the file system. If you reorganize or change these folders, Windows 8 can't locate and start the applications stored in those folders. Likewise, you should not make changes to the folder (usually named Windows) that contains the Windows 8 operating system.

Level 2 of the file system also includes a folder for your user account, such as the User folder. This folder contains all of your system settings, preferences, and other user account information. It also contains subfolders, such as the My Documents folder, for your personal files. The folders in Level 3 of the file system are designed to contain subfolders for your personal files. You can create as many subfolders at Level 4 of the file system as you need to store other folders and files and keep them organized.

Figure 4 shows how you could organize your files on a hard disk if you were taking a full semester of business classes. To duplicate this organization, you would open the main folder for your documents, such as My Documents, create four folders—one each for the Basic Accounting, Computer Concepts, Management Skills, and Professional Writing courses—and then store the writing assignments you complete in the Professional Writing folder.

If you store your files on removable media, such as a USB drive, you can use a simpler organization because you do not have to account for system files. In general, the larger the storage medium, the more levels of folders you should use because large media can store more files and, therefore, need better organization. For example, if you were organizing your files on a 12 GB USB drive, you could create folders in the top level of the USB drive for each general category of documents you store—one each for Courses, Creative, Financials, and Vacation. The Courses folder could then include one folder for each course (Basic Accounting, Computer Concepts, Management Skills, and Professional Writing), and each of those folders could contain the appropriate files.

PROSKILLS

Decision Making: Determining Where to Store Files

When you create and save files on your computer's hard disk, you should store them in subfolders. The top level of the hard disk is off-limits for your files because they could interfere with system files. If you are working on your own computer, store your files within the My Documents folder in the Documents library, which is where many applications save your files by default. When you use a computer on the job, your employer might assign a main folder to you for storing your work. In either case, if you simply store all your files in one folder, you will soon have trouble finding the files you want. Instead, you should create subfolders within a main folder to separate files in a way that makes sense for you.

Even if you store most of your files on removable media, such as USB drives, you still need to organize those files into folders and subfolders. Before you start creating folders, whether on a hard disk or removable disk, you need to plan the organization you will use. Following your plan increases your efficiency because you don't have to pause and decide which folder to use when you save your files. A file organization plan also makes you more productive in your computer work—the next time you need a particular file, you'll know where to find it.

Exploring Files and Folders

As shown in the Visual Overview, you use File Explorer in Windows 8 to explore the files and folders on your computer. File Explorer displays the contents of your computer by using icons to represent drives, folders, and files. When you open File Explorer, it shows the contents of the Windows built-in libraries by default. Windows provides these libraries so you can organize files by category—documents, music, pictures, and video. A library can display these categories of files together, no matter where the files are actually stored. For example, you might keep some music files in a folder named Albums on your hard disk. You might also keep music files in a Songs folder on a USB drive. Although the Albums and Songs folders are physically stored in different locations, you can set up the Music library to display both folders in the same File Explorer window. You can then search and arrange the files as a single collection to quickly find the music you want to open and play. In this way, you use libraries to organize your files into categories so you can easily locate and work with files.

The File Explorer window is divided into two sections, called panes. The left pane is the navigation pane, which contains icons and links to locations on your computer. The right pane displays the contents of the location selected in the navigation pane. If the navigation pane showed all the contents on your computer at once, it could be a very long list. Instead, you open drives and folders only when you want to see what they contain. For example, to display the hierarchy of the folders and other locations on your computer, you select the Computer icon in the navigation pane, and then select the icon for a drive, such as Local Disk (C:) or Removable Disk (F:). You can then open and explore folders on that drive.

If a folder contains undisplayed subfolders, an expand icon appears to the left of the folder icon. (The same is true for drives.) To view the folders contained in an object, you click the expand icon. A collapse icon then appears next to the folder icon; click the collapse icon to hide the folder's subfolders. To view the files contained in a folder, you click the folder icon, and the files appear in the right pane. See Figure 5.

Figure 5   **Viewing files in File Explorer**

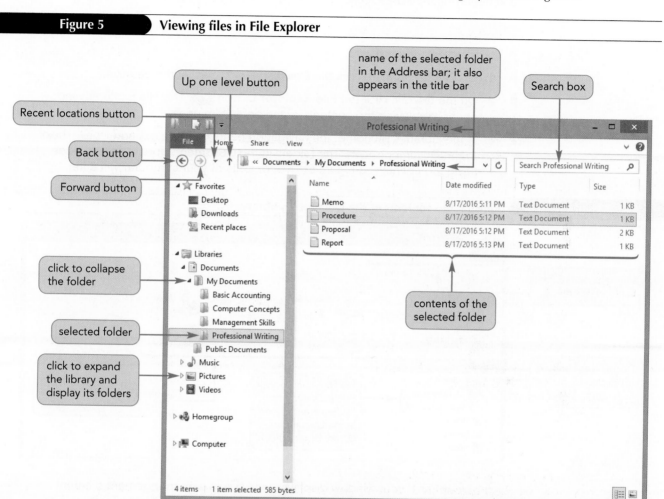

Using the navigation pane helps you explore your computer and orients you to your current location. As you move, copy, delete, and perform other tasks with the files and folders in the right pane of File Explorer, you can refer to the navigation pane to see how your changes affect the overall organization of the selected location.

In addition to using the navigation pane, you can explore your computer in File Explorer using the following navigation techniques:

- Opening drives and folders in the right pane—To view the contents of a drive or folder, double-click the drive or folder icon in the right pane of File Explorer.
- Using the Address bar—You can use the Address bar to navigate to a different folder. The Address bar displays the file path for your current folder. (Recall that a file path shows the location of a folder or file.) Click a folder name such as My Documents in the Address bar to navigate to that folder, or click an arrow button to navigate to a different location in the folder's hierarchy.
- Clicking the Back, Forward, Recent locations, and Up to buttons—Use the Back, Forward, and Recent locations buttons to navigate to other folders you have already opened. Use the Up to button to navigate up to the folder containing the current folder.
- Using the Search box—To find a file or folder stored in the current folder or its subfolders, type a word or phrase in the Search box. The search begins as soon as you

start typing. Windows finds files based on text in the filename, text within the file, and other properties of the file.

You'll practice using some of these navigation techniques later in the tutorial. Right now, you'll show Matt how to open File Explorer. Your computer should be turned on and displaying the Start screen.

To open File Explorer:

▶ **1.** On the Start screen, click the **Desktop** tile to display the desktop.

▶ **2.** On the taskbar, click the **File Explorer** button [icon]. The File Explorer window opens, displaying the contents of the default libraries.

▶ **3.** In the Libraries section of the navigation pane, click the **expand** icon [▷] next to the Documents icon. The folders in the Documents library appear in the navigation pane; see Figure 6. The contents of your computer will differ.

| Figure 6 | Viewing the contents of the Documents library |

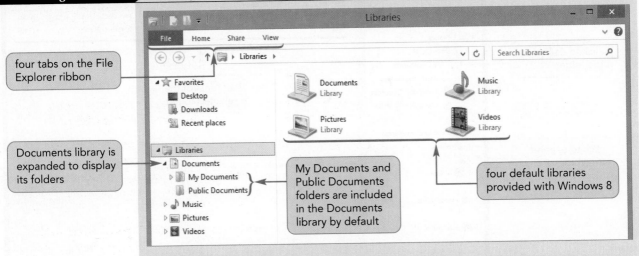

four tabs on the File Explorer ribbon

Documents library is expanded to display its folders

My Documents and Public Documents folders are included in the Documents library by default

four default libraries provided with Windows 8

Trouble? If your window displays icons in a size or arrangement different from the one shown in the figure, you can still explore files and folders. The same is true for all the figures in this tutorial.

▶ **4.** In the navigation pane, click the **My Documents** folder to display its contents in the right pane.

TIP

When you are working in the navigation pane, you only need to click a folder to open it; you do not need to double-click it.

As Figure 6 shows, the File Explorer window includes a ribbon, which is collapsed by default so it displays only tab names, such as File, Home, Share, and View. The Visual Overview shows the expanded ribbon, which displays the options for the selected tab. You'll work with the ribbon and learn how to expand it later in the tutorial.

Navigating to Your Data Files

To navigate to the files you want, it helps to know the file path because the file path tells you exactly where the file is stored in the hierarchy of drives and folders on your computer. For example, Matt has a file named "Logo," which contains an image of the company's logo. If Matt stored the Logo file in a folder named "Marketing" and saved that folder in a folder named "Savvy Traveler" on drive F (a USB drive) on his computer, the Address bar would show the following file path for the Logo file:

Computer ▸ Removable Disk (F:) ▸ Savvy Traveler ▸ Marketing ▸ Logo.png

This path has five parts, with each part separated by an arrow button:

- Computer—The main container for the file, such as "Computer" or "Network"
- Removable Disk (F:)—The drive name, including the drive letter followed by a colon, which indicates a drive rather than a folder
- Savvy Traveler—The top-level folder on drive F
- Marketing—A subfolder in the Savvy Traveler folder
- Logo.png—The name of the file

Although File Explorer uses arrow buttons to separate locations in a file path, printed documents use backslashes (\ ). For example, if you read an instruction to open the Logo file in the Savvy Traveler\Marketing folder on your USB drive, you know you must navigate to the USB drive attached to your computer, open the Savvy Traveler folder, and then open the Marketing folder to find the Logo file.

File Explorer displays the file path in the Address bar so you can keep track of your current location as you navigate between drives and folders. You can use File Explorer to navigate to the Data Files you need for this tutorial. Before you perform the following steps, you should know where you stored your Data Files, such as on a USB drive. The following steps assume that drive is Removable Disk (F:), a USB drive. If necessary, substitute the appropriate drive on your system when you perform the steps.

To navigate to your Data Files:

1. Make sure your computer can access your Data Files for this tutorial. For example, if you are using a USB drive, insert the drive into the USB port.

   Trouble? If you don't have the starting Data Files, you need to get them before you can proceed. Your instructor will either give you the Data Files or ask you to obtain them from a specified location (such as a network drive). If you have any questions about the Data Files, see your instructor or technical support person for assistance.

2. In the navigation pane of File Explorer, click the **expand** icon ▷ next to the Computer icon to display the drives on your computer, if necessary.

3. Click the **expand** icon ▷ next to the drive containing your Data Files, such as Removable Disk (F:). A list of the folders on that drive appears below the drive name.

4. If the list of folders does not include the FM folder, continue clicking the **expand** icon ▷ to navigate to the folder that contains the FM folder.

5. Click the **expand** icon ▷ next to the FM folder to expand the folder, and then click the **FM** folder so that its contents appear in the navigation pane and in the right pane of the folder window. The FM folder contains the Case1, Case2, Review, and Tutorial folders, as shown in Figure 7. The other folders on your computer might vary.

| Figure 7 | Navigating to the FM folder |

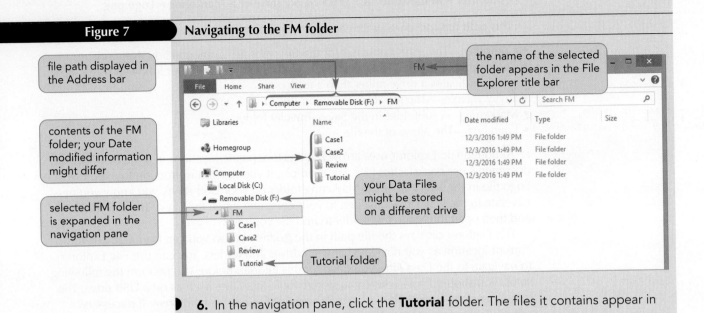

file path displayed in the Address bar

the name of the selected folder appears in the File Explorer title bar

contents of the FM folder; your Date modified information might differ

your Data Files might be stored on a different drive

selected FM folder is expanded in the navigation pane

Tutorial folder

▶ **6.** In the navigation pane, click the **Tutorial** folder. The files it contains appear in the right pane.

You can change the appearance of the File Explorer window to suit your preferences. You'll do so next so you can see more details about folders and files.

Changing the View

TIP

The default view for any folder in the Pictures library is Large icons view, which provides a thumbnail image of the file contents.

File Explorer provides eight ways to view the contents of a folder: Extra large icons, Large icons, Medium icons, Small icons, List, Details, Tiles, and Content. For example, the files in the Tutorial folder are currently displayed in Details view, which is the default view for all folders except those stored in the Pictures library. Details view displays a small icon to identify each file's type and lists file details in columns, such as the date the file was last modified, the file type, and the size of the file. Although only Details view lists the file details, you can see these details in any other view by pointing to a file to display a ScreenTip.

To change the view of File Explorer to any of the eight views, you use the View tab on the ribbon. To switch to Details view or Large icons view, you can use the view buttons on the status bar.

REFERENCE

Changing the View in File Explorer

• Click a view button on the status bar.

or

• Click the View tab on the ribbon.
• In the Layout group, click the view option; or click the More button, if necessary, and then click a view option.

You'll show Matt how to change the view of the Tutorial folder in the File Explorer window.

To change the view of the Tutorial folder in File Explorer:

▸ **1.** On the ribbon, click the **View** tab.

▸ **2.** In the Layout group, click **Medium icons**. The files appear in Medium icons view in File Explorer. See Figure 8.

Figure 8   **Files in the Tutorial folder in Medium icons view**

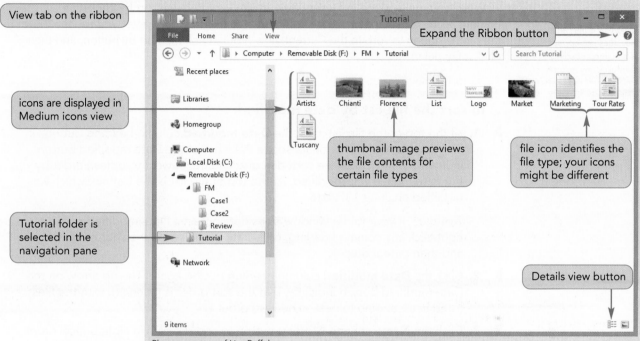

View tab on the ribbon

icons are displayed in Medium icons view

Tutorial folder is selected in the navigation pane

Expand the Ribbon button

thumbnail image previews the file contents for certain file types

file icon identifies the file type; your icons might be different

Details view button

Photos courtesy of Lisa Ruffolo

Because the icons used to identify types of files depend on the applications installed on your computer, the file icons that appear in your window might be different.

▸ **3.** On the status bar, click the **Large icons view** button ▣. The window shows the files with large icons and no file details.

TIP

When you change the view, it only changes the view for the currently selected folder.

When you clicked the View tab in the previous steps, the ribbon expanded so you could select an option and then collapsed after you clicked the Medium icons option. You can keep the ribbon expanded in the File Explorer window so you can easily access all of its options. You'll show Matt how to expand the ribbon and then use the View tab to switch to Details view.

To expand the ribbon in File Explorer:

▸ **1.** Click the **Expand the Ribbon** button ⌄ to expand the ribbon. The Expand the Ribbon button changes to the Minimize the Ribbon button, which you could click if you wanted to collapse the ribbon.

▸ **2.** On the View tab, in the Layout group, click **Details**. The window shows the files with small icons and lists the file details.

No matter which view you use, you can sort the file list by the name of the files or another detail, such as size, type, or date. When you **sort** files, you list them in ascending order (A to Z, 0 to 9, or earliest to latest date) or descending order (Z to A, 9 to 0, or latest to earliest date) by a file detail. If you're viewing music files, you can sort by details such as contributing artists or album title; and if you're viewing picture files, you can sort by details such as date taken or size. Sorting can help you find a particular file in a long file listing. For example, suppose you want to work on a document that you know you edited on June 4, 2016, but you can't remember the name of the file. You can sort the file list by date modified to find the file you want.

When you are working in Details view in File Explorer, you sort by clicking a column heading that appears at the top of the file list. In other views, you use the View tab on the ribbon to sort. In the Current view group, click the Sort by button, and then click a file detail.

TIP

To sort by a file detail that does not appear as a column heading, right-click any column heading and then select a file detail.

To sort the file list by date modified:

1. At the top of the file list, click the **Date modified** column heading button. The down arrow that appears above the label of the Date modified button indicates that the files are sorted in descending (newest to oldest) order by the date the file was modified. At the top of the list is the List file, which was modified on June 18, 2016.

   Trouble? If your folder window does not contain a Date modified column, right-click any column heading, click Date modified on the shortcut menu, and then repeat Step 1.

2. Click the **Date modified** column heading button again. The up arrow on the Date modified button indicates that the sort order is reversed, with the files listed in ascending (oldest to newest) order.

3. Click the **Name** column heading button to sort the files in alphabetical order by name. The Artists file is now listed first.

Now that Matt is comfortable working in File Explorer, you're ready to show him how to manage his files and folders.

Managing Files and Folders

As discussed earlier, you manage your personal files and folders by storing them according to a logical organization so that they are easy to find later. You can organize files as you create, edit, and save them, or you can do so later by creating folders, if necessary, and then moving and copying files into the folders.

To create a file-organization plan for Matt's files, you can review Figure 8 and look for files that logically belong together. In the Tutorial folder, Chianti, Florence, Logo, and Market are all graphics files that Matt uses for marketing and sales. He created the Artists and Tuscany files to describe Italian tours. The Marketing and Tour Rates files relate to business finances. Matt thinks the List file contains a task list for completing a project, but he isn't sure of its contents. He does recall creating the file using WordPad.

If the List file does contain a project task list, you can organize the files by creating four folders—one for graphics, one for tours, another for the financial files, and a fourth folder for projects. When you create a folder, you give it a name, preferably one that describes its contents. A folder name can have up to 255 characters, and any character is allowed, except / \ : * ? " < > and |. Considering these conventions, you could create four folders to contain Matt's files, as follows:

- Marketing Graphics folder—Chianti, Florence, Logo, and Market files
- Tours folder—Artists and Tuscany files
- Financial folder—Marketing and Tour Rates files
- Projects folder—List file

Before you start creating folders according to this plan, you need to verify the contents of the List file. You can do so by opening the file.

Opening a File

TIP

To select the default application for opening a file, right-click the file in File Explorer, point to Open with, and then click Choose default application. Click an application in the list that opens, and then click OK.

You can open a file from a running application or from File Explorer. To open a file in a running application, you select the application's Open command to access the Open dialog box, which you use to navigate to the file you want, select the file, and then open it. In the Open dialog box, you use the same tools that are available in File Explorer to navigate to the file you want to open. If the application you want to use is not running, you can open a file by double-clicking it in the right pane of File Explorer. The file usually opens in the application that you used to create or edit it.

Occasionally, File Explorer will open the file in an application other than the one you want to use to work with the file. For example, double-clicking a digital picture file usually opens the picture in a picture viewer application. If you want to edit the picture, you must open the file in a graphics editing application. When you need to specify an application to open a file, you can right-click the file, point to Open with on the shortcut menu, and then click the name of the application that you want to use.

Matt says that he might want to edit the List file to add another task. You'll show him how to use File Explorer to open the file in WordPad, which he used to create the file, and then edit it.

To open and edit the List file:

1. In the right pane of File Explorer, right-click the **List** file, and then point to **Open with** on the shortcut menu to display a list of applications that can open the file. See Figure 9.

   Trouble? If a list does not appear when you point to Open with on the shortcut menu, click Open with to display a window asking how you want to open this file.

| Figure 9 | Shortcut menu for opening a file |

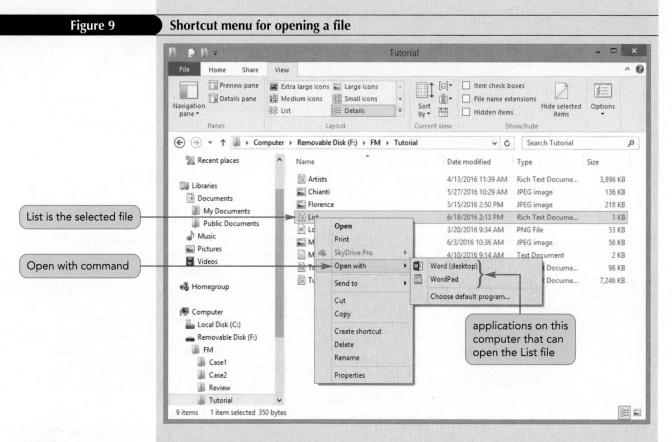

List is the selected file

Open with command

applications on this computer that can open the List file

TIP

In File Explorer, you can also double-click a file to open it in the default application for that file type.

2. Click **WordPad** to open the List file in WordPad. The file contains a task list for the marketing project, which includes three items.

Trouble? If you had to click Open with instead of pointing to it, in the window that asks how you want to open this file, click Keep using WordPad.

3. Press the **Ctrl+End** keys to move the insertion point to the end of the document, press the **Enter** key if necessary to start a new line, and then type **4. Review the Tours in Italy webpage.**

Now that you've added text to the List file, you need to save it to preserve the changes you made.

Saving a File

As you are creating or editing a file, you should save it frequently so you don't lose your work. When you save a file, you need to decide what name to use for the file and where to store it. Most applications provide a default location for saving a file, which makes it easy to find the file again later. However, you can select a different location depending on where you want to store the file.

Besides a storage location, every file must have a filename, which provides important information about the file, including its contents and purpose. A filename such as Italian Tours.docx has the following three parts:

- Main part of the filename—When you save a file, you need to provide only the main part of the filename, such as "Italian Tours."
- Dot—The dot (.) separates the main part of the filename from the extension.
- Extension—The **extension** includes the three or four characters that follow the dot in the filename and identify the file's type.

Similar to folder names, the main part of a filename can have up to 255 characters. This gives you plenty of room to name your file accurately enough so that you'll recognize the contents of the file just by looking at the filename. You can use spaces and certain punctuation symbols in your filenames. However, filenames cannot contain the symbols / \ : * ? " < > or | because these characters have special meanings in Windows 8.

Windows and other software add the dot and the extension to a filename, though File Explorer does not display them by default. Instead, File Explorer shows the file icon associated with the extension or a thumbnail for some types of files, such as graphics. For example, in a file named Italian Tours.docx, the docx extension identifies the file as one created in Microsoft Word, a word-processing application. File Explorer displays this file using a Microsoft Word icon and the main part of its filename. For a file named Italian Tours.png, the png extension identifies the file as one created in a graphics application such as Paint. In Details view or List view, File Explorer displays this file using a Paint icon and the main part of its filename. In other views, File Explorer does not use an icon, but displays the file contents in a thumbnail. File Explorer treats the Italian Tours.docx and Italian Tours.png files differently because their extensions distinguish them as different types of files, even though the main parts of their filenames are identical.

When you save a new file, you use the Save As dialog box to provide a filename and select a location for the file. You can create a folder for the new file at the same time you save the file. When you edit a file you saved previously, you can use the application's Save command to save your changes to the file, keeping the same name and location. If you want to save the edited file with a different name or in a different location, however, you need to use the Save As dialog box to specify the new name or location.

As with the Open dialog box, you specify the file location in the Save As dialog box using the same navigation techniques and tools that are available in File Explorer. You might need to click the Browse Folders button to expand the Save As dialog box so it displays these tools. In addition, the Save As dialog box always includes a File name box where you specify a filename.

INSIGHT

Saving Files on SkyDrive

Some Windows 8 applications, such as Microsoft Office, include SkyDrive as a location for saving and opening files. **SkyDrive** is a Microsoft service that provides up to 7 GB of online storage space for your files at no charge. You can purchase additional space if you need it. For example, if you create a document in Microsoft Word, your SkyDrive appears as a location for saving the document. (Your SkyDrive appears with your username, such as Matt's SkyDrive.) If you have a Microsoft account, you can select a folder on your SkyDrive to save the document online. (If you don't have a Microsoft account, you can sign up for one by visiting the SkyDrive website.) Because the file is stored online, it takes up no storage space on your computer and is available from any computer with an Internet connection. You access the document by opening it in Word or by visiting the SkyDrive website, and then signing in to your Microsoft account. To share the document with other people, you can send them a link to the document via email. They can use the link to access the document even if they do not have a Microsoft account.

One reason that Matt had trouble remembering the contents of the List file is that "List" is not a descriptive name. A better name for this file is Task List. You will save this document in the Tutorial subfolder of the FM folder provided with your Data Files. You will also use the Save As dialog box to specify a new name for the file as you save it.

To save the List file with a new name:

1. On the ribbon in the WordPad window, click the **File** tab to display commands for working with files.

2. Click **Save as** to open the Save As dialog box, as shown in Figure 10. The Tutorial folder is selected as the storage location for this file because you opened the file from this folder.

Figure 10   **Saving a file using the Save As dialog box**

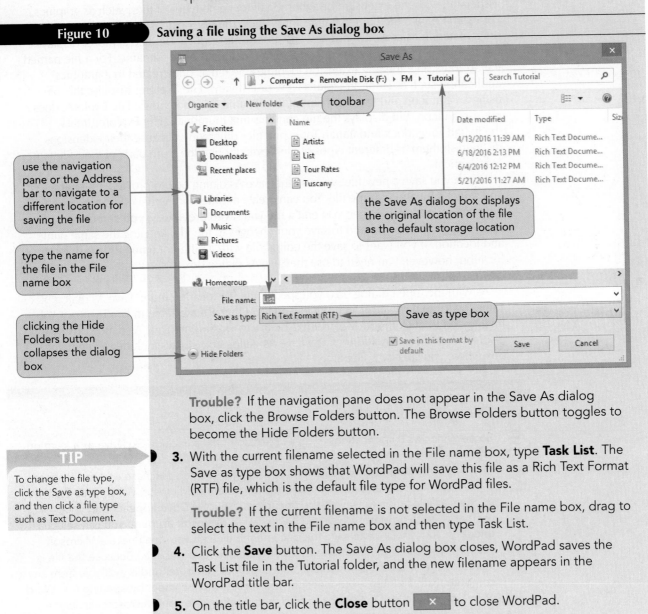

use the navigation pane or the Address bar to navigate to a different location for saving the file

type the name for the file in the File name box

clicking the Hide Folders button collapses the dialog box

the Save As dialog box displays the original location of the file as the default storage location

Save as type box

Trouble? If the navigation pane does not appear in the Save As dialog box, click the Browse Folders button. The Browse Folders button toggles to become the Hide Folders button.

TIP

To change the file type, click the Save as type box, and then click a file type such as Text Document.

3. With the current filename selected in the File name box, type **Task List**. The Save as type box shows that WordPad will save this file as a Rich Text Format (RTF) file, which is the default file type for WordPad files.

Trouble? If the current filename is not selected in the File name box, drag to select the text in the File name box and then type Task List.

4. Click the **Save** button. The Save As dialog box closes, WordPad saves the Task List file in the Tutorial folder, and the new filename appears in the WordPad title bar.

5. On the title bar, click the **Close** button [×] to close WordPad.

Now you're ready to start creating the folders you need to organize Matt's files.

Creating Folders

You originally proposed creating four new folders for Matt's files: Marketing Graphics, Tours, Financial, and Projects. Matt asks you to create these folders now. After that, you'll move his files to the appropriate folders. You create folders in File Explorer using one of three methods: using the New folder button in the New group on the Home tab; using the New folder button on the Quick Access Toolbar; or right-clicking to display a shortcut menu that includes the New command.

INSIGHT

Guidelines for Creating Folders

Consider the following guidelines as you create folders:

- Keep folder names short yet descriptive of the folder's contents. Long folder names can be more difficult to display in their entirety in folder windows, so use names that are short but clear. Choose names that will be meaningful later, such as project names or course numbers.
- Create subfolders to organize files. If a file list in File Explorer is so long that you must scroll the window, you should probably organize those files into subfolders.
- Develop standards for naming folders. Use a consistent naming scheme that is clear to you, such as one that uses a project name as the name of the main folder, and includes step numbers in each subfolder name (for example, 1-Outline, 2-First Draft, 3-Final Draft, and so on).

In the following steps, you will create the four folders for Matt in your Tutorial folder. Because it is easier to work with files using large file icons, you'll switch to Large icons view first.

To create the folders:

1. On the status bar in the File Explorer window, click the **Large icons view** button ▣ to switch to Large icons view.

2. Click the **Home** tab to display the Home tab on the ribbon.

3. In the New group, click the **New folder** button. A folder icon with the label "New folder" appears in the right pane of the File Explorer window. See Figure 11.

Figure 11   Creating a new folder in the Tutorial folder

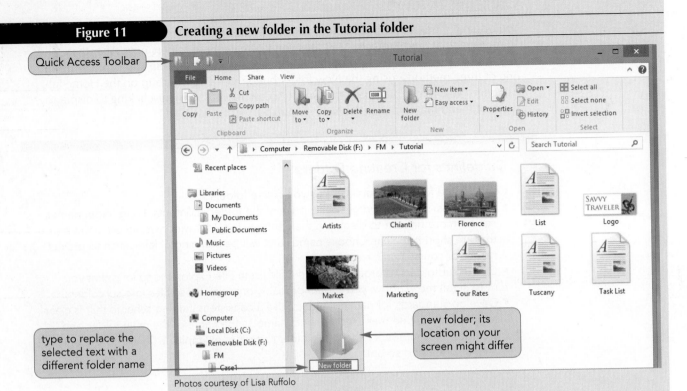

Photos courtesy of Lisa Ruffolo

> **Trouble?** If the "New folder" name is not selected, right-click the new folder, click Rename on the shortcut menu, and then continue with Step 4.
>
> Windows uses "New folder" as a placeholder, and selects the text so that you can replace it immediately by typing a new name. You do not need to press the Backspace or Delete key to delete the text.

4. Type **Marketing Graphics** as the folder name, and then press the **Enter** key. The new folder is named Marketing Graphics and is the selected item in the right pane. To create a second folder, you can use a shortcut menu.

5. In the right pane, right-click a blank area, point to **New** on the shortcut menu, and then click **Folder**. A folder icon appears in the right pane with the "New folder" text selected.

6. Type **Tours** as the name of the new folder, and then press the **Enter** key. To create the third folder, you can use the Quick Access Toolbar.

7. On the Quick Access Toolbar, click the **New folder** button, type **Financial**, and then press the **Enter** key to create and name the folder.

8. Create a new folder in the Tutorial folder named **Projects**.

After creating four folders, you're ready to organize Matt's files by moving them into the appropriate folders.

Moving and Copying Files and Folders

You can either move or copy a file from its current location to a new location. **Moving** a file removes it from its current location and places it in a new location that you specify. **Copying** a file places a duplicate version of the file in a new location that you specify, while leaving the original file intact in its current location. You can also move and copy folders. When you do, you move or copy all the files contained in the folder. (You'll practice copying folders in a Case Problem at the end of this tutorial.)

In File Explorer, you can move and copy files by using the Move to or Copy to buttons in the Organize group on the Home tab; using the Copy and Cut commands on a file's shortcut menu; or using keyboard shortcuts. When you copy or move files using these methods, you are using the **Clipboard**, a temporary storage area for files and information that you copy or move from one location to place in another.

You can also move files by dragging the files in the File Explorer window. You will now organize Matt's files by moving them to the appropriate folders you have created. You'll start by moving the Marketing file to the Financial folder by dragging the file.

To move the Marketing file by dragging it:

1. In File Explorer, point to the **Marketing** file in the right pane, and then press and hold the mouse button.

2. While still pressing the mouse button, drag the **Marketing** file to the **Financial** folder. See Figure 12.

| Figure 12 | Dragging a file to move it to a folder |

3. When the Move to Financial ScreenTip appears, release the mouse button. The Marketing file is removed from the main Tutorial folder and stored in the Financial subfolder.

   Trouble? If you released the mouse button before the Move to Financial ScreenTip appeared, press the Ctrl+Z keys to undo the move, and then repeat Steps 1–3.

   Trouble? If you moved the Market file instead of the Marketing file, press the Ctrl+Z keys to undo the move, and then repeat Steps 1–3.

4. In the right pane, double-click the **Financial** folder to verify that it contains the Marketing file.

TIP

If you drag a file or folder to a location on a different drive, the file is copied, not moved, to preserve the file in its original location.

Trouble? If the Marketing file does not appear in the Financial folder, you probably moved it to a different folder. Press the Ctrl+Z keys to undo the move, and then repeat Steps 1–3.

5. Click the **Back** button ⊛ on the Address bar to return to the Tutorial folder.

You'll move the remaining files into the folders using the Clipboard.

To move files using the Clipboard:

1. Right-click the **Artists** file, and then click **Cut** on the shortcut menu. Although the file icon still appears selected in the right pane of File Explorer, Windows removes the Artists file from the Tutorial folder and stores it on the Clipboard.

2. In the right pane, right-click the **Tours** folder, and then click **Paste** on the shortcut menu. Windows pastes the Artists file from the Clipboard to the Tours folder. The Artists file icon no longer appears in the File Explorer window, which is currently displaying the contents of the Tutorial folder.

3. In the navigation pane, click the **expand** icon ▷ next to the Tutorial folder, if necessary, to display its contents, and then click the **Tours** folder to view its contents in the right pane. The Tours folder now contains the Artists file. See Figure 13.

| Figure 13 | Artists file in its new location |

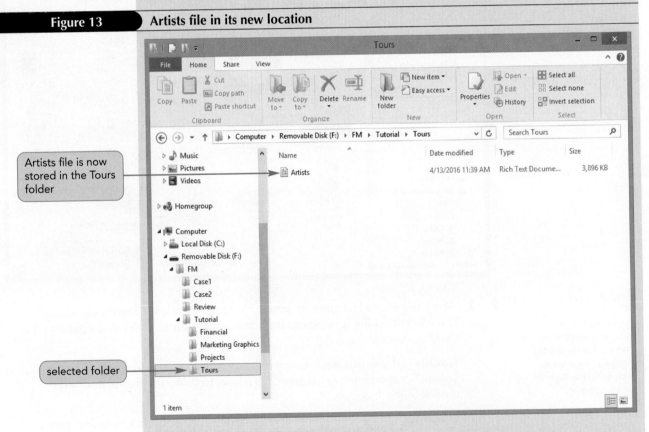

Artists file is now stored in the Tours folder

selected folder

Next, you'll use the Clipboard again to move the Tuscany file from the Tutorial folder to the Tours folder. But this time, you'll access the Clipboard using the ribbon.

4. On the Address bar, point to the **Up to** button ⬆ to display its ScreenTip (Up to "Tutorial"), click the **Up to** button ⬆ to return to the Tutorial folder, and then click the **Tuscany** file to select it.

5. On the Home tab, in the Clipboard group, click the **Cut** button to remove the Tuscany file from the Tutorial folder and temporarily store it on the Clipboard.

6. In the Address bar, click the **arrow** button ▶ to the right of "Tutorial" to display a list of subfolders in the Tutorial folder, and then click **Tours** to display the contents of the Tours folder in File Explorer.

7. In the Clipboard group, click the **Paste** button to paste the Tuscany file in the Tours folder. The Tours folder now contains the Artists and Tuscany files.

Finally, you'll move the Task List file from the Tutorial folder to the Projects folder using the Move to button in the Organize group on the Home tab. This button and the Copy to button are ideal when you want to move or copy files without leaving the current folder. When you select a file and then click the Move to or Copy to button, a list of locations appears, including all of the Windows libraries and one or more folders you open frequently. You can click a location in the list to move the selected file to that library or folder. You can also select the Choose location option to open the Move Items or Copy Items dialog box, and then select a location for the file, which you'll do in the following steps.

To move the Task List file using the Move to button:

1. In the Address bar, click **Tutorial** to return to the Tutorial folder, and then click the **Task List** file to select it.

2. On the Home tab, in the Organize group, click the **Move to** button to display a list of locations to which you can move the selected file. The Projects folder is not included on this list because you haven't opened it yet.

3. Click **Choose location** to open the Move Items dialog box. See Figure 14.

Figure 14   Move Items dialog box

locations on your computer; yours might differ

4. If necessary, scroll the list of locations, and then click the **expand** icon ▷ next to the drive containing your Data Files, such as Removable Disk (F:).

  5. Navigate to the FM ► Tutorial folder, and then click the **Projects** folder to select it.

  6. Click the **Move** button to close the dialog box and move the Task List file to the Projects folder.

  7. Open the Projects folder to confirm that it contains the Task List file.

One way to save steps when moving or copying multiple files or folders is to select all the files and folders you want to move or copy, and then work with them as a group. You can use several techniques to select multiple files or folders at the same time, which are described in Figure 15.

Figure 15   Selecting multiple files or folders

Items to Select in the Right Pane of File Explorer	Method
Files or folders listed together	Click the first item, press and hold the Shift key, click the last item, and then release the Shift key.
	or
	Drag the pointer to create a selection box around all the items you want to include.
Files or folders not listed together	Press and hold the Ctrl key, click each item you want to select, and then release the Ctrl key.
All files and folders	On the Home tab, in the Select group, click the Select all button.

Items to Deselect in the Right Pane of File Explorer	Method
Single file or folder in a selected group	Press and hold the Ctrl key, click each item you want to remove from the selection, and then release the Ctrl key.
All selected files and folders	Click a blank area of the File Explorer window.

© 2014 Cengage Learning

Next, you'll copy the four graphics files from the Tutorial folder to the Marketing Graphics folder using the Clipboard. To do this efficiently, you will select multiple files at once.

To copy multiple files at once using the Clipboard:

  1. Display the contents of the Tutorial folder in File Explorer.

  2. Click the **Chianti** file, press and hold the **Shift** key, click the **Market** file, and then release the **Shift** key.

  3. Press and hold the **Ctrl** key, click the **List** file to deselect it, and then release the **Ctrl** key. Four files—Chianti, Florence, Logo, and Market—are selected in the Tutorial folder window.

  4. Right-click a selected file, and then click **Copy** on the shortcut menu. Windows copies the selected files to the Clipboard.

  5. Right-click the **Marketing Graphics** folder, and then click **Paste** on the shortcut menu.

  6. Open the **Marketing Graphics** folder to verify it contains the four files you copied, and then return to the Tutorial folder.

> **7.** Right-click the **Tour Rates** file, and then click **Copy** on the shortcut menu.

> **8.** In the right pane, double-click the **Financial** folder to open it, right-click a blank area of the right pane, and then click **Paste** on the shortcut menu.

INSIGHT

Duplicating Your Folder Organization

If you work on two computers, such as one computer at an office or school and another computer at home, you can duplicate the folders you use on both computers to simplify the process of transferring files from one computer to another. For example, if you have four folders in your My Documents folder on your work computer, create these same four folders on a USB drive and in the My Documents folder of your home computer. If you change a file on the hard disk of your home computer, you can copy the most recent version of the file to the corresponding folder on your USB drive so the file is available when you are at work. You also then have a **backup**, or duplicate copy, of important files. Having a backup of your files is invaluable if your computer has a fatal error.

All the files that originally appeared in the Tutorial folder are now stored in appropriate subfolders. You can streamline the organization of the Tutorial folder by deleting the duplicate files you no longer need.

Deleting Files and Folders

TIP

In most cases, a file deleted from a USB drive does not go into the Recycle Bin. Instead, it is deleted when Windows 8 removes its icon, and the file cannot be recovered.

You should periodically delete files and folders you no longer need so that your main folders and disks don't get cluttered. In File Explorer, you delete a file or folder by deleting its icon. When you delete a file from a hard disk, Windows 8 removes the file from the folder but stores the file contents in the Recycle Bin. The Recycle Bin is an area on your hard disk that holds deleted files until you remove them permanently. When you delete a folder from the hard disk, the folder and all of its files are stored in the Recycle Bin. If you change your mind and want to retrieve a deleted file or folder, you can double-click the Recycle Bin on the desktop, right-click the file or folder you want to retrieve, and then click Restore. However, after you empty the Recycle Bin, you can no longer recover the files it contained.

Because you copied the Chianti, Florence, Logo, Market, and Tour Rates files to the subfolders in the Tutorial folder, you can safely delete the original files. You can also delete the List file because you no longer need it. You can delete a file or folder using various methods, including using a shortcut menu or selecting one or more files and then pressing the Delete key.

To delete files in the Tutorial folder:

> **1.** Display the Tutorial folder in the File Explorer window.

> **2.** In the right pane, click **Chianti**, press and hold the **Shift** key, click **Tour Rates**, and then release the **Shift** key. All files in the Tutorial folder are now selected. None of the subfolders should be selected.

> **3.** Right-click the selected files, and then click **Delete** on the shortcut menu. A message box appears, asking if you're sure you want to permanently delete these files.

Make sure you have copied the selected files to the Marketing Graphics and Financial folders before completing this step.

> **4.** Click the **Yes** button to confirm that you want to delete the files.

Renaming Files

After creating and naming a file or folder, you might realize that a different name would be more meaningful or descriptive. You can easily rename a file or folder by using the Rename command on the file's shortcut menu.

Now that you've organized Matt's files into folders, he reviews your work and notes that the Artists file was originally created to store text specifically about Florentine painters and sculptors. You can rename that file to give it a more descriptive filename.

To rename the Artists file:

TIP

To rename a file, you can also click the file, pause, click it again to select the filename, and then type to enter a new filename.

1. In the right pane of the File Explorer window, double-click the **Tours** folder to display its contents.

2. Right-click the **Artists** file, and then click **Rename** on the shortcut menu. The filename is highlighted and a box appears around it.

3. Type **Florentine Artists**, and then press the **Enter** key. The file now appears with the new name.

   Trouble? If you make a mistake while typing and you haven't pressed the Enter key yet, press the Backspace key until you delete the mistake and then complete Step 3. If you've already pressed the Enter key, repeat Steps 2 and 3 to rename the file again.

   Trouble? If your computer is set to display filename extensions, a message might appear asking if you are sure you want to change the filename extension. Click the No button, and then repeat Steps 2 and 3.

Working with Compressed Files

You compress a file or a folder of files so it occupies less space on the disk. It can be useful to compress files before transferring them from one location to another, such as from your hard disk to a removable disk or vice versa, or from one computer to another via email. You can then transfer the files more quickly. Also, if you or your email contacts can send and receive files only up to a certain size, compressing large files might make them small enough to send and receive. Compare two folders—a folder named Photos that contains files totaling about 8.6 MB, and a compressed folder containing the same files but requiring only 6.5 MB of disk space. In this case, the compressed files use about 25 percent less disk space than the uncompressed files.

You can compress one or more files in File Explorer using the Zip button, which is located in the Send group on the Share tab of the ribbon. Windows stores the compressed files in a special type of folder called an **archive**, or a compressed folder. File Explorer uses an icon of a folder with a zipper to represent a compressed folder. To compress additional files or folders, you drag them into the compressed folder. You can open a file directly from a compressed folder, although you cannot modify the file. To edit and save a compressed file, you must extract it first. When you **extract** a file, you create an uncompressed copy of the file in a folder you specify. The original file remains in the compressed folder.

Matt suggests that you compress the files and folders in the Tutorial folder so that you can more quickly transfer them to another location.

To compress the folders and files in the Tutorial folder:

TIP

Another way to compress files is to select the files, right-click the selection, point to Send to on the shortcut menu, and then click Compressed (zipped) folder.

1. In File Explorer, navigate to the Tutorial folder, and then select all the folders in the Tutorial folder.

2. Click the **Share** tab on the ribbon.

3. In the Send group, click the **Zip** button. After a few moments, a new compressed folder appears in the Tutorial window with the filename selected. By default, File Explorer uses the name of the first selected item as the name of the compressed folder. You'll replace the name with a more descriptive one.

4. Type **Savvy Traveler**, and then press the **Enter** key to rename the compressed folder. See Figure 16.

| Figure 16 | Compressing files and folders |

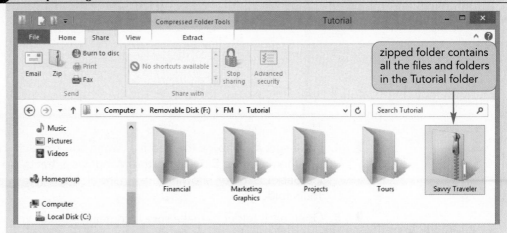

zipped folder contains all the files and folders in the Tutorial folder

5. Double-click the **Savvy Traveler** compressed folder to open it, open the **Tours** folder, and then note the size of the compressed Tuscany file, which is 1,815 KB.

6. Navigate back to the Tutorial folder.

You can move and copy the files and folders from an opened compressed folder to other locations, although you cannot rename the files. More often, you extract all of the files from the compressed folder to a new location that you specify, preserving the files in their original folders as appropriate.

To extract the compressed files:

1. Click the **Savvy Traveler** compressed folder to select it, and then click the **Compressed Folder Tools Extract** tab on the ribbon.

2. In the Extract all group, click the **Extract all** button. The Extract Compressed (Zipped) Folders Wizard starts and opens the Select a Destination and Extract Files dialog box.

3. Press the **End** key to deselect the path in the box and move the insertion point to the end of the path, press the **Backspace** key as many times as necessary to delete the Savvy Traveler text, and then type **Backups**. The final three parts of the path in the box should be \FM\Tutorial\Backups. See Figure 17.

Figure 17   **Extracting files from a compressed folder**

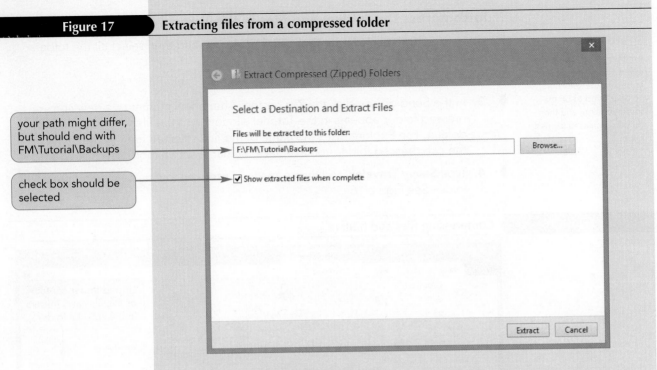

your path might differ,
but should end with
FM\Tutorial\Backups

check box should be
selected

4. Make sure the Show extracted files when complete check box is checked,
and then click the **Extract** button. Windows extracts the files and then opens
the Backups folder, showing the Financial, Marketing Graphics, Projects, and
Tours folders.

5. Open each folder to make sure it contains the files you worked with in this
tutorial. When you open the Tours folder, note the uncompressed size of the
Tuscany file, which is about four times as large as its compressed version.

6. Close all open windows.

In this tutorial, you examined the purpose of organizing files and folders, and you
planned and created an organization for a set of related files and folders. You also
explored your computer using File Explorer and learned how to navigate to your Data
Files using the navigation pane. You used File Explorer to manage files and folders by
opening and saving files; creating folders; and selecting, moving, and copying files.
You also renamed and deleted files according to your organization plan. Finally, you
compressed and extracted files.

Quick Check

REVIEW

1. You organize files by storing them in _____.
2. What is the purpose of the Address bar in File Explorer?
3. A filename _____ identifies the file's type and indicates the application that created the file.
4. Explain how to use File Explorer to navigate to a file in the following location: E: ▸ Courses ▸ Computer Basics ▸ Operating Systems.txt.
5. One way to move files and folders is to use the _____, a temporary storage area for files and information that you copied or moved from one place and plan to use somewhere else.
6. What happens if you click the first file in a folder window, press the Shift key, click the last file, and then release the Shift key?
7. When you delete a file from a hard disk, Windows removes the file from the folder but stores the file contents in the _____.
8. Describe how to compress a file or folder.
9. What are the benefits of compressing files and folders?

PRACTICE

Review Assignments

Data Files needed for the Review Assignments: Banner.png, Colosseum.jpg, Lectures.xlsx, Rome.jpg, Rome.rtf, Schedule.rtf, Tours.rtf

Matt has saved a few files from his old computer to a removable disk. He gives you these files in a single, unorganized folder, and asks you to organize them logically into subfolders. To do this, you will need to devise a plan for managing the files, and then create the subfolders you need. Next, you will rename, copy, move, and delete files, and then perform other management tasks to make it easy for Matt to work with these files and folders. Complete the following steps:

1. Use File Explorer to navigate to and open the FM ▸ Review folder provided with your Data Files. Examine the seven files in this folder and consider the best way to organize the files.
2. Open the **Rome** text file in WordPad, and then add the following tip to the end of the document: **Dine on the Italian schedule, with the main meal in the middle of the day.**
3. Save the document as **Rome Dining Tips** in the Review folder. Close the WordPad window.
4. In the Review folder, create three folders: **Business**, **Destinations**, and **Supplements**.
5. To organize the files into the correct folders, complete the following steps:
   - Move the Banner and Schedule files from the Review folder to the Business folder.
   - Move the Colosseum and Rome JPEG image files and the Rome Dining Tips and Tours text files to the Destinations folder.
   - Copy the Lectures file to the Supplements folder.
6. Copy the Tours file in the Destinations folder to the Business folder.
7. Rename the Schedule file in the Business folder as **2016 Schedule**. Rename the Lectures file in the Supplements folder as **On-site Lectures**.
8. Delete the Lectures file and the Rome text file from the Review folder.
9. Create a compressed (zipped) folder in the Review folder named **Rome** that contains all the files and folders in the Review folder.
10. Extract the contents of the Rome compressed folder to a new folder named **Rome Backups** in the Review folder. (*Hint:* The file path will end with \FM\Review\Rome Backups.)
11. Close the File Explorer window.

Case Problem 1

See the Starting Data Files section at the beginning of this tutorial for the list of Data Files needed for this Case Problem.

Bay Shore Arts Center   Casey Sullivan started the Bay Shore Arts Center in Monterey, California, to provide workshops and courses on art and photography. Attracting students from the San Francisco and San José areas, Casey's business has grown and she now holds classes five days a week. She recently started a course on fine art landscape photography, which has quickly become her most popular offering. Casey hired you to help her design new classes and manage other parts of her growing business, including maintaining electronic business files and communications. Your first task is to organize the files on her new Windows 8 computer. Complete the following steps:

1. Open File Explorer. In the FM ▶ Case1 folder provided with your Data Files, create three folders: **Classes**, **Landscapes**, and **Management**.
2. Move the Fall Classes, Spring Classes, Summer Classes, and Winter Classes files from the Case1 folder to the Classes folder.
3. Rename the four files in the Classes folder by deleting the word "Classes" from each filename.
4. Move the four JPEG image files from the Case1 folder to the Landscapes folder.
5. Copy the remaining two files to the Management folder.
6. Copy the Workshops file to the Classes folder.
7. Delete the Instructors and Workshops files from the Case1 folder.
8. Make a copy of the Landscapes folder in the Case1 folder. The name of the duplicate folder appears as Landscapes – Copy. Rename the Landscapes – Copy folder as **California Photos**.
9. Copy the Workshops file from the Classes folder to the California Photos folder. Rename this file **California Workshops**.
10. Compress the graphics files in the California Photos folder in a new compressed folder named **Photos**.
11. Move the compressed Photos folder to the Case1 folder.
12. Close File Explorer.

TROUBLESHOOT

Case Problem 2

See the Starting Data Files section at the beginning of this tutorial for the list of Data Files needed for this Case Problem.

Charlotte Area Business Incubator Antoine Jackson is the director of the Charlotte Area Business Incubator, a service run by the University of North Carolina in Charlotte to consult with new and struggling small businesses. You work as an intern at the business incubator and spend part of your time organizing client files. Since Antoine started using Windows 8, he has been having trouble finding files on his computer. He sometimes creates duplicates of files and then doesn't know which copy is the most current. Complete the following steps:

1. Navigate to the FM ▸ Case2 folder provided with your Data Files, and then examine the files in this folder. Based on the filenames and file types, begin to create an organization plan for the files.

⚙ **Troubleshoot** 2. Open the Tips1 and the Tips1 – Copy files and consider the problem these files could cause. Close the files and then fix the problem, renaming one or more files as necessary to reflect the contents.

⚙ **Troubleshoot** 3. Open the Tips2 and the Tips2 – Copy files and compare their contents. Change the filenames to clarify the purpose and contents of the files.

4. Complete the organization plan for Antoine's files. In the FM ▸ Case2 folder, create the subfolders you need according to your plan.

5. Move the files in the Case2 folder to the subfolders you created. When you finish, the Case2 folder should contain at least two subfolders containing files.

6. Rename the spreadsheet files in each subfolder according to the following descriptions.

   - Budget1: **Website budget**
   - Budget2: **Marketing budget**
   - Report1: **Travel expense report**
   - Report2: **Project expense report**
   - Report3: **Balance sheet**
   - Report4: **Event budget**

⚙ **Troubleshoot** 7. Make sure all files have descriptive names that accurately reflect their contents.

⚙ **Troubleshoot** 8. Based on the work you did in Steps 6 and 7, move files as necessary to improve the file organization.

9. Close File Explorer.

Getting Started with Excel

Creating a Customer Order Report

OBJECTIVES

Session 1.1
- Open and close a workbook
- Navigate through a workbook and worksheet
- Select cells and ranges
- Plan and create a workbook
- Insert, rename, and move worksheets
- Enter text, dates, and numbers
- Undo and redo actions
- Resize columns and rows

Session 1.2
- Enter formulas and the SUM and COUNT functions
- Copy and paste formulas
- Move or copy cells and ranges
- Insert and delete rows, columns, and ranges
- Create patterned text with Flash Fill
- Add cell borders and change font size
- Change worksheet views
- Prepare a workbook for printing
- Save a workbook with a new filename

Case | *Sparrow & Pond*

Sally Hughes is part owner of Sparrow & Pond, a small bookstore in Hudson, New Hampshire. Among her many tasks is to purchase new books from publishers. She also purchases rare and first edition books from online auctions as well as local library, estate, and garage sales.

Sally needs to quickly track sales data, compile customer profiles, and generate financial reports. She can perform all of these tasks with **Microsoft Excel 2013** (or **Excel**), an application used to enter, analyze, and present quantitative data. Sally asks you to use Excel to record a recent book order from a regular Sparrow & Pond customer.

STARTING DATA FILES

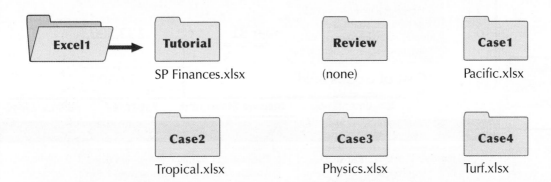

Excel1 → Tutorial
SP Finances.xlsx

Review
(none)

Case1
Pacific.xlsx

Case2
Tropical.xlsx

Case3
Physics.xlsx

Case4
Turf.xlsx

Session 1.1 Visual Overview:

The ribbon is organized into tabs. Each **tab** has commands related to particular activities or tasks.

The **formula bar** displays the value or formula entered in the active cell.

Excel stores spreadsheets in files called **workbooks**. The name of the current workbook appears in the title bar.

The **ribbon** contains buttons that you click to execute commands to work with Excel. You can pin the ribbon to leave it fully displayed, as shown here.

The **Name box** displays the cell reference of the active cell. In this case, the active cell is cell B104.

A group of cells in a rectangular block is called a **cell range** (or **range**). If the blocks are not connected, as shown here, it is a **nonadjacent range**.

The currently selected cell is the **active cell**.

The **row headings** are numbers along the left side of the workbook window that identify the different rows of the worksheet.

A workbook is made up of **sheets**. Each sheet is identified by a sheet name, which appears in a **sheet tab**.

The **status bar** provides information about the workbook.

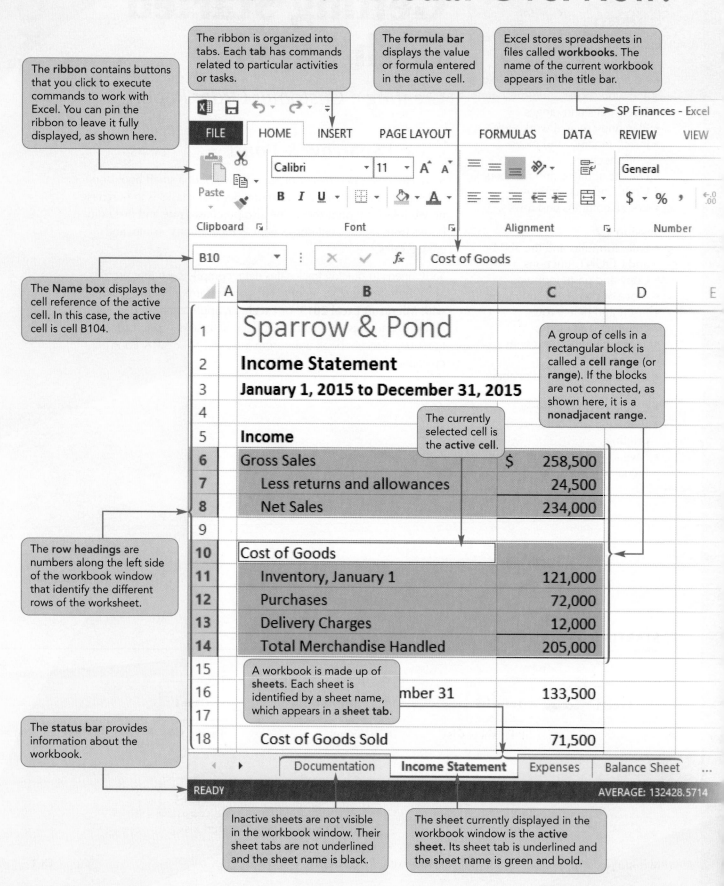

Inactive sheets are not visible in the workbook window. Their sheet tabs are not underlined and the sheet name is black.

The sheet currently displayed in the workbook window is the **active sheet**. Its sheet tab is underlined and the sheet name is green and bold.

The Excel Window

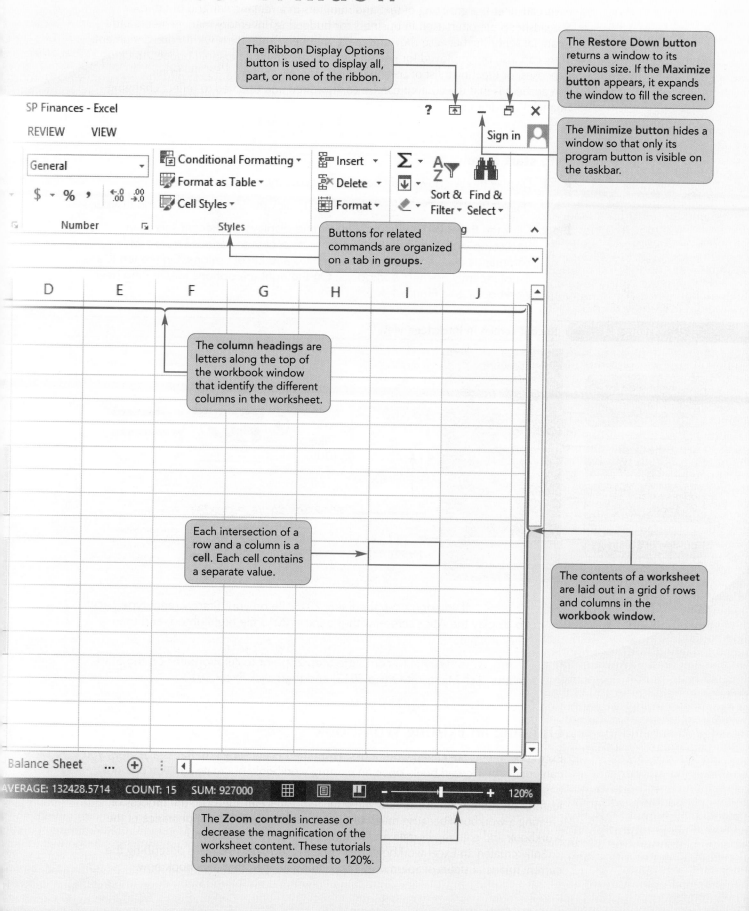

The Ribbon Display Options button is used to display all, part, or none of the ribbon.

The **Restore Down button** returns a window to its previous size. If the Maximize **button** appears, it expands the window to fill the screen.

The **Minimize button** hides a window so that only its program button is visible on the taskbar.

Buttons for related commands are organized on a tab in **groups**.

The **column headings** are letters along the top of the workbook window that identify the different columns in the worksheet.

Each intersection of a row and a column is a **cell**. Each cell contains a separate value.

The contents of a **worksheet** are laid out in a grid of rows and columns in the **workbook window**.

The **Zoom controls** increase or decrease the magnification of the worksheet content. These tutorials show worksheets zoomed to 120%.

SP Finances - Excel

REVIEW   VIEW

Sign in

General

$ ▾ % , .00 .00

Conditional Formatting ▾
Format as Table ▾
Cell Styles ▾

Insert ▾
Delete ▾
Format ▾

Sort & Filter ▾   Find & Select ▾

Number   Styles

Balance Sheet ... ⊕

AVERAGE: 132428.5714   COUNT: 15   SUM: 927000   120%

Introducing Excel and Spreadsheets

A **spreadsheet** is a grouping of text and numbers in a rectangular grid or table. Spreadsheets are often used in business for budgeting, inventory management, and financial reporting because they unite text, numbers, and charts within one document. They can also be employed for personal use for planning a personal budget, tracking expenses, or creating a list of personal items. The advantage of an electronic spreadsheet is that the content can be easily edited and updated to reflect changing financial conditions.

To start Excel:

▶ **1.** Display the Windows Start screen, if necessary.

Using Windows 7? To complete Step 1, click the Start button on the taskbar.

▶ **2.** Click the **Excel 2013** tile. Excel starts and displays the Recent screen in Backstage view. **Backstage view** provides access to various screens with commands that allow you to manage files and Excel options. On the left is a list of recently opened workbooks. On the right are options for creating new workbooks. See Figure 1-1.

Figure 1-1	Recent screen in Backstage view

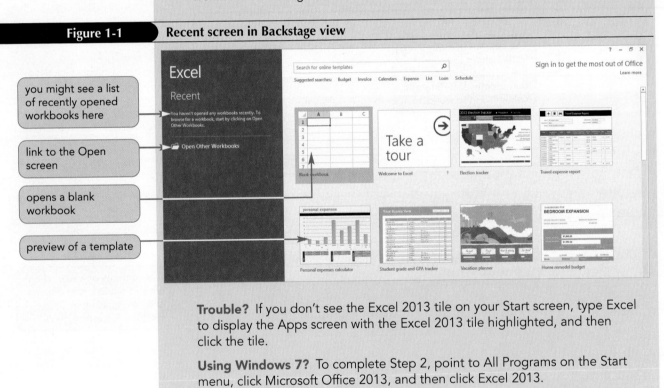

you might see a list of recently opened workbooks here

link to the Open screen

opens a blank workbook

preview of a template

Trouble? If you don't see the Excel 2013 tile on your Start screen, type Excel to display the Apps screen with the Excel 2013 tile highlighted, and then click the tile.

Using Windows 7? To complete Step 2, point to All Programs on the Start menu, click Microsoft Office 2013, and then click Excel 2013.

Opening an Existing Workbook

Excel documents are called workbooks. From the Recent screen in Backstage view, you can open a blank workbook, open an existing workbook, or create a new workbook based on a template. A **template** is a preformatted workbook with many design features and some content already filled in. Templates can speed up the process of creating a workbook because much of the work in designing the appearance of the workbook and entering its data and formulas is already done for you.

Sally created an Excel workbook that contains several worksheets describing the current financial status of Sparrow & Pond. You will open that workbook now.

To switch between Touch Mode and Mouse Mode:

1. On the Quick Access Toolbar, click the **Customize Quick Access Toolbar** button ⏷. A menu opens listing buttons you can add to the Quick Access Toolbar as well as other options for customizing the toolbar.

Trouble? If the Touch/Mouse Mode command on the menu has a checkmark next to it, press the Esc key to close the menu, and then skip Step 2.

2. Click **Touch/Mouse Mode**. The Quick Access Toolbar now contains the Touch/Mouse Mode button 👆, which you can use to switch between Mouse Mode, the default display, and Touch Mode.

3. On the Quick Access Toolbar, click the **Touch/Mouse Mode** button 👆. A menu opens listing Mouse and Touch, and the icon next to Mouse is shaded to indicate it is selected.

Trouble? If the icon next to Touch is shaded, press the Esc key to close the menu and skip Step 4.

4. Click **Touch**. The display switches to Touch Mode with more space between the commands and buttons on the ribbon. See Figure 1-4.

Figure 1-4	Ribbon displayed in Touch Mode

Touch/Mouse Mode button

buttons are larger with more space around them

Now you'll return to Mouse Mode.

Trouble? If you are working with a touchscreen and want to use Touch Mode, skip Steps 5 and 6.

5. On the Quick Access Toolbar, click the **Touch/Mouse Mode** button 👆, and then click **Mouse**. The ribbon returns to the Mouse Mode display shown in Figure 1-2.

6. On the Quick Access Toolbar, click the **Customize Quick Access Toolbar** button ⏷, and then click **Touch/Mouse Mode** to deselect it. The Touch/Mouse Mode button is removed from the Quick Access Toolbar.

Exploring a Workbook

Workbooks are organized into separate pages called sheets. Excel supports two types of sheets: worksheets and chart sheets. A worksheet contains a grid of rows and columns into which you can enter text, numbers, dates, and formulas, and display charts. A **chart sheet** contains a chart that provides a visual representation of worksheet data. The contents of a workbook are shown in the workbook window.

Changing the Active Sheet

The sheets in a workbook are identified in the sheet tabs at the bottom of the workbook window. The SP Finances workbook includes five sheets labeled Documentation, Income Statement, Expenses, Balance Sheet, and Cash Flow. The sheet currently displayed in the workbook window is the active sheet, which in this case is the Documentation sheet. To make a different sheet active and visible, you click its sheet tab. You can tell which sheet is active because its name appears in bold green.

If a workbook includes so many sheets that not all of the sheet tabs can be displayed at the same time in the workbook window, you can use the sheet tab scrolling buttons to scroll through the list of tabs. Scrolling the sheet tabs does not change the active sheet; it only changes which sheet tabs are visible.

You will view the different sheets in the SP Finances workbook.

To change the active sheet:

▶ **1.** Click the **Income Statement** sheet tab. The Income Statement worksheet becomes the active sheet, and its name is in bold green type. See Figure 1-5.

| Figure 1-5 | Income Statement worksheet |

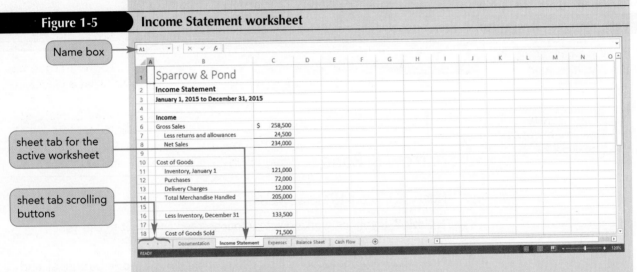

▶ **2.** Click the **Expenses** sheet tab to make it the active sheet. The Expenses sheet is an example of a chart sheet containing only an Excel chart. See Figure 1-6.

| Figure 1-6 | Expenses chart sheet |

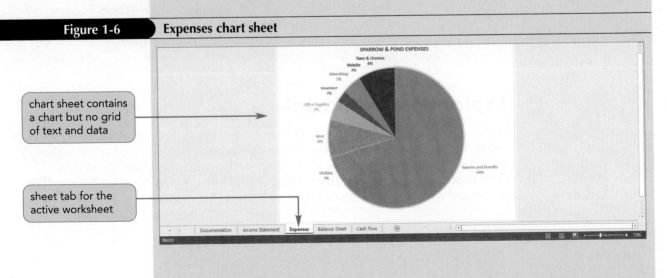

TIP

You can move to the previous or next sheet in the workbook by pressing the Ctrl+PgUp or Ctrl+PgDn keys.

▶ **3.** Click the **Balance Sheet** sheet tab to make it the active sheet. Note that this sheet contains a chart embedded into the grid of data values. A worksheet can contain data values, charts, pictures, and other design elements.

▶ **4.** Click the **Cash Flow** sheet tab. The worksheet with information about the company's cash flow is now active.

▶ **5.** Click the **Income Statement** sheet tab to make the Income Statement worksheet the active sheet.

Navigating Within a Worksheet

The worksheet is organized into individual cells. Each cell is identified by a **cell reference**, which is based on the cell's column and row location. For example, in Figure 1-5, the company name, Sparrow & Pond, is in cell B1, which is the intersection of column B and row 1. The column letter always appears before the row number in any cell reference. The cell that is currently selected in the worksheet is referred to as the active cell. The active cell is highlighted with a thick green border, its cell reference appears in the Name box, and the corresponding column and row headings are highlighted. The active cell in Figure 1-5 is cell A1.

Row numbers range from 1 to 1,048,576, and column labels are letters in alphabetical order. The first 26 column headings range from A to Z. After Z, the next column headings are labeled AA, AB, AC, and so forth. Excel allows a maximum of 16,384 columns in a worksheet (the last column has the heading XFD). This means that you can create large worksheets whose content extends well beyond what is visible in the workbook window.

To move different parts of the worksheet into view, you can use the horizontal and vertical scroll bars located at the bottom and right edges of the workbook window, respectively. A scroll bar has arrow buttons that you can click to shift the worksheet one column or row in the specified direction, and a scroll box that you can drag to shift the worksheet in the direction you drag.

You will scroll the active worksheet so you can review the rest of the Sparrow & Pond income statement.

To scroll through the Income Statement worksheet:

▶ **1.** On the vertical scroll bar, click the down arrow button ▼ to scroll down the Income Statement worksheet until you see cell C36, which displays the company's net income value of $4,600.

▶ **2.** On the horizontal scroll bar, click the right arrow button ▶ three times. The worksheet scrolls three columns to the right, moving columns A through C out of view.

▶ **3.** On the horizontal scroll bar, drag the scroll box to the left until you see column A.

▶ **4.** On the vertical scroll bar, drag the scroll box up until you see the top of the worksheet and cell A1.

Scrolling the worksheet does not change the location of the active cell. Although the active cell might shift out of view, you can always see the location of the active cell in the Name box. To make a different cell active, you can either click a new cell or use the keyboard to move between cells, as described in Figure 1-7.

Figure 1-7 **Excel navigation keys**

Press	To move the active cell
↑ ↓ ← →	Up, down, left, or right one cell
Home	To column A of the current row
Ctrl+Home	To cell A1
Ctrl+End	To the last cell in the worksheet that contains data
Enter	Down one row or to the start of the next row of data
Shift+Enter	Up one row
Tab	One column to the right
Shift+Tab	One column to the left
PgUp, PgDn	Up or down one screen
Ctrl+PgUp, Ctrl+PgDn	To the previous or next sheet in the workbook

© 2014 Cengage Learning

You will use both your mouse and your keyboard to change the location of the active cell in the Income Statement worksheet.

To change the active cell:

1. Move your pointer over cell **B5**, and then click the mouse button. The active cell moves from cell A1 to cell B5. A green border appears around cell B5, the column heading for column B and the row heading for row 5 are both highlighted, and the cell reference in the Name box changes from A1 to B5.

2. Press the → key. The active cell moves one cell to the right to cell C5.

3. Press the **PgDn** key. The active cell moves down one full screen.

4. Press the **PgUp** key. The active cell moves up one full screen, returning to cell C5.

5. Press the **Ctrl+Home** keys. The active cell returns to the first cell in the worksheet, cell A1.

The mouse and keyboard provide quick ways to navigate the active worksheet. For larger worksheets that span several screens, you can move directly to a specific cell using the Go To command or by typing a cell reference in the Name box. You will try both of these methods.

To use the Go To dialog box and the Name box:

1. On the HOME tab, in the Editing group, click the **Find & Select** button, and then click **Go To** on the menu that opens (or press the **F5** key). The Go To dialog box opens.

2. Type **C36** in the Reference box. See Figure 1-8.

Figure 1-8	Go To dialog box

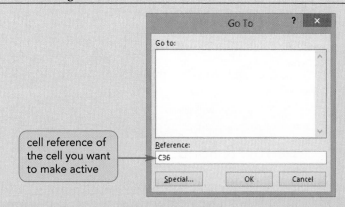

cell reference of
the cell you want
to make active

> **3.** Click the **OK** button. Cell C36 becomes the active cell, displaying $4,600, which is Sparrow & Pond's net income for the year. Because cell C36 is the active cell, its cell reference appears in the Name box.

> **4.** Click in the Name box, type **A1**, and then press the **Enter** key. Cell A1 is again the active cell.

Selecting a Cell Range

Many tasks in Excel require you to work with a group of cells. You can use your mouse or keyboard to select those cells. A group of cells in a rectangular block is called a cell range (or simply a range). Each range is identified with a **range reference** that includes the cell reference of the upper-left cell of the rectangular block and the cell reference of the lower-right cell separated by a colon. For example, the range reference A1:G5 refers to all of the cells in the rectangular block from cell A1 through cell G5.

As with individual cells, you can select cell ranges using your mouse, the keyboard, or commands. You will select a range in the Income Statement worksheet.

TIP

You can also select a range by clicking the upper-left cell of the range, holding down the Shift key as you click the lower-right cell in the range, and then releasing the Shift key.

To select a cell range:

> **1.** Click cell **B5** to select it, and without releasing the mouse button, drag down to cell **C8**.

> **2.** Release the mouse button. The range B5:C8 is selected. See Figure 1-9. The selected cells are highlighted and surrounded by a green border. The first cell you selected in the range, cell B5, is the active cell in the worksheet. The active cell in a selected range is white. The Quick Analysis button appears, providing options for working with the range; you will use this button in another tutorial.

Figure 1-9 **Range B5:C8 selected**

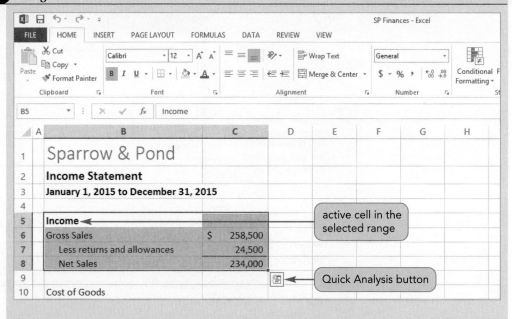

3. Click cell **A1** to deselect the range.

A nonadjacent range is a collection of separate ranges. The range reference for a nonadjacent range includes the range reference to each range separated by a semicolon. For example, the range reference A1:G5;A10:G15 includes two ranges—the first range is the rectangular block of cells from cell A1 to cell G5, and the second range is the rectangular block of cells from cell A10 to cell G15.

You will select a nonadjacent range in the Income Statement worksheet.

To select a nonadjacent range in the Income Statement worksheet:

1. Click cell **B5**, hold down the **Shift** key as you click cell **C8**, and then release the **Shift** key to select the range B5:C8.

2. Hold down the **Ctrl** key as you select the range **B10:C14**, and then release the **Ctrl** key. The two separate blocks of cells in the nonadjacent range B5:C8;B10:C14 are selected. See Figure 1-10.

Figure 1-10	Nonadjacent range B5:C8;B10:C14 selected

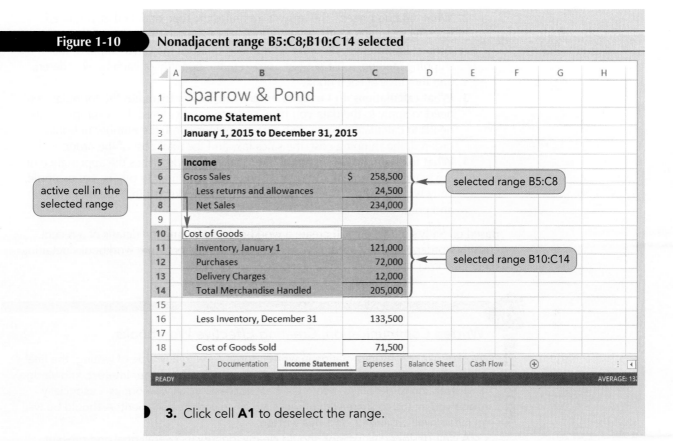

> **3.** Click cell **A1** to deselect the range.

Closing a Workbook

When you close a workbook, a dialog box might open, asking whether you want to save the workbook. If you have made changes that you want to keep, you should save the workbook. You have finished reviewing the SP Finances workbook, so you will close it. You will not save the workbook because you want the original version to remain unchanged.

To close the SP Finances workbook:

> **1.** On the ribbon, click the **FILE** tab to display Backstage view, and then click **Close** in the navigation bar (or press the **Ctrl+W** keys).

> **2.** If a dialog box opens asking whether you want to save your changes to the workbook, click the **Don't Save** button. The workbook closes without saving any changes. Excel remains opens, ready for you to create or open another workbook.

Planning a Workbook

Before you begin creating a new workbook, you should develop a plan. You can do this by using a **planning analysis sheet**, which includes the following questions that help you think about the workbook's purpose and how to achieve your desired results:

1. **What problems do I want to solve?** The answer identifies the goal or purpose of the workbook. For example, Sally needs an easy way to record customer orders and analyze details from these orders.

2. **What data do I need?** The answer identifies the type of data that you need to collect and enter into the workbook. For example, Sally needs customer contact information, an order ID number, the date the order shipped, the shipping method, a list of books ordered, the quantity of each book ordered, and the price of each book.

3. **What calculations do I need to enter?** The answer identifies the formulas you need to apply to the data you have collected and entered. For example, Sally needs to calculate the charge for each book ordered, the number of books ordered, the shipping cost, the sales tax, and the total cost of the order.

4. **What form should my solution take?** The answer describes the appearance of the workbook content and how it should be presented to others. For example, Sally wants the information stored in a single worksheet that is easy to read and prints clearly.

Based on Sally's plan, you will create a workbook containing the details of a recent customer order. Sally will use this workbook as a model for future workbooks detailing other customer orders.

PROSKILLS

Written Communication: Creating Effective Workbooks

Workbooks convey information in written form. As with any type of writing, the final product creates an impression and provides an indicator of your interest, knowledge, and attention to detail. To create the best impression, all workbooks—especially those you intend to share with others such as coworkers and clients—should be well planned, well organized, and well written.

A well-designed workbook should clearly identify its overall goal and present information in an organized format. The data it includes—both the entered values and the calculated values—should be accurate. The process of developing an effective workbook includes the following steps:

- Determine the workbook's purpose, content, and organization before you start.
- Create a list of the sheets used in the workbook, noting each sheet's purpose.
- Insert a documentation sheet that describes the workbook's purpose and organization. Include the name of the workbook author, the date the workbook was created, and any additional information that will help others to track the workbook to its source.
- Enter all of the data in the workbook. Add labels to indicate what the values represent and, if possible, where they originated so others can view the source of your data.
- Enter formulas for calculated items rather than entering the calculated values into the workbook. For more complicated calculations, provide documentation explaining them.
- Test the workbook with a variety of values; edit the data and formulas to correct errors.
- Save the workbook and create a backup copy when the project is completed. Print the workbook's contents if you need to provide a hard-copy version to others or for your files.
- Maintain a history of your workbook as it goes through different versions, so that you and others can quickly see how the workbook has changed during revisions.

By including clearly written documentation, explanatory text, a logical organization, and accurate data and formulas, you will create effective workbooks that others can use easily.

Creating a New Workbook

You create new workbooks from the New screen in Backstage view. Similar to the Recent screen that opened when you started Excel, the New screen include templates for a variety of workbook types. You can see a preview of what the different workbooks will look like. You will create a new workbook from the Blank workbook template, in which you can add all of the content and design Sally wants for the Sparrow & Pond customer order worksheet.

TIP

You can also create a new, blank workbook by pressing the Ctrl+N keys.

To start a new, blank workbook:

▶ **1.** On the ribbon, click the **FILE** tab to display Backstage view.

▶ **2.** Click **New** in the navigation bar to display the New screen, which includes access to templates for a variety of workbooks.

▶ **3.** Click the **Blank workbook** tile. A blank workbook opens. See Figure 1-11.

Figure 1-11	Blank workbook

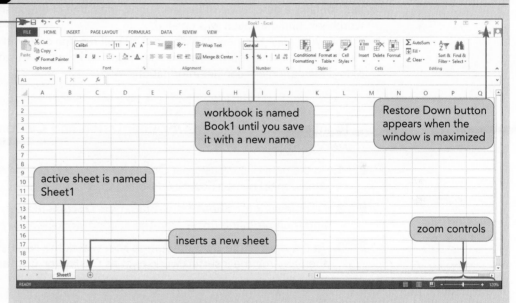

Save button on the Quick Access Toolbar

workbook is named Book1 until you save it with a new name

Restore Down button appears when the window is maximized

active sheet is named Sheet1

inserts a new sheet

zoom controls

In these tutorials, the workbook window is zoomed to 120% for better readability. If you want to zoom your workbook window to match the figures, complete Step 4. If you prefer to work in the default zoom of 100% or at another zoom level, read but do not complete Step 4; you might see more or less of the worksheet on your screen, but this will not affect your work in the tutorials.

▶ **4.** If you want your workbook window zoomed to 120% to match the figures, click the **Zoom In** button ➕ on the status bar twice to increase the zoom level to 120%. The 120% magnification increases the size of each cell, but reduces the number of worksheet cells visible in the workbook window.

The name of the active workbook, Book1, appears in the title bar. If you open multiple blank workbooks, they are named Book1, Book2, Book3, and so forth until you save them with a more descriptive name.

Renaming and Inserting Worksheets

Blank workbooks open with a single blank sheet named Sheet1. You can give sheets more descriptive and meaningful names. This is a good practice so that you and others can easily tell what a sheet contains. Sheet names cannot exceed 31 characters, but they can contain blank spaces and include upper- and lowercase letters.

Because Sheet1 is not a very descriptive name, Sally wants you to rename the worksheet as Customer Order.

To rename the Sheet1 worksheet:

▶ **1.** Double-click the **Sheet1** tab. The Sheet1 label in the tab is selected.

▶ **2.** Type **Customer Order** as the new name, and then press the **Enter** key. The width of the sheet tab expands to fit the longer sheet name.

Many workbooks include multiple sheets so that data can be organized in logical groups. A common business practice is to include a worksheet named Documentation that contains a description of the workbook, the name of the person who prepared the workbook, and the date it was created.

You will create two new worksheets. You will rename one worksheet as Documentation and you will rename the other worksheet as Customer Contact to record the customer's contact information.

To insert and name the Documentation and Customer Contact worksheets:

▶ **1.** To the right of the Customer Order sheet tab, click the **New sheet** button ⊕. A new sheet named Sheet2 is inserted to the right of the Customer Order sheet.

▶ **2.** Double-click the **Sheet2** sheet tab, type **Documentation** as the new name, and then press the **Enter** key. The second worksheet is renamed.

▶ **3.** To the right of the Documentation sheet, click the **New sheet** button ⊕, and then rename the inserted worksheet as **Customer Contact**.

Moving Worksheets

A good practice is to place the most important sheets at the beginning of the workbook (the leftmost sheet tabs) and less important sheets at the end (the rightmost sheet tabs). To change the placement of sheets in a workbook, you drag them by their sheet tabs to the new location.

Sally wants you to move the Documentation worksheet to the front of the workbook, so that it appears before the Customer Order sheet.

To move the Documentation worksheet:

▶ **1.** Point to the **Documentation** sheet tab.

TIP

To copy a sheet, hold down the Ctrl key as you drag and drop its sheet tab.

▶ **2.** Press and hold the mouse button. The pointer changes to ⬚, and a small arrow appears in the upper-left corner of the tab.

▶ **3.** Drag to the left until the small arrow appears in the upper-left corner of the Customer Order sheet tab, and then release the mouse button. The Documentation worksheet is now the first sheet in the workbook.

Deleting Worksheets

In some workbooks, you will want to delete an existing sheet. The easiest way to delete a sheet is by using a **shortcut menu**, which is a list of commands related to a selection that opens when you click the right mouse button. Sally asks you to include the customer's contact information on the Customer Order worksheet so all of the information is on one sheet.

To delete the Customer Contact worksheet from the workbook:

▸ **1.** Right-click the **Customer Contact** sheet tab. A shortcut menu opens.

▸ **2.** Click **Delete**. The Customer Contact worksheet is removed from the workbook.

Saving a Workbook

As you modify a workbook, you should save it regularly—every 10 minutes or so is a good practice. The first time you save a workbook, the Save As dialog box opens so you can name the file and choose where to save it. You can save the workbook on your computer or network, or to your account on SkyDrive.

To save your workbook for the first time:

▸ **1.** On the Quick Access Toolbar, click the **Save** button 🖫 (or press the **Ctrl+S** keys). The Save As screen in Backstage view opens.

▸ **2.** Click **Computer** in the Places list, and then click the **Browse** button. The Save As dialog box opens.

   Trouble? If your instructor wants you to save your files to your SkyDrive account, click SkyDrive, and then log in to your account, if necessary.

▸ **3.** Navigate to the location specified by your instructor.

▸ **4.** In the File name box, select **Book1** (the suggested name) if it is not already selected, and then type **SP Customer Order**.

▸ **5.** Verify that **Excel Workbook** appears in the Save as type box.

▸ **6.** Click the **Save** button. The workbook is saved, the dialog box closes, and the workbook window reappears with the new filename in the title bar.

As you modify the workbook, you will need to resave the file. Because you already saved the workbook with a filename, the next time you save, the Save command saves the changes you made to the workbook without opening the Save As dialog box.

Entering Text, Dates, and Numbers

Workbook content is entered into worksheet cells. Those cells can contain text, numbers, or dates and times. **Text data** is any combination of letters, numbers, and symbols. Text data is often referred to as a **text string** because it contains a series, or string, of text characters. **Numeric data** is any number that can be used in a mathematical calculation. **Date** and **time data** are commonly recognized formats for date and time values. For example, Excel interprets the cell entry April 15, 2016 as a date and not as text. New data is placed into the active cell of the current worksheet. As you enter data, the entry appears in both the active cell and the formula bar. By default, text is left-aligned in cells, and numbers, dates, and times are right-aligned.

Entering Text

Text is often used in worksheets to label other data and to identify areas of a sheet. Sally wants you to enter some of the information from the planning analysis sheet into the Documentation sheet.

To enter the text for the Documentation sheet:

▸ 1. Press the **Ctrl+Home** keys to make sure cell A1 is the active cell on the Documentation sheet.

▸ 2. Type **Sparrow and Pond** in cell A1. As you type, the text appears in cell A1 and in the formula bar.

▸ 3. Press the **Enter** key twice. The text is entered into cell A1 and the active cell moves down two rows to cell A3.

▸ 4. Type **Author** in cell A3, and then press the **Tab** key. The text is entered and the active cell moves one column to the right to cell B3.

▸ 5. Type your name in cell B3, and then press the **Enter** key. The text is entered and the active cell moves one cell down and to the left to cell A4.

▸ 6. Type **Date** in cell A4, and then press the **Tab** key. The text is entered and the active cell moves one column to the right to cell B4, where you would enter the date you created the worksheet. For now, you will leave the cell for the date blank.

▸ 7. Click cell **A5** to make it the active cell, type **Purpose** in the cell, and then press the **Tab** key. The active cell moves one column to the right to cell B5.

▸ 8. Type **To record customer book orders**. in cell B5, and then press the **Enter** key. Figure 1-12 shows the text entered in the Documentation sheet.

| Figure 1-12 | Documentation sheet |

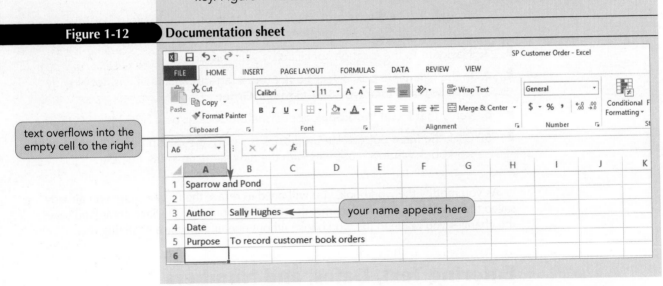

The text you entered in cell A1 is so long that it appears to overflow into cell B1. The same is true for the text you entered in cells B3 and B5. Any text you enter in a cell that doesn't fit within that cell will cover the adjacent cells to the right as long as they are empty. If the adjacent cells contain data, only the text that fits into the cell is displayed. The rest of the text entry is hidden from view. The text itself is not affected. The complete text is still entered in the cell; it is just not displayed. (You will learn how to display all text in a cell in the next session.)

Undoing and Redoing an Action

As you enter data in a workbook, you might need to undo a previous action. Excel maintains a list of the actions you performed in the workbook during the current session, so you can undo most of your actions. You can use the Undo button on the Quick Access Toolbar or press the Ctrl+Z keys to reverse your most recent actions one at a time. If you want to undo more than one action, you can click the Undo button arrow and then select the earliest action you want to undo—all of the actions after the earliest action you selected are also undone.

You will undo the most recent change you made to the Documentation sheet—the text you entered into cell B5. Then you will enter more descriptive and accurate description of the worksheet's purpose.

To undo the text entry in cell B5:

▶ **1.** On the Quick Access Toolbar, click the **Undo** button ↺ (or press the **Ctrl+Z** keys). The last action is reversed, removing the text you entered in cell B5.

▶ **2.** In cell B5, type **To record book orders from a Sparrow & Pond customer.** and then press the **Enter** key.

If you want to restore actions you have undone, you can redo them. To redo one action at a time, you can click the Redo button ↻ on the Quick Access Toolbar or press the Ctrl+Y keys. To redo multiple actions at once, you can click the Redo button arrow and then click the earliest action you want to redo. After you undo or redo an action, Excel continues the action list starting from any new changes you make to the workbook.

Editing Cell Content

As you work, you might find mistakes you need to correct or entries that you want to change. If you want to replace all of the content in a cell, you simply select the cell and then type the new entry to overwrite the previous entry. However, if you need to replace only part of a cell's content, you can work in **Edit mode**. To switch to Edit mode, you double-click the cell. A blinking insertion point indicates where the new content you type will be inserted. In the cell or formula bar, the pointer changes to an I-beam, which you can use to select text in the cell. Anything you type replaces the selected content.

You need to edit the text in cell A1 to Sparrow & Pond. You will switch to Edit mode to correct the text.

To edit the text in cell A1:

▶ **1.** Double-click cell **A1** to select the cell and switch to Edit mode. A blinking insertion point appears within the text of cell A1. The status bar displays EDIT instead of READY to indicate that the cell is in Edit mode.

▶ **2.** Press the arrow keys to move the insertion point directly to the right of the word "and" in the company name.

▶ **3.** Press the **Backspace** key three times to delete the word "and."

▶ **4.** Type **&** to enter the new text, and then press the **Enter** key. The cell text changes to Sparrow & Pond. See Figure 1-13.

| Figure 1-13 | **Revised Documentation sheet** |

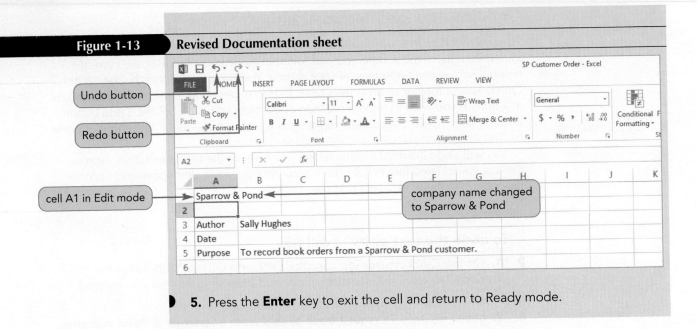

5. Press the **Enter** key to exit the cell and return to Ready mode.

Understanding AutoComplete

As you type text in the active cell, Excel tries to anticipate the remaining characters by displaying text that begins with the same letters as a previous entry in the same column. This feature, known as **AutoComplete**, helps make entering repetitive text easier. To accept the suggested text, press the Tab or Enter key. To override the suggested text, continue to type the text you want to enter in the cell. AutoComplete does not work with dates or numbers, or when a blank cell is between the previous entry and the text you are typing.

Next, you will enter the contact information for Tobias Gregson, a customer who recently placed an order with Sparrow & Pond. You will enter the contact information on the Customer Order worksheet.

To enter Tobias Gregson's contact information:

1. Click the **Customer Order** sheet tab to make it the active sheet.

2. In cell A1, type **Customer Order** as the worksheet title, and then press the **Enter** key twice. The worksheet title is entered in cell A1, and the active cell is cell A3.

3. Type **Ship To** in cell A3, and then press the **Enter** key. The label is entered in the cell, and the active cell is now cell A4.

4. In the range A4:A10, enter the following labels, pressing the **Enter** key after each entry and ignoring any AutoComplete suggestions: **First Name**, **Last Name**, **Address**, **City**, **State**, **Postal Code**, and **Phone**.

5. Click cell **B4** to make that cell the active cell.

> **6.** In the range B4:B10, enter the following contact information, pressing the **Enter** key after each entry and ignoring any AutoComplete suggestions: **Tobias**, **Gregson**, **412 Apple Grove St.**, **Nashua**, **NH**, **03061**, and **(603) 555-4128**. See Figure 1-14.

Figure 1-14   **Text entered in the Customer Order worksheet**

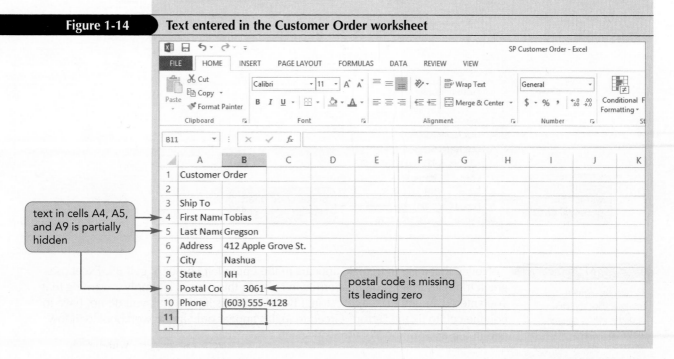

text in cells A4, A5, and A9 is partially hidden

postal code is missing its leading zero

Displaying Numbers as Text

When you type numbers in the active cell, Excel treats the entry as a number and ignores any leading zero. For example, in cell B9, the first digit of the postal code 03061 is missing; Excel displays 3061 because the numbers 3061 and 03061 have the same value. To specify that a number entry should be considered text and all digits should be displayed, you include an apostrophe (') before the numbers.

You will make this change in cell B9 so that Excel treats the postal code as text and displays all of the digits you type.

To enter the postal code as text:

> **1.** Click cell **B9** to select it. Notice that the postal code is right-aligned in the cell, unlike the other text entries, which are left-aligned—another indication that the entry is being treated as a number.

> **2.** Type **'03061** in cell B9, and then press the **Enter** key. The text 03061 appears in cell B9 and is left-aligned in the cell, matching all of the other text entries. See Figure 1-15.

Figure 1-15 | Number displayed as text

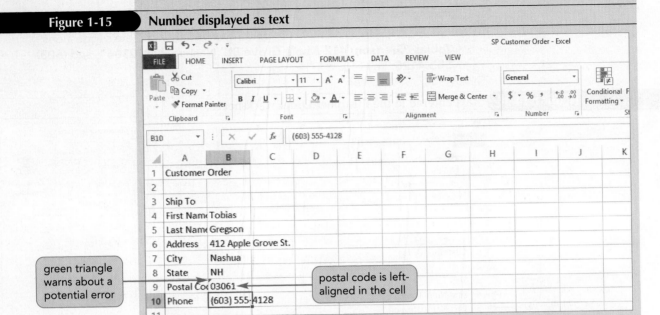

green triangle warns about a potential error

postal code is left-aligned in the cell

Notice that a green triangle appears in the upper-left corner of cell B9. Excel uses green triangles to flag potential errors in cells. In this case, it is simply a warning that you entered a number as a text string. Because this is intentional, you do not have to edit the cell to fix the "error." Green triangles appear only in the workbook window and not in any printouts of the worksheet.

Entering Dates

You can enter dates in any of the standard date formats. For example, all of the following entries are recognized by Excel as the same date:

- 4/6/2016
- 4/6/16
- 4-6-2016
- April 6, 2016
- 6-Apr-16

Even though you enter a date as text, Excel stores the date as a number equal to the number of days between the specified date and January 0, 1900. Times are also entered as text and stored as fractions of a 24-hour day. For example, the date and time April 4, 2016 @ 6:00 PM is stored by Excel as 42,464.75. Dates and times are stored as numbers so that Excel can easily perform date and time calculations, such as determining the elapsed time between one date and another.

Based on the default date format your computer uses, Excel might alter the format of a date after you type it. For example, if you enter the date 4/6/16 into the active cell, Excel might display the date with the four-digit year value, 4/6/2016; if you enter the text April 6, 2016, Excel might convert the date format to 6-Apr-16. Changing the date or time format does not affect the underlying date or time value.

International Date Formats

As business transactions become more international in scope, you may need to adopt international standards for expressing dates, times, and currency values in your workbooks. For example, a worksheet cell might contain 06/05/16. This format could represent any of the following dates: the 5th of June, 2016; the 6th of May, 2016; and the 16th of May, 2006.

The date depends on which country the workbook has been designed for. You can avoid this problem by entering the full date, as in June 5, 2016. However, this might not work with documents written in foreign languages, such as Japanese, that use different character symbols.

To solve this problem, many international businesses adopt ISO (International Organization for Standardization) dates in the format *yyyy-mm-dd*, where *yyyy* is the four-digit year value, *mm* is the two-digit month value, and *dd* is the two-digit day value. So, a date such as June 5, 2016 is entered as 2016/06/05. If you choose to use this international date format, make sure that people using your workbook understand this format so they do not misinterpret the dates. You can include information about the date format in the Documentation sheet.

For the SP Customer Order workbook, you will enter dates in the format *mm/dd/yyyy*, where *mm* is the 2-digit month number, *dd* is the 2-digit day number, and *yyyy* is the 4-digit year number.

To enter the current date into the Documentation sheet:

1. Click the **Documentation** sheet tab to make the Documentation sheet the active worksheet.

2. Click cell **B4** to make it active, type the current date in the *mm/dd/yyyy* format, and then press the **Enter** key. The date is entered in the cell.

   Trouble? Depending on your system configuration, Excel might change the date to the date format *dd-mmm-yy*. This difference will not affect your work.

3. Make the **Customer Order** worksheet the active sheet.

The next part of the Customer Order worksheet will list the books the customer purchased from Sparrow & Pond. As shown in Figure 1-16, the list includes identifying information about each book, its price, and the quantity ordered.

Figure 1-16   **Book order from Tobias Gregson**

ISBN	CATEGORY	BINDING	TITLE	AUTHOR(S)	PRICE	QTY
0-374-25385-4	Used	Hardcover	Samurai William: The Englishman Who Opened Japan	Milton, Giles	$5.95	2
4-889-96213-1	New	Softcover	Floral Origami Globes	Fuse, Tomoko	$24.95	3
0-500-27062-7	New	Hardcover	Tao Magic: The Secret Language of Diagrams and Calligraphy	Legeza, Laszlo	$8.95	1
0-785-82169-4	Used	Hardcover	The Holy Grail	Morgan, Giles	$3.75	1
0-854-56516-7	New	Softcover	Murder on the Links	Christie, Agatha	$7.50	2

You will enter the first five columns of the book order into the worksheet.

To enter the first part of the book order:

1. In the Customer Order worksheet, click cell **A12** to make it the active cell, type **ISBN** as the column label, and then press the **Tab** key to move to cell B12.

2. In the range B12:E12, type the following labels, pressing the **Tab** key to move to the next cell: **CATEGORY**, **BINDING**, **TITLE**, and **AUTHOR(S)**.

3. Press the **Enter** key to go to the next row of the worksheet, making cell A13 the active cell.

4. In the range A13:E17, enter the ISBN, category, binding, title, and author text for the five books listed in Figure 1-16, pressing the **Tab** key to move from one cell to the next, and pressing the **Enter** key to move to a new row. See Figure 1-17. The text in some cells will be partially hidden; you will fix that problem shortly.

| Figure 1-17 | Tobias Gregson's partial book order |

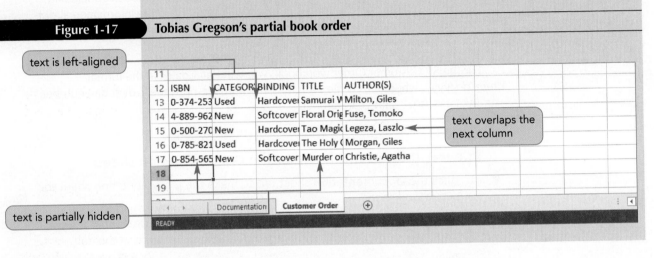

text is left-aligned

text overlaps the next column

text is partially hidden

Entering Numbers

In Excel, numbers can be integers such as 378, decimals such as 1.95, or negatives such as −5.2. In the case of currency and percentages, you can include the currency symbol and percent sign when you enter the value. Excel treats a currency value such as $87.25 as the number 87.25, and a percentage such as 95% as the decimal 0.95. Much like dates, currency and percentages are formatted in a convenient way for you to read, but only the number is stored within the cell. This makes it easier to perform calculations with currency and percentage values.

You will complete the information for Tobias Gregson's order by entering the price for each title and the quantity of each title he ordered.

To enter the price and quantity of books ordered:

1. In the range F12:G12, enter **PRICE** and **QTY** as the labels.

2. In cell F13, enter **$5.95** as the price of the first book. The book price is stored as a number but displayed with the $ symbol.

3. In cell G13, enter **2** as the quantity of books ordered.

4. In the range F14:G17, enter the remaining prices and quantities shown in Figure 1-16. See Figure 1-18.

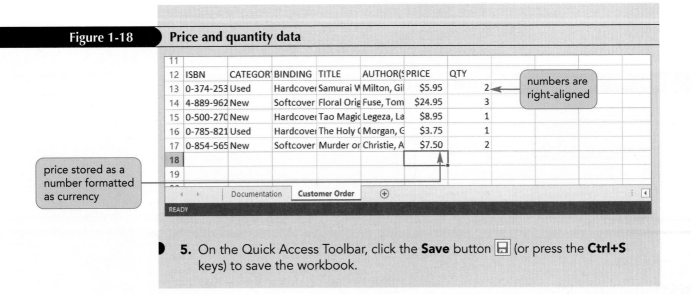

Figure 1-18   Price and quantity data

price stored as a number formatted as currency

numbers are right-aligned

> **5.** On the Quick Access Toolbar, click the **Save** button 🖫 (or press the **Ctrl+S** keys) to save the workbook.

Resizing Columns and Rows

Much of the information in the Customer Order worksheet is difficult to read because of the hidden text. You can make the cell content easier to read by changing the size of the columns and rows in the worksheet.

Changing Column Widths

Column widths are expressed as the number of characters the column can contain. The default column width is 8.43 standard-sized characters. In general, this means that you can type eight characters in a cell; any additional text is hidden or overlaps the adjacent cell. Column widths are also expressed in terms of pixels. A **pixel** is a single point on a computer monitor or printout. A column width of 8.43 characters is equivalent to 64 pixels.

INSIGHT

Setting Column Widths

On a computer monitor, pixel size is based on screen resolution. As a result, cell contents that look fine on one screen might appear very different when viewed on a screen with a different resolution. If you work on multiple computers or share your workbooks with others, you should set column widths based on the maximum number of characters you want displayed in the cells rather than pixel size. This ensures that everyone sees the cell contents the way you intended.

You will increase the width of column A so that the contact information labels in cells A4 and A5 and the ISBN numbers in the range A13:A17 are completely displayed.

To increase the width of column A:

> **1.** Move the pointer over the right border of the column A heading until the pointer changes to ✛.

> **2.** Click and drag to the right until the width of the column heading reaches **15** characters, but do not release the mouse button. The ScreenTip that appears as you resize the column shows the new column width in characters and in pixels.

> **3.** Release the mouse button. The width of column A expands to 15 characters, and all of the text within that column is visible within the cells. See Figure 1-19.

Figure 1-19 | Width of column A increased

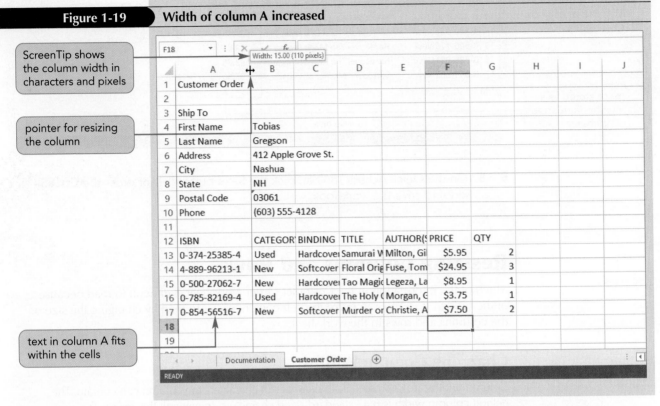

ScreenTip shows the column width in characters and pixels

pointer for resizing the column

text in column A fits within the cells

You will increase the widths of columns B and C to 18 characters so that their complete entries are visible. Rather than resizing each column separately, you can select both columns and adjust their widths at the same time.

To increase the widths of columns B and C:

> **1.** Click the **column B** heading. The entire column is selected.

> **2.** Hold down the **Ctrl** key, click the **column C** heading, and then release the **Ctrl** key. Both columns B and C are selected.

> **3.** Move the pointer to the right border of the column C heading until the pointer changes to ✛.

> **4.** Drag to the right until the column width changes to **18** characters, and then release the mouse button. Both column widths increase to 18 characters and display all of the entered text.

TIP

To select multiple columns, you can also click and drag the pointer over multiple column headings.

The book titles in column D are partially hidden. You will increase the width of this column to 30 characters. Rather than using your mouse, you can set the column width using the Format command on the HOME tab. The Format command gives you precise control over setting column widths and row heights.

To set the width of column D with the Format command:

▶ **1.** Click the **column D** heading. The entire column is selected.

▶ **2.** On the HOME tab, in the Cells group, click the **Format** button, and then click **Column Width**. The Column Width dialog box opens.

▶ **3.** Type **30** in the Column width box to specify the new column width.

▶ **4.** Click the **OK** button. The width of column D changes to 30 characters.

▶ **5.** Change the width of column E to **15** characters.

▶ **6.** Click cell **A1**. The revised column widths are shown in Figure 1-20.

Figure 1-20   **Resized columns**

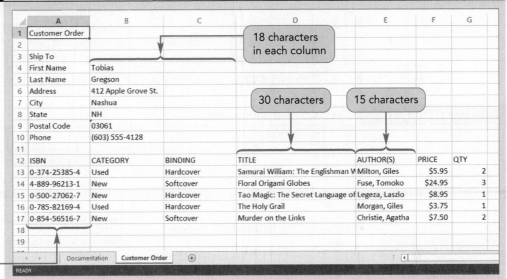

Even with the width of column D increased, some of the book titles still don't fit within the allotted space. Instead of manually changing the column width to display all of the text, you can autofit the column. **AutoFit** changes the column width or row height to display the longest or tallest entry within the column or row. You autofit a column or a row by double-clicking the right border of the column heading or the bottom border of the row heading.

TIP

If the row or column is blank, autofitting restores its default height or width.

To autofit the contents of column D:

▶ **1.** Move the pointer over the right border of column D until the pointer changes to ✛.

▶ **2.** Double-click the right border of the column D heading. The width of column D increases to about 54 characters so that the longest book title is completely visible.

Wrapping Text Within a Cell

Sometimes, resizing a column width to display all of the text entered in the cells makes the worksheet more difficult to read. This is the case with column D in the Customer Order worksheet. Another way to display long text entries is to wrap text to a new line when it extends beyond the column width. When text wraps within a cell, the row height increases so that all of the text within the cell is displayed.

You will resize column D, and then wrap the text entries in the column.

To wrap text in column D:

 1. Resize the width of column D to **30** characters.

 2. Select the range **D13:D17**. These cells include the titles that extend beyond the new cell width.

 3. On the HOME tab, in the Alignment group, click the **Wrap Text** button. The Wrap Text button is toggled on, and text in the selected cells that exceeds the column width wraps to a new line.

 4. Click cell **A12** to make it the active cell. See Figure 1-21.

| Figure 1-21 | Text wrapped within cells |

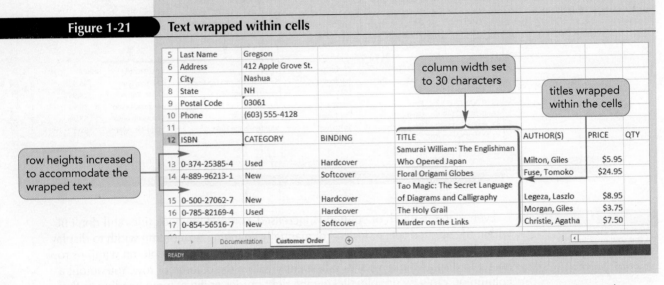

If you want to create a new line within a cell, press the Alt+Enter keys to move the insertion point to the next line within the cell. Whatever you type next will appear on the new line in the cell.

Changing Row Heights

The height of a row is measured in points or pixels. A **point** is approximately 1/72 of an inch. The default row height is 15 points or 20 pixels. Row heights are set in the same way as column widths. You can drag the bottom border of the row heading to a new row height, specify a row height using the Format command, or autofit the row's height to match its content.

Sanjit wants you add more space above the labels in the book list by resizing row 12.

To increase the height of row 12:

1. Move the pointer over the bottom border of the row 12 heading until the pointer changes to ✛.

2. Drag the bottom border down until the height of the row is equal to **30** points (or **40** pixels), and then release the mouse button. The height of row 12 is set to 30 points.

3. Press the **Ctrl+S** keys to save the workbook.

You have entered most of the data for Tobias Gregson's order at Sparrow & Pond. In the next session, you will calculate the total charge for the order and print the worksheet.

REVIEW

Session 1.1 Quick Check

1. What are the two types of sheets used in a workbook?
2. What is the cell reference for the cell located in the fourth column and third row of a worksheet?
3. What is the range reference for the block of cells B10 through C15?
4. What is the reference for the nonadjacent block of cells B10 through C15 and cells B20 through D25?
5. What keyboard shortcut changes the active cell to cell A1?
6. What is text data?
7. Cell A4 contains *May 3, 2016*; why doesn't Excel consider this entry a text string?
8. How do you resize a column or row?

Session 1.2 Visual Overview:

The font size refers to how big the text is.

You use the PAGE LAYOUT tab to change how the worksheet will appear on the printed page.

In Excel, every formula begins with an equal sign (=).

When the active cell contains a formula, the formula appears in the formula bar but the result of the formula appears in the cell.

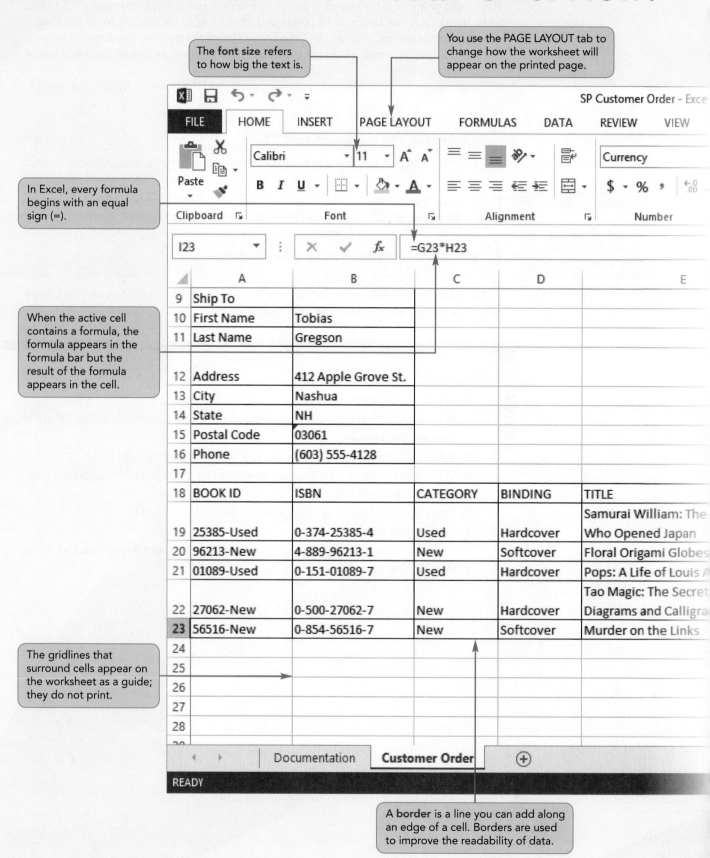

	A	B	C	D	E
9	Ship To				
10	First Name	Tobias			
11	Last Name	Gregson			
12	Address	412 Apple Grove St.			
13	City	Nashua			
14	State	NH			
15	Postal Code	03061			
16	Phone	(603) 555-4128			
17					
18	BOOK ID	ISBN	CATEGORY	BINDING	TITLE
19	25385-Used	0-374-25385-4	Used	Hardcover	Samurai William: The Who Opened Japan
20	96213-New	4-889-96213-1	New	Softcover	Floral Origami Globes
21	01089-Used	0-151-01089-7	Used	Hardcover	Pops: A Life of Louis A
22	27062-New	0-500-27062-7	New	Hardcover	Tao Magic: The Secret Diagrams and Calligra
23	56516-New	0-854-56516-7	New	Softcover	Murder on the Links
24					
25					
26					
27					
28					

Formula bar: =G23*H23

Cell reference box: I23

Currency format, Calibri, 11

The gridlines that surround cells appear on the worksheet as a guide; they do not print.

Documentation | **Customer Order** | +

READY

A **border** is a line you can add along an edge of a cell. Borders are used to improve the readability of data.

Formulas and Functions

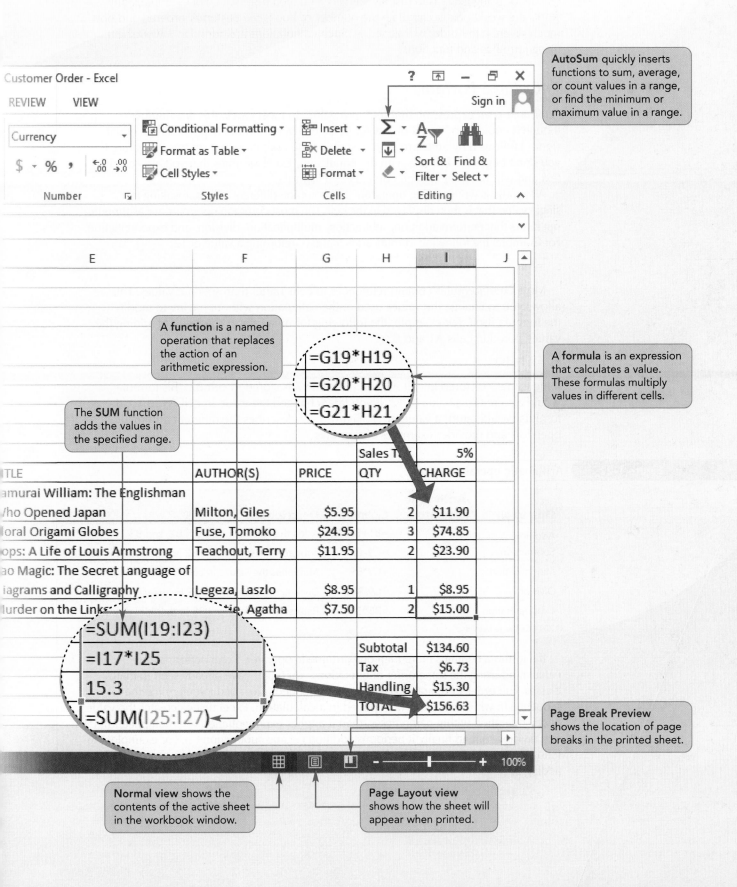

AutoSum quickly inserts functions to sum, average, or count values in a range, or find the minimum or maximum value in a range.

A **function** is a named operation that replaces the action of an arithmetic expression.

A **formula** is an expression that calculates a value. These formulas multiply values in different cells.

The **SUM** function adds the values in the specified range.

=G19*H19
=G20*H20
=G21*H21

TLE	AUTHOR(S)	PRICE	QTY	CHARGE
			Sales T	5%
amurai William: The Englishman				
/ho Opened Japan	Milton, Giles	$5.95	2	$11.90
loral Origami Globes	Fuse, Tomoko	$24.95	3	$74.85
ops: A Life of Louis Armstrong	Teachout, Terry	$11.95	2	$23.90
ao Magic: The Secret Language of				
iagrams and Calligraphy	Legeza, Laszlo	$8.95	1	$8.95
urder on the Links	ie, Agatha	$7.50	2	$15.00

=SUM(I19:I23)
=I17*I25
15.3
=SUM(I25:I27)

Subtotal	$134.60
Tax	$6.73
Handling	$15.30
TOTAL	$156.63

Page Break Preview shows the location of page breaks in the printed sheet.

Normal view shows the contents of the active sheet in the workbook window.

Page Layout view shows how the sheet will appear when printed.

100%

Adding Formulas to a Worksheet

So far you have entered text, numbers, and dates in the worksheet. However, the main reason for using Excel is to display values calculated from data. For example, Sally wants the workbook to calculate the number of books the customer ordered and how much revenue the order will generate. Such calculations are added to a worksheet using formulas and functions.

Entering a Formula

A formula is an expression that returns a value. In most cases, this is a number— though it could also be text or a date. In Excel, every formula begins with an equal sign (=) followed by an expression describing the operation that returns the value. If you don't begin the formula with the equal sign, Excel assumes that you are entering text and will not treat the cell contents as a formula.

A formula is written using **operators** that combine different values, resulting in a single value that is then displayed in the cell. The most common operators are **arithmetic operators** that perform addition, subtraction, multiplication, division, and exponentiation. For example, the following formula adds 5 and 7, returning a value of 12:

=5+7

Most Excel formulas contain references to cells rather than specific values. This allows you to change the values used in the calculation without having to modify the formula itself. For example, the following formula returns the result of adding the values stored in cells A1 and B2:

=A1+B2

If the value 5 is stored in cell A1 and the value 7 is stored in cell B2, this formula would also return a value of 12. If you later changed the value in cell A1 to 10, the formula would return a value of 17. Figure 1-22 describes the different arithmetic operators and provides examples of formulas.

Figure 1-22   Arithmetic operators

Operation	Arithmetic Operator	Example	Description
Addition	+	=B1+B2+B3	Adds the values in cells B1, B2, and B3
Subtraction	–	=C9–B2	Subtracts the value in cell B2 from the value in cell C9
Multiplication	*	=C9*B9	Multiplies the values in cells C9 and B9
Division	/	=C9/B9	Divides the value in cell C9 by the value in cell B9
Exponentiation	^	=B5^3	Raises the value of cell B5 to the third power

© 2014 Cengage Learning

If a formula contains more than one arithmetic operator, Excel performs the calculation using the same order of operations you might have already seen in math classes. The **order of operations** is a set of predefined rules used to determine the sequence in which operators are applied in a calculation. Excel first calculates the value of any operation within parentheses, then it applies exponentiation (^), multiplication (*), and division (/), and finally it performs addition (+) and subtraction (–). For example, the following formula returns the value 23 because multiplying 4 by 5 takes precedence over adding 3:

=3+4*5

If a formula contains two or more operators with the same level of priority, the operators are applied in order from left to right. In the following formula, Excel first multiplies 4 by 10 and then divides that result by 8 to return the value 5:

=4*10/8

When parentheses are used, the value inside them is calculated first. In the following formula, Excel calculates (3+4) first, and then multiplies that result by 5 to return the value 35:

=(3+4)*5

Figure 1-23 shows how slight changes in a formula affect the order of operations and the result of the formula.

Figure 1-23   **Order of operations applied to Excel formulas**

Formula	Application of the Order of Operations	Result
=50+10*5	10*5 calculated first and then 50 is added	100
=(50+10)*5	(50+10) calculated first and then 60 is multiplied by 5	300
=50/10–5	50/10 calculated first and then 5 is subtracted	0
=50/(10–5)	(10–5) calculated first and then 50 is divided by that value	10
=50/10*5	Two operators at same precedence level, so the calculation is done left to right in the expression	25
=50/(10*5)	(10*5) is calculated first and then 50 is divided by that value	1

© 2014 Cengage Learning

Sally wants the Customer Order worksheet to include the total amount charged for each book. The charge is equal to the number of books ordered multiplied by the book's price. You already entered this information in columns F and G. Now you will enter a formula to calculate the charge for books ordered in column H.

To enter the formula to calculate the charge for the first book order:

1. Make cell **H12** the active cell, type **CHARGE** as the column label, and then press the **Enter** key. The label text is entered in cell H12, and cell H13 is now the active cell.

2. Type **=F13*G13** (the price of the book multiplied by the quantity of books ordered). As you type the formula, a list of Excel function names appears in a ScreenTip, which provides a quick method for entering functions. The list will close when you complete the formula. You will learn more about Excel functions shortly. Also, as you type each cell reference, Excel color codes the cell reference with the cell. See Figure 1-24.

Figure 1-24   **Formula being entered in a cell**

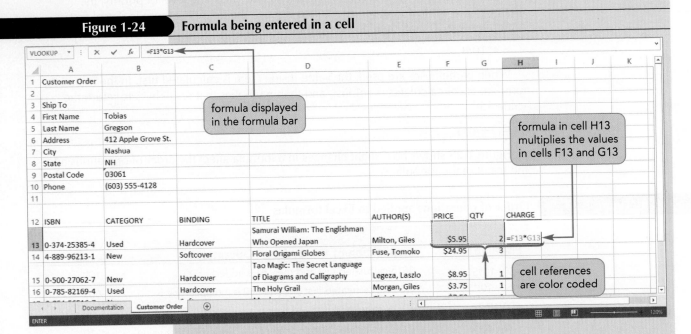

3. Press the **Enter** key. The formula is entered in cell H13, which displays the value $11.90. The result is displayed as currency because cell F13, which is referenced in the formula, contains a currency value.

4. Click cell **H13** to make it the active cell. The cell displays the result of the formula, and the formula bar displays the formula you entered.

For the first book, you entered the formula by typing each cell reference in the expression. You can also insert a cell reference by clicking the cell as you type the formula. This technique reduces the possibility of error caused by typing an incorrect cell reference. You will use this method to enter the formula to calculate the charge for the second book.

To enter the cell references in the formula using the mouse:

1. Click cell **H14** to make it the active cell.

2. Type **=**. The equal sign indicates that you are entering a formula. Any cell you click from now on inserts the cell reference of the selected cell into the formula until you complete the formula by pressing the Enter or Tab key.

3. Click cell **F14**. The cell reference is inserted into the formula in the formula bar. At this point, any cell you click changes the cell reference used in the formula. The cell reference isn't locked until you type an operator.

4. Type ***** to enter the multiplication operator. The cell reference for cell F14 is locked in the formula, and the next cell you click will be inserted after the operator.

5. Click cell **G14** to enter its cell reference in the formula. The formula is complete.

6. Press the **Enter** key. Cell H14 displays the value $74.85, which is the total charge for the second book.

Be sure to type = as the first part of the entry; otherwise, Excel will not interpret the entry as a formula.

Copying and Pasting Formulas

Sometimes you will need to repeat the same formula throughout a worksheet. Rather than retyping the formula, you can copy a formula from one cell and paste it into another cell. When you copy a formula, Excel places the formula into the **Clipboard**, which is a temporary storage location for text and graphics. When you paste, Excel takes the formula from the Clipboard and inserts it into the selected cell or range. Excel adjusts the cell references in the formula to reflect the formula's new location in the worksheet. This occurs because you usually want to copy the actions of a formula rather than the specific value the formula generates. In this case, the formula's action is to multiply the price of the book by the quantity. By copying and pasting the formula, you can quickly repeat that action for every book listed in the worksheet.

You will copy the formula you entered in cell H14 to the range H15:H17 to calculate the charges on the remaining three books in Tobias Gregson's order. By copying and pasting the formula, you will save time and avoid potential mistakes from retyping the formula.

To copy and paste the formula:

1. Click cell **H14** to select the cell that contains the formula you want to copy.

2. On the HOME tab, in the Clipboard group, click the **Copy** button (or press the **Ctrl+C** keys). Excel copies the formula to the Clipboard.

3. Select the range **H15:H17**. You want to paste the formula into these cells.

4. In the Clipboard group, click the **Paste** button (or press the **Ctrl+V** keys). Excel pastes the formula into the selected cells, adjusting each formula so that the total charges calculated for the books are based on the corresponding values within each row. A button appears below the selected range, providing options for pasting formulas and values. See Figure 1-25.

Figure 1-25   **Copied and pasted formula**

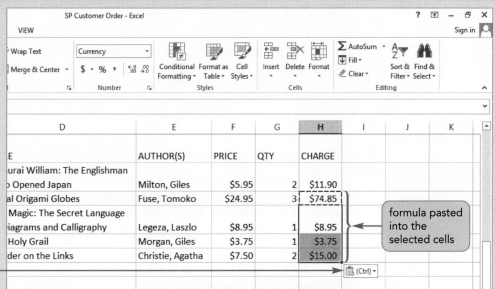

button provides more options for pasting formulas and values

formula pasted into the selected cells

▶ **5.** Click cell **H15** and verify that the formula =F15*G15 appears in the formula bar. The formula was updated to reflect the cell references in the corresponding row.

▶ **6.** Click the other cells in column H and verify that the corresponding formulas are entered in those cells.

Simplifying Formulas with Functions

In addition to cell references and operators, formulas can also contain functions. A function is a named operation that replaces the arithmetic expression in a formula. Functions are used to simplify long or complex formulas. For example, to add the values from cells A1 through A10, you could enter the following long formula:

=A1+A2+A3+A4+A5+A6+A7+A8+A9+A10

Or, you could use the SUM function to calculate the sum of those cell values by entering the following formula:

=SUM(A1:A10)

In both instances, Excel adds the values in cells A1 through A10, but the SUM function is faster and simpler to enter and less prone to a typing error. You should always use a function, if one is available, in place of a long, complex formula. Excel supports more than 300 different functions from the fields of finance, business, science, and engineering. Excel provides functions that work with numbers, text, and dates.

Introducing Function Syntax

Every function follows a set of rules, or **syntax**, which specifies how the function should be written. The general syntax of all Excel functions is

FUNCTION (argument1, argument2, …)

where FUNCTION is the function name, and argument1, argument2, and so forth are values used by that function. For example, the SUM function shown above uses a single argument, A1:A10, which is the range reference of the cells whose values will be added. Some functions do not require any arguments and are entered as FUNCTION(). Functions without arguments still require the opening and closing parentheses, but do not include a value within the parentheses.

Entering Functions with AutoSum

A fast and convenient way to enter commonly used functions is with AutoSum. The AutoSum button includes options to insert the SUM, AVERAGE, COUNT, MIN, and MAX functions to generate the following:

- Sum of the values in the specified range
- Average value in the specified range
- Total count of numeric values in the specified range
- Minimum value in the specified range
- Maximum value in the specified range

After you select one of the AutoSum options, Excel determines the most appropriate range from the available data and enters it as the function's argument. You should always verify that the range included in the AutoSum function matches the range that you want to use.

You will use AutoSum to enter the SUM function to add the total charges for Tobias Gregson's order.

To use AutoSum to enter the SUM function:

▶ **1.** Click cell **G18** to make it the active cell, type **Subtotal** as the label, and then press the **Tab** key to make cell H18 the active cell.

▶ **2.** On the HOME tab, in the Editing group, click the **AutoSum button arrow**. The button's menu opens and displays five common summary functions: Sum, Average, Count Numbers, Max (for maximum), and Min (for minimum).

▶ **3.** Click **Sum** to enter the SUM function. The formula =SUM(H13:H17) is entered in cell H18. The cells involved in calculating the sum are selected and highlighted on the worksheet so you can quickly confirm that Excel selected the most appropriate range from the available data. A ScreenTip appears below the formula describing the function's syntax. See Figure 1-26.

| Figure 1-26 | SUM function being entered with the AutoSum button |

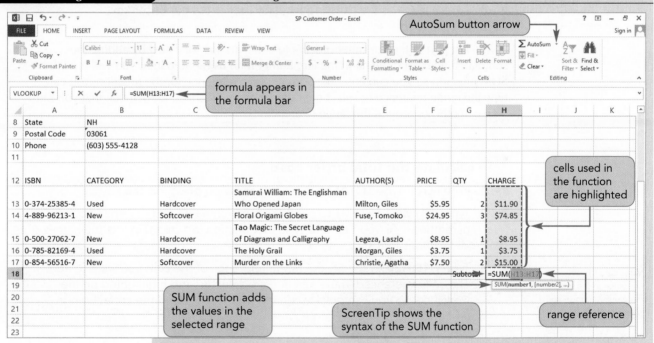

▶ **4.** Press the **Enter** key to accept the formula. The subtotal of the book charges returned by the SUM function is $114.45.

AutoSum makes entering a commonly used formula such as the SUM function fast and easy. However, AutoSum can determine the appropriate range reference to include only when the function is adjacent to the cells containing the values you want to summarize. If you need to use a function elsewhere in the worksheet, you will have to select the range reference to include or type the function yourself.

Each sale made by Sparrow & Pond is subject to a 5 percent sales tax and a $15.30 handling fee. You will add these to the Customer Order worksheet so you can calculate the total charge for the order.

To add the sales tax and handling fee to the worksheet:

▶ **1.** Click cell **G11**, type **Sales Tax** as the label, and then press the **Tab** key to make cell H11 the active cell.

▶ **2.** In cell H11, type **5%** as the sales tax rate, and then press the **Enter** key. The sales tax rate is entered in the cell, and can be used in other calculations. The value is displayed with the % symbol, but is stored as the equivalent decimal value 0.05.

▶ **3.** Click cell **G19** to make it the active cell, type **Tax** as the label, and then press the **Tab** key to make cell H19 the active cell.

▶ **4.** Type **=H11*H18** as the formula to calculate the sales tax on the book order, and then press the **Enter** key. The formula multiples the sales tax value in cell H11 by the order subtotal value in cell H18. The value $5.72 is displayed in cell H19, which is 5 percent of the book order subtotal of $114.45.

▶ **5.** In cell G20, type **Handling** as the label, and then press the **Tab** key to make cell H20 the active cell. You will enter the handling fee in this cell.

▶ **6.** Type **$15.30** as the handling fee, and then press the **Enter** key.

The last part of the customer order is to calculate the total cost by adding the subtotal, the tax, and the handling fee. Rather than using AutoSum, you will type the SUM function so you can enter the correct range reference for the function. You can type the range reference or select the range in the worksheet. Remember, that you must type parentheses around the range reference.

To calculate the total order cost:

▶ **1.** In cell G21, type **TOTAL** as the label, and then press the **Tab** key.

▶ **2.** Type **=SUM(** in cell H21 to enter the function name and the opening parenthesis. As you begin to type the function, a ScreenTip lists the names of all functions that start with S.

▶ **3.** Type **H18:H20** to specify the range reference of the cells you want to add. The cells referenced in the function are selected and highlighted on the worksheet so you can quickly confirm that you entered the correct range reference.

Make sure the cell reference in the function matches the range you want to calculate.

4. Type **)** to complete the function, and then press the **Enter** key. The value of the SUM function appears in cell H21, indicating that the total charge for the order is $135.47. See Figure 1-27.

Figure 1-27 | Total charge for the customer order

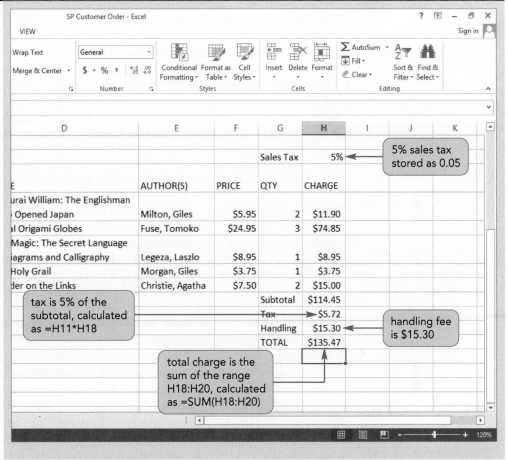

The SUM function makes it simple to quickly add the values in a group of cells.

Problem Solving: Writing Effective Formulas

You can use formulas to quickly perform calculations and solve problems. First, identify the problem you need to solve. Then, gather the data needed to solve the problem. Finally, create accurate and effective formulas that use the data to answer or resolve the problem. Follow these guidelines:

- **Keep formulas simple.** Use functions in place of long, complex formulas whenever possible. For example, use the SUM function instead of entering a formula that adds individual cells, which makes it easier to confirm that the formula is making an accurate calculation as it provides answers needed to evaluate the problem.

- **Do not hide data values within formulas.** The worksheet displays formula results, not the actual formula. For example, to calculate a 5 percent interest rate on a currency value in cell A5, you could enter the formula =0.05*A5. However, this doesn't show how the value is calculated. A better approach places the value 0.05 in a cell accompanied by a descriptive label and uses the cell reference in the formula. If you place 0.05 in cell A6, the formula =A6*A5 would calculate the interest value. Other people can then easily see the interest rate as well as the resulting interest, ensuring that the formula is solving the right problem.

- **Break up formulas to show intermediate results.** When a worksheet contains complex computations, other people can more easily comprehend how the formula results are calculated when different parts of the formula are distinguished. For example, the formula =SUM(A1:A10)/SUM(B1:B10) calculates the ratio of two sums, but hides the two sum values. Instead, enter each SUM function in a separate cell, such as cells A11 and B11, and use the formula =A11/B11 to calculate the ratio. Other people can see both sums and the value of their ratio in the worksheet and better understand the final result, which makes it more likely that the best problem resolution will be selected.

- **Test formulas with simple values.** Use values you can calculate in your head to confirm that your formula works as intended. For example, using 1s or 10s as the input values lets you easily figure out the answer and verify the formula.

Finding a solution to a problem requires accurate data and analysis. With workbooks, this means using formulas that are easy to understand, clearly show the data being used in the calculations, and demonstrate how the results are calculated. Only then can you be confident that you are choosing the best problem resolution.

Modifying a Worksheet

As you develop a worksheet, you might need to modify its content and structure to create a more logical organization. Some ways you can modify a worksheet include moving cells and ranges, inserting rows and columns, deleting rows and columns, and inserting and deleting cells.

Moving and Copying a Cell or Range

One way to move a cell or range is to select it, position the pointer over the bottom border of the selection, drag the selection to a new location, and then release the mouse button. This technique is called **drag and drop** because you are dragging the range and dropping it in a new location. If the drop location is not visible, drag the selection to the edge of the workbook window to scroll the worksheet, and then drop the selection.

You can also use the drag-and-drop technique to copy cells by pressing the Ctrl key as you drag the selected range to its new location. A copy of the original range is placed in the new location without removing the original range from the worksheet.

Moving or Copying a Cell or Range

- Select the cell or range you want to move or copy.
- Move the pointer over the border of the selection until the pointer changes shape.
- To move the range, click the border and drag the selection to a new location (or to copy the range, hold down the Ctrl key and drag the selection to a new location).

or

- Select the cell or range you want to move or copy.
- On the HOME tab, in the Clipboard group, click the Cut or Copy button (or right-click the selection, and then click Cut or Copy on the shortcut menu, or press the Ctrl+X or Ctrl+C keys).
- Select the cell or the upper-left cell of the range where you want to paste the content.
- In the Clipboard group, click the Paste button (or right-click the selection and then click Paste on the shortcut menu, or press the Ctrl+V keys).

Sally wants the subtotal, tax, handling, and total values in the range G18:H21 moved down one row to the range G19:H22 to provide more space from the book orders. You will use the drag-and-drop method to move the range.

To drag and drop the range G18:H21:

1. Select the range **G18:H21**. These are the cells you want to move.

2. Move the pointer over the bottom border of the selected range so that the pointer changes to ⛯.

3. Press and hold the mouse button to change the pointer to ⬚, and then drag the selection down one row. Do not release the mouse button. A ScreenTip appears, indicating that the new range of the selected cells will be G19:H22. A darker border also appears around the new range. See Figure 1-28.

| Figure 1-28 | Range G18:H21 being moved to range G19:H22 |

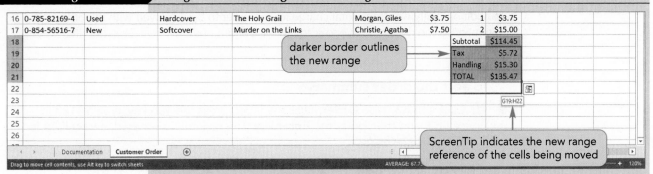

4. Make sure the ScreenTip displays the range **G19:H22**, and then release the mouse button. The selected cells move to their new location.

Some people find dragging and dropping a difficult and awkward way to move a selection, particularly if the selected range is large or needs to move a long distance in the worksheet. In those situations, it is often more efficient to cut or copy and paste the cell contents. Cutting moves the selected content, whereas copying duplicates the selected content. Pasting places the selected content in the new location.

Sally wants the worksheet to include a summary of the customer order starting in row 3. You will cut the customer contact information and the book listing from range A3:A22 and paste it into range A9:H23, freeing up space for the order information.

To cut and paste the customer contact information and book listing:

▶ **1.** Click cell **A3** to select it.

▶ **2.** Press the **Ctrl+Shift+End** keys to extend the selection to the last cell in the lower-right corner of the worksheet (cell H22).

▶ **3.** On the HOME tab, in the Clipboard group, click the **Cut** button (or press the **Ctrl+X** keys). The range is surrounded by a moving border, indicating that it has been cut.

▶ **4.** Click cell **A9** to select it. This is the upper-left corner of the range where you want to paste the range that you cut.

▶ **5.** In the Clipboard group, click the **Paste** button (or press the **Ctrl+V** keys). The range A3:H22 is pasted into the range A9:H28. All of the formulas in the moved range were automatically updated to reflect their new locations.

Using the COUNT Function

Sometimes you will want to know how many unique items are included in a range, such as the number of different books in the customer order. To calculate that value, you use the COUNT function, which has the syntax

=COUNT(*range*)

where *range* is the range of cells containing numeric values to be counted. Note that any cell in the range containing a non-numeric value is not counted in the final tally.

You will include the count of the number of different books for the order in the summary information. The summary will also display the order ID (a unique number assigned by Sparrow & Pond to the order), the shipping date, and the type of delivery (overnight, two-day, or standard) in the freed-up space at the top of the worksheet. In addition, Sally wants the total charge for the order to be displayed with the order summary so she does not have to scroll to the bottom of the worksheet to find that value.

To add the order summary:

▶ **1.** Click cell **A3**, type **Order ID** as the label, press the **Tab** key, type **14123** in cell B3, and then press the **Enter** key. The order ID is entered, and cell A4 is the active cell.

▶ **2.** Type **Shipping Date** as the label in cell A4, press the **Tab** key, type **4/3/2016** in cell B4, and then press the **Enter** key. The shipping date is entered, and cell A5 is the active cell.

▶ **3.** Type **Delivery** as the label in cell A5, press the **Tab** key, type **Overnight** in cell B5, and then press the **Enter** key. The delivery type is entered, and cell A6 is the active cell.

▶ **4.** Type **Items Ordered** as the label in cell A6, and then press the **Tab** key. Cell B6 is the active cell. You will enter the COUNT function to determine the number of different books ordered.

▶ **5.** In cell B6, type **=COUNT(** to begin the function.

6. With the insertion point still blinking in cell B6, select the range **G19:G23**. The range reference is entered as the argument for the COUNT function.

7. Type **)** to complete the function, and then press the **Enter** key. Cell B6 displays the value 5, indicating that five items were ordered by Tobias Gregson. Cell A7 is the active cell.

8. Type **Total Charge** as the label in cell A7, and then press the **Tab** key to make cell B7 the active cell.

9. Type **=** to start the formula, and then click cell **H28** to enter its cell reference in the formula in cell B7. The formula =H28 tells Excel to display the contents of cell H28 in the current cell.

10. Press the **Enter** key to complete the formula. See Figure 1-29.

Figure 1-29   **Customer order summary**

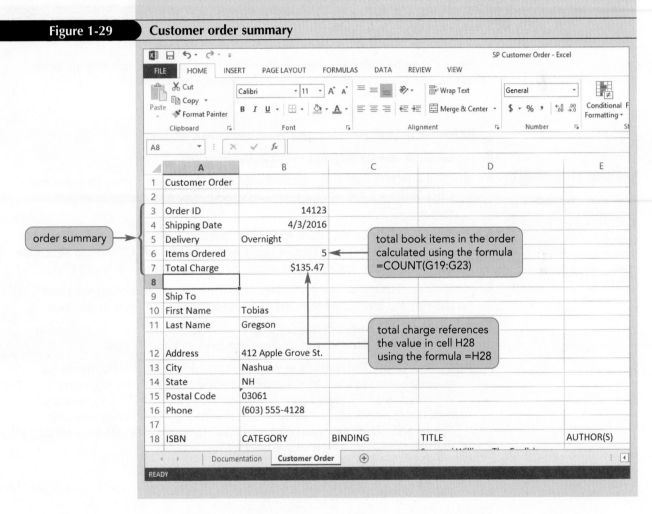

Inserting a Column or Row

You can insert a new column or row anywhere within a worksheet. When you insert a new column, the existing columns are shifted to the right and the new column has the same width as the column directly to its left. When you insert a new row, the existing rows are shifted down and the new row has the same height as the row above it. Because inserting a new row or column moves the location of the other cells in the worksheet, any cell references in a formula or function are updated to reflect the new layout.

REFERENCE

Inserting or Deleting a Column or Row

To insert a column or row:
- Select the column(s) or row(s) where you want to insert the new column(s) or row(s). Excel will insert the same number of columns or rows as you select to the *left* of the selected columns or *above* the selected rows.
- On the HOME tab, in the Cells group, click the Insert button (or right-click a column or row heading or selected column and row headings, and then click Insert on the shortcut menu; or press the Ctrl+Shift+= keys).

To delete a column or row:
- Select the column(s) or row(s) you want to delete.
- On the HOME tab, in the Cells group, click the Delete button (or right-click a column or row heading or selected column and row headings, and then click Delete on the shortcut menu; or press the Ctrl+– keys).

Tobias Gregson's order is missing an item. You need to insert a row directly below *Floral Origami Globes* in which to enter the additional book.

To insert a new row for the missing book order:

▶ 1. Click the **row 21** heading to select the entire row.

TIP

You can insert multiple columns or rows by selecting that number of column or row headings, and then clicking the Insert button or pressing the Ctrl+Shift+= keys.

▶ 2. On the HOME tab, in the Cells group, click the **Insert** button (or press the **Ctrl+Shift+=** keys). A new row is inserted below row 20 and becomes the new row 21.

▶ 3. Enter **0-151-01089-7** in cell A21, enter **Used** in cell B21, enter **Hardcover** in cell C21, enter **Pops: A Life of Louis Armstrong** in cell D21, enter **Teachout, Terry** in cell E21, enter **$11.95** in cell F21, and then enter **2** in cell G21.

▶ 4. Click cell **H20** to select the cell with the formula for calculating the book charge, and then press the **Ctrl+C** keys to copy the formula in that cell.

▶ 5. Click cell **H21** to select the cell where you want to insert the formula, and then press the **Ctrl+V** keys to paste the formula into the cell.

▶ 6. Click cell **H26**. The formula in this cell is now =SUM(H19:H24); the range reference was updated to reflect the inserted row. Also, the tax amount increased to $6.92 based on the new subtotal value of $138.35, and the total charge increased to $160.57 because of the added book order. See Figure 1-30. Also, the result of the COUNT function in cell B6 increased to 6 to reflect the item added to the book order.

| Figure 1-30 | New row inserted |

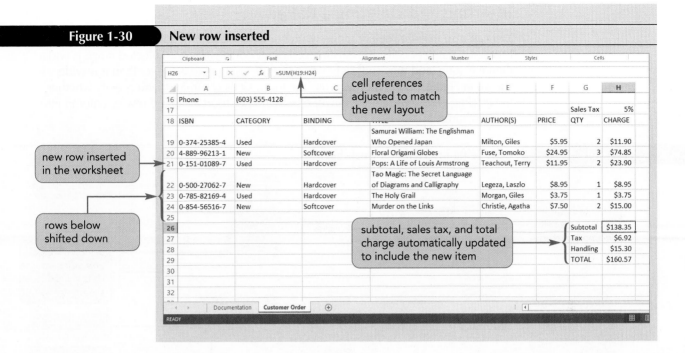

Deleting a Row or Column

You can delete rows or columns from a worksheet. **Deleting** removes the data from the row or column as well as the row or column itself. The rows below the deleted row shift up to fill the vacated space. Likewise, the columns to the right of the deleted column shift left to fill the vacated space. Also, all cell references in the worksheet are adjusted to reflect the change. You click the Delete button in the Cells group on the HOME tab to delete selected rows or columns.

Deleting a column or row is not the same as clearing a column or row. **Clearing** removes the data from the selected row or column but leaves the blank row or column in the worksheet. You press the Delete key to clear the contents of the selected row or column, which leaves the worksheet structure unchanged.

Tobias Gregson did not order *The Holy Grail* by Giles Morgan, so that book needs to be removed from the order. You will delete the row containing that book.

To delete the *The Holy Grail* row from the book order:

▶ **1.** Click the **row 23** heading to select the entire row.

▶ **2.** On the HOME tab, in the Cells group, click the **Delete** button (or press the **Ctrl+–** keys). Row 23 is deleted, and the rows below it shift up to fill the space.

All of the cell references in the worksheet are again updated automatically to reflect the impact of deleting row 23. The subtotal value in cell H25 now returns a value of $134.60 based on the sum of the cells in the range H19:H23. The sales tax amount in cell H26 decreases to $6.73. The total cost of the order decreases to $156.63. Also, the result of the COUNT function in cell B6 decreases to 5 to reflect the item deleted from the book order. As you can see, one of the great advantages of using Excel is that it modifies the formulas to reflect the additions and deletions you make to the worksheet.

Inserting and Deleting a Range

You can also insert or delete ranges within a worksheet. When you use the Insert button to insert a range of cells, the existing cells shift down when the selected range is wider than it is long, and they shift right when the selected range is longer than it is wide, as shown in Figure 1-31. When you use the Insert Cells command, you specify whether the existing cells shift right or down, or whether to insert an entire row or column into the new range.

Figure 1-31	Cells being inserted in a worksheet

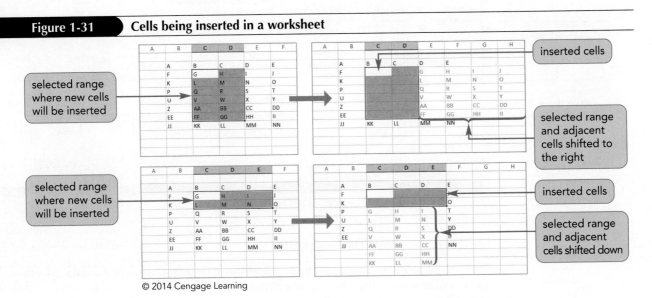

selected range where new cells will be inserted

inserted cells

selected range and adjacent cells shifted to the right

selected range where new cells will be inserted

inserted cells

selected range and adjacent cells shifted down

© 2014 Cengage Learning

The process works in reverse when you delete a range. As with deleting a row or column, the cells adjacent to the deleted range either move up or left to fill in the space vacated by the deleted cells. The Delete Cells command lets you specify whether you want to shift the adjacent cells left or up, or whether you want to delete the entire column or row.

When you insert or delete a range, cells that shift to a new location adopt the width of the columns they move into. As a result, you might need to resize columns and rows in the worksheet.

REFERENCE

Inserting or Deleting a Range

- Select a range that matches the range you want to insert or delete.
- On the HOME tab, in the Cells group, click the Insert button or the Delete button.

or

- Select the range that matches the range you want to insert or delete.
- On the HOME tab, in the Cells group, click the Insert button arrow and then click Insert Cells, or click the Delete button arrow and then click Delete Cells (or right-click the selected range, and then click Insert or Delete on the shortcut menu).
- Click the option button for the direction to shift the cells, columns, or rows.
- Click the OK button.

Sally wants you to insert cells in the book list that will contain the Sparrow & Pond book ID for each book. You will insert these new cells into the range A17:A28, shifting the adjacent cells to the right.

To insert a range in the book list:

1. Select the range **A17:A28**. You want to insert cells in this range.

2. On the HOME tab, in the Cells group, click the **Insert button arrow**. A menu of insert options appears.

3. Click **Insert Cells**. The Insert dialog box opens.

4. Verify that the **Shift cells right** option button is selected.

5. Click the **OK** button. New cells are inserted into the selected range, and the adjacent cells move to the right. The cell contents do not fit well in the columns and rows they shifted into, so you will resize the columns and rows.

6. Resize columns C and D to **12** characters, resize column E to **30** characters, and then resize column F to **15** characters. The text is easier to read in the resized columns.

7. Select the row **19** through row **23** headings.

8. In the Cells group, click the **Format** button, and then click **AutoFit Row Height**. The selected rows autofit to their contents.

TIP

You can also autofit by double-clicking the bottom border of row 23.

9. Click cell **A18**, type **BOOK ID** as the label, and then press the **Enter** key. See Figure 1-32.

Figure 1-32   **Range added to the worksheet**

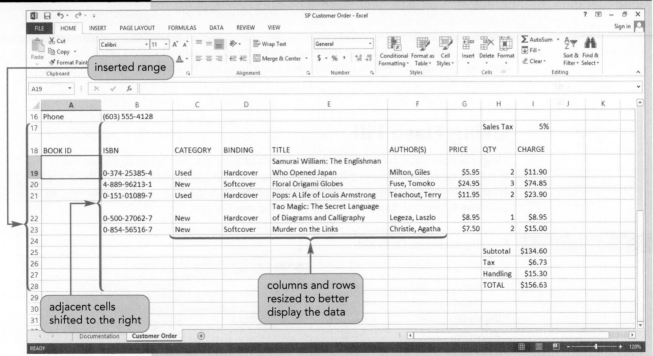

Why did you insert cells in the range A17:A28 even though the book ID values will be entered only in the range A18:A23? You did this to retain the layout of the page design. Selecting the additional rows ensures that the sales tax and summary values still line up with the QTY and CHARGE columns. Whenever you insert a new range, be sure to consider its impact on the layout of the entire worksheet.

INSIGHT

Hiding and Unhiding Rows, Columns, and Worksheets

Workbooks can become long and complicated, filled with formulas and data that are important for performing calculations but are of little interest to readers. In those situations, you can simplify these workbooks for readers by **hiding** rows, columns, and even worksheets. Although the contents of hidden cells cannot be seen, the data in those cells is still available for use in formulas and functions throughout the workbook.

Hiding a row or column essentially decreases that row height or column width to 0 pixels. To a hide a row or column, select the row or column heading, click the Format button in the Cells group on the HOME tab, point to Hide & Unhide on the menu that appears, and then click Hide Rows or Hide Columns. The border of the row or column heading is doubled to mark the location of hidden rows or columns.

A worksheet often is hidden when the entire worksheet contains data that is not of interest to the reader and is better summarized elsewhere in the document. To hide a worksheet, make that worksheet active, click the Format button in the Cells group on the HOME tab, point to Hide & Unhide, and then click Hide Sheet.

Unhiding redisplays the hidden content in the workbook. To unhide a row or column, click in a cell below the hidden row or to the right of the hidden column, click the Format button, point to Hide & Unhide, and then click Unhide Rows or Unhide Columns. To unhide a worksheet, click the Format button, point to Hide & Unhide, and then click Unhide Sheet. The Unhide dialog box opens. Click the sheet you want to unhide, and then click the OK button. The hidden content is redisplayed in the workbook.

Although hiding data can make a worksheet and workbook easier to read, be sure never to hide information that is important to the reader.

Sally wants you to add one more piece of data to the worksheet—a book ID that is used by Sparrow & Pond to identify each book in stock. You will use Flash Fill to create the book IDs.

Using Flash Fill

Flash Fill enters text based on patterns it finds in the data. As shown in Figure 1-33, Flash Fill generates customer names from the first and last names stored in the adjacent columns in the worksheet. To enter the rest of the names, you press the Enter key; to continue typing the names yourself, you press the Esc key.

Figure 1-33   **Entering text with Flash Fill**

	A	B	C	D	E
1	First	M.I.	Last	Full Name	
2	Tobias	A.	Gregson	Tobias Gregson	you enter the full name twice to begin the pattern
3	Maria	R.	Sanchez	Maria Sanchez	
4	Andrew	T.	Lewis	Andrew Lewis	
5	Brett	K.	Carls	Brett Carls	Flash Fill generates the remaining full names based on the pattern in the first two cells
6	Carmen	A.	Hzu	Carmen Hzu	
7	Karen	M.	Schultz	Karen Schultz	
8	Howard	P.	Gary	Howard Gary	
9	Natalia	N.	Shapiro	Natalia Shapiro	
10	Paul	O.	Douglas	Paul Douglas	
11					

Flash Fill works best when the pattern is clearly recognized from the values in the data. Be sure to enter the data pattern in the column or row right next to the related data. The data used to generate the pattern must be in a rectangular grid and cannot have blank columns or rows. Also, Flash Fill enters text, not formulas. If you edit or replace an entry originally used by Flash Fill, the content generated by Flash Fill will not be updated.

The Sparrow & Pond book ID combines five digits of the book's ISBN and its category (used or new). For example, *Floral Origami Globes* has the ISBN 4-889-96213-1 and is new, so its book ID is 96213-New. The book IDs follow a consistent and logical pattern. Rather than typing every book ID, you will use Flash Fill to enter the book IDs into the worksheet.

To enter the book IDs using Flash Fill:

▶ **1.** Make sure that cell **A19** is the active cell.

▶ **2.** Type **25385-Used** as the ID for the first book in the list, and then press the **Enter** key.

▶ **3.** Type **9** in cell A20. As soon as you start typing, Flash Fill generates the remaining entries in the column based on the pattern you entered. See Figure 1-34.

| Figure 1-34 | Book IDs generated by Flash Fill |

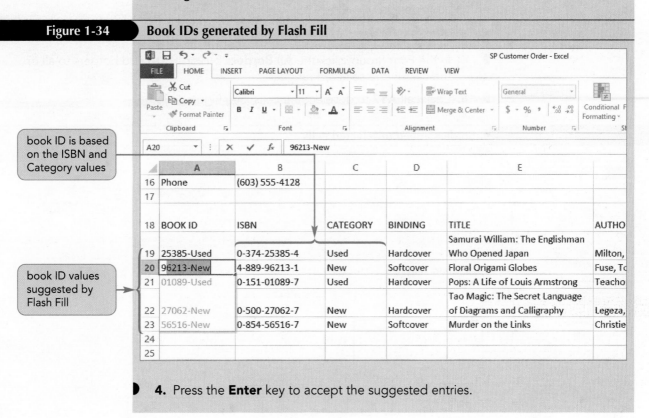

▶ **4.** Press the **Enter** key to accept the suggested entries.

Formatting a Worksheet

Formatting changes a workbook's appearance to make the content of a worksheet easier to read. Two common formatting changes are adding borders to cells and changing the font size of text.

Adding Cell Borders

Sometimes you want to include lines along the edges of cells to enhance the readability of rows and columns of data. You can do this by adding borders to the left, top, right, or bottom edge of a cell or range. You can also specify the thickness of and the number of lines in the border. This is especially helpful when a worksheet is printed because the gridlines that surround the cells are not printed by default; they appear on the worksheet only as a guide.

Sally wants add borders around the cells that contain content in the Customer Order worksheet to make the content easier to read.

To add borders around the worksheet cells:

1. Select the range **A3:B7**. You will add borders around all of the cells in the selected range.

2. On the HOME tab, in the Font group, click the **Borders button arrow** 🔲 ▾, and then click **All Borders**. Borders are added around each cell in the range. The Borders button changes to reflect the last selected border option, which in this case is All Borders. The name of the selected border option appears in the button's ScreenTip.

3. Select the nonadjacent range **A9:B16;H17:I17**. You will add borders around each cell in the selected range.

4. In the Font group, click the **All Borders** button ⊞ to add borders to all of the cells in the selected range.

5. Click cell **A17** to deselect the cells. See Figure 1-35.

Figure 1-35   Borders added to selected cells

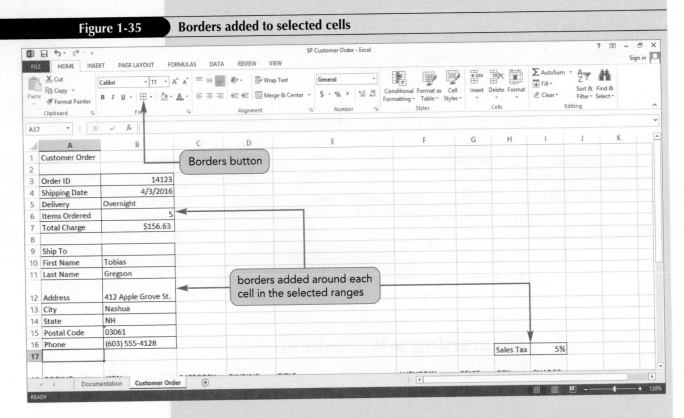

---

6. Select the nonadjacent range **A18:I23;H25:I28**, and then click the **All Borders** button ⊞ to add borders to all of the cells in the selected range.

Changing the Font Size

Changing the size of text in a sheet provides a way to identify different parts of a worksheet, such as distinguishing a title or section heading from data. The size of the text is referred to as the font size and is measured in points. The default font size for worksheets is 11 points, but it can be made larger or smaller as needed. You can resize text in selected cells using the Font Size button in the Font group on the HOME tab. You can also use the Increase Font Size and Decrease Font Size buttons to resize cell content to the next higher or lower standard font size.

Sally wants you to increase the size of the worksheet title to 26 points to make it stand out more.

To change the font size of the worksheet title:

▶ **1.** Click cell **A1** to select it. The worksheet title is in this cell.

▶ **2.** On the HOME tab, in the Font group, click the **Font Size button arrow** to display a list of font sizes, and then click **28**. The worksheet title changes to 28 points. See Figure 1-36.

Figure 1-36	**Font size of cell content increased**

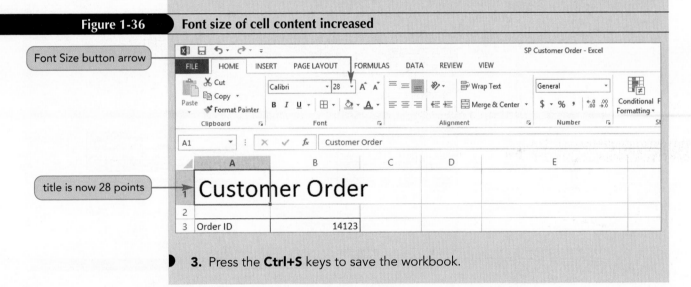

Font Size button arrow

title is now 28 points

▶ **3.** Press the **Ctrl+S** keys to save the workbook.

Printing a Workbook

Now that you have finished the workbook, Sally wants you to print a copy of the book order. Before you print a workbook, you should preview it to ensure that it will print correctly.

Changing Worksheet Views

You can view a worksheet in three ways. Normal view, which you have been using throughout this tutorial, shows the contents of the worksheet. Page Layout view shows how the worksheet will appear when printed. Page Break Preview displays the location of the different page breaks within the worksheet. This is useful when a worksheet will span several printed pages and you need to control what content appears on each page.

Sally wants you to see how the Customer Order worksheet will appear on printed pages. You will do this by switching between views.

To switch the Customer Order worksheet to different views:

▶ 1. Click the **Page Layout** button 📧 on the status bar. The page layout of the worksheet appears in the workbook window.

▶ 2. Drag the **Zoom slider** to reduce the zoom level to 50%. The reduced magnification makes it clear that the worksheet will spread over two pages when printed. See Figure 1-37.

Figure 1-37 | **Worksheet in Page Layout view**

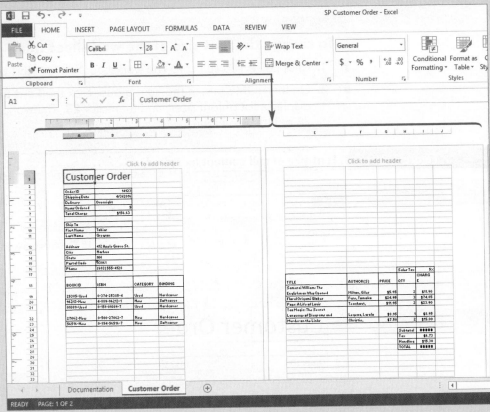

worksheet will span
two printed pages

▶ 3. Click the **Page Break Preview** button 📙 on the status bar. The view switches to Page Break Preview, which shows only those parts of the current worksheet that will print. A dotted blue border separates one page from another.

▶ 4. Zoom the worksheet to **70%** so that you can more easily read the contents of the worksheet. See Figure 1-38.

TIP

You can relocate a page break by dragging the dotted blue border in the Page Break Preview window.

Figure 1-38   **Worksheet in Page Break Preview**

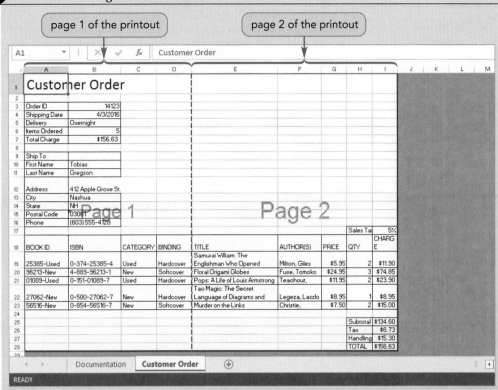

page 1 of the printout   page 2 of the printout

5. Click the **Normal** button 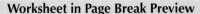 on the status bar. The worksheet returns to Normal view. A dotted black line indicates where the page break will occur.

Changing the Page Orientation

Page orientation specifies in which direction content is printed on the page. In **portrait orientation**, the page is taller than it is wide. In **landscape orientation**, the page is wider than it is tall. By default, Excel displays pages in portrait orientation. Changing the page orientation affects only the active sheet.

As you saw in Page Layout view and Page Break Preview, the Customer Order worksheet will print on two pages—columns A through D will print on the first page, and columns E through I will print on the second page, although the columns that print on each page may differ slightly depending on the printer. Sally wants the entire worksheet to print on a single page, so you'll change the page orientation from portrait to landscape.

To change the page orientation of the Customer Order worksheet:

1. On the ribbon, click the **PAGE LAYOUT** tab. The tab includes options for changing how the worksheet is arranged.

2. In the Page Setup group, click the **Orientation** button, and then click **Landscape**. The worksheet switches to landscape orientation.

3. Click the **Page Layout** button on the status bar to switch to Page Layout view. The worksheet will still print on two pages.

Setting the Scaling Options

You change the size of the worksheet on the printed page by **scaling** it. You can scale the width or the height of the printout so that all of the columns or all of the rows fit on a single page. You can also scale the printout to fit the entire worksheet (both columns and rows) on a single page. If the worksheet is too large to fit on one page, you can scale the print to fit on the number of pages you select. You can also scale the worksheet to a percentage of its size. For example, scaling a worksheet to 50% reduces the size of the sheet by half when it is sent to the printer. When scaling a printout, make sure that the worksheet is still readable after shrinking. Scaling affects only the active worksheet, so you can scale each worksheet to best fit its contents.

Sally asks you to scale the printout so that all of the Customer Order worksheet fits on one page in landscape orientation.

To scale the printout of the Customer Order worksheet:

1. On the PAGE LAYOUT tab, in the Scale to Fit group, click the **Width arrow**, and then click **1 page** on the menu that appears. All of the columns in the worksheet now fit on one page.

2. In the Scale to Fit group, click the **Height arrow**, and then click **1 page**. All of the rows in the worksheet now fit on one page. See Figure 1-39.

Figure 1-39   **Printout scaled to fit on one page**

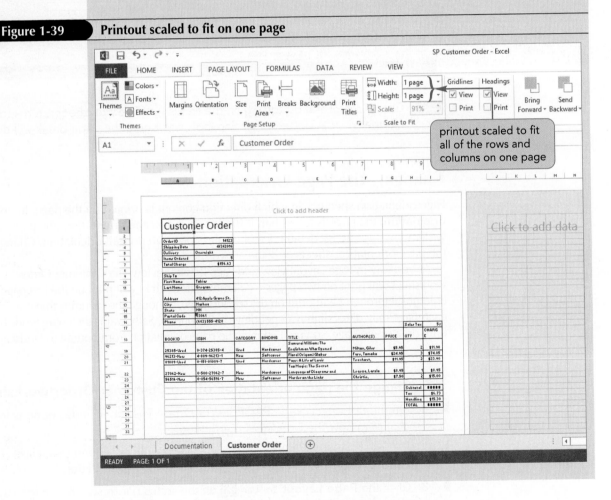

printout scaled to fit all of the rows and columns on one page

Setting the Print Options

TIP

To print the gridlines or the column and row headings, click the corresponding Print check box in the Sheet Options group on the PAGE LAYOUT tab.

You can print the contents of a workbook by using the Print screen in Backstage view. The Print screen provides options for choosing where to print, what to print, and how to print. For example, you can specify the number of copies to print, which printer to use, and what to print. You can choose to print only the selected cells, only the active sheets, or all of the worksheets in the workbook that contain data. The printout will include only the data in the worksheet. The other elements in the worksheet, such as the row and column headings and the gridlines around the worksheet cells, will not print by default. The preview shows you exactly how the printed pages will look with the current settings. You should always preview before printing to ensure that the printout looks exactly as you intended and avoid unnecessary reprinting.

Sally asks you to preview and print the Sparrow & Pond workbook now.

Note: Check with your instructor first to make sure you should complete the steps for printing the workbook.

To preview and print the workbook:

▸ **1.** On the ribbon, click the **FILE** tab to display Backstage view.

▸ **2.** Click **Print** in the navigation bar. The Print screen appears with the print options and a preview of the Customer Order worksheet printout. See Figure 1-40.

Figure 1-40	Print screen in Backstage view

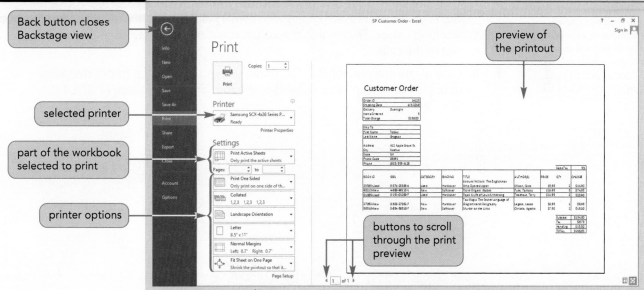

Back button closes Backstage view

selected printer

part of the workbook selected to print

printer options

preview of the printout

buttons to scroll through the print preview

▸ **3.** Click the **Printer** button, and then click the printer to which you want to print, if it is not already selected. By default, Excel will print only the active sheet.

▸ **4.** In the Settings options, click the top button, and then click **Print Entire Workbook** to print all of the sheets in the workbook—in this case, both the Documentation and the Customer Order worksheets. The preview shows the first sheet in the workbook—the Documentation worksheet. Note that this sheet is still in the default portrait orientation.

▸ **5.** Below the preview, click the **Next Page** button ▸ to view the Customer Order worksheet. As you can see, the Customer Order worksheet will print on a single page in landscape orientation.

▶ **6.** If you are instructed to print, click the **Print** button to send the contents of the workbook to the specified printer. If you are not instructed to print, click the **Back** button ◉ in the navigation bar to exit Backstage view.

Viewing Worksheet Formulas

Most of the time, you will be interested in only the final results of a worksheet, not the formulas used to calculate those results. However, in some cases, you might want to view the formulas used to develop the workbook. This is particularly useful when you encounter unexpected results and you want to examine the underlying formulas, or you want to discuss your formulas with a colleague. You can display the formulas instead of the resulting values in cells.

If you print the worksheet while the formulas are displayed, the printout shows the formulas instead of the values. To make the printout easier to read, you should print the worksheet gridlines as well as the row and column headings so that cell references in the formulas are easy to find in the printed version of the worksheet.

You will look at the Customer Order worksheet with the formulas displayed.

To display the formulas in cells in the Customer Order worksheet:

▶ **1.** Make sure the Customer Order worksheet is in Page Layout view.

TIP

You can also display formulas in a worksheet by clicking the Show Formulas button in the Formula Auditing group on the FORMULAS tab.

▶ **2.** Press the **Ctrl+`** keys (the grave accent symbol ` is usually located above the Tab key). The worksheet changes to display all of the formulas instead of the resulting values. Notice that the columns widen to display all of the formula text in the cells.

▶ **3.** Look at the entry in cell B4. The underlying numeric value of the shipping date (42463) is displayed instead of the formatted date value (4/3/2016). See Figure 1-41.

| Figure 1-41 | Worksheet with formulas displayed |

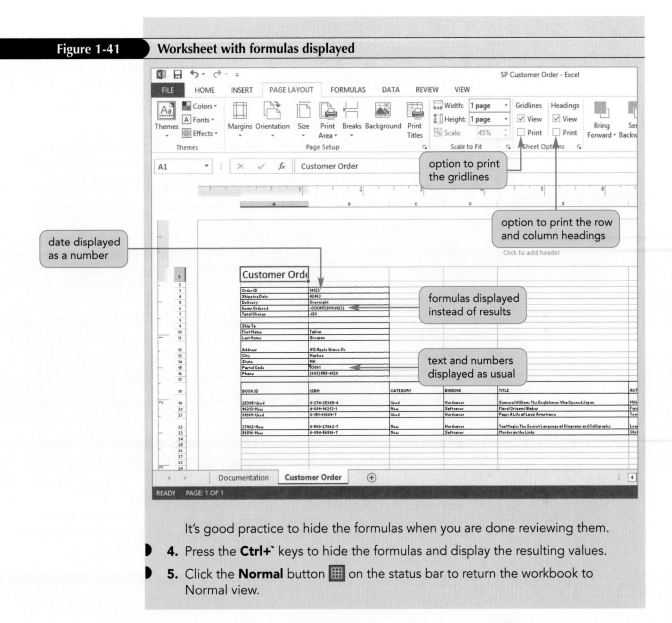

It's good practice to hide the formulas when you are done reviewing them.

 4. Press the **Ctrl+`** keys to hide the formulas and display the resulting values.

 5. Click the **Normal** button ▦ on the status bar to return the workbook to Normal view.

Saving a Workbook with a New Filename

Whenever you click the Save button on the Quick Access Toolbar or press the Ctrl+S keys, the workbook file is updated to reflect the latest content. If you want to save a copy of the workbook with a new filename or to a different location, you need to use the Save As command. When you save a workbook with a new filename or to a different location, the previous version of the workbook remains stored as well.

You have completed the SP Customer Order workbook. Sally wants to use the workbook as a model for other customer order reports. You will save the workbook with a new filename to avoid overwriting the Tobias Gregson book order. Then you'll clear the information related to Tobias Gregson, leaving the formulas intact. This new, revised workbook will then be ready for a new customer order.

To save the workbook with a new filename:

1. Press the **Ctrl+S** keys to save the workbook. This ensures that the final copy of the SP Customer Order workbook contains the latest content.

2. On the ribbon, click the **FILE** tab to display Backstage view, and then click **Save As** on the navigation bar. The Save As screen is displayed.

3. Click **Computer**, and then click the **Browse** button. The Save As dialog box opens so you can save the workbook with a new filename or to a new location.

4. Navigate to the location specified by your instructor.

TIP

Save the workbook with the new name *before* making your changes to avoid inadvertently saving your edits to the wrong file.

5. In the File name box, type **SP Customer Order Form** as the new filename.

6. Click the **Save** button. The workbook is saved with the new filename and is open in Excel.

7. Select the range **B3:B5**, right-click the selected range to open the shortcut menu, and then click **Clear Contents** to clear the contents of the order ID, shipping date, and delivery type cells.

8. Select the nonadjacent range **B10:B16;A19:H23**, and then press the **Delete** key to clear the contact information for Tobias Gregson and the list of books he ordered from those cells.

9. Select cell **I27**, and then clear the handling fee.

10. Click cell **A3** to make that cell the active cell. The next time someone opens this workbook, cell A3 will still be the active cell.

11. Press the **Ctrl+S** keys to save the workbook.

12. Click the **Close** button ✖ on the title bar (or press the **Ctrl+W** keys). The workbook closes, and the Excel program closes.

Sally is pleased with the workbook you created. With the calculations already in place in the new workbook, she will be able to quickly enter new customer orders and see the calculated book charges without having to recreate the worksheet.

Session 1.2 Quick Check

1. What formula would you enter to add the values in cells B4, B5, and B6? What function would you enter to achieve the same result?

2. What formula would you enter to count the number of numeric values in the range B2:B100?

3. What formula would you enter to find the maximum value of the cells in the range B2:B100?

4. If you insert cells into the range C1:D10 shifting the cells to the right, what is the new location of the data that was previously in cell E5?

5. Cell E11 contains the formula =SUM(E1:E10). How does this formula change if a new row is inserted above row 5?

6. Describe four ways of viewing the content of a workbook in Excel.

7. How are page breaks indicated in Page Break Preview?

8. How do you display the formulas used in a worksheet instead of the formula results?

SAM Projects

Put your skills into practice with SAM Projects! SAM Projects for this tutorial can be found online. If you have a SAM account, go to www.cengage.com/sam2013 to download the most recent Project Instructions and Start Files.

Review Assignments

There are no Data Files needed for the Review Assignments.

Sally wants you to create a workbook to record the recent book purchases made by Sparrow & Pond. The workbook should list the recent acquisitions from private sellers, libraries, and other vendors; include a description of each book; and calculate the total number of books acquired and the total amount spent by Sparrow & Pond. Complete the following:

1. Create a new, blank workbook, and then save the workbook as **Book List** in the location specified by your instructor.
2. Rename the Sheet1 worksheet as **Documentation**, and then enter the data shown in Figure 1-42 in the specified cells.

Figure 1-42   **Documentation sheet data**

Cell	Data
A1	Sparrow & Pond
A3	Author
A4	Date
A5	Purpose
B3	*your name*
B4	*current date*
B5	To record book acquisitions by Sparrow & Pond

© 2014 Cengage Learning

3. Set the font size of the title text in cell A1 to 26 points.
4. Add a new worksheet after the Documentation sheet, and then rename the sheet as **Books**.
5. In cell A1, enter the text **Book Acquisitions**. Set the font size of this text to 26 points.
6. In cell A2, enter the text **DATE** as the label. In cell B2, enter the date **4/3/2016**.
7. In the range A4:G9, enter the data shown in Figure 1-43.

Figure 1-43   Book list

ISBN	STATUS	BINDING	TITLE	AUTHOR	CONDITION	PRICE
0-670-02103-2	New	Softcover	Rocket Men: The Epic Story of the First Men on the Moon	Nelson, Craig	Excellent	$12.95
0-195-09076-4	Used	Hardcover	Buildings of Colorado	Noel, Thomas J.	Good	$22.50
0-375-70365-9	New	Softcover	American Visions: The Epic History of Art in America	Hughes, Robert	Excellent	$22.50
1-564-77848-7	New	Softcover	Simple Comforts: 12 Cozy Lap Quilts	Diehl, Kim	Very Good	$9.25
1-851-70006-4	Used	Hardcover	Beautiful Stories About Children	Dickens, Charles	Good	$33.50

© 2014 Cengage Learning

8. Insert cells into the range A4:A9, shifting the other cells to the right.

9. Enter the label **BOOK ID** in cell A4, type **02103-New** in cell A5, and then type **09076-Used** in cell A6.

10. Use Flash Fill to fill in the remaining book IDs.

11. Set the width of columns A through D to 15 characters each. Set the width of column E to 30 characters. Set the width of column F to 20 characters. Set the width of column G to 15 characters.

12. Set the book titles in the range E4:E9 to wrap to a new line.

13. Autofit the heights of rows 4 through 9.

14. Move the book list in the range A4:H9 to the range A8:H13.

15. In cell G15, enter the text **TOTAL**. In cell H15, enter a function to add the prices in the range H9:H13.

16. In cell A4, enter the text **TOTAL BOOKS**. In cell B4, enter a function to count the number of numeric values in the range H9:H13.

17. In cell A5, enter the text **TOTAL PRICE**. In cell B5, display the value from cell H15.

18. In cell A6, enter the text **AVERAGE PRICE**. In cell B6, enter a formula to calculate the total price paid for the books (listed in cell B5) divided by the number of books purchased (listed in cell B4).

19. Add borders around each cell in the nonadjacent range A4:B6;A8:H13;G15:H15.

20. For the Books worksheet, change the page orientation to landscape and scale the worksheet to print on a single page for both the width and the height. If you are instructed to print, print the entire workbook.

21. Display the formulas in the Books worksheet, and set the gridlines and row/column headings to print. If you are instructed to print, print the entire worksheet.

22. Save and close the workbook.

Case Problem 1

APPLY

Data File needed for this Case Problem: Pacific.xlsx

American Wheel Tours   Kevin Bennett is a tours manager at American Wheel Tours, a bicycle touring company located in Philadelphia, Pennsylvania, that specializes in one- and two-week supported tours in destinations across the United States. Kevin wants you to create a workbook that details the itinerary of the company's Pacific Coast tour. The workbook will list the tour itinerary shown in Figure 1-44 and calculate the total number of riding days, total mileage, and average mileage per ride.

Figure 1-44	Pacific Tour itinerary

DATE	START	FINISH	CAMPSITE	MILES	DESCRIPTION
10-Oct-16	Eugene	Eugene	Richardson Park		Orientation day. Meet at Richardson Park, located at the Fern Ridge Reservoir.
11-Oct-16	Eugene	Florence	Honeyman State Park	66	Cycle over Low Pass to Honeyman State Park.
12-Oct-16	Florence	Charleston	Sunset Bay State Park	56	Cycle through Oregon Dunes National Recreation Area to Sunset Bay State Park.
13-Oct-16	Charleston	Port Orford	Humbug Mountain State Park	60	Cycle around Bullards Beach State Park and camp at Humbug Mountain State Park.
14-Oct-16	Port Orford	Brookings	Harris Beach State Park	52	Cycle past the mouth of the Rogue River to Harris Beach State Park.
15-Oct-16	Brookings	Crescent City	Jedediah State Park	48	Pass into California and camp at Jedediah State Park.
16-Oct-16	Crescent City	Eureka	Eureka Fairgrounds	72	A long day through Del Norte Coast Redwoods State Park to Eureka.

© 2014 Cengage Learning

Complete the following:

1. Open the **Pacific** workbook located in the Excel1 ▶ Case1 folder included with your Data Files, and then save the workbook as **Pacific Coast** in the location specified by your instructor.
2. In the Documentation worksheet, enter your name in cell B3 and the date in cell B4.
3. Add a new sheet to the end of the workbook and rename it as **Itinerary**.
4. In cell A1, enter the text **Pacific Coast Tour** and set the font size to 28 points.
5. In the range A3:A8, enter the following labels: **Start Date**, **End Date**, **Total Days**, **Riding Days**, **Total Miles**, and **Miles per Day**.
6. Enter the date **October 10, 2016** in cell B3, and then enter the date **October 16, 2016** in cell B4.
7. In the range D3:D8, enter the labels **Type**, **Surface**, **Difficulty**, **Tour Leader**, **Cost**, and **Deposit**.
8. In the range E3:E8, enter **Van Supported**, **Paved**, **Intermediate**, **Kevin Bennett**, **$1,250**, and **$350**.
9. In the range A11:F18, enter the data shown in Figure 1-44, including the column labels. Leave the mileage value for October 10th blank.
10. In cell B5, enter a formula to calculate the total number of days in the tour by subtracting the starting date (cell B3) from the ending date (cell B4) and adding 1.

11. In cell B6, enter a function to count the total number of riding days based on the numbers in the range E12:E18.

12. In cell B7, enter a function to add the total number of miles in the range E12:E18.

13. In cell B8, enter a formula to calculate the average miles per day by dividing the total miles by the number of riding days.

14. Insert cells in the range A11:A18, shifting the cells to the right. In cell A11, enter **DAY**. In the range A12:A18, enter the numbers 1 through 7 to number each day of the tour.

15. Set the column widths so that column A is 12 characters, columns B through E are 14 characters each, column F is 6 characters, and column G is 50 characters.

16. Wrap text in the range A11:G18 as needed so that any hidden entries are displayed on multiple lines within the cell.

17. Autofit the height of rows 11 through 18.

18. Add borders around the ranges A3:B8, D3:E8, and A11:G18.

19. Format the Itinerary worksheet so that it prints on a single page in landscape orientation. If you are instructed to print, print the entire workbook.

20. Display the formulas in the Itinerary worksheet, and set the gridlines and column/row headings to print. If you are instructed to print, print the worksheet.

21. Return the Itinerary worksheet to Normal view, hide the formulas, set the gridlines and column/row headings so that they won't print, and then save the workbook.

22. Save the workbook as **Pacific Coast Revised** in the location specified by your instructor.

23. Determine what the total mileage and average mileage per day of the tour would be if Kevin adds a 10-mile warm-up ride on October 10th but decreases the length of the October 15th ride to 41 miles. Save the workbook.

Case Problem 2

APPLY

Data File needed for this Case Problem: Tropical.xlsx

Tropical Foods   Tropical Foods is a health food grocery store located in Keizer, Oregon. Monica Li is working on the store's annual financial report. One part of the financial report will be the company's balance sheet for the previous two years. Monica already entered the labels for the balance sheet. You will enter the numeric data and formulas to perform the financial calculations. Complete the following:

1. Open the **Tropical** workbook located in the Excel1 ▶ Case2 folder included with your Data Files, and then save the workbook as **Tropical Foods Balance Sheet** in the location specified by your instructor.

2. In cells B3 and B4 of the Documentation sheet, enter your name and the date. In cell A1, increase the font size of the title to 28 points.

3. Go to the Balance Sheet worksheet. Increase the font size of the title in cell A1 to 28 points, and then increase the font size of the subtitle in cell A2 to 20 points.

4. In the corresponding cells of columns C and D, enter the numbers shown in Figure 1-45 for the company's assets and liabilities.

Figure 1-45   **Tropical Foods assets and liabilities**

		2015	2014
Assets	Cash	$645,785	$627,858
	Accounts Receivable	431,982	405,811
	Inventories	417,615	395,648
	Prepaid Expenses	2,152	4,151
	Other Assets	31,252	26,298
	Fixed Assets @ Cost	1,800,000	1,750,000
	Accumulated Depreciation	82,164	$77,939
Liabilities	Accounts Payable	$241,191	$193,644
	Accrued Expenses	31,115	32,151
	Current Portion of Debt	120,000	100,000
	Income Taxes Payable	144,135	126,524
	Long-Term Debt	815,000	850,000
	Capital Stock	1,560,000	1,525,000
	Retain Earnings	335,181	304,508

© 2014 Cengage Learning

5. Set the width of column A to 12 characters, column B to 28 characters, columns C and D to 14 characters each, column E to 2 characters, and column F to 10 characters.

6. In cells C8 and D8, enter formulas to calculate the current assets value for 2014 and 2015, which is equal to the sum of the cash, accounts receivable, inventories, and prepaid expenses values.

7. In cells C14 and D14, enter formulas to calculate the net fixed assets value for 2014 and 2015, which is equal to the difference between the fixed assets value and the accumulated depreciation value.

8. In cells C16 and D16, enter formulas to calculate the total assets value for 2014 and 2015, which is equal to the sum of the current assets, other assets, and net fixed assets value.

9. In cells C23 and D23, enter formulas to calculate the sum of the accounts payable, accrued expenses, current portion of debt, and income taxes payable values for 2014 and 2015.

10. In cells C29 and D29, enter formulas to calculate the shareholders' equity value for 2014 and 2015, which is equal to the sum of the capital stock and retained earnings.

11. In cells C31 and D31, enter formulas to calculate the total liabilities & equity value for 2014 and 2015, which is equal to the sum of the current liabilities, long-term debt, and shareholders' equity.

12. In a balance sheet, the total assets should equal the total liabilities & equity. Compare the values in cells C16 and C31, and then compare the values in cells D16 and D31 to confirm that this is the case for the Tropical Foods balance sheet in 2014 and 2015. If the account doesn't balance, check your worksheet for errors in either values or formulas.

13. In cell F4, enter a formula to calculate the percentage change in cash from 2014 to 2015, which is equal to (C4–D4)/D4.

14. Copy the formula in cell F4 and paste it in the nonadjacent range F5:F8;F10;F12:F14;F16; F19:F23;F25;F27:F29;F31 to show the percentage change in all values of the balance sheet.

15. Add borders around the cells in columns B, C, D, and F of the balance sheet, excluding the cells in rows 9, 11, 15, 17, 18, 24, 26, and 30.

16. Set the page layout of the Balance Sheet worksheet to portrait orientation and scaled to print on a single page. If you are instructed to print, print the entire workbook.

17. Display the formulas in the Balance Sheet worksheet, and then set the gridlines and row/column headings to print. If you are instructed to print, print the worksheet.

18. Display the Balance Sheet worksheet in Normal view, hide the formulas, set the gridlines and column/row headings so that they won't print, and then save the workbook.

Case Problem 3

CHALLENGE

Data File needed for this Case Problem: Physics.xlsx

Gladstone Country Day School Beatrix Melendez teaches Introduction to Physics at Gladstone Country Day School in Gladstone, Missouri. She wants to record students' quiz scores, and then calculate each student's total and average scores. She also wants to calculate the class average, high score, and low score for each quiz in her records. Beatrix has entered scores from 10 quizzes for 20 students in a worksheet. You will summarize these grades by student and by quiz using the functions listed in Figure 1-46.

Figure 1-46	Excel summary functions

Function	Description
=AVERAGE (range)	Calculates the average of the values from the specified range
=MEDIAN (range)	Calculates the median or midpoint of the values from the specified range
=MIN (range)	Calculates the minimum of the values from the specified range
=MAX (range)	Calculates the maximum of the values from the specified range

© 2014 Cengage Learning

Complete the following:

1. Open the **Physics** workbook located in the Excel1 ▶ Case3 folder included with your Data Files, and then save the workbook as **Physics Grading Sheet** in the location specified by your instructor.

2. In the Documentation sheet, enter your name in cell B3 and the date in cell B4. Increase the font size of the title in cell A1 to 28 points.

3. Go to the Grades worksheet. Increase the font size of cell A1 to 28 points, and then increase the font size of cell A2 to 22 points.

⊕ **Explore** 4. In cell M5, enter a formula to calculate the median or midpoint of the quiz scores for Debra Alt. In cell N5, enter a formula to calculate the average of Debra Alt's quiz scores.

5. Copy the formulas in the range M5:N5 to the range M6:N24 to summarize the scores for the remaining students.

⊕ **Explore** 6. In cell B26, enter a formula to calculate the minimum class score from the first quiz. In cell B27, enter a formula to calculate the median class score.

⊕ **Explore** 7. In cell B28, use the MAX function to calculate the high score from the first quiz.

8. In cell B30, enter a formula to calculate the average score from the first quiz.

9. Copy the formulas in the range B26:B30 to the range C26:K30 to calculate the summary statistics for the rest of the quizzes.

10. Insert 10 new rows above row 4, shifting the student grade table and summary from the range A4:N30 to the range A14:N40. You will enter a summary of all of the students from all of the quizzes at the top of the worksheet.

11. In cell A4, enter the text **Class Size**. In cell B4, enter a formula to calculate the count of scores from the range N15:N34.

12. In the range A6:A9, enter the labels **Overall Scores**, **Lowest Average**, **Median Average**, and **Highest Average**. In cell A11, enter **Class Average**.

13. Using the average scores in the range N15:N34, enter formulas to calculate the overall lowest average score in cell B7, the median of the class averages in cell B8, the overall highest average in cell B9, and the average overall class score in cell B11.

14. Add cell borders around the ranges A4:B4, A7:B9, A11:B11, A14:K34, M14:N34, A36:K38, and A40:K40.

15. Set the page layout of the Grades worksheet to landscape orientation and scaled to print on a single page. If you are instructed to print, print the entire workbook.

16. Display the formulas in the Grades worksheet. Set the gridlines and the row/column headings to print. If you are instructed to print, print the worksheet.

17. Display the Grades worksheet in Normal view, hide the formulas, set the gridlines and column/row headings so that they won't print, and then save the workbook.

18. Determine the effect of raising each student's score on the first quiz by 10 points to curve the results. Report what impact this has on the overall class average from all 10 quizzes.

19. Save the workbook as **Physics Grading Sheet Revised**. If you are instructed to print, print the Grades worksheet.

Case Problem 4

TROUBLESHOOT

Data File needed for this Case Problem: Turf.xlsx

Turf Toughs   Tim Gables is the owner and operator of Turf Toughs, a lawn and tree removal service located in Chicopee, Massachusetts. He created a workbook to record and analyze the service calls made by his company. So far, the workbook calculates the cost of each service call, the total charges for all of the calls, and the total number of billable hours. Unfortunately, the workbook contains several errors. You will fix these errors and then complete the workbook. Complete the following:

1. Open the **Turf** workbook located in the Excel1 ▸ Case4 folder included with your Data Files, and then save the workbook as **Turf Toughs Service Calls** in the location specified by your instructor.

2. In the Documentation sheet, enter your name in cell B3 and the date in cell B4.

3. Go to the Service Log worksheet. The log lists the contact information and the service calls for each customer.

   Tim wants you to insert a column of IDs for each customer. The customer ID is in the form *last-phone*, where *last* is the customer's last name and *phone* is the last four digits of the customer's phone number.

4. Insert cells in the range A4:A34, shifting the other cells to the right. Type **Cust ID** in cell A4, and then enter **Morris-4380** as the customer ID for Michael Morris. Use Flash Fill to fill in the remaining customer IDs in the column.

5. Add borders around the cells in the range A4:A32.

⚙ **Troubleshoot** 6. There is a problem with the all of the customer zip codes. Each zip code should begin with zero. Make the necessary changes to fix this problem.

7. Resize the columns of the worksheet so that all of the column labels in the service calls list are displayed entirely.

⚙ **Troubleshoot** 8. The formula in cell L5 is not correctly calculating the number of hours for each service call. Fix the formula so that it multiplies the difference between the starting and ending time by 24.

9. Copy the formula you created for cell L5 to the range L6:L32, replacing the previous calculated values.

10. Calculate the service charge for each service call so that it equals the base fee added to the hourly rate times the number of hours worked.

⚙ **Troubleshoot** 11. Cell N34 contains a formula to calculate the total service charges for all customer visits. Is it calculating the value correctly? If not, edit the formula to fix any errors you find.

12. Above row 4, insert six new rows, shifting the range A4:N34 down to the range A10:N40.

13. In the range A4:A8, enter the labels **From**, **To**, **Total Service Calls**, **Billable Hours**, and **Total Charges**.

14. In cell B4, calculate the starting date of the service calls by entering a formula that finds the minimum value of the dates in the Date column.

15. In cell B5, calculate the ending date of the service calls by entering a formula that finds the maximum value of the dates in the Date column.

16. In cell B6, enter a formula that counts the total number of service calls using the values in the Date column.

17. In cell B7, enter a formula that calculates the sum of hours from the Hours column.

18. In cell B8, enter a formula that references the value of cell N40.

19. Add borders around each cell in the range A4:B8.

20. Set the page layout of the Service Log worksheet so that it prints on a single page in landscape orientation. If you are instructed to print, print the entire workbook.

21. Display the formulas in the Service Log worksheet, scale the worksheet to fit on a single page, and then set the gridlines and row/column headings to print. If you are instructed to print, print the Service Log worksheet.

22. Return the Service Log worksheet to Normal view, hide the formulas, set the gridlines and column/row headings so that they won't print, and then save the workbook.

TUTORIAL 2

OBJECTIVES

Session 2.1
- Change fonts, font style, and font color
- Add fill colors and a background image
- Create formulas to calculate sales data
- Apply Currency and Accounting formats and the Percent style
- Format dates and times
- Align, indent, and rotate cell contents
- Merge a group of cells

Session 2.2
- Use the AVERAGE function
- Apply cell styles
- Copy and paste formats with the Format Painter
- Find and replace text and formatting
- Change workbook themes
- Highlight cells with conditional formats
- Format a worksheet for printing
- Set the print area, insert page breaks, add print titles, create headers and footers, and set margins

Formatting Workbook Text and Data

Designing a Sales Report

Case | *Big Red Wraps*

Sanjit Chandra is a sales manager for Big Red Wraps, a growing restaurant chain that specializes in preparing made-to-order sandwich wraps, seasonal soups, and fresh salads. The first Big Red Wraps opened in Madison, Wisconsin, and has since expanded to 20 restaurants across six states. Four of these restaurants were opened this year. Each spring, the company has a sales conference where the restaurant managers meet to discuss sales concerns and review marketing plans for the upcoming year. Sanjit created a workbook that summarizes the sales data for the previous year and is part of a sales report that will be given to all conference attendees. He wants you to calculate some summary statistics and format the workbook.

STARTING DATA FILES

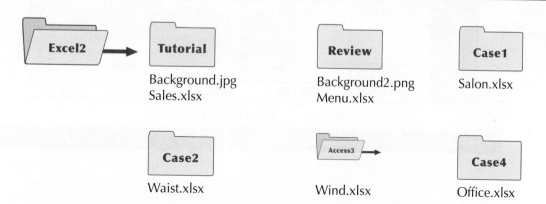

Excel2 → Tutorial	Review	Case1
Background.jpg Sales.xlsx	Background2.png Menu.xlsx	Salon.xlsx

Case2	Access3 →	Case4
Waist.xlsx	Wind.xlsx	Office.xlsx

Microsoft product screenshots used with permission from Microsoft Corporation.

Session 2.1 Visual Overview:

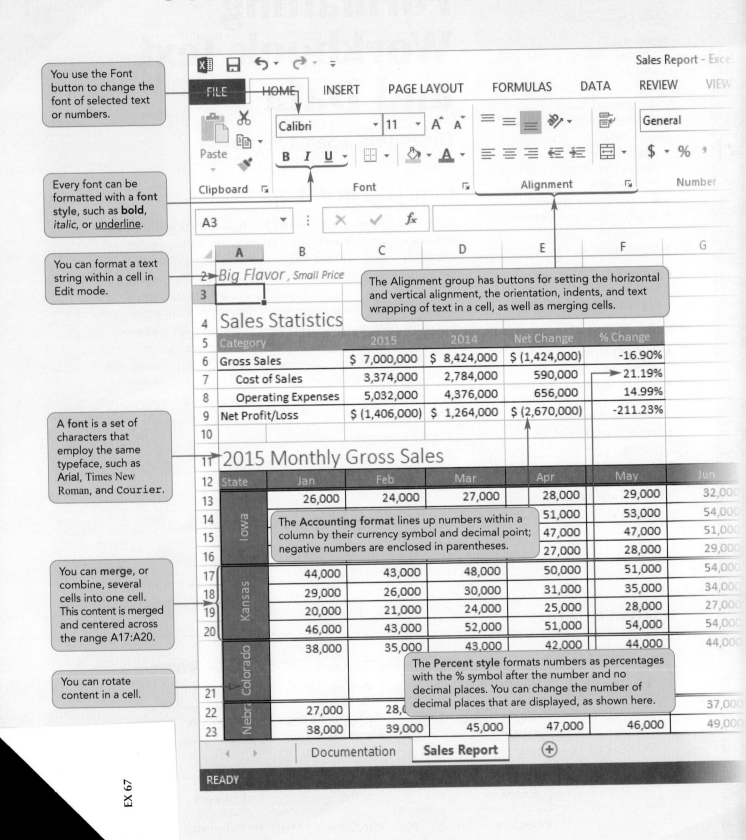

You use the Font button to change the font of selected text or numbers.

Every font can be formatted with a **font style**, such as **bold**, *italic*, or <u>underline</u>.

You can format a text string within a cell in Edit mode.

A **font** is a set of characters that employ the same typeface, such as Arial, Times New Roman, and Courier.

You can **merge**, or combine, several cells into one cell. This content is merged and centered across the range A17:A20.

You can rotate content in a cell.

The Alignment group has buttons for setting the horizontal and vertical alignment, the orientation, indents, and text wrapping of text in a cell, as well as merging cells.

The **Accounting format** lines up numbers within a column by their currency symbol and decimal point; negative numbers are enclosed in parentheses.

The **Percent style** formats numbers as percentages with the % symbol after the number and no decimal places. You can change the number of decimal places that are displayed, as shown here.

Worksheet with Formatting

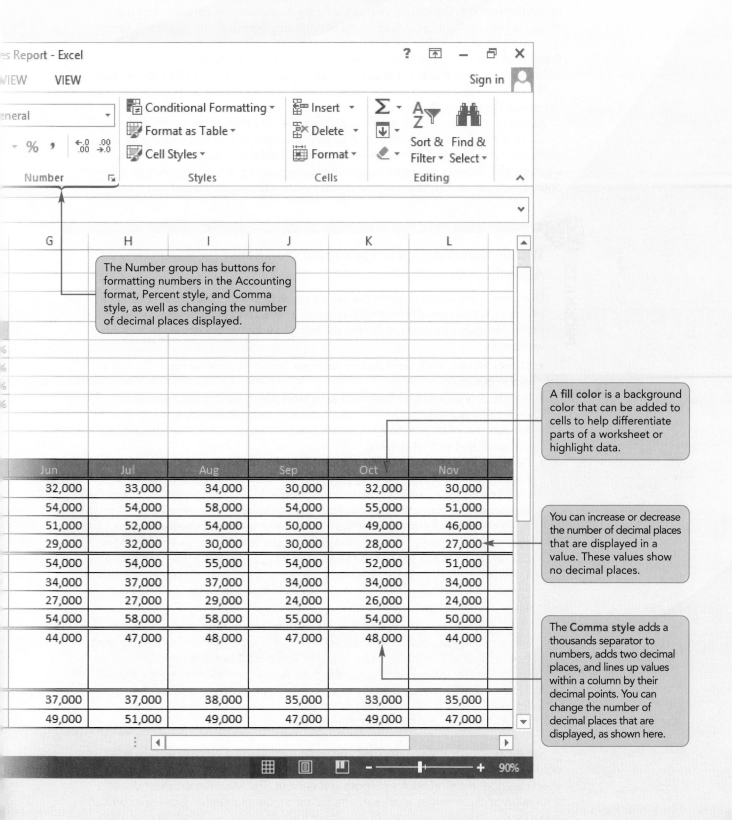

The Number group has buttons for formatting numbers in the Accounting format, Percent style, and Comma style, as well as changing the number of decimal places displayed.

A **fill color** is a background color that can be added to cells to help differentiate parts of a worksheet or highlight data.

You can increase or decrease the number of decimal places that are displayed in a value. These values show no decimal places.

The **Comma** style adds a thousands separator to numbers, adds two decimal places, and lines up values within a column by their decimal points. You can change the number of decimal places that are displayed, as shown here.

Jun	Jul	Aug	Sep	Oct	Nov	
32,000	33,000	34,000	30,000	32,000	30,000	
54,000	54,000	58,000	54,000	55,000	51,000	
51,000	52,000	54,000	50,000	49,000	46,000	
29,000	32,000	30,000	30,000	28,000	27,000	
54,000	54,000	55,000	54,000	52,000	51,000	
34,000	37,000	37,000	34,000	34,000	34,000	
27,000	27,000	29,000	24,000	26,000	24,000	
54,000	58,000	58,000	55,000	54,000	50,000	
44,000	47,000	48,000	47,000	48,000	44,000	
37,000	37,000	38,000	35,000	33,000	35,000	
49,000	51,000	49,000	47,000	49,000	47,000	

Formatting Cell Text

You can add formatting to a workbook by choosing its fonts, styles, colors, and decorative features. Formatting changes only the appearance of data—it does not affect the data itself. In Excel, formatting options are organized into themes. A **theme** is a collection of formatting for text, colors, and graphical effects that are applied throughout a workbook to create a specific look and feel. Each theme has a name. Although the Office theme is the default theme, you can apply other themes or create your own. You can also add formatting to a workbook using fonts and colors that are not part of the current theme.

As you format a workbook, galleries and Live Preview show how a workbook would be affected by a formatting selection. A **gallery** is a menu or grid that shows a visual representation of the options available for the selected button. As you point to options in a gallery, **Live Preview** shows the results of clicking each option. By pointing to different options, you can quickly see different results before selecting the format you want.

PROSKILLS

Written Communication: Formatting Workbooks for Readability and Appeal

Designing a workbook requires the same care as designing any written document or report. A well-formatted workbook is easy to read and establishes a sense of professionalism with readers. Do the following to improve the appearance of your workbooks:

- **Clearly identify each worksheet's purpose.** Include column or row titles and a descriptive sheet name.
- **Include only one or two topics on each worksheet.** Don't crowd individual worksheets with too much information. Place extra topics on separate sheets. Readers should be able to interpret each worksheet with a minimal amount of horizontal and vertical scrolling.
- **Place worksheets with the most important information first in the workbook.** Position worksheets summarizing your findings near the front of the workbook. Position worksheets with detailed and involved analysis near the end as an appendix.
- **Use consistent formatting throughout the workbook.** If negative values appear in red on one worksheet, format them in the same way on all sheets. Also, be consistent in the use of thousands separators, decimal places, and percentages.
- **Pay attention to the format of the printed workbook.** Make sure your printouts are legible with informative headers and footers. Check that the content of the printout is scaled correctly to the page size, and that page breaks divide the information into logical sections.

Excel provides many formatting tools. However, too much formatting can be intrusive, overwhelm data, and make the document difficult to read. Remember that the goal of formatting is not simply to make a "pretty workbook," but also to accentuate important trends and relationships in the data. A well-formatted workbook should seamlessly convey your data to the reader. If the reader is thinking about how your workbook looks, it means he or she is not thinking about your data.

Sanjit has already entered the data and some formulas in a workbook, which is only a rough draft of what he wants to submit to the company. The Documentation sheet describes the workbook's purpose and content. The Sales Report sheet displays a summary of the previous year's sales including a table of monthly gross sales broken down by the 20 franchise stores. In its current form, the data is difficult to read and interpret. Sanjit wants you to format the contents of the workbook to improve its readability and visual appeal.

To open the workbook:

▶ 1. Open the **Sales** workbook located in the Excel2 ▸ Tutorial folder included with your Data Files, and then save the workbook as **Sales Report** in the location specified by your instructor.

▶ 2. In the Documentation sheet, enter your name in cell B4 and the date in cell B5.

Applying Fonts and Font Styles

Excel organizes fonts into theme and non-theme fonts. A **theme font** is associated with a particular theme and used for headings and body text in the workbook. These fonts change automatically when you change the theme applied to the workbook. Text formatted with a **non-theme font** retains its appearance no matter what theme is used with the workbook.

Fonts appear in different character styles. **Serif fonts**, such as Times New Roman, have extra strokes at the end of each character that aid in reading passages of text. **Sans serif fonts**, such as Arial, do not include these extra strokes. Other fonts are purely decorative, such as a font used for specialized logos. Every font can be further formatted with a font style such as *italic*, **bold**, or ***bold italic***; with <u>underline</u>; and with special effects such as ~~strikethrough~~ and color. You can also increase or decrease the font size.

REFERENCE

Formatting Cell Content

- To change the font, select the cell or range. On the HOME tab, in the Font group, click the Font arrow, and then click a font.
- To change the font size, select the cell or range. On the HOME tab, in the Font group, click the Font Size arrow, and then click a font size.
- To change a font style, select the cell or range. On the HOME tab, in the Font group, click the Bold, Italic, or Underline button.
- To change a font color, select the cell or range. On the HOME tab, in the Font group, click the Font Color button arrow, and then click a color.
- To format a text selection, double-click the cell to enter Edit mode, and then select the text to format. Change the font, size, style, or color, and then press the Enter key.

Sanjit wants the company name at the top of each worksheet to appear in large, bold letters using the default heading font from the Office theme. He wants the slogan "Big Flavor, Small Price" displayed below the company name to appear in the heading font, but in smaller, italicized letters.

To format the company name and slogan in the Documentation sheet:

▶ 1. In the Documentation sheet, select cell **A1** to make it the active cell. The cell with the company name is selected.

▶ 2. On the HOME tab, in the Font group, click the **Font button arrow** to display a gallery of fonts available on your computer. Each name is displayed in its corresponding font. When you point to a font in the gallery, Live Preview shows how the text in the selected cell will look with that font. The first two fonts are the theme fonts for headings and body text—Calibri Light and Calibri.

3. Point to **Algerian** (or another font) in the All Fonts list. Live Preview shows the effect of the Algerian font on the text in cell A1. See Figure 2-1.

Figure 2-1   **Font gallery**

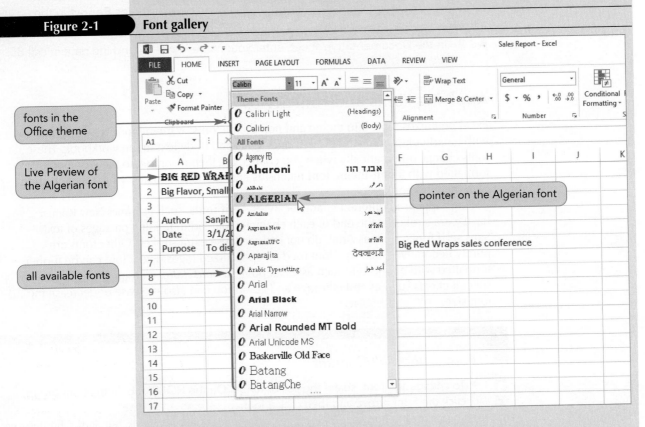

- fonts in the Office theme
- Live Preview of the Algerian font
- all available fonts
- pointer on the Algerian font

4. Point to three other fonts in the Font gallery to see the Live Preview showing how cell A1 could look with those fonts.

5. Click **Calibri Light** in the Theme Fonts list. The company name in cell A1 changes to the Calibri Light font, the default headings font in the current theme.

6. In the Font group, click the **Font Size button arrow** to display a list of font sizes, and then click **26**. The company name changes to 26 points.

7. In the Font group, click the **Bold** button **B** (or press the **Ctrl+B** keys). The company name is set in bold.

8. Select cell **A2** to make it active. The cell with the slogan text is selected.

9. In the Font group, click the **Font Size button arrow**, and then click **10**. The slogan text changes to 10 points.

10. In the Font group, click the **Italic** button *I* (or press the **Ctrl+I** keys). The slogan in cell A2 is italicized.

11. Select the range **A4:A6**, and then press the **Ctrl+B** keys to change the font to bold.

12. Select cell **A7** to deselect the range. The column labels are set in bold. See Figure 2-2.

Figure 2-2   **Formatted cell text**

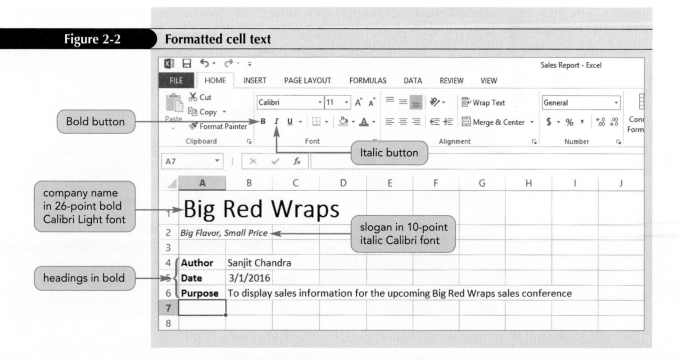

Applying a Font Color

Color can transform a plain workbook filled with numbers and text into a powerful presentation that captures the user's attention and adds visual emphasis to the points you want to make. By default, Excel displays text in a black font color.

Like fonts, colors are organized into theme and non-theme colors. **Theme colors** are the 12 colors that belong to the workbook's theme. Four colors are designated for text and backgrounds, six colors are used for accents and highlights, and two colors are used for hyperlinks (followed and not followed links). These 12 colors are designed to work well together and to remain readable in all combinations. Each theme color has five variations, or accents, in which a different tint or shading is applied to the theme color.

Ten **standard colors**—dark red, red, orange, yellow, light green, green, light blue, blue, dark blue, and purple—are always available regardless of the workbook's theme. You can open an extended palette of 134 standard colors. You can also create a custom color by specifying a mixture of red, blue, and green color values, making available 16.7 million custom colors—more colors than the human eye can distinguish. Some dialog boxes have an automatic color option that uses your Windows default text and background colors, usually black text on a white background.

Creating Custom Colors

Custom colors let you add subtle and striking colors to a formatted workbook. To create custom colors, you use the **RGB Color model** in which each color is expressed with varying intensities of red, green, and blue. RGB color values are often represented as a set of numbers in the format

(*red*, *green*, *blue*)

where *red* is an intensity value assigned to red light, *green* is an intensity value assigned to green light, and *blue* is an intensity value assigned to blue light. The intensities are measured on a scale of 0 to 255—0 indicates no intensity (or the absence of the color) and 255 indicates the highest intensity. So, the RGB color value (255, 255, 0) represents a mixture of high-intensity red (255) and high-intensity green (255) with the absence of blue (0), which creates the color yellow.

To create colors in Excel using the RGB model, click the More Colors option located in a color menu or dialog box to open the Colors dialog box. In the Colors dialog box, click the Custom tab, and then enter the red, green, and blue intensity values. A preview box shows the resulting RGB color.

Sanjit wants the labels in the Documentation sheet to stand out, so you will change the Big Red Wraps company name and slogan to red.

To change the company name and slogan font color:

1. Select the range **A1:A2**. The company name and slogan are selected.

2. On the HOME tab, in the Font group, click the **Font Color button arrow** ![A] to display the gallery of theme and standard colors. (The two colors for hyperlinked text are not shown.)

3. Point to the **Red** color (the second color) in the Standard Colors section. The color name appears in a ScreenTip and you see a Live Preview of the text with the red font color. See Figure 2-3.

Figure 2-3   Font color gallery

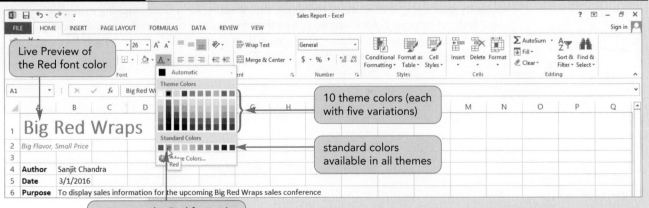

4. Click the **Red** color. The company name and slogan change to red.

Formatting Text Selections

TIP

The **Mini toolbar** contains buttons for common formatting options used for the selection. These same buttons appear on the ribbon.

In Edit mode, you can select and format selections of text within a cell. When the Big Red Wraps slogan is used in marketing materials, "Big Flavor" is set slightly larger than "Small Price." Sanjit wants you to recreate this effect in the workbook by increasing the font size of "Big Flavor" while leaving the rest of the text unchanged. You will use Edit mode to apply a different format to part of the cell text.

To format part of the company slogan:

1. Double-click cell **A2** to select the cell and enter Edit mode (or click cell **A2** and press the **F2** key). The status bar shows EDIT to indicate that you are working with the cell in Edit mode. The pointer changes to the I-beam pointer.

2. Drag the pointer over the phrase **Big Flavor** to select it. The Mini toolbar appears above the selected text with buttons to change the font, size, style, and color of the selected text in the cell. See Figure 2-4.

Figure 2-4   Mini toolbar in Edit mode

Mini toolbar includes common formatting options

3. On the Mini toolbar, click the **Font Size button arrow**, and then click **14**. The font size of the selected text increases to 14 points.

4. Select cell **A7** to deselect cell A2. See Figure 2-5.

Figure 2-5   Formatted text selection

font size increased to 14 points

Working with Fill Colors and Backgrounds

Another way to distinguish sections of a worksheet is by formatting the cell background. You can fill the cell background with color or an image. Sanjit wants you to add fill colors and background images to the Documentation worksheet.

INSIGHT

Using Color to Enhance a Workbook

When used wisely, color can enhance any workbook. However, when used improperly, color can distract the user, making the workbook more difficult to read. As you format a workbook, keep in mind the following tips:

- Use colors from the same theme to maintain a consistent look and feel across the worksheets. If the built-in themes do not fit your needs, you can create a custom theme.
- Use colors to differentiate types of cell content and to direct users where to enter data. For example, format a worksheet so that formula results appear in cells without a fill color and users enter data in cells with a light gray fill color.
- Avoid color combinations that are difficult to read.
- Print the workbook on both color and black-and-white printers to ensure that the printed copy is readable in both versions.
- Understand your printer's limitations and features. Colors that look good on your monitor might not look as good when printed.
- Be sensitive to your audience. About 8 percent of all men and 0.5 percent of all women have some type of color blindness and might not be able to see the text when certain color combinations are used. Red-green color blindness is the most common, so avoid using red text on a green background or green text on a red background.

Changing a Fill Color

TIP

You can also change a sheet tab's color. Right-click a sheet tab, point to Tab Color on the shortcut menu, and then click a color.

By default, worksheet cells do not include any background color. But background colors, also known as fill colors, can be helpful for distinguishing different parts of a worksheet or adding visual interest. You add fill colors to selected cells in the worksheet from the Fill Color gallery, which has the same options as the Font Color gallery.

Sanjit wants the labels and text in the Documentation sheet to stand out. You will format the labels in a white font on a red background, and then you'll format the author's name, current date, and purpose of the worksheet in a red font on a white background.

To change the fill and font colors in the Documentation worksheet:

1. Select the range **A4:A6**.

2. On the HOME tab, in the Font group, click the **Fill Color button arrow** 🖌 ▾, and then click the **Red** color (the second color) in the Standard Colors section.

3. In the Font group, click the **Font Color button arrow** 🅰 ▾, and then click the **White, Background 1** color in the Theme Colors section. The labels are formatted in white text on a red background.

4. Select the range **B4:B6**, and then format the cells with a red font and a white background.

5. Increase the width of column B to **30** characters, and then wrap the text in the selected range. *Alt + Enter*

6. Select the range **A4:B6**, and then add all borders around each of the selected cells.

7. Click cell **A7** to deselect the range. See Figure 2-6.

| Figure 2-6 | Font and fill colors in the Documentation sheet |

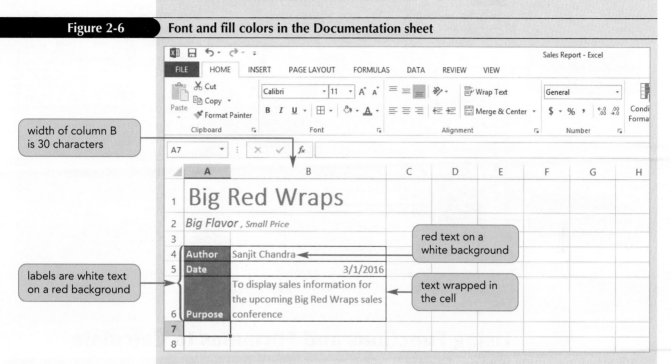

width of column B is 30 characters

labels are white text on a red background

red text on a white background

text wrapped in the cell

Adding a Background Image

A background image can provide a textured appearance, like that of granite, wood, or fibered paper, to a worksheet. The image is repeated until it fills the entire sheet. The background image does not affect any cell's format or content. Fill colors added to cells appear on top of the image, covering that portion of the image. Background images are visible only on the screen; they do not print.

Sanjit has provided an image that he wants you to use as the background of the Documentation sheet.

To add a background image to the Documentation sheet:

1. On the ribbon, click the **PAGE LAYOUT** tab to display the page layout options.

2. In the Page Setup group, click the **Background** button. The Insert Pictures dialog box opens with options to select a picture from a file, select Office.com Clip Art, or perform a Bing Image Search.

3. Click the **Browse** button next to the From a file label. The Sheet Background dialog box opens.

4. Navigate to the **Excel2 ▸ Tutorial** folder included with your Data Files, click the **Background** JPEG image file, and then click the **Insert** button. The image is added to the background of the Documentation sheet, and the Background button changes to the Delete Background button, which you can use to remove the background image. See Figure 2-7.

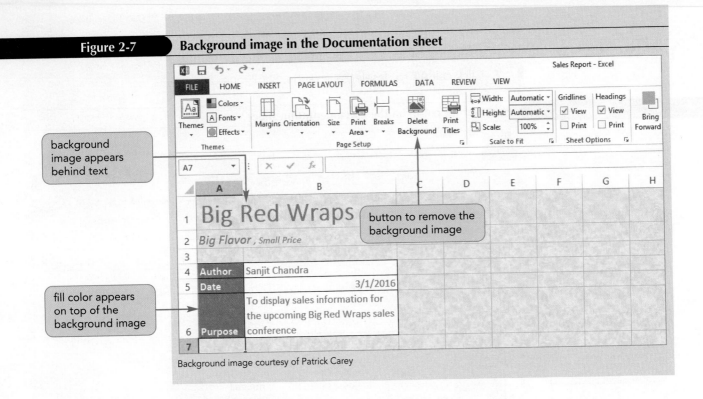

Figure 2-7   **Background image in the Documentation sheet**

background image appears behind text

button to remove the background image

fill color appears on top of the background image

Background image courtesy of Patrick Carey

Using Functions and Formulas to Calculate Sales Data

In the Sales Report worksheet, you will format the gross sales from each of the store's 20 restaurants and the summary statistics for those stores. The Sales Report worksheet is divided into two areas. The table at the bottom of the worksheet displays gross sales for the past year for each month by restaurant. The section at the top of the worksheet summarizes the sales data for the past two years. Sanjit collected the following sales data:

- **Gross Sales**—the total amount of sales at all of the restaurants
- **Cost of Sales**—the cost of producing the store's menu items
- **Operating Expenses**—the cost of running the stores including the employment and insurance costs
- **Net Profit/Loss**—the difference between the income from the gross sales and the total cost of sales and operating expenses
- **Units Sold**—the total number of menu items sold by the company during the year
- **Customers Served**—the total number of customers served by the company during the year

Sanjit wants you to calculate these sales statistics for the entire company and per store so he can track how well the stores are performing. First, you will calculate the total gross sales for Big Red Wraps and the company's overall net profit and loss.

To calculate the company's sales and profit/loss:

▶ **1.** Click the **Sales Report** sheet tab to make the Sales Report worksheet active.

2. Click cell **C6**, type the formula **=SUM(C27:N46)** to calculate the total gross sales from all stores in the previous year, and then press the **Enter** key. Cell C6 displays 9514000, which means that Big Red Wraps' total gross sales for the previous year were more than $9.5 million.

TIP

To enter content in a cell, you select the cell, type the specified content, and then press the Enter key.

3. In cell **C9**, enter the formula **=C6–(C7+C8)** to calculate the current year's net profit/loss, which is equal to the difference between the gross sales and the sum of the cost of sales and operating expenses. Cell C9 displays 1108000, which means that the company's net profit for 2015 was more than $1.1 million.

4. Copy the formula in cell **C9**, and then paste it into cell **D9** to calculate the net profit/loss for 2014. Cell D9 displays 1264000, which means that the company's net profit for that year was more than $1.26 million.

Next, Sanjit asks you to summarize the sales statistics for each store. Sanjit wants the same per-store statistics calculated for the 2015 and 2014 sales data. Per-store sales statistics are calculated by dividing the overall statistics by the number of stores. In this case, you will divide the overall statistics by the value in cell C23, which contains the total number of stores in the Big Red Wraps chain. After you enter the 2015 formulas, you can copy and paste them to calculate the 2014 results.

To calculate the per-store statistics:

1. In cell **C16**, enter the formula **=C6/C23** to calculate the gross sales per store in 2015. The formula returns 475700, which means that the annual gross sales amount for a Big Red Wraps store in 2015 was more than $475,000.

2. In cell **C17**, enter the formula **=C7/C23** to calculate the cost of sales per store in 2015. The formula returns the value 168700, which means that the cost of sales for a Big Red Wraps store in 2015 was typically $168,700.

3. In cell **C18**, enter the formula **=C8/C23** to calculate the operating expenses per store in 2015. The formula returns the value 251600, which means that operating expenses of a typical store in 2015 were $251,600.

4. In cell **C19**, enter the formula **=C9/C23** to calculate the net profit/loss per store in 2015. The formula returns the value 55400, indicating that the net profit/loss of a typical store in 2015 was $55,400.

5. In cell **C21**, enter the formula **=C11/C23** to calculate the units sold per store in 2015. The formula returns the value 67200, indicating that a typical store sold 67,200 units during 2015.

6. In cell **C22**, enter the formula **=C12/C23** to calculate the customers served per store in 2015. The formula returns the value 7770, indicating that a typical store served 7,770 customers during that year.

7. Copy the formulas in the range **C16:C22** and paste them into the range **D16:D22**. The cell references in the formulas change to calculate the sales data for the year 2014.

8. Select cell **B24** to deselect the range. See Figure 2-8.

Figure 2-8 Sales statistics for the entire company and per store

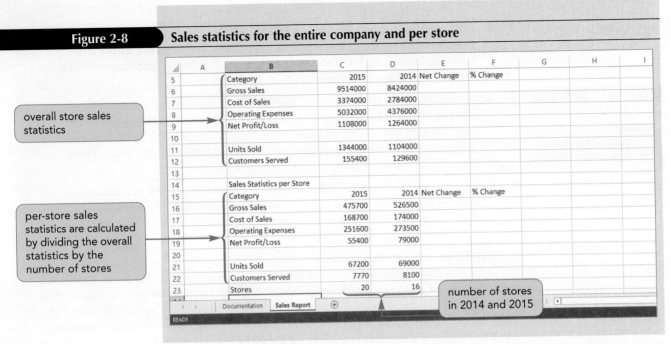

overall store sales statistics

per-store sales statistics are calculated by dividing the overall statistics by the number of stores

number of stores in 2014 and 2015

Sanjit also wants to explore how the company's sales and expenses have changed from 2014 to 2015. To do this, you will calculate the net change in sales from 2014 to 2015 as well as the percent change. The percent change is calculated using the following formula:

$$percent\ change = \frac{2015\ value - 2014\ value}{2014\ value}$$

You will calculate the net and percent changes for all of the sales statistics.

To calculate the net and percent changes for 2015 and 2014:

1. In cell **E6**, enter the formula **=C6–D6** to calculate the difference between the 2015 and 2014 gross sales. The formula returns 1090000, indicating that gross sales increased by $1.09 million between 2014 and 2015.

2. In cell **F6**, enter the formula **=(C6–D6)/D6** to calculate the percent change in gross sales from 2014 to 2015. The formula returns 0.129392213, indicating a nearly 13% increase in gross sales from 2014 to 2015.

   Next, you'll copy and paste the formulas in cells E6 and F6 to the rest of the sales data to calculate the net change and percent change from 2014 to 2015.

3. Select the range **E6:F6**, and then copy the selected range. The two formulas are copied to the Clipboard.

4. Select the nonadjacent range **E7:F9;E11:F12;E16:F19;E21:F23**, and then paste the formulas from the Clipboard into the selected range. The net and percent changes are calculated for the remaining sales data.

5. Click cell **B24** to deselect the range, and then scroll the worksheet up to display row 5. See Figure 2-9.

Be sure to include the parentheses as shown to calculate the percent change correctly.

| Figure 2-9 | Net and percent changes calculated |

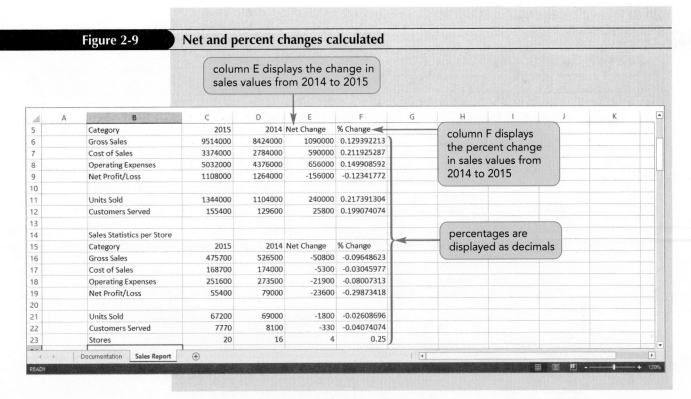

column E displays the change in sales values from 2014 to 2015

column F displays the percent change in sales values from 2014 to 2015

percentages are displayed as decimals

	A	B	C	D	E	F	G	H	I	J	K
5		Category	2015	2014	Net Change	% Change					
6		Gross Sales	9514000	8424000	1090000	0.129392213					
7		Cost of Sales	3374000	2784000	590000	0.211925287					
8		Operating Expenses	5032000	4376000	656000	0.149908592					
9		Net Profit/Loss	1108000	1264000	-156000	-0.12341772					
10											
11		Units Sold	1344000	1104000	240000	0.217391304					
12		Customers Served	155400	129600	25800	0.199074074					
13											
14		Sales Statistics per Store									
15		Category	2015	2014	Net Change	% Change					
16		Gross Sales	475700	526500	-50800	-0.09648623					
17		Cost of Sales	168700	174000	-5300	-0.03045977					
18		Operating Expenses	251600	273500	-21900	-0.08007313					
19		Net Profit/Loss	55400	79000	-23600	-0.29873418					
20											
21		Units Sold	67200	69000	-1800	-0.02608696					
22		Customers Served	7770	8100	-330	-0.04074074					
23		Stores	20	16	4	0.25					

Documentation   Sales Report

READY

The bottom part of the worksheet contains the sales for each restaurant from 2015. You will use the SUM function to calculate the total gross sales for each restaurant during the entire year, the total monthly sales of all 20 restaurants, and the total gross sales of all restaurants and months.

To calculate different subtotals of the gross sales:

1. Select cell **O26**, type **TOTAL** as the label, and then press the **Enter** key. Cell O27 is now the active cell.

2. On the HOME tab, in the Editing group, click the **AutoSum** button, and then press the **Enter** key to accept the suggested range reference and enter the formula =SUM(C27:N27) in cell O27. The cell displays 355000, indicating gross sales in 2015 for the 411 Elm Drive restaurant were $355,000.

3. Copy the formula in cell **O27**, and then paste that formula into the range **O28:O46** to calculate the total sales for each of the remaining 19 restaurants in the Big Red Wraps chain.

4. Select cell **B47**, type **TOTAL** as the label, and then press the **Tab** key. Cell C47 is now the active cell.

5. Select the range **C47:O47** so that you can calculate the total monthly sales for all of the stores.

6. On the HOME tab, in the Editing group, click the **AutoSum** button, and then press the **Enter** key to calculate the total sales for each month as well as the total sales for all months. For example, cell C47 displays 680000, indicating that monthly sales for January 2015 for all stores were $680,000.

7. Select cell **O48** to deselect the range. See Figure 2-10.

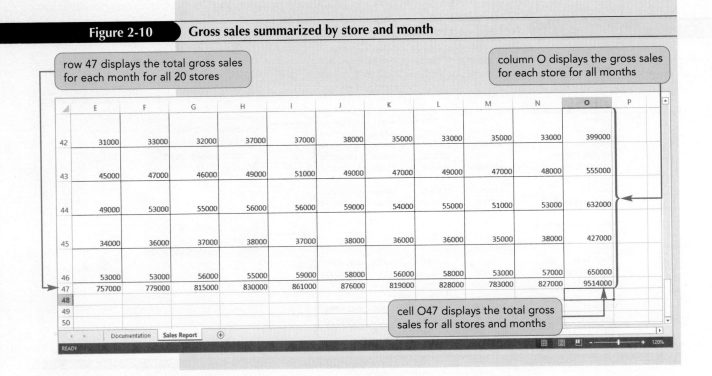

Figure 2-10   **Gross sales summarized by store and month**

row 47 displays the total gross sales for each month for all 20 stores

column O displays the gross sales for each store for all months

	E	F	G	H	I	J	K	L	M	N	O	P
42	31000	33000	32000	37000	37000	38000	35000	33000	35000	33000	399000	
43	45000	47000	46000	49000	51000	49000	47000	49000	47000	48000	555000	
44	49000	53000	55000	56000	56000	59000	54000	55000	51000	53000	632000	
45	34000	36000	37000	38000	37000	38000	36000	36000	35000	38000	427000	
46	53000	53000	56000	55000	59000	58000	56000	58000	53000	57000	650000	
47	757000	779000	815000	830000	861000	876000	819000	828000	783000	827000	9514000	
48												
49												
50												

cell O47 displays the total gross sales for all stores and months

Documentation   Sales Report

READY   120%

Formatting Numbers

The goal in formatting any workbook is to make the content easier to interpret. For numbers, this can mean adding a comma to separate thousands, setting the number of decimal places, and using percentage and currency symbols to make numbers easier to read and understand. Sanjit asks you to format the numbers in the Sales Report worksheet to improve their readability.

Applying Number Formats

You can use a number format to display values in a way that makes them easier to read and understand. Changing the number format of the displayed value does not affect the stored value. Numbers are originally formatted in the **General format**, which, for the most part, displays numbers exactly as they are typed. If the number is calculated from a formula or function, the cell displays as many digits after the decimal point as will fit in the cell with the last digit rounded. Calculated values too large to fit into the cell are displayed in scientific notation.

The General format is fine for small numbers, but some values require additional formatting to make the numbers easier to interpret. For example, you might want to:

- Change the number of digits displayed to the right of the decimal point
- Add commas to separate thousands in large numbers
- Apply currency symbols to numbers to identify the monetary unit being used
- Display percentages using the % symbol

TIP

To apply the Currency format, click the Number Format button arrow and click Currency, or press the Ctrl+Shift+$ keys.

Excel supports two monetary formats: currency and accounting. Both formats add a thousands separator to the currency values and display two digits to the right of the decimal point. However, the **Currency format** places a currency symbol directly to the left of the first digit of the currency value and displays negative numbers with a negative sign. The **Accounting format** fixes a currency symbol at the left edge of the column, and displays negative numbers within parentheses and zero values with a dash. It also slightly indents the values from the right edge of the cell to allow room for parentheses around negative values. Figure 2-11 compares the two formats.

| Figure 2-11 | Currency and Accounting number formats |

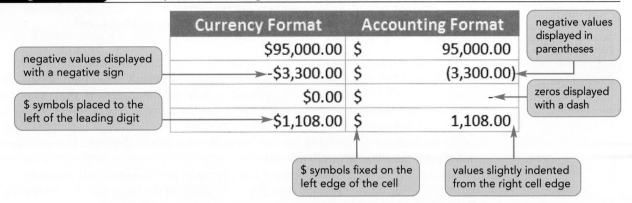

negative values displayed with a negative sign

$ symbols placed to the left of the leading digit

negative values displayed in parentheses

zeros displayed with a dash

$ symbols fixed on the left edge of the cell

values slightly indented from the right cell edge

	Currency Format	Accounting Format
	$95,000.00	$ 95,000.00
	-$3,300.00	$ (3,300.00)
	$0.00	$ -
	$1,108.00	$ 1,108.00

PROSKILLS

Written Communication: Formatting Monetary Values

Spreadsheets commonly include monetary values. To make these values simpler to read and comprehend, keep in mind the following guidelines when formatting the currency data in a worksheet:

- **Format for your audience.** For general financial reports, round values to the nearest hundred, thousand, or million. Investors are generally more interested in the big picture than in exact values. However, for accounting reports, accuracy is important and often legally required. So, for those reports, be sure to display the exact monetary value.
- **Use thousands separators.** Large strings of numbers can be challenging to read. For monetary values, use a thousands separator to make the amounts easier to comprehend.
- **Apply the Accounting format to columns of monetary values.** The Accounting format makes columns of numbers easier to read than the Currency format. Use the Currency format for individual cells that are not part of long columns of numbers.
- **Use only two currency symbols in a column of monetary values.** Standard accounting format displays one currency symbol with the first monetary value in the column, and optionally displays a second currency symbol with the last value in that column. Use the Accounting format to fix the currency symbols, lining them up within the column.

Following these standard accounting principles will make your financial data easier to read both on the screen and in printouts.

Sanjit wants you to format the gross sales amounts in the Accounting format so that they are easier to read.

To format the gross sales in the Accounting format:

1. Select the range **C6:E6** with the gross sales.

2. On the HOME tab, in the Number group, click the **Accounting Number Format** button $. The numbers are formatted in the Accounting format. You cannot see the format because the cells display ##########.

The cells display ########## because the formatted number doesn't fit into the column. One reason for this is that monetary values, by default, show both dollars and cents in the cell. However, you can increase or decrease the number of decimal places displayed in a cell. The displayed value might then be rounded. For example, the stored value 11.7 will appear in the cell as 12 if no decimal places are displayed to the right of the decimal point. Changing the number of decimal places displayed in a cell does not change the value stored in the cell.

Because Sanjit and the other conference attendees are interested only in whole dollar amounts, he wants you to hide the cents values of the gross sales by decreasing the number of decimal places to zero.

To decrease the number of decimal places displayed in the gross sales:

1. Make sure the range **C6:E6** is selected.

2. On the HOME tab, in the Number group, click the **Decrease Decimal** button twice. The cents are hidden for gross sales.

3. Select cell **C4** to deselect the range. See Figure 2-12.

Figure 2-12 **Formatted gross sales values**

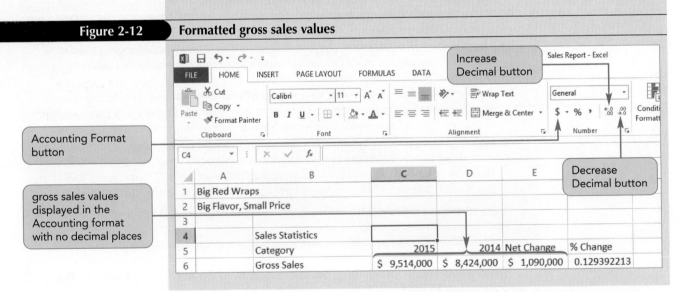

The Comma style is identical to the Accounting format except that it does not fix a currency symbol to the left of the number. The advantage of using the Comma style and the Accounting format together is that the numbers will be aligned in the column.

Sanjit asks you to apply the Comma style to the remaining sales statistics.

To apply the Comma style to the sales statistics:

▶ **1.** Select the nonadjacent range **C7:E9;C11:E12** containing the sales figures for all stores in 2014 and 2015.

▶ **2.** On the HOME tab, in the Number group, click the **Comma Style** button ⟨ ⟩. In some instances, the number is now too large to be displayed in the cell.

▶ **3.** In the Number group, click the **Decrease Decimal** button twice to remove two decimal places. Digits to the right of the decimal point are hidden for all of the selected cells.

▶ **4.** Select cell **C13** to deselect the range. See Figure 2-13.

Figure 2-13	Formatted sales values

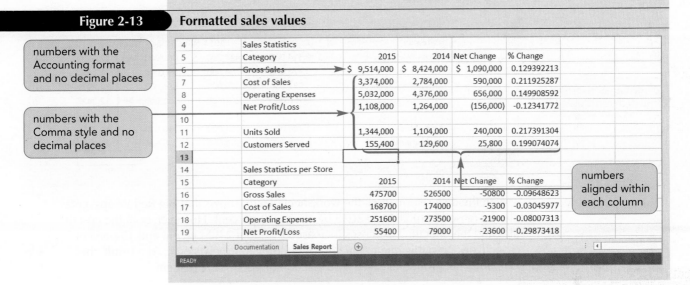

numbers with the Accounting format and no decimal places

numbers with the Comma style and no decimal places

numbers aligned within each column

4	Sales Statistics				
5	Category	2015	2014	Net Change	% Change
6	Gross Sales	$ 9,514,000	$ 8,424,000	$ 1,090,000	0.129392213
7	Cost of Sales	3,374,000	2,784,000	590,000	0.211925287
8	Operating Expenses	5,032,000	4,376,000	656,000	0.149908592
9	Net Profit/Loss	1,108,000	1,264,000	(156,000)	-0.12341772
10					
11	Units Sold	1,344,000	1,104,000	240,000	0.217391304
12	Customers Served	155,400	129,600	25,800	0.199074074
13					
14	Sales Statistics per Store				
15	Category	2015	2014	Net Change	% Change
16	Gross Sales	475700	526500	-50800	-0.09648623
17	Cost of Sales	168700	174000	-5300	-0.03045977
18	Operating Expenses	251600	273500	-21900	-0.08007313
19	Net Profit/Loss	55400	79000	-23600	-0.29873418

Documentation   **Sales Report**   ⊕

READY

The Percent style formats numbers as percentages. When you format values as percentages, the % symbol appears after the number and no digits appear to the right of the decimal point. You can always change how many decimal places are displayed in the cell if that is important to show with your data.

Sanjit wants you to format the percent change from the 2014 to 2015 sales statistics with a percent symbol to make the percent values easier to read.

To format percentages:

▶ **1.** Select the nonadjacent range **F6:F9;F11:F12** containing the percent change values.

▶ **2.** On the HOME tab, in the Number group, click the **Percent Style** button % (or press the **Ctrl+Shift+%** keys). The values are displayed as percentages.

▶ **3.** In the Number group, click the **Increase Decimal** button twice. The displayed number includes two decimal places.

▶ **4.** Select cell **F13** to deselect the range. See Figure 2-14.

Figure 2-14   **Formatted percent changes**

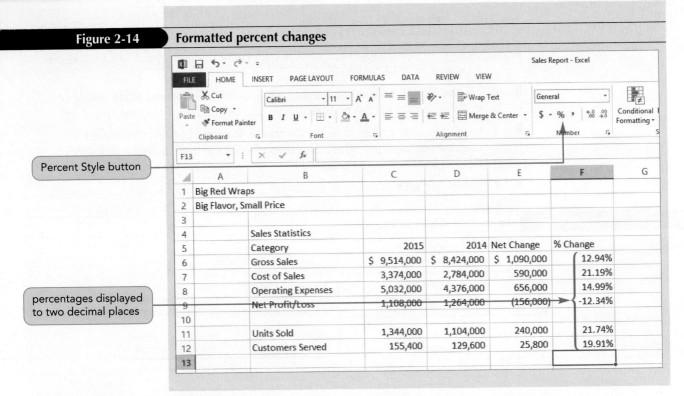

Percent Style button

percentages displayed to two decimal places

With the data reformatted, the worksheet clearly shows that Big Red Wraps' gross sales increased from 2014 to 2015 by almost 13 percent. However, both the cost of sales and the operating expenses increased by about 21.2 percent and 15 percent, respectively, probably due to the cost of building four new stores. As a result, the company's net profit decreased by $156,000 or about 12.3 percent.

Formatting Dates and Times

TIP

To view the underlying date and time value, apply the General format to the cell or display the formulas instead of the formula results.

Because Excel stores dates and times as numbers and not as text, you can apply different formats without affecting the date and time value. The abbreviated format, *mm/dd/yyyy*, entered in the Documentation sheet is referred to as the **Short Date format**. You can also apply a **Long Date format** that displays the day of the week and the full month name in addition to the day of the month and the year. Other built-in formats include formats for displaying time values in 12- or 24-hour time format.

You will change the date in the Documentation sheet to the Long Date format.

To format the date in the Long Date format:

1. Go to the **Documentation** sheet, and then select cell **B5**.

2. On the ribbon, make sure the HOME tab is displayed.

3. In the Number group, click the **Number Format button arrow** to display a list of number formats, and then click **Long Date**. The date is displayed with the weekday name, month name, day, and year. Notice that the date in the formula bar did not change because you changed only the display format, not the date value.

Formatting Worksheet Cells

You can format the appearance of individual cells by modifying the alignment of text within the cell, indenting cell text, or adding borders of different styles and colors.

Aligning Cell Content

By default, text is aligned with the left and bottom borders of a cell, and numbers are aligned with the right and bottom borders. You might want to change the alignment to make the text and numbers more readable or visually appealing. In general, you should center column titles, left-align other text, and right-align numbers to keep their decimal places lined up within a column. Figure 2-15 describes the buttons you use to set these alignment options, which are located in the Alignment group on the HOME tab.

Figure 2-15   **Alignment buttons**

Button	Name	Description
	Top Align	Aligns the cell content with the cell's top edge
	Middle Align	Vertically centers the cell content within the cell
	Bottom Align	Aligns the cell content with the cell's bottom edge
	Align Left	Aligns the cell content with the cell's left edge
	Center	Horizontally centers the cell content within the cell
	Align Right	Aligns the cell content with the cell's right edge
	Decrease Indent	Decreases the size of the indentation used in the cell
	Increase Indent	Increases the size of the indentation used in the cell
	Orientation	Rotates the cell content to any angle within the cell
	Wrap Text	Forces the cell text to wrap within the cell borders
	Merge & Center	Merges the selected cells into a single cell

© 2014 Cengage Learning

The date in the Documentation sheet is right-aligned in the cell because Excel treats dates and times as numbers. Sanjit wants you to left-align the date and center the column titles in the Sales Report worksheet.

To left-align the date and center the column titles:

1. In the Documentation sheet, make sure cell **B5** is still selected.

2. On the HOME tab, in the Alignment group, click the **Align Left** button ☰. The date shifts to the left edge of the cell.

3. Make the **Sales Report** worksheet the active worksheet.

4. Select the range **C5:F5**. The column titles are selected.

5. In the Alignment group, click the **Center** button ☰. The column titles are centered in the cells.

Indenting Cell Content

Sometimes you want a cell's content moved a few spaces from the cell's left edge. This is particularly useful to create subsections in a worksheet or to set off some entries from others. You can increase the indent to shift the contents of a cell away from the left edge of the cell, or you can decrease the indent to shift a cell's contents closer to the left edge of the cell.

Sanjit wants the Cost of Sales and Operating Expenses labels in the sales statistics table offset from the other labels because they represent expenses to the company. You will increase the indent for the expense categories.

To indent the expense categories:

▶ 1. Select the range **B7:B8** containing the expense categories.

▶ 2. On the HOME tab, in the Alignment group, click the **Increase Indent** button ▤ twice to indent each label two spaces in its cell.

Adding Cell Borders

Common accounting practices provide guidelines on when to add borders to cells. In general, a single black border appears above a subtotal, a single bottom border is added below a calculated number, and a double black bottom border appears below the total.

Sanjit wants you to follow these common accounting practices in the Sales Report worksheet. You will add borders below the column titles and below the gross sales values. You will add a top border to the net profit/loss values. Finally, you will add a top and bottom border to the Units Sold and Customers Served rows.

To add borders to the sales statistics data:

▶ 1. Select the range **B5:F5** containing the table headings.

▶ 2. On the HOME tab, in the Font group, click the **All Borders button arrow** ⊞ ▾, and then click **Bottom Border**. A border is added below the column titles.

▶ 3. Select the range **B6:F6** containing the gross sales amounts.

▶ 4. In the Font group, click the **Bottom Border** button ▦ to add a border below the selected gross sales amounts.

▶ 5. Select the range **B9:F9**, click the **Bottom Border button arrow** ▦ ▾, and then click **Top Border** to add a border above the net profit/loss amounts.

     The Units Sold and Customers Served rows do not contain monetary values as the other rows do. You will distinguish these rows by adding a top and bottom border.

▶ 6. Select the range **B11:F12**, click the **Top Border button arrow** ▦ ▾, and then click **Top and Bottom** to add a border above the number of units sold and below the number of customers served.

▶ 7. Select cell **B3** to deselect the range. See Figure 2-16.

| Figure 2-16 | Worksheet with formatted cells |

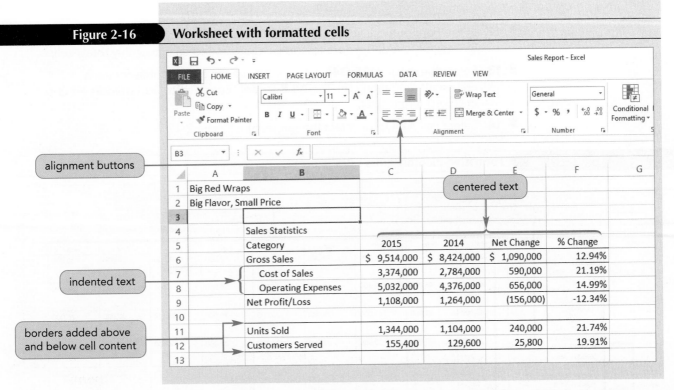

You can apply multiple formats to the same cell to create the look that best fits the data. For example, one cell might be formatted with a number format, alignments, borders, indents, fonts, font sizes, and so on. The monthly sales data needs to be formatted with number styles, alignment, indents, and borders. You'll add these formats now.

To format the monthly sales table:

▶ 1. Click the **Name** box to select the cell reference, type **C27:O47**, and then press the **Enter** key to quickly select the range C27:O47 containing the monthly gross sales for each restaurant.

▶ 2. On the HOME tab, in the Number group, click the **Comma Style** button ⟩ to add a thousands separator to the values.

▶ 3. In the Number group, click the **Decrease Decimal** button ⟨.00→.0⟩ twice to hide the cents from the sales results.

▶ 4. In the Alignment group, click the **Top Align** button ≡ to align the sales numbers with the top of each cell.

▶ 5. Select the range **C26:O26** containing the labels for the month abbreviations and the TOTAL column.

▶ 6. In the Alignment group, click the **Center** button ≡ to center the column labels.

▶ 7. Select the range **B27:B46** containing the store addresses.

▶ 8. Reduce the font size of the store addresses to **9** points.

▶ 9. In the Alignment group, click the **Increase Indent** button ≣→ to indent the store addresses.

▶ 10. In the Alignment group, click the **Top Align** button ≡ to align the addresses at the top of each cell.

▶ 11. Select the range **B47:O47** containing the monthly totals.

▶ **12.** In the Font group, click the **Top and Bottom Borders button arrow** 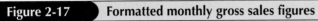,
and then click **All Borders** to add borders around each monthly totals cell.

▶ **13.** Select the range **O26:O46**, which contains the annual totals for each
restaurant, and then click the **All Borders** button ⊞ to add borders around
each restaurant total.

▶ **14.** Select cell **A24** to deselect the range. See Figure 2-17.

| Figure 2-17 | Formatted monthly gross sales figures |

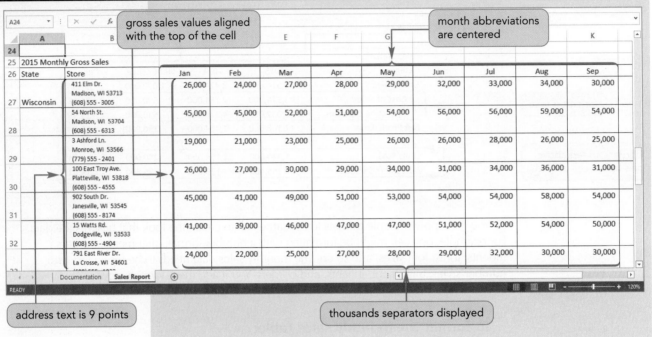

address text is 9 points   thousands separators displayed

Merging Cells

You can merge, or combine, several cells into one cell. A merged cell contains two or
more cells with a single cell reference. When you merge cells, only the content from
the upper-left cell in the range is retained. The cell reference for the merged cell is the
upper-left cell reference. So, if you merge cells A1 and A2, the merged cell reference
is cell A1. After you merge cells, you can align the content within the merged cell.
The Merge & Center button in the Alignment group on the HOME tab includes the
following options:

- **Merge & Center**—merges the range into one cell and horizontally centers the content
- **Merge Across**—merges each row in the selected range across the columns in the range
- **Merge Cells**—merges the range into a single cell, but does not horizontally center
  the cell content
- **Unmerge Cells**—reverses a merge, returning the merged cell to a range of individual cells

The first column of the monthly sales data lists the states in which Big Red Wraps
has stores. You will merge the cells for each state name.

To merge the state name cells:

▶ **1.** Select the range **A27:A33** containing the cells for the Wisconsin stores. You
will merge these seven cells into a single cell.

2. On the HOME tab, in the Alignment group, click the **Merge & Center** button. The range A27:A33 merges into one cell with the cell reference A27, and the text is centered and bottom-aligned within the cell.

3. Select the range **A34:A36**, and then click the **Merge & Center** button in the Alignment group to merge and center the Minnesota cells.

4. Select the range **A37:A40**, and then click the **Merge & Center** button to merge and center the Iowa cells.

5. Select cell **A41**, and then center it horizontally to align the Colorado text with the text in the other state cells.

6. Merge and center the range **A42:A43** containing the Nebraska cells.

7. Merge and center the range **A44:A46** containing the Kansas cells. See Figure 2-18. The merged cells make it easier to distinguish restaurants in each state.

Figure 2-18	Merged cells

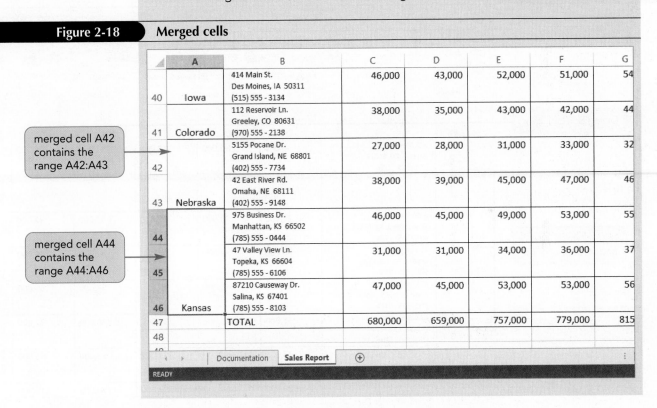

merged cell A42 contains the range A42:A43

merged cell A44 contains the range A44:A46

	A	B	C	D	E	F	G
40	Iowa	414 Main St. Des Moines, IA 50311 (515) 555 - 3134	46,000	43,000	52,000	51,000	54
41	Colorado	112 Reservoir Ln. Greeley, CO 80631 (970) 555 - 2138	38,000	35,000	43,000	42,000	44
42		5155 Pocane Dr. Grand Island, NE 68801 (402) 555 - 7734	27,000	28,000	31,000	33,000	32
43	Nebraska	42 East River Rd. Omaha, NE 68111 (402) 555 - 9148	38,000	39,000	45,000	47,000	46
44		975 Business Dr. Manhattan, KS 66502 (785) 555 - 0444	46,000	45,000	49,000	53,000	55
45		47 Valley View Ln. Topeka, KS 66604 (785) 555 - 6106	31,000	31,000	34,000	36,000	37
46	Kansas	87210 Causeway Dr. Salina, KS 67401 (785) 555 - 8103	47,000	45,000	53,000	53,000	56
47		TOTAL	680,000	659,000	757,000	779,000	815
48							

Documentation   **Sales Report**   ⊕

READY

Rotating Cell Contents

Text and numbers are displayed horizontally within cells. However, you can rotate cell text to any angle to save space or to provide visual interest to a worksheet. The state names at the bottom of the merged cells would look better and take up less room if they were rotated vertically within their cells. Sanjit asks you to rotate the state names.

To rotate the state names:

1. Select the merged cell **A27**.

2. On the HOME tab, in the Alignment group, click the **Orientation** button to display a list of rotation options, and then click **Rotate Text Up**. The state name rotates 90 degrees counterclockwise.

   3. In the Alignment group, click the **Middle Align** button ☰ to vertically center the rotated text in the merged cell.

   4. Select the merged cell range **A34:A44**, and then repeat Steps 2 and 3 to rotate and vertically center the rest of the state names in their cells.

   5. Select cell **A41** to deselect the range, and then increase the height of row 41 (the Colorado row) to **75** points (**100** pixels) so that the entire state name appears in the cell.

   6. Reduce the width of column A to **7** characters because the rotated state names take up less space.

   7. Select cell **A47**. See Figure 2-19.

Figure 2-19   **Rotated cell content**

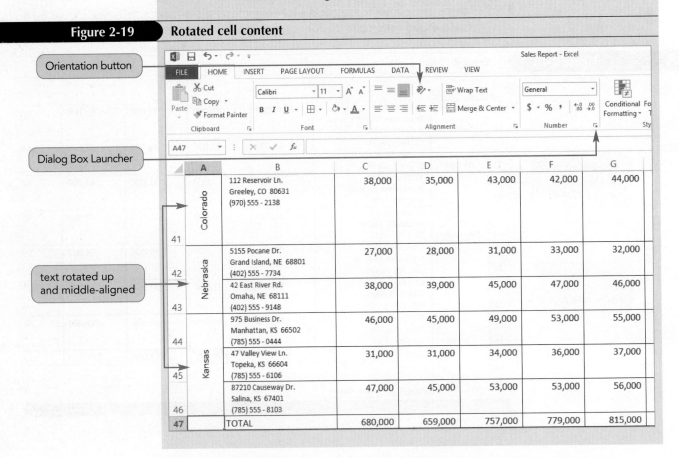

Exploring the Format Cells Dialog Box

The buttons on the HOME tab provide quick access to the most commonly used formatting choices. For more options, you can use the Format Cells dialog box. You can apply the formats in this dialog box to the selected worksheet cells. The Format Cells dialog box has six tabs, each focusing on a different set of formatting options, as described below:

- **Number**—provides options for formatting the appearance of numbers, including dates and numbers treated as text such as telephone or Social Security numbers
- **Alignment**—provides options for how data is aligned within a cell
- **Font**—provides options for selecting font types, sizes, styles, and other formatting attributes such as underlining and font colors

- **Border**—provides options for adding and removing cell borders as well as selecting a line style and color
- **Fill**—provides options for creating and applying background colors and patterns to cells
- **Protection**—provides options for locking or hiding cells to prevent other users from modifying their contents

Although you have applied many of these formats from the HOME tab, the Format Cells dialog box presents them in a different way and provides more choices. You will use the Font and Fill tabs to format the column titles with a white font on a red background.

To use the Format Cells dialog box to format the column labels:

TIP

You can also open the Format Cells dialog box by right-clicking the selected range, and then clicking Format Cells on the shortcut menu.

1. Select the range **A26:O26** containing the column labels for the table.

2. On the HOME tab, in the Number group, click the **Dialog Box Launcher** located to the right of the group name (refer to Figure 2-19). The Format Cells dialog box opens with the Number tab displayed.

3. Click the **Font** tab to display the font formatting options.

4. Click the **Color** box to display the color palette, and then click the **White, Background 1** theme color. The font is set to white. See Figure 2-20.

| Figure 2-20 | Font tab in the Format Cells dialog box |

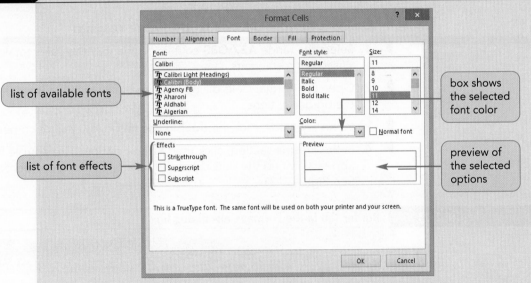

5. Click the **Fill** tab to display background options.

6. In the Background Color palette, click the **red** standard color (the second color in the last row). The background is set to red, as you can see in the Sample box.

7. Click the **OK** button. The dialog box closes, and the font and fill options you selected are applied to the column titles.

You will also use the Format Cells dialog box to change the appearance of the row titles. You'll format them to be displayed in a larger white font on a gray background.

To format the row labels:

▶ **1.** Select the range **A27:A46** containing the rotated state names.

▶ **2.** Right-click the selected range, and then click **Format Cells** on the shortcut menu. The Format Cells dialog box opens with the last tab used displayed—in this case, the Fill tab.

▶ **3.** In the Background Color palette, click the **gray** theme color (the first color in the seventh column). Its preview is shown in the Sample box.

▶ **4.** Click the **Font** tab to display the font formatting options.

▶ **5.** Click the **Color** box, and then click the **White, Background 1** theme color to set the font color to white.

▶ **6.** Scroll down the **Size** box, and then click **16** to set the font size to 16 points.

▶ **7.** Click the **OK** button. The dialog box closes, and the font and fill formats are applied to the state names.

The Border tab in the Format Cells dialog box provides options for changing the border style and color as well as placing the border anywhere around a cell or cells in a selected range. Sanjit wants you to format the borders in the monthly sales data so that the sales result from each state is surrounded by a double border.

To add a double border to the state results:

▶ **1.** Select the range **A27:O33** containing the monthly sales totals for the Wisconsin restaurants.

▶ **2.** Open the Format Cells dialog box, and then click the **Border** tab to display the border options.

▶ **3.** In the Style box, click the **double line** in the lower-right corner of the box.

▶ **4.** In the Presets section, click the **Outline** option. The double border appears around the outside of the selected cells in the Border preview. See Figure 2-21.

Figure 2-21   **Border tab in the Format Cells dialog box**

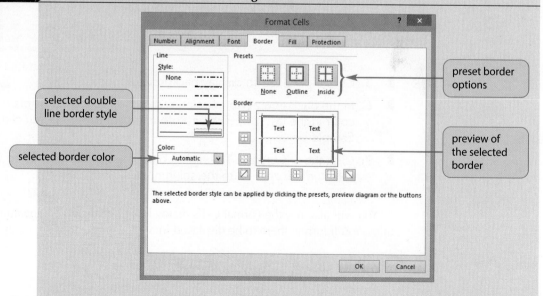

> **5.** Click the **OK** button. The selected border is applied to the Wisconsin monthly sales.

> **6.** Repeat Steps 2 through 5 to apply double borders to the ranges **A34:O36**, **A37:O40**, **A41:O41**, **A42:O43**, and **A44:O46**.

> **7.** Select cell **A48** to deselect the range. See Figure 2-22.

Figure 2-22   **Worksheet with font, fill, and border formatting**

state names in a 16-point white font on a gray background

double borders around state sales rows

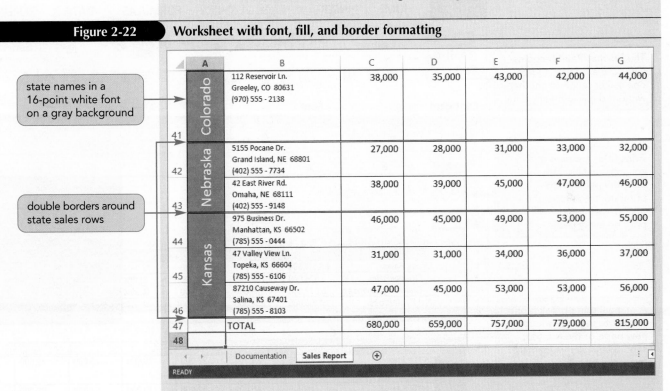

	A	B	C	D	E	F	G
	Colorado	112 Reservoir Ln. Greeley, CO 80631 (970) 555 - 2138	38,000	35,000	43,000	42,000	44,000
41							
42	**Nebraska**	5155 Pocane Dr. Grand Island, NE 68801 (402) 555 - 7734	27,000	28,000	31,000	33,000	32,000
43		42 East River Rd. Omaha, NE 68111 (402) 555 - 9148	38,000	39,000	45,000	47,000	46,000
44	**Kansas**	975 Business Dr. Manhattan, KS 66502 (785) 555 - 0444	46,000	45,000	49,000	53,000	55,000
45		47 Valley View Ln. Topeka, KS 66604 (785) 555 - 6106	31,000	31,000	34,000	36,000	37,000
46		87210 Causeway Dr. Salina, KS 67401 (785) 555 - 8103	47,000	45,000	53,000	53,000	56,000
47		TOTAL	680,000	659,000	757,000	779,000	815,000
48							

Documentation   **Sales Report**   ⊕

READY

> **8.** Save the Sales Report worksheet.

You have completed much of the formatting that Sanjit wants in the Sales Report worksheet for the Big Red Wraps sales conference. In the next session, you will explore other formatting options.

REVIEW

Session 2.1 Quick Check

1. What is the difference between a serif font and a sans serif font?

2. What is the difference between a theme color and a standard color?

3. A cell containing a number displays ######. Why does this occur and what can you do to fix it?

4. What is the General format?

5. Describe the differences between Currency format and Accounting format.

6. The range A1:C5 is merged into a single cell. What is its cell reference?

7. How do you format text so that it is set vertically within the cell?

8. Where can you access all the formatting options for worksheet cells?

Session 2.2 Visual Overview:

The PAGE LAYOUT tab has options for setting how the worksheet will print.

The Format Painter copies and pastes formatting from one cell or range to another without duplicating any data.

Print titles are rows and columns that are included on every page of the printout. In this case, the text in rows 1 and 2 will print on every page.

A manual page break is one you set to indicate where a new page of the printout should start and is identified by a solid blue line.

Sales Report - E

| FILE | HOME | INSERT | PAGE LAYOUT | FORMULAS | DATA | REVIEW | VI |

Calibri   11   A^ A^   General

B I U   A $ %

Clipboard   Font   Alignment   Number

A3   fx

Big Red Wraps

Big Flavor , Small Price

Sales Statistics   Page 1

Category	2015	2014	Net Change	% Change
Gross Sales	$9,514,000	########	$1,090,000	12.94%
Cost of Sales	3,374,000	2,784,000	590,000	21.19%
Operating Expenses	5,032,000	4,376,000	656,000	14.99%
Net Profit/Loss	1,108,000	1,264,000	(156,000)	-12.34%

2015 Monthly Gross Sales

Page 2

State	Store	Jan	Feb	Mar	Apr	May	Jun	Jul
Wisconsin	411 Elm Drive, Madison, WI 53713, (608) 555-3005	26,000	24,000	27,000	28,000	29,000	32,000	33,000
	54 North Street, Madison, WI 53704, (608) 555-6313	45,000	45,000	52,000	51,000	54,000	56,000	56,000
	3 Ashford Lane, Monroe, WI 53566, (779) 555-2401	19,000	21,000	23,000	25,000	26,000	26,000	28,000
	100 East Troy Avenue, Platteville, WI 53818, (608) 555-4555	26,000	27,000	30,000	29,000	34,000	31,000	34,000
	902 South Drive, Janesville, WI 53545, (608) 555-8174	45,000	41,000	49,000	51,000	53,000	54,000	54,000
	15 Watts Road, Dodgeville, WI 53533, (608) 555-4904	41,000	39,000	46,000	47,000	47,000	51,000	52,000
	791 East River Drive, La Crosse, WI 54601, (608) 555-1003	24,000	22,000	25,000	27,000	28,000	29,000	32,000
Minnesota	681 Main Avenue, Rochester, MN 55902, (507) 381-4002	34,000	34,000	38,000	39,000	42,000	42,000	43,000
	100 Business Drive, Owatonna, MN 55060, (507) 555-8994	31,000	30,000	33,000	33,000	36,000	35,000	36,000
	531 Eldorado Avenue, Mankato, MN 56001, (507) 555-2130	23,000	20,000	25,000	28,000	28,000	26,000	30,000
	55 Bluff Drive	44,000	43,000	48,000	50,000	51,000	54,000	54,000

◄ ►   Documentation   **Sales Report**   ⊕

READY

Worksheet Formatted for Printing

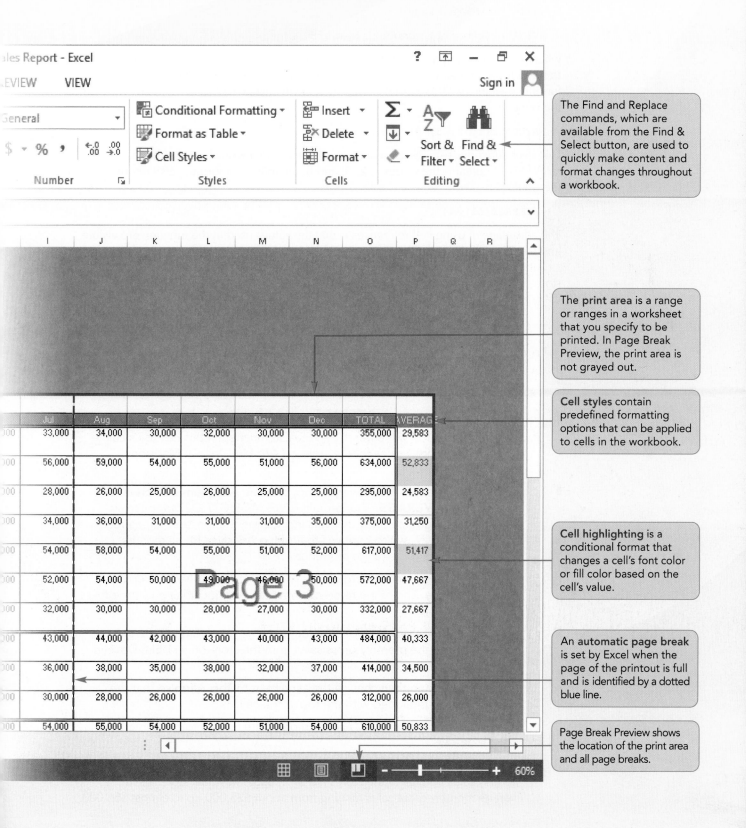

The Find and Replace commands, which are available from the Find & Select button, are used to quickly make content and format changes throughout a workbook.

The **print area** is a range or ranges in a worksheet that you specify to be printed. In Page Break Preview, the print area is not grayed out.

Cell styles contain predefined formatting options that can be applied to cells in the workbook.

Cell highlighting is a conditional format that changes a cell's font color or fill color based on the cell's value.

An **automatic page break** is set by Excel when the page of the printout is full and is identified by a dotted blue line.

Page Break Preview shows the location of the print area and all page breaks.

Using the Average Function

The **AVERAGE function** calculates the average value from a collection of numbers. The syntax of the Average function is

    AVERAGE (number1, number2, number3, …)

where *number1*, *number2*, *number3*, and so forth are either numbers or cell references to the cells or a range where the numbers are stored. For example, the following formula uses the AVERAGE function to calculate the average of 1, 2, 5, and 8, returning the value 4:

    =AVERAGE(1, 2, 5, 8)

However, functions usually reference values entered in a worksheet. So, if the range A1:A4 contains the values 1, 2, 5, and 8, the following formula also returns the value 4:

    =AVERAGE(A1:A4)

The advantage of using cell references is that the values used in the function are visible and can be easily edited.

Sanjit wants to show the average monthly sales for each of the 20 Big Red Wraps stores in addition to the total sales for each store. You will use the AVERAGE function to calculate these values.

To calculate the average monthly sales for each store:

1. If you took a break after the previous session, make sure the Sales Report workbook is open and the Sales Report worksheet is active.

2. In cell **P26**, enter the text **AVERAGE** as the label.

3. Select cell **P27**. You will enter the AVERAGE function in this cell to calculate the average monthly sales for the store on 411 Elm Drive in Madison, Wisconsin.

4. On the HOME tab, in the Editing group, click the **AutoSum button arrow**, and then click **AVERAGE**. The formula =AVERAGE(C27:O27) appears in the cell. The range reference that was included in the function is incorrect. It includes cell O27, which contains the total gross sales for all months. You need to correct the range reference.

5. Select **O27** in the function's argument, and then click cell **N27** to replace the cell reference. The range reference now correctly includes only the gross sales for each month.

6. Press the **Enter** key to complete the formula. The formula results show 29,583, which is the monthly gross sales from the store on 411 Elm Drive in Madison, Wisconsin.

7. Select cell **P27**, and then change the alignment to **Top Align** so that the calculated value is aligned with the top of the cell.

8. Copy the formula in cell **P27**, and then paste the copied formula into the range **P28:P47**.

9. Select cell **P48** to deselect the range. As shown in Figure 2-23, the average monthly sales from all of the stores are $792,833. Individual stores have average monthly gross sales ranging from about $25,000 up to almost $55,000.

Figure 2-23   **AVERAGE function results**

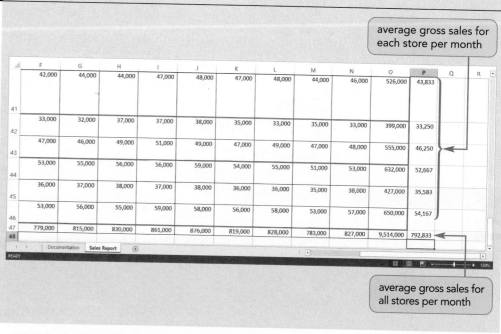

average gross sales for each store per month

average gross sales for all stores per month

With the last formulas added to the worksheet, Sanjit wants you to continue formatting the workbook.

Applying Cell Styles

A workbook often contains several cells that store the same type of data. For example, each worksheet might have a cell displaying the sheet title, or a range of financial data might have several cells containing totals and averages. It is good design practice to apply the same format to worksheet cells that contain the same type of data.

One way to ensure that similar data is displayed consistently is with styles. A **style** is a collection of formatting options that include a specified font, font size, font styles, font color, fill color, and borders. The Cell Styles gallery includes a variety of built-in styles that you can use to format titles and headings, different types of data such as totals or calculations, and cells that you want to emphasize. For example, you can use the Heading 1 style to display sheet titles in a bold, blue-gray, 15-point Calibri font with no fill color and a blue bottom border. You can then apply the Heading 1 style to all titles in the workbook. If you later revise the style, the appearance of any cell formatted with that style is updated automatically. This saves you the time and effort of reformatting each cell individually.

You already used built-in styles when you formatted data in the Sales Report worksheet with the Accounting, Comma, and Percent styles. You can also create your own cell styles by clicking New Cell Style at the bottom of the Cell Styles gallery.

Sanjit wants you to add more color and visual interest to the Sales Report worksheet. You'll use some of the styles in the Cell Styles gallery to do this.

To apply cell styles to the Sales Report worksheet:

▸ 1. Select cell **B4** containing the text "Sales Statistics."

▸ 2. On the HOME tab, in the Styles group, click the **Cell Styles** button. The Cell Styles gallery opens.

▸ 3. Point to the **Heading 1** style in the Titles and Headings section. Live Preview shows cell B4 in a 15-point, bold font with a solid blue bottom border. See Figure 2-24.

| Figure 2-24 | Cell Styles gallery |

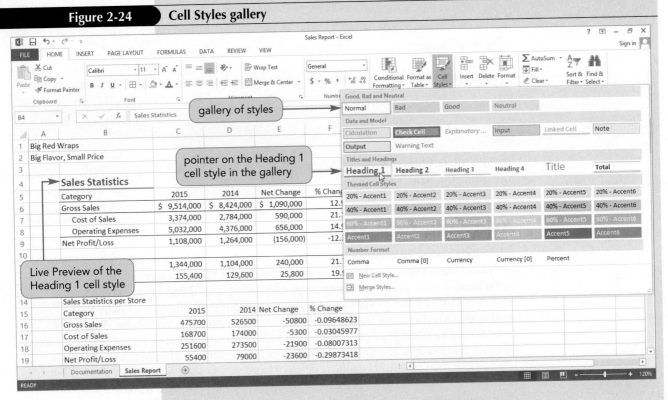

▸ 4. Move the pointer over different styles in the Cell Styles gallery to see cell B4 with a Live Preview of each style.

▸ 5. Click the **Title** style. The Title style is applied to cell B4.

▸ 6. Select the range **B5:F5** containing the column labels for the Sales Statistics data.

▸ 7. In the Styles group, click the **Cell Styles** button, and then click the **Accent3** style in the Themed Cell Styles section of the Cell Styles gallery.

▸ 8. Select cell **A25** containing the text "2015 Monthly Gross Sales," and then apply the **Title** cell style to the cell.

▸ 9. Select cell **A3**. See Figure 2-25.

Figure 2-25 **Cell styles applied to the worksheet**

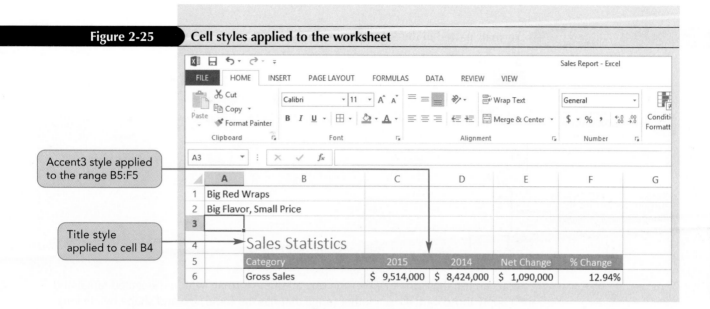

Accent3 style applied to the range B5:F5

Title style applied to cell B4

Copying and Pasting Formats

Large workbooks often use the same formatting on similar data throughout the workbook, sometimes in widely scattered cells. Rather than repeating the same steps to format these cells, you can copy the format of one cell or range and paste it to another.

Copying Formats with the Format Painter

The Format Painter provides a fast and efficient way of copying and pasting formats, ensuring that a workbook has a consistent look and feel. The Format Painter does not copy formatting applied to selected text within a cell, and it does not copy data.

Sanjit wants the Sales Report worksheet to use the same formats you applied to the Big Red Wraps company name and slogan in the Documentation sheet. You will use the Format Painter to copy and paste the formats.

To use the Format Painter to copy and paste a format:

1. Go to the **Documentation** worksheet, and then select the range **A1:A2**.

2. On the HOME tab, in the Clipboard group, click the **Format Painter** button. The formats from the selected cells are copied to the Clipboard, and a flashing border appears around the selected range and the pointer changes to ⊕🖌.

3. Return to the **Sales Report** worksheet, and then click cell **A1**. The formatting from the Documentation worksheet is removed from the Clipboard and applied to the range A1:A2. Notice that the larger font size you applied to the text "Big Flavor" was not included in the pasted formats.

4. Double-click cell **A2** to enter Edit mode, select **Big Flavor**, and then increase the font size to **14** points. The format for the slogan now matches the slogan on the Documentation sheet.

5. Select cell **A3** to exit Edit mode. See Figure 2-26.

TIP

To paste the same format multiple times, double-click the Format Painter button to leave the Format Painter on until you click the button again or press the Esc key.

Figure 2-26 Formats pasted in the Sales Report worksheet

Format Painter button

format copied from Documentation sheet

You can use the Format Painter to copy all of the formats within a selected range and then apply those formats to another range that has the same size and shape by clicking the upper-left cell of the range. Sanjit wants you to copy all of the formats you applied to the Sales Statistics data to the sales statistics per store.

To copy and paste multiple formats:

1. Select the range **B4:F12** in the Sales Report worksheet.

2. On the HOME tab, in the Clipboard group, click the **Format Painter** button.

3. Click cell **B14**. All of the number formats, cell borders, fonts, and fill colors are pasted into the range B14:F22.

4. Select the range **C23:E23**.

5. On the HOME tab, in the Number group, click the **Comma Style** button, and then click the **Decrease Decimal** button twice to remove the decimal places to the right of the decimal point. The numbers are vertically aligned in their columns.

6. Select cell **F23**.

7. In the Number group, click the **Percent Style** button to change the number to a percentage, and then click the **Increase Decimal** button twice to display two decimal places in the percentage.

8. Click cell **B24**. See Figure 2-27.

TIP

If the range in which you paste the formats is bigger than the range you copied, Format Painter will repeat the copied formats to fill the pasted range.

Figure 2-27   **Formats pasted from a range**

copied formats

pasted formats

	A	B	C	D	E	F	G	H
6		Gross Sales	$ 9,514,000	$ 8,424,000	$ 1,090,000	12.94%		
7		Cost of Sales	3,374,000	2,784,000	590,000	21.19%		
8		Operating Expenses	5,032,000	4,376,000	656,000	14.99%		
9		Net Profit/Loss	1,108,000	1,264,000	(156,000)	-12.34%		
10								
11		Units Sold	1,344,000	1,104,000	240,000	21.74%		
12		Customers Served	155,400	129,600	25,800	19.91%		
13								
14		Sales Statistics per Store						
15		Category	2015	2014	Net Change	% Change		
16		Gross Sales	$ 475,700	$ 526,500	$ (50,800)	-9.65%		
17		Cost of Sales	168,700	174,000	(5,300)	-3.05%		
18		Operating Expenses	251,600	273,500	(21,900)	-8.01%		
19		Net Profit/Loss	55,400	79,000	(23,600)	-29.87%		
20								
21		Units Sold	67,200	69,000	(1,800)	-2.61%		
22		Customers Served	7,770	8,100	(330)	-4.07%		
23		Stores	20	16	4	25.00%		
24								

Documentation | **Sales Report** | (+)

READY

Copying Formats with the Paste Options Button

Another way to copy and paste formats is with the Paste Options button  (Ctrl) ▾, which provides options for pasting only values, only formats, or some combination of values and formats. Each time you paste, the Paste Options button appears in the lower-right corner of the pasted cell or range. You click the Paste Options button to open a list of pasting options, shown in Figure 2-28, such as pasting only the values or only the formatting. You can also click the Transpose button to paste the column data into a row, or to paste the row data into a column.

Figure 2-28   **Paste Options button**

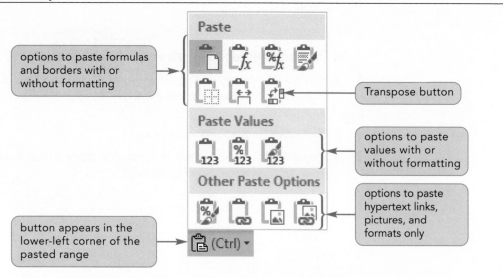

options to paste formulas and borders with or without formatting

Transpose button

options to paste values with or without formatting

options to paste hypertext links, pictures, and formats only

button appears in the lower-left corner of the pasted range

Copying Formats with Paste Special

The Paste Special command provides another way to control what you paste from the Clipboard. To use Paste Special, select and copy a range, select the range where you want to paste the Clipboard contents, click the Paste button arrow in the Clipboard group on the HOME tab, and then click Paste Special to open the dialog box shown in Figure 2-29.

Figure 2-29   Paste Special dialog box

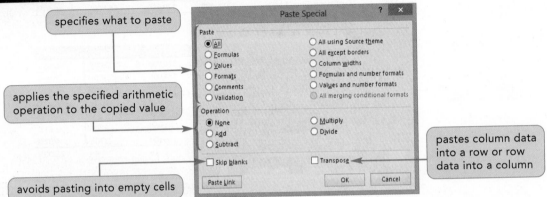

From the Paste Special dialog box, you can control exactly how to paste the copied range.

Finding and Replacing Text and Formats

The Find and Replace commands let you make content and design changes to a worksheet or the entire workbook quickly. The Find command searches through the current worksheet or workbook for the content or formatting you want to locate, and the Replace command then substitutes it with the new content or formatting you specify.

Sanjit wants you to replace all the street title abbreviations (such as Ave.) in the Sales Report with their full names (such as Avenue). You will use Find and Replace to make these changes.

To find and replace the street title abbreviations:

▶ 1. On the HOME tab, in the Editing group, click the **Find & Select** button, and then click **Replace** (or press the **Ctrl+H** keys). The Find and Replace dialog box opens.

▶ 2. Type **Ave.** in the Find what box.

▶ 3. Press the **Tab** key to move the insertion point to the Replace with box, and then type **Avenue**. See Figure 2-30.

Figure 2-30 **Find and Replace dialog box**

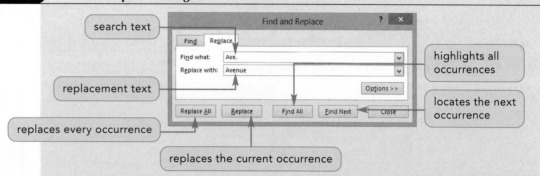

You can choose to find each occurrence of the search text one at a time and decide whether to replace it. You can choose to highlight all occurrences of the search text in the worksheet. Or, you can choose to replace all occurrences at once without reviewing them. In this case, you want to replace every occurrence of the search text with the replacement text.

4. Click the **Replace All** button to replace all occurrences of the search text without reviewing them. A dialog box opens, reporting that three replacements were made in the worksheet.

5. Click the **OK** button to return to the Find and Replace dialog box.

    Next, you will replace the other street title abbreviations.

6. Repeat Steps 2 through 5 to replace all occurrences of each of the following: **St.** with **Street**, **Ln.** with **Lane**, **Dr.** with **Drive**, and **Rd.** with **Road**.

7. Click the **Close** button to close the Find and Replace dialog box.

8. Scroll through the Sales Report worksheet to verify that all street title abbreviations were replaced with their full names.

The Find and Replace dialog box can also be used to replace one format with another or to replace both text and a format simultaneously. Sanjit wants you to replace all occurrences of the white text in the Sales Report worksheet with light yellow text. You'll use the Find and Replace dialog box to make this formatting change.

To replace white text with yellow text:

1. On the HOME tab, in the Editing group, click the **Find & Select** button, and then click **Replace** (or press the **Ctrl+H** keys). The Find and Replace dialog box opens.

2. Click the **Options** button to expand the dialog box.

3. Click the **Format** button in the Find what row to open the Find Format dialog box, which is similar to the Format Cells dialog box you used earlier to format a range.

4. Click the **Font** tab to make it active, click the **Color** box, and then click the **White, Background 1** theme color.

5. Click the **OK** button to close the dialog box and return to the Find and Replace dialog box.

6. Click the **Format** button in the Replace with row to open the Replace Format dialog box.

7. Click the **Color** box, and then click the **Yellow** standard color.

8. Click the **OK** button to close the dialog box and return to the Find and Replace dialog box. See Figure 2-31.

Figure 2-31   **Expanded Find and Replace dialog box**

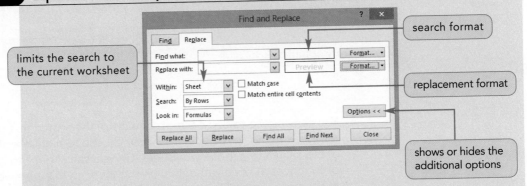

limits the search to the current worksheet

search format

replacement format

shows or hides the additional options

9. Verify that the Within box lists **Sheet** to limit the search to the current worksheet.

10. Click the **Replace All** button to replace all occurrences of white text in the Sales Report worksheet with yellow text. A dialog box appears, reporting that 32 replacements were made.

11. Click the **OK** button to return to the Find and Replace dialog box.

It is a good idea to clear the find and replace formats after you are done so that they won't affect any future searches and replacements. You'll remove the formats from the Find and Replace dialog box.

12. Click the **Format button arrow** in the Find what row, and then click **Clear Find Format**. The search format is removed.

13. Click the **Format button arrow** in the Replace with row, and then click **Clear Replace Format**. The replacement format is removed.

14. Click the **Close** button to return to the worksheet. Notice that every cell in the worksheet that had white text now has yellow text.

Working with Themes

Recall that a theme is a coordinated selection of fonts, colors, and graphical effects that are applied throughout a workbook to create a specific look and feel. When you switch to a different theme, the theme-related fonts, colors, and effects change throughout the workbook to reflect the new theme. The appearance of non-theme fonts, colors, and effects remains unchanged no matter which theme is applied to the workbook.

Most of the formatting you have applied to the Sales Report workbook is based on the Office theme. Sanjit wants you to change the theme to see how it affects the workbook's appearance.

To change the workbook's theme:

▶ **1.** Click the **PAGE LAYOUT** tab on the ribbon.

▶ **2.** In the Themes group, click the **Themes** button. The Themes gallery opens. Office—the current theme—is the default.

▶ **3.** Point to the **Organic** theme in the Themes gallery. Live Preview shows how the appearance of the Sales Report worksheet will change if you select the Organic theme. See Figure 2-32.

Figure 2-32   **Live Preview of the Organic theme**

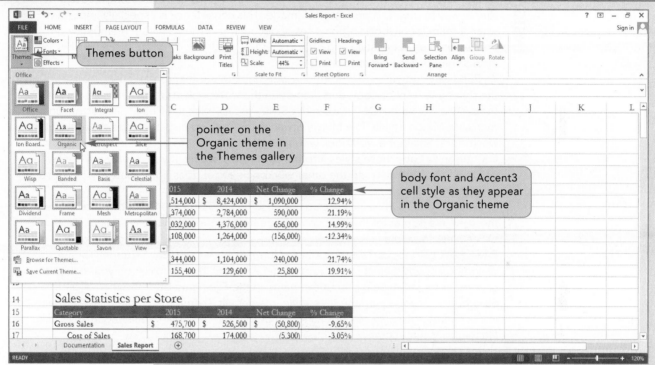

▶ **4.** Point to several other themes in the Themes gallery to see how the worksheet appearance would change.

▶ **5.** Click the **Wisp** theme to apply that theme to the workbook.

Changing the theme made a significant difference in the worksheet's appearance. The most obvious changes to the worksheet are the fill colors and the fonts. Only formatting options directly tied to a theme change when you select a different theme. Any formatting options you selected that were not theme-based remain unaffected by the change. For example, the yellow standard color you just applied to the different column labels is still yellow, even with the Wisp theme applied, because yellow is not a theme color. For the same reason, the red fill color used in the column labels of the monthly sales table remains unchanged under the new theme.

Sanjit informs you that Big Red Wraps requires all documents to be formatted with the Office theme. You will reapply the Office theme to the workbook.

> **To reapply the Office theme to the workbook:**
>
>   **1.** On the PAGE LAYOUT tab, in the Themes group, click the **Themes** button, and then click the **Office** theme from the gallery of themes.

The workbook now complies with the company's standard formatting.

Sharing Styles and Themes

Using a consistent look and feel for all the files you create in Microsoft Office is a simple way to project a professional image. This consistency is especially important when a team is collaborating on a set of documents. When all team members work from a common set of style and design themes, readers will not be distracted by inconsistent or clashing formatting.

To quickly copy the styles from one workbook to another, open the workbook with the styles you want to copy, and then open the workbook in which you want to copy those styles. On the HOME tab, in the Styles group, click the Cell Styles button, and then click Merge Styles. The Merge Styles dialog box opens, listing the currently open workbooks. Select the workbook with the styles you want to copy, and then click the OK button to copy those styles into the current workbook. If you modify any styles, you must copy the styles to the other workbook; Excel does not update styles between workbooks.

Because other Office files, including those created with Word or PowerPoint, use the same file format for themes, you can create one theme to use with all of your Office files. To save a theme, click the Themes button in the Themes group on the PAGE LAYOUT tab, and then click Save Current Theme. The Save Current Theme dialog box opens. Select a save location (in a default Theme folder on your computer or another folder), type a descriptive name in the File name box, and then click the Save button. If you saved the theme file in a default Theme folder, the theme appears in the Themes gallery, and any changes made to the theme are reflected in any Office file that uses that theme.

Highlighting Cells with Conditional Formats

Conditional formats are often used to help analyze data. A **conditional format** applies formatting to a cell when its value meets a specified condition. For example, a conditional format can be used to format negative numbers in red and positive numbers in black. Conditional formats are dynamic, which means that the formatting can change when the cell's value changes. Each conditional format has a set of rules that define how the formatting should be applied and under what conditions the format will be changed.

Highlighting Cells with a Conditional Format

- Select the range in which you want to highlight cells.
- On the HOME tab, in the Styles group, click the Conditional Formatting button, point to Highlight Cells Rules or Top/Bottom Rules, and then click the appropriate rule.
- Select the appropriate options in the dialog box.
- Click the OK button.

Excel has four conditional formats—data bars, highlighting, color scales, and icon sets. In this tutorial, you will apply cell highlighting, which changes the cell's font color or fill color based on the cell's value, as described in Figure 2-33. You can enter a value or a cell reference if you want to compare other cells with the value in a certain cell.

Figure 2-33	Highlight Cells rules

Rule	Highlights Cell Values
Greater Than	Greater than a specified number
Less Than	Less than a specified number
Between	Between two specified numbers
Equal To	Equal to a specified number
Text that Contains	That contain specified text
A Date Occurring	That contain a specified date
Duplicate Values	That contain duplicate or unique values

© 2014 Cengage Learning

Highlighting Cells Based on Their Values

Sanjit wants to highlight important trends and sales values in the Sales Report worksheet. He wants you to use a conditional format to display sales statistics that showed a negative net or percent change in a red font so that they stand out. You will do this by creating a rule to format the cells in ranges E6:F12 and E16:F22 with numbers that are less than 0.

To highlight negative numbers in red:

1. Select the nonadjacent range **E6:F12;E16:F22** in the Sales Report worksheet.

2. On the ribbon, click the **HOME** tab.

3. In the Styles group, click the **Conditional Formatting** button, and then point to **Highlight Cells Rules** to display a menu of the available rules.

4. Click **Less Than**. The Less Than dialog box opens so you can select the value and formatting to highlight negative values.

5. Type **0** (a zero) in the Format cells that are LESS THAN box, click the **with** arrow, and then click **Red Text**. Live Preview shows that the rule formats any cells in the selected range that have a negative value in a red font. See Figure 2-34.

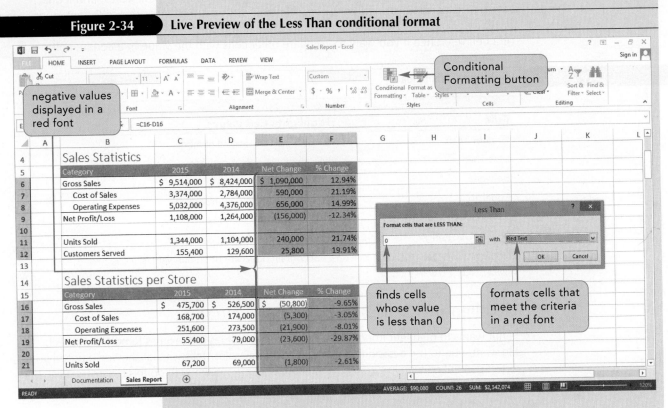

Figure 2-34   **Live Preview of the Less Than conditional format**

> **6.** Click the **OK** button to apply the highlighting rule. You will verify that this format is conditional.
>
> **7.** In cell D8, enter **4,576,000** to change the Operating Expenses value. The now positive values in cells E9 and F9 are formatted in a black font.
>
> **8.** Press the **Ctrl+Z** keys to return the value in cell D8 to 4,376,000. The values in cells E9 and F9 are again negative and in a red font.

The highlighted values show at a glance that Big Red Wraps' gross sales, units sold, and customers served increased from 2014 to 2015, while the company's net profit declined during the same period. The average gross sales per store also declined in 2015. Big Red Wraps opened four new stores in 2015, and Sanjit will argue that the cost of this expansion and low sales from the new stores caused this apparent decline.

Highlighting Cells with a Top/Bottom Rule

Another way of applying conditional formats is with the Quick Analysis tool. The **Quick Analysis tool**, which appears whenever you select a range of cells, provides access to the most common tools for data analysis and formatting. The FORMATTING category includes buttons for the Greater Than and Top 10% conditional formatting rules. You can highlight cells based on their values in comparison to other cells. For example, you can highlight cells with the 10 highest or lowest values in a selected range, or you can highlight the cells with above-average values in a range.

Sanjit wants you to highlight the five stores in the Big Red Wraps chain that had the highest gross sales in the last fiscal year. You will use a Top/Bottom rule to do this.

To use a Top/Bottom Rule to highlight the stores with the highest gross sales:

▶ **1.** Select the range **P27:P46** containing the average monthly gross sales for each of the 20 Big Red Wraps stores. The Quick Analysis button appears in the lower-right corner of the selected range.

▶ **2.** Click the **Quick Analysis** button 📧, and then point to **Top 10%**. Live Preview colors the cells in the top 10 percent with red font and a red fill. See Figure 2-35.

Figure 2-35	Quick Analysis tool

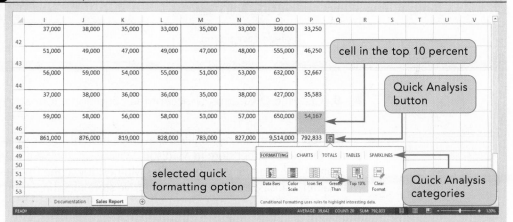

Sanjit wants to see the top five items rather than the cells with values in the top 10 percent, so you won't apply this conditional formatting.

▶ **3.** Press the **Esc** key to close the Quick Analysis tool. The range P27:P46 remains selected.

▶ **4.** On the HOME tab, in the Styles group, click the **Conditional Formatting** button, and then point to **Top/Bottom Rules** to display a menu of available rules.

▶ **5.** Click **Top 10 Items** to open the Top 10 Items dialog box.

▶ **6.** Click the down arrow on the spin box five times to change the value from 10 to 5. This specifies that the top five values in the selected range will be formatted.

▶ **7.** Click the **with** arrow, and then click **Green Fill with Dark Green Text** to specify the formatting to apply to the five cells with the top values. Live Preview highlights the top five stores in terms of gross sales. See Figure 2-36.

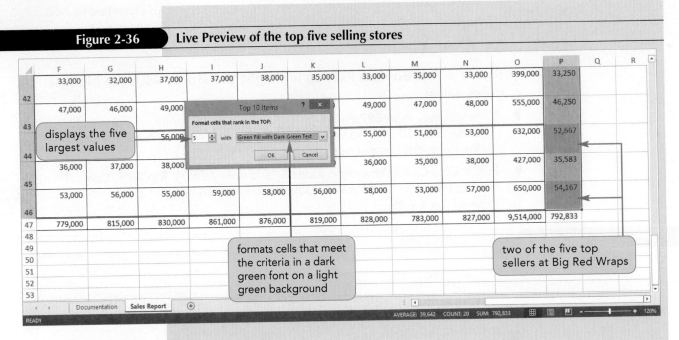

Figure 2-36   Live Preview of the top five selling stores

> **8.** Click the **OK** button to accept the conditional formatting.

The Top/Bottom rule highlights the average monthly gross sales for the five top-selling stores: the North Street store in Madison, Wisconsin; the South Drive store in Janesville, Wisconsin; the Main Street store in Des Moines, Iowa; the Business Drive store in Manhattan, Kansas; and the Causeway Drive store in Salina, Kansas.

Clearing a Conditional Format

You can remove a conditional format at any time without affecting the underlying data by selecting the range containing the conditional format, clicking the Conditional Formatting button, and then clicking the Clear Rules button. A menu opens, providing options to clear the conditional formatting rules from the selected cells or the entire worksheet. You can also click the Quick Analysis button that appears in the lower-right corner of the selected range, and then click the Clear Format button in the FORMATTING category.

Creating a Conditional Formatting Legend

When you use conditional formatting to highlight cells in a worksheet, the purpose of the formatting is not always immediately apparent. To ensure that everyone knows why certain cells are highlighted, you should include a **legend**, which is a key that identifies each color and its meaning.

You will add a legend to the Sales Report worksheet to document the Top 5 highlighting rule you just created.

To create a conditional formatting legend:

> **1.** Select cell **P49**, type **light green**, and then press the **Enter** key. You will use a highlight rule to fill this cell with a dark green font on a light green fill.

> **2.** Select cell **P49** to make it the active cell.

> **3.** On the HOME tab, in the Styles group, click the **Conditional Formatting** button, point to **Highlight Cells Rules**, and then click **Text that Contains**. The Text That Contains dialog box opens.

▶ **4.** Verify that **light green** appears in the Format cells that contain the text box. The box shows the text entered in the selected cell.

▶ **5.** Click the **with** arrow, and then click **Green Fill with Dark Green Text** to format cell P49 with the same format used for the top five gross sales.

▶ **6.** Click the **OK** button. Cell P49 remains selected.

▶ **7.** In the Alignment group, click the **Center** button to center the text in the cell.

▶ **8.** In cell **O49**, enter **Top 5 Stores** to identify the format's purpose, and then select cell **O49**.

▶ **9.** In the Styles group, click the **Cell Styles** button, and then click the **Explanatory Text** style (the third style in the first row of the Data and Model section). The cell style is applied to the selected cell.

▶ **10.** Click cell **O51**. The legend is complete, as shown in Figure 2-37.

| Figure 2-37 | **Conditional formatting legend** |

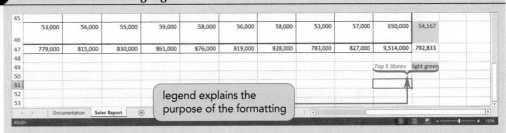

The conditional formatting makes the top-selling stores stand out.

Written Communication: Using Conditional Formatting Effectively

PROSKILLS

Conditional formatting is an excellent way to highlight important trends and data values to clients and colleagues. However, be sure to use it judiciously. Overusing conditional formatting might obscure the very data you want to emphasize. Keep in mind the following tips as you make decisions about what to highlight and how it should be highlighted:

- **Document the conditional formats you use.** If a bold, green font means that a sales number is in the top 10 percent of all sales, include that information in a legend in the worksheet.
- **Don't clutter data with too much highlighting.** Limit highlighting rules to one or two per data set. Highlights are designed to draw attention to points of interest. If you use too many, you will end up highlighting everything—and, therefore, nothing.
- **Use color sparingly in worksheets with highlights.** It is difficult to tell a highlight color from a regular fill color, especially when fill colors are used in every cell.
- **Consider alternatives to conditional formats.** If you want to highlight the top 10 sales regions, it might be more effective to simply sort the data with the best-selling regions at the top of the list.

Remember that the goal of highlighting is to provide a strong visual clue to important data or results. Careful use of conditional formatting helps readers to focus on the important points you want to make rather than distracting them with secondary issues and facts.

Formatting a Worksheet for Printing

You should format any worksheets you plan to print so that they are easy to read and understand. You can do this using the print settings, which enable you to set the page orientation, the print area, page breaks, print titles, and headers and footers. Print settings can be applied to an entire workbook or to individual sheets. Because other people will likely see your printed worksheets, you should format the printed output as carefully as you format the electronic version. Sanjit wants you to format the Sales Report worksheet so he can distribute the printed version at the upcoming sales conference.

Using Page Break Preview

Page Break Preview shows only those parts of the active sheet that will print and how the content will be split across pages. A dotted blue border indicates a page break, which separates one page from another. As you format the worksheet for printing, you can use this view to control what content appears on each page.

Sanjit wants to know how the Sales Report worksheet would print in portrait orientation and how many pages would be required. You will look at the worksheet in Page Break Preview to find these answers.

To view the Sales Report worksheet in Page Break Preview:

1. Click the **Page Break Preview** button on the status bar. The worksheet switches to Page Break Preview.

2. Change the zoom level of the worksheet to **30%** so you can view the entire contents of this large worksheet. See Figure 2-38.

Figure 2-38 | **Sales Report worksheet in Page Break Preview**

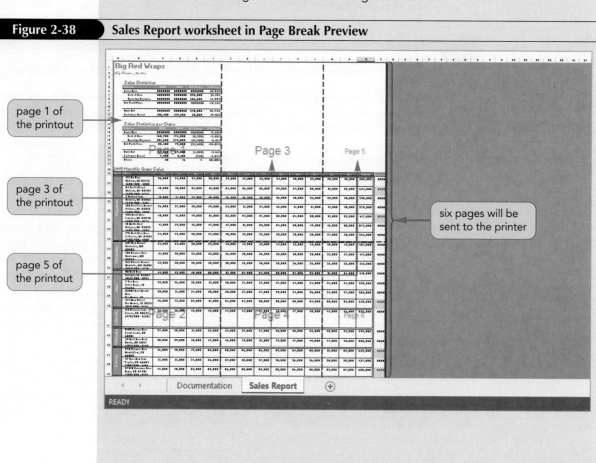

page 1 of the printout

page 3 of the printout

page 5 of the printout

six pages will be sent to the printer

Trouble? If you see a different page layout or the worksheet is split onto a different number of pages, don't worry. Each printer is different, so the layout and pages might differ from what is shown in Figure 2-38.

Page Break Preview shows that a printout of the Sales Report worksheet requires six pages in portrait orientation, and that pages 3 and 5 would be mostly blank. Note that each printer is different, so your Page Break Preview might show a different number of pages. With this layout, each page would be difficult to interpret because the data is separated from the descriptive labels. Sanjit wants you to fix the layout so that the contents are easier to read and understand.

Defining the Print Area

By default, all cells in a worksheet containing text, formulas, or values are printed. If you want to print only part of a worksheet, you can set a print area, which is the region of the worksheet that is sent to the printer. Each worksheet has its own print area. Although you can set the print area in any view, Page Break Preview shades the areas of the worksheet that are not included in the print area, making it simple to confirm what will print.

Sanjit doesn't want the empty cells in the range G1:O24 to print, so you will set the print area to eliminate those cells.

To set the print area of the Sales Report worksheet:

1. Change the zoom level of the worksheet to **80%** to make it easier to select cells and ranges.

2. Select the nonadjacent range **A1:F24;A25:P49** containing the cells with content.

3. On the ribbon, click the **PAGE LAYOUT** tab.

4. In the Page Setup group, click the **Print Area** button, and then click **Set Print Area**. The print area changes to cover only the nonadjacent range A1:F24;A25:P49. The rest of the worksheet content is shaded to indicate that it will not be part of the printout.

5. Select cell **A1** to deselect the range.

6. Change the zoom level to **50%** so you can view more of the worksheet. See Figure 2-39.

Figure 2-39   **Print area set for the Sales Report worksheet**

range A1:F24 prints on its own page

print area covers the nonadjacent range A1:F24;A25:P49

solid line indicates a manual page break

dotted lines indicate automatic page breaks

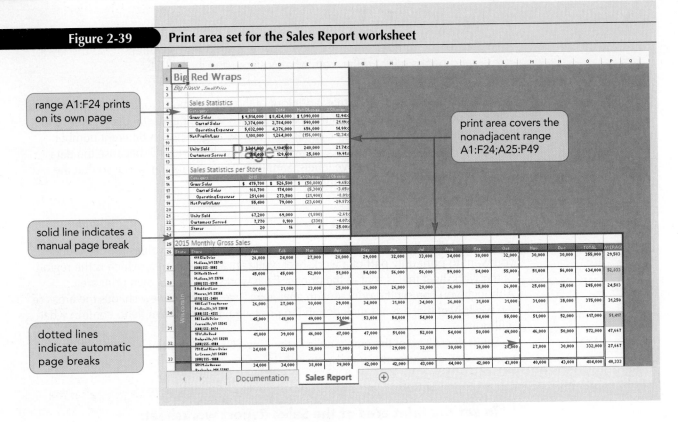

Inserting Page Breaks

Often, the contents of a worksheet will not fit onto a single printed page. When this happens, Excel prints as much of the content that fits on a single page without resizing, and then inserts automatic page breaks to continue printing the remaining worksheet content on successive pages. The resulting printouts might split worksheet content in awkward places, such as within a table of data.

To split the printout into logical segments, you can insert manual page breaks. Page Break Preview identifies manual page breaks with a solid blue line and automatic page breaks with a dotted blue line. When you specify a print area for a nonadjacent range, as you did for the Sales Report worksheet, you also insert manual page breaks around the adjacent ranges. So a manual page break already appears in the print area you defined (see Figure 2-39). You can remove a page break in Page Break Preview by dragging it out of the print area.

REFERENCE

Inserting and Removing Page Breaks

To insert a page break:
- Click the first cell below the row where you want to insert a page break, click a column heading, or click a row heading.
- On the PAGE LAYOUT tab, in the Page Setup group, click the Breaks button, and then click Insert Page Break.

To remove a page break:
- Select any cell below or to the right of the page break you want to remove.
- On the PAGE LAYOUT tab, in the Page Setup group, click the Breaks button, and then click Remove Page Break.

or
- In Page Break Preview, drag the page break line out of the print area.

The Sales Report worksheet has automatic page breaks along columns F and L. You will remove these automatic page breaks from the Sales Report worksheet.

To remove the automatic page breaks and insert manual page breaks:

▶ **1.** Point to the dotted blue page break directly to the right of column L until the pointer changes to ◀╫▶.

▶ **2.** Drag the page break to the right and out of the print area. The page break is removed from the worksheet.

▶ **3.** Point to the page break located in cell F31 until the pointer changes to ◀╫▶, and then drag the page break to the right and out of the print area.

   On the PAGE LAYOUT tab, in the Scale to Fit section, notice that the Scale box shows 43%. After removing the two page breaks from the Sales Report printout, Excel scaled the printout from 100% of its actual size to 43% to fit the printout onto two pages.

▶ **4.** Click the **column I** heading to select the entire column. You will add a manual page break between columns H and I to split the monthly gross sales data onto two pages so the printout will be larger and easier to read.

▶ **5.** On the PAGE LAYOUT tab, in the Page Setup group, click the **Breaks** button, and then click **Insert Page Break**. A manual page break is added between columns H and I, forcing the monthly gross sales onto a new page after the June data.

▶ **6.** Select cell **A1** to deselect the column. The printout of the Sales Report worksheet is now limited to three pages. However, the gross sales data in the range A25:O49 is split across pages. See Figure 2-40.

| Figure 2-40 | Manual page break added to the print area |

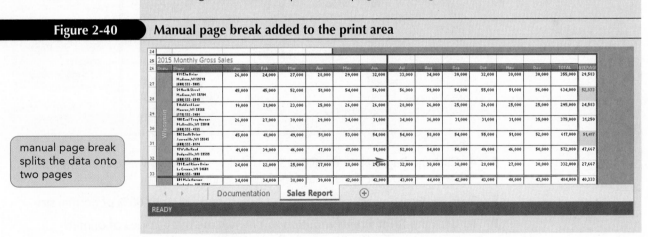

manual page break splits the data onto two pages

Adding Print Titles

It is a good practice to include descriptive information such as the company name, logo, and worksheet title on each page of a printout in case a page becomes separated from the other pages. You can repeat information, such as the company name, by specifying which rows or columns in the worksheet act as print titles. If a worksheet contains a large table, you can print the table's column headings and row headings on every page of the printout by designating those columns and rows as print titles.

In the Sales Report worksheet, the company name and slogan currently appear on the first page of the printout, but do not appear on subsequent pages. Also, the descriptive row labels for the monthly sales table in column A do not appear on the third page of the printout. You will add print titles to fix these issues.

To set the print titles:

TIP

You can also open the Page Setup dialog box by clicking the Dialog Box Launcher in the Page Setup group on the PAGE LAYOUT tab.

1. On the PAGE LAYOUT tab, in the Page Setup group, click the **Print Titles** button. The Page Setup dialog box opens with the Sheet tab displayed.

2. In the Print titles section, click the **Rows to repeat at top** box, move the pointer over the worksheet, and then select the range **A1:A2**. A flashing border appears around the first two rows of the worksheet to indicate that the contents of the first two rows will be repeated on each page of the printout. The row reference $1:$2 appears in the Rows to repeat at top box.

3. Click the **Columns to repeat at left** box, and then select columns A and B from the worksheet. The column reference $A:$B appears in the Columns to repeat at left box. See Figure 2-41.

Figure 2-41	Sheet tab in the Page Setup dialog box

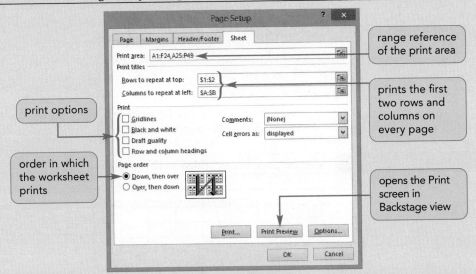

4. Click the **Page** tab in the Page Setup dialog box. You will rescale the worksheet so that it doesn't appear too small in the printout.

5. In the Scaling section, change the Adjust to amount to **65%** of normal size.

6. Click the **Print Preview** button to preview the three pages of printed material on the Print screen in Backstage view.

7. Verify that each of the three pages has the Big Red Wraps title and slogan at the top of the page, and that the state and store names appear in the leftmost columns of pages 2 and 3. See Figure 2-42.

Figure 2-42	Print titles on page 3 of the Sales Report worksheet

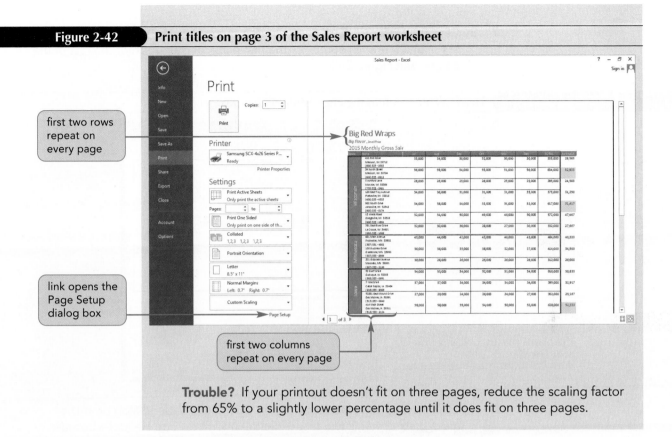

first two rows
repeat on
every page

link opens the
Page Setup
dialog box

first two columns
repeat on every page

Trouble? If your printout doesn't fit on three pages, reduce the scaling factor from 65% to a slightly lower percentage until it does fit on three pages.

Creating Headers and Footers

You can also use headers and footers to repeat information on each printed page. A **header** appears at the top of each printed page; a **footer** appears at the bottom of each printed page. Headers and footers contain helpful and descriptive text that is usually not found within the worksheet, such as the workbook's author, the current date, or the workbook's filename. If the printout spans multiple pages, you can display the page number and the total number of pages in the printout to help ensure you and others have all the pages.

Each header and footer has three sections—a left section, a center section, and a right section. Within each section, you type the text you want to appear, or you insert elements such as the worksheet name or the current date and time. These header and footer elements are dynamic; if you rename the worksheet, for example, the name is automatically updated in the header or footer. Also, you can create one set of headers and footers for even and odd pages, and you can create another set for the first page in the printout.

Sanjit wants the printout to display the workbook's filename in the header's left section, and the current date in the header's right section. He wants the center footer to display the page number and the total number of pages in the printout, and the right footer to display your name as the workbook's author.

To create the header and footer:

▶ 1. Click the **Page Setup** link near the bottom of the Print screen to open the Page Setup dialog box.

▶ 2. Click the **Header/Footer** tab to display the header and footer options.

3. Click the **Different first page** check box to select it. This lets you create one set of headers and footers for the first page, and one set for the rest of the pages. See Figure 2-43.

Figure 2-43   **Header/Footer tab in the Page Setup dialog box**

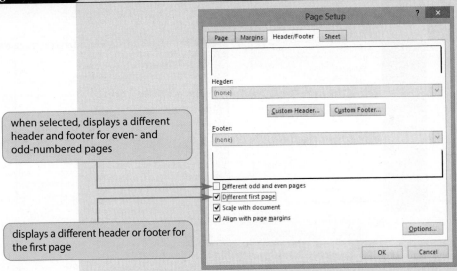

when selected, displays a different header and footer for even- and odd-numbered pages

displays a different header or footer for the first page

4. Click the **Custom Header** button to open the Header dialog box. The dialog box contains two tabs—Header and First Page Header—because you selected the Different first page option.

TIP

You can create or edit headers and footers in Page Layout view by clicking in the header/footer section and using the tools on the DESIGN tab.

5. On the Header tab, type **Filename:** in the Left section box, press the **spacebar**, and then click the **Insert File Name** button 🗋. The code &[File], which displays the filename of the current workbook, is added to the left section of the header.

6. Press the **Tab** key twice to move to the right section of the header, and then click the **Insert Current Date** button 🗓. The code &[Date] is added to the right section of the header. See Figure 2-44.

Figure 2-44   **Header dialog box**

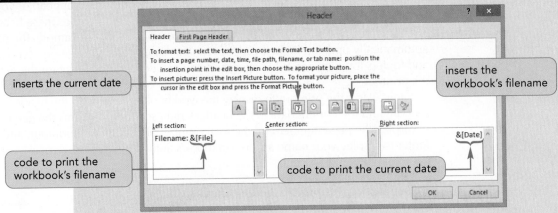

inserts the current date

inserts the workbook's filename

code to print the workbook's filename

code to print the current date

7. Click the **OK** button to return to the Header/Footer tab in the Page Setup dialog box. You did not define a header for the first page of the printout, so no header information will be added to that page.

Now you will format the page footer for all pages of the printout.

▶ **8.** Click the **Custom Footer** button to open the Footer dialog box, which is similar to the Header dialog box.

▶ **9.** Click the **Center section** box, type **Page**, press the **spacebar**, and then click the **Insert Page Number** button 🖹. The code &[Page], which inserts the current page number, appears after the label "Page."

▶ **10.** Press the **spacebar**, type **of**, press the **spacebar**, and then click the **Insert Number of Pages** button 🖺. The code &[Pages], which inserts the total number of pages in the printout, is added to the Center section box. See Figure 2-45.

Figure 2-45   Footer dialog box

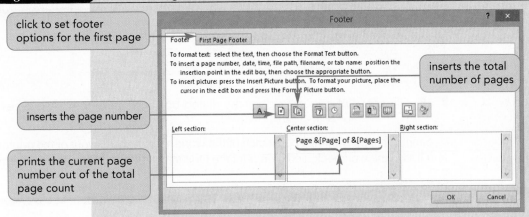

- click to set footer options for the first page
- inserts the page number
- prints the current page number out of the total page count
- inserts the total number of pages

▶ **11.** Click the **First Page Footer** tab so you can create the footer for the first page of the printout.

▶ **12.** Click the **Right section** box, type **Prepared by:**, press the **spacebar**, and then type your name.

▶ **13.** Click the **OK** button to return to the Page Setup dialog box.

Setting the Page Margins

A **margin** is the space between the page content and the edges of the page. By default, Excel sets the page margins to 0.7 inch on the left and right sides, and 0.75 inch on the top and bottom; and it allows for 0.3-inch margins around the header and footer. You can reduce or increase these margins as needed by selecting predefined margin sizes or setting your own.

Sanjit's reports need a wider margin along the left side of the page to accommodate the binding. He asks you to increase the left margin for the printout from 0.7 inch to 1 inch.

To set the left margin:

TIP

To select preset margins, click the Margins button in the Page Setup group on the PAGE LAYOUT tab.

▶ **1.** Click the **Margins** tab in the Page Setup dialog box to display options for changing the page margins.

▶ **2.** Double-click the **Left** box to select the setting, and then type **1** to increase the size of the left margin. See Figure 2-46.

Figure 2-46 Margins tab in the Page Setup dialog box

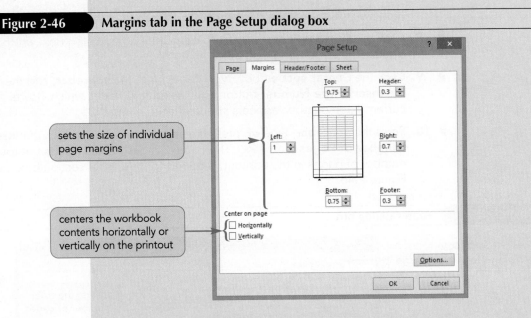

sets the size of individual page margins

centers the workbook contents horizontally or vertically on the printout

3. Click the **OK** button to close the dialog box and return to the worksheet.

Sanjit is happy with the appearance of the worksheet and the layout of the printout. You'll save the workbook, and then print the Documentation and Sales Report sheets.

To save and print the workbook:

1. Return the Sales Report worksheet to **Normal** view, and then save the workbook.

2. Display the Print screen in Backstage view, and then change the first Settings box to **Print Entire Workbook**. Both the Sales Report worksheet and the Documentation sheet appear in the preview. As you can see, the printout will include a header with the filename and date on every page except the first page, and a footer with your name on the first page and the page number along with the total number of pages on subsequent pages.

3. If you are instructed to print, print the entire workbook, and then close it.

Session 2.2 Quick Check

REVIEW

1. Describe two methods of applying the same format to different ranges.
2. Red is a standard color. What happens to red text when you change the workbook's theme?
3. What is a conditional format?
4. How would you highlight the top five values in the range A1:C20?
5. How do you insert a manual page break in a worksheet?
6. What is a print area?
7. What are print titles?
8. Describe how to add the workbook filename to the center section of the footer on every page of the printout.

ASSESS

SAM Projects

Put your skills into practice with SAM Projects! SAM Projects for this tutorial can be found online. If you have a SAM account, go to www.cengage.com/sam2013 to download the most recent Project Instructions and Start Files.

Review Assignments

Data Files needed for the Review Assignments: Menu.xlsx, Background2.png

Sanjit has a worksheet that details the sales of individual items from the Big Red Wraps menu. He asks you to format the sales figures and design a layout for the printed sheet as you did for the Sales Report workbook. Complete the following:

1. Open the **Menu** workbook located in the Excel2 ► Review folder included with your Data Files, and then save the workbook as **Menu Sales** in the location specified by your instructor.
2. In the Documentation sheet, enter your name in cell B4 and the date in cell B5.
3. Make the following formatting changes to the Documentation sheet:
   a. Set the background image to the **Background2.png** file located in the Excel2 ► Review folder.
   b. Format the text in cell A1 in red 26-point bold Calibri Light.
   c. Format the text in cell A2 to red 10-point italic Calibri Light. Change the text string "Big Flavor" to 14 points.
   d. Apply the Accent2 cell style to the range A4:A6.
   e. Change the font color of range B4:B6 to red and change its fill color to white.
   f. Format the date in the Long Date format and left-align the cell contents.
4. Use the Format Painter to copy the formatting in the range A1:A2 in the Documentation sheet and paste it to the same range in the Menu Sales worksheet. (*Hint*: You must increase the size of the text "Big Flavor" manually.)
5. Apply the Title cell style to the titles in cells B4, B12, and A20.
6. Make the following changes to the Units Sold table in the range B5:F10:
   a. In cell C6, calculate the total number of wraps sold by the company (found in the range C22:N31). In cell C7, calculate the total number of soups. In cell C8, calculate the total number of sides. In cell C9, calculate the total number of salads.
   b. In cell C10, calculate the sum of the range C6:C9. Copy the formula to cell D10.
   c. In the range E6:E10, calculate the difference between the 2015 and 2014 values. In the range F6:F10, calculate the percent change from 2014 to 2015.
   d. Apply the Accent2 cell style to the headings in the range B5:F5. Center the headings in the range C5:F5.
   e. Apply the Comma style to the values in the range C6:E10. Do not display any numbers to the right of the decimal point.
   f. Apply the Percent style to the values in the range F6:F10 and show two decimal places.
   g. Add a top border to the values in the range B10:F10.
7. Make the following changes to the range B13:F18:
   a. In cells C18 and D18, calculate the totals of the 2014 and 2015 sales. In the range E14:F18, calculate the change in sales and the percent change.
   b. Copy the format from the range B5:F10 and paste it into the range B13:F18.
   c. Change the format for the values in the ranges C14:E14 and C18:E18 to Accounting format with no decimal places.

8. Make the following changes to the Units Sold per Month table in the range A21:O46:

   a. In the range O22:O45, calculate the total units sold for each menu item. In the range C46:O46, calculate the total items sold per month and overall.

   b. Format the headings in the range A21:O21 with the Accent2 cell style. Center the headings in the range C21:O21.

   c. Format the units sold values in the range C22:O46 with the Comma style and no decimal places.

   d. Change the fill color of the subtotals in the range O22:O45 and C46:N46 to White, Background 1, Darker 15% (the first color in the third row of the theme colors).

   e. Merge each of the menu categories in the range A22:A45 into single cells. Rotate the text of the cells up. Increase the font size to 18 points and middle-align the cell contents.

   f. Format cell A22 with the "Wraps" label in a white font on a Gray-25%, Background 2, Darker 50% fill. Format cell A32 with the "Soups" label in a white font on Blue, Accent 1, Darker 25% fill. Format of cell A37 with the "Sides" label in a white font on a Gold, Accent 4, Darker 25% fill. Format cell A42 with the "Salads" label in a white font on a Green, Accent 6, Darker 25% fill.

   g. Add a thick box border around each category of menu item in the ranges A22:O31, A32:O36, A37:O41, and A42:O45.

9. Create a conditional format for the subtotals in the range O22:O45 highlighting the top five selling items with a yellow fill and dark yellow text.

10. Create a legend for the conditional format. Enter the text **Top 5 Sellers** in cell O48. Add a thick box border around the cell, and then use a conditional format that displays this text in dark yellow text on a yellow fill.

11. Set the following print formats for the Menu Sales worksheet:

    a. Set the print area to the nonadjacent range A1:F19;A20:O48.

    b. Remove any automatic page breaks in the large Units Sold table. Insert a manual page break to separate the June and July sales figures. The printout of the Menu Sales worksheet should fit on three pages.

    c. Scale the printout to 70 percent of normal size.

    d. Define the print titles to repeat the first three rows at the top of the sheet, and the first two columns at the left of the sheet.

    e. Increase the left margin of the printout from 0.7 inch to 1 inch.

    f. Create headers and footers for the printout with a different header for the first page.

    g. For the first page header, print **Prepared by *your name*** in the right section. For every other page, print **Filename: *file*** in the left section and ***date*** in the right section, where *file* is the name of the workbook file and *date* is the current date. (*Hint:* Use the buttons in the Header dialog box to insert the filename and date.)

    h. For every footer, print **Page *page* of *pages*** in the center section, where *page* is the page number and *pages* is the total number of pages in the printout.

12. If you are instructed to print, print the entire workbook in portrait orientation. Verify that the company name and slogan appear on every page of the Menu Sales worksheet printout, and that the menu category and menu item name appear on both pages with the Units Sold table.

13. Save and close the workbook.

Case Problem 1

Data File needed for this Case Problem: Salon.xlsx

Special Highlights Hair Salon Sarah Jones is developing a business plan for a new hair salon, Special Highlights Hair Salon, located in Hatton, North Dakota. As part of the business plan, she needs a projected income statement for the company. You will help her develop and format the income statement. Complete the following:

1. Open the **Salon** workbook located in the Excel2 ▸ Case1 folder included with your Data Files, and then save the workbook as **Salon Income Statement** in the location specified by your instructor.

2. In the Documentation sheet, enter your name in cell B3 and the date in cell B4.

3. Apply the following formatting to the Documentation sheet:
   a. Format cell A1 using the Title cell style.
   b. Format the range A3:A5 using the Accent6 cell style.
   c. In cell B4, format the date value using the long date format, and left-align the cell contents.
   d. In cell B5, format the text string "Special Highlights Hair Salon" in italic.

4. In the Income Statement worksheet, format cell A1 using the Title cell style.

5. Calculate the following items in the Income Statement worksheet:
   a. In cell C7, calculate the Gross Profit, which is equal to the Gross Sales minus the Cost of Sales.
   b. In cell C21, calculate the Total Operating Expenses, which is equal to the sum of the operating expenses.
   c. In cell C22, calculate the Total Operating Profit/Loss, which is equal to the Gross Profit minus the Total Operating Expenses.
   d. In cell C23, calculate the projected Income Taxes, which is equal to 35 percent of the Total Operating Profit/Loss.
   e. In cell C24, calculate the Net Profit/Loss, which is equal to the Total Operating Profit/Loss minus the projected Income Taxes.

6. Set the following formats to the Income Statement worksheet:
   a. Format cells A3 and A26 using the Heading 2 cell style.
   b. Format cells A4 and A9 and the range A27:A38 in bold.
   c. Format cells B5, C7, B10, C21, and C24 using the Accounting format with no decimal places.
   d. Format cells B6, B11:B19, C22, and C23 using the Comma style with no decimal places.
   e. Indent the text in the ranges A5:A6 and A10:A19 two spaces. Indent the text in cell A7 and the range A21:A24 four spaces.
   f. Add a bottom border to cells B6, C7, C21, C22, and C23. Add a double bottom border to cell C24.

7. Merge cells A26:E26 and then left-align the merged cell's contents.

8. Merge the contents of the range B27:E27. Left-align the merged cell's contents and wrap the text within the cell. Increase the height of row 27 to display the entire contents of the cell.

9. Top-align and left-align the range A27:B38.

10. Copy the format from the range A27:B27 to the range A28:B38. Merge columns B through E in each row, left-align the text, and resize the row heights to display the complete contents of the cells.

11. Italicize the text string "National Salon News" in cells B27 and B28.

12. Set the following printing formats to the Income Statement worksheet:

   a. Insert a manual page break directly above row 26 so that the Income Statement prints on two pages.

   b. Set rows 1 and 2 as a print title to print on both pages.

   c. Change the page margins to 1 inch on every side.

   d. On the first page of the printout, print **Prepared by** *your name* in the left section of the header, where *your name* is your name. Print the **current date** in the right section of the header. Do not display header text on any other page.

   e. For every page, add a footer that prints the workbook *filename* in the left section, **Page** *page* in the center section, and the *worksheet name* in the right section.

13. If you are instructed to print, print the entire contents of the workbook in portrait orientation.

14. Save and close the workbook.

Case Problem 2

Data File needed for this Case Problem: Waist.xlsx

Waist Trainers   Alexandra Roulez is a dietician at Waist Trainers, a company in Fort Smith, Arkansas, that specializes in personal improvement, particularly in areas of health and fitness. Alexandra wants to create a meal-planning workbook for her clients who want to lose weight and improve their health. One goal of meal planning is to decrease the percentage of fat in the diet. Alexandra thinks it would be helpful to highlight foods that have a high percentage of fat as well as list their total fat calories. She already created a workbook that contains a few sample food items and lists the number of calories and grams of fat in each item. She wants you to format this workbook. Complete the following:

1. Open the **Waist** workbook located in the Excel2 ▶ Case2 folder included with your Data Files, and then save the workbook as **Waist Trainers Nutrition Table** in the location specified by your instructor.

2. In the Documentation sheet, enter your name in cell B3 and the date in cell B4.

3. Set the following formatting to the Documentation sheet:

   a. In cell A1, apply the Title cell style, increase the font size to 24 points, and then change the font color to a medium orange.

   b. Apply the Accent2 cell style to the range A3:A5.

   c. Wrap the text within the range B3:B5, and then left- and top-align the text in the cells.

   d. Change the format of the date in cell B4 to the long date format.

   e. Add borders around all of the cells in the range A3:B5.

4. Copy the cell format for cell A1 in the Documentation sheet to cell A1 in the Meal Planner worksheet.

5. In cell F4, enter the text **Calories from Fat**. In cell G4, enter the text **Fat Percentage**.

6. In the range F5:F54, calculate the calories from fat for each food item, which is equal to the Grams of Fat multiplied by 9. In the range G5:G54, calculate the fat percentage of each food item, which is equal to the Calories from Fat divided by the Calories.

7. Format cell A3 using the Heading 4 cell style.

8. Format the range A4:G4 using the Accent2 cell style.

9. Format the range D5:F54 with the Comma style and display one decimal place.

10. Format the range G5:G54 with the Percent style and display two decimal places.

11. Merge the cells in the range A5:A8, rotate the text up, and then center-align the cell content both horizontally and vertically. Change the fill color to medium gold, increase the font size to 14 points, and then change the font color to white.

12. Place a thick box border around the beef food items in the range A5:G8.

13. Repeat Steps 11 and 12 for the other six food categories.

14. For good health, the FDA recommends that the fat percentage in a person's diet should not exceed 30 percent of the total calories per day. Create a Conditional Formatting rule for the fat percentages to highlight those food items that exceed the FDA recommendation in dark red text on a light red fill.

15. In cell G2, enter the text **High Fat Food**. Center the text in the cell. Change the format of the cell to dark red text on a light red fill. Add a thick black border around the cell.

16. Set the following print formats for the Meal Planner worksheet:

    a. Change the page orientation to landscape.

    b. Scale the printout so that the width of the worksheet fits on a single page.

    c. If necessary, create manual page breaks directly above row 25 and above row 44. The worksheet should print on three separate pages.

    d. Repeat the first four rows of the worksheet on every printed page.

    e. For every page, add a footer that prints **Prepared by** *your name* in the left section, **Page** *page* in the center section, and the *worksheet name* in the right section.

17. If you are instructed to print, print the entire contents of the workbook.

18. Save and close the workbook.

Case Problem 3

Data File needed for this Case Problem: Wind.xlsx

Winds of Change   Odette Ferris is a researcher at Winds of Change, a privately run wind farm providing supplemental power for communities near Topeka, Kansas. One of Odette's jobs is to record wind speeds from different sectors of the wind farm. She has entered the wind speed data into a workbook as a table with wind speed measures laid out in a grid. Because the numbers are difficult to read and interpret, she wants you to color code the wind speed values using conditional formatting. Complete the following:

1. Open the **Wind** workbook located in the Excel2 ▸ Case3 folder included with your Data Files, and then save the workbook as **Wind Speed Grid** in the location specified by your instructor.

2. In the Documentation sheet, enter your name in cell B3 and the date in cell B4.

3. In the Wind Speed Grid worksheet, merge the range A1:V1, and then apply the Heading 1 cell style to the merged cell and set the font size to 20 points.

4. Format the range B3:V3 as white text on a black background. Copy this formatting to the grid coordinates in the range A4:A64.

✦ **Explore** 5. Create a conditional format that highlights cells in the range B4:V64 whose value equals 18 with fill color equal to (99, 37, 35). (*Hint:* In the Equal To dialog box, select Custom Format in the with box to open the Format Cells dialog box. On the Fill tab, in the Background Color section, click the More Colors button, and then click the Custom tab to enter the RGB color value.)

✦ **Explore** 6. Repeat Step 5 to continue creating conditional formats that set highlight colors for the wind speed values in the range B4:V64 using the wind speeds and color values shown in Figure 2-47.

CHALLENGE

Figure 2-47   **Wind speed color values**

Wind Speed	RGB Color Value
16 m/s	(150, 54, 52)
14 m/s	(218, 150, 148)
12 m/s	(230, 184, 183)
10 m/s	(242, 220, 219)
8 m/s	(242, 242, 242)
6 m/s	(255, 255, 255)
4 m/s	(197, 217, 241)
2 m/s	(141, 180, 226)
0 m/s	(83, 141, 213)

© 2014 Cengage Learning

7. Reduce the font size of the values in the range B4:V64 to 1 point.

⊕ **Explore** 8. Enclose each cell in the range B4:V64 in a light gray border. (*Hint*: Use the Border tab in the Format Cells dialog box.)

9. Use the Format Painter to copy the formats from the range B4:V64 and apply them to the range X3:X12. Increase the font size of the cells in that range to 11 points.

10. Merge the range Y3:Y12, center the contents of the merged cell horizontally and vertically, and then rotate the text down. Format the text in a bold 18-point font.

11. Set the following print formats to the Wind Speed Grid worksheet:

   a Change the page orientation to landscape.

   b. Set the print area to the range A1:Y64.

   c. Scale the worksheet so that the width and the height of the sheet fit on a single page.

   d. Add a header to the printed page with your name in the left section of the header and the worksheet name in the right section of the header.

12. Save and close the workbook.

Case Problem 4

CREATE

Data File needed for this Case Problem: Office.xlsx

Office Cart   Robert Trenton is a shipping manager at Office Cart, an online office supply store located in Muncie, Indiana. He wants to use an Excel workbook to track shipping orders. Robert asks you to create and format a worksheet that he can use to enter information for packing slips. Complete the following:

1. Open the **Office** workbook located in the Excel2 ▶ Case4 folder included with your Data Files, and then save the workbook as **Office Cart Packing Slip** in the location specified by your instructor.

2. In the Documentation sheet, enter your name in cell B3 and the date in cell B4.

3. Set the following formats in the Documentation sheet:

   a. Merge cells A1 and B1, and then left-align the contents of the merged cell. Change the font to 28-point white Calibri Light on a dark green background.

   b. Change the font of the range A3:A5 to 14-point white Calibri Light on a dark green background.

   c. Change the format of the date value in cell B4 to the Long Date style, and then left-align the date in the cell.

   d. Italicize the text "Office Cart" in cell B5.

   e. Add a border around each cell in the range A3:B5.

4. Insert a new worksheet at the end of the workbook and name it **Packing Slip**.

5. In the Packing Slip worksheet, select all of the cells in the worksheet. (*Hint*: Click the Select All button at the intersection of the row and column headings, or press the Ctrl+A keys.) Change the font to 10-point dark green Calibri.

6. Add a thick box border around the range A1:D40.

7. For the range A1:D3, change the format to a white Calibri Light font on a dark green background.

8. Set the width of column A to 15 characters. Set the width of column B to 20 characters. Set the width of column C to 30 characters. Set the width of column D to 20 characters.

9. Merge the range A1:B3. Merge the range C1:D3, and then right- and top-align the merged cell. Set the row height of row 1 to 36 points and the heights of rows 2 and 3 to 15 points.

10. In cell A1, enter the following three lines of text, pressing the Alt+Enter keys to start a new line within the cell:
    Office Cart
    14 Trenke Lane
    Muncie, IN 47303
    Format the first line in a 26-point bold font.

11. In cell C1, enter **Packing Slip**, and then format the text in a 26-point bold font using the Headings font of the current theme.

12. In the range A5:A7, enter the following three lines of text in a bold font, and then right-align the text and indent the text one character:
    Order Date
    Order Number
    Purchase Order

13. Format cell B5 in the Long Date format and left-align the cell contents. Insert border lines around each of the cells in the range B5:B7.

14. In the range C5:C7, enter the following three lines of text, and then use the Format Painter to copy the formats from the range A5:B7 to the range C5:D7:
    Date
    Sales Rep
    Account Num

15. In cell B9, enter **Ship To**. In cell D9, enter **Bill To**. Format the text in both cells in bold.

16. In cell A10, enter **Address**, format the text in bold, right-align the text, and then indent it one character.

17. Merge the cells in the range B10:B15, left- and top-align the cell contents, insert a border around the merged cell, and then wrap the text within this cell.

18. In cell C10, enter **Address**. Copy the format from the range A10:B15 to the range C10:D15.

19. Enter the following data in the indicated cells in the worksheet:
    cell A17: **Item**
    cell B17: **Product No.**
    cell C17: **Description**
    cell D17: **Order Quantity**

20. Format the range A17:D17 in bold white Calibri on a dark green background.

21. Format the range A18:D18 with a bottom border and a light green background. Format the range A19:D19 with a bottom border and a white background. Copy the format in the range A18:D19 to the range A20:D27.

22. Apply a Top and Double Bottom Border to the range A28:D28. Merge the contents of the range A28:C28. Enter **Total** in cell A28, bold the text, and right-align the cell contents.

23. In cell D28, enter a formula to calculate the sum of the values in the range D18:D27. Bold the text.

24. In cell A30, enter **Comments** and then bold the text.

25. Merge the range A31:D39, left- and top-align the cell contents, and then add a thick box border around the merged cell.

26. In cell D40, enter **Thank you for your business!** in italic 16-point Calibri, and then right-align the cell contents.

27. Make sure the worksheet is set to portrait orientation, and then add a footer that displays your name in the left section, the filename in the center section, and the current date in the right section. Scale the printout so that it fits onto a single page.

28. Enter the packing slip data shown in Figure 2-48. Save and close the workbook.

Figure 2-48   **Office Cart packing slip form**

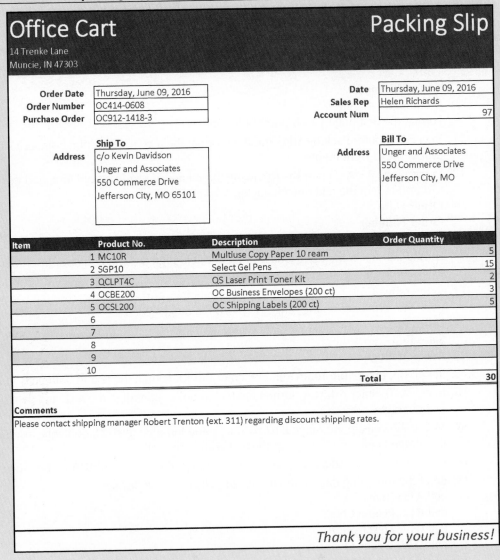

Calculating Data with Formulas and Functions

Creating a Fitness Tracker

OBJECTIVES

Session 3.1
- Make a workbook user-friendly
- Translate an equation into an Excel formula
- Understand function syntax
- Enter formulas and functions with the Quick Analysis tool
- Enter functions with the Insert Function dialog box
- Interpret error values
- Change cell references between relative and absolute

Session 3.2
- Use the AutoFill tool to enter formulas and data and complete a series
- Display the current date with the TODAY function
- Find the next weekday with the WORKDAY function
- Use the COUNT and COUNTA functions to tally cells
- Use an IF function to return a value based on a condition
- Perform an exact match lookup with the VLOOKUP function
- Perform what-if analysis using trial and error and Goal Seek

Case | *Fit Fathers Inc.*

Ken Dorsett is a certified fitness professional and founder of Fit Fathers Inc., which is a fitness program he developed to help fathers stay fit and active. From its beginnings in Blue Springs, Missouri, where Ken led daily workouts with three other dads, his program has grown to an enrollment of 318 fathers in five different cities in the northwest corner of the state.

Ken wants to help his members evaluate their fitness goals and track their workouts. He has been working on an Excel workbook that can assess each participant's fitness level and track his workout progress. Ken has developed the basic structure of the workbook, but still needs to enter the formulas to calculate the different statistics and data that are important for his clients. He asks you to enter the appropriate formulas to complete the workbook. To do this, you will use a variety of formulas and functions.

STARTING DATA FILES

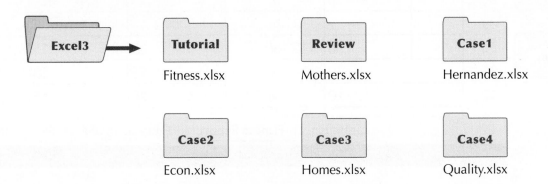

Excel3 → Tutorial
Fitness.xlsx

Review
Mothers.xlsx

Case1
Hernandez.xlsx

Case2
Econ.xlsx

Case3
Homes.xlsx

Case4
Quality.xlsx

Session 3.1 Visual Overview:

Functions are organized by category in the Function Library group. Select a function to open the Function Arguments dialog box.

The Insert Function button opens the Insert Function dialog box from which you can select a function.

The SUM function adds the values in the range.

The AVERAGE function calculates the average value of the range.

The MEDIAN function determines the middle value in the range.

The MAX function displays the maximum value in the range.

The MIN function displays the minimum value in the range.

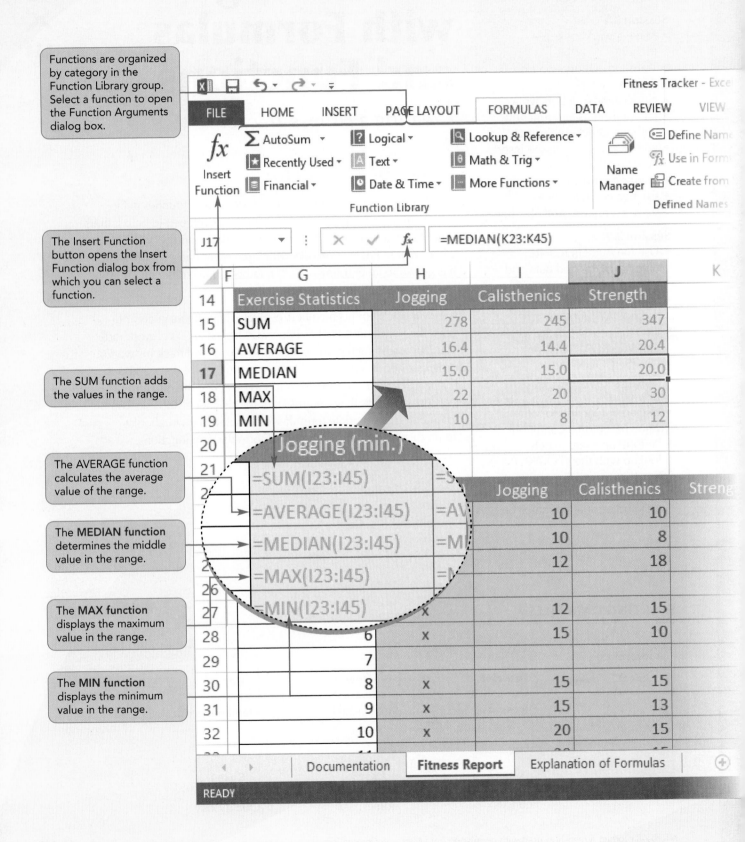

Fitness Tracker - Exce

FILE   HOME   INSERT   PAGE LAYOUT   FORMULAS   DATA   REVIEW   VIEW

fx Insert Function

Σ AutoSum ▾
Recently Used ▾
Financial ▾

Logical ▾
Text ▾
Date & Time ▾

Lookup & Reference ▾
Math & Trig ▾
More Functions ▾

Name Manager

Define Name
Use in Form
Create from

Function Library

Defined Names

J17 · : × ✓ *fx* =MEDIAN(K23:K45)

	F	G	H	I	J	K
14		Exercise Statistics	Jogging	Calisthenics	Strength	
15		SUM	278	245	347	
16		AVERAGE	16.4	14.4	20.4	
17		MEDIAN	15.0	15.0	20.0	
18		MAX	22	20	30	
19		MIN	10	8	12	

Jogging (min.)

=SUM(I23:I45)
=AVERAGE(I23:I45)
=MEDIAN(I23:I45)
=MAX(I23:I45)
=MIN(I23:I45)

	Jogging	Calisthenics	Streng
	10	10	
	10	8	
	12	18	
27	12	15	x
28	6	15	10	x
29	7		
30	8	15	15	x
31	9	15	13	x
32	10	20	15	x

◄ ► Documentation **Fitness Report** Explanation of Formulas ⊕

READY

Functions and Cell References

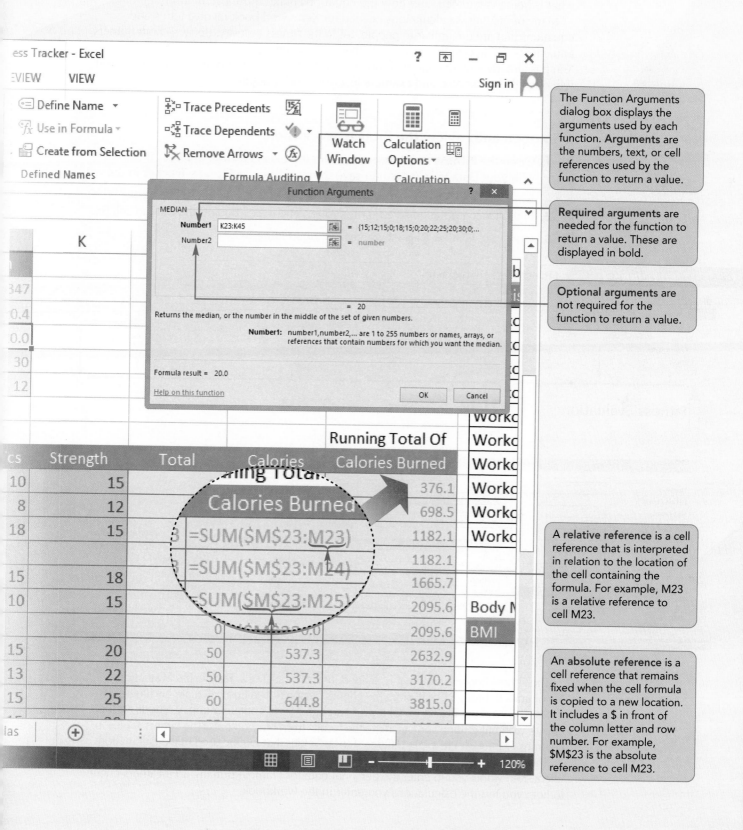

The Function Arguments dialog box displays the arguments used by each function. **Arguments** are the numbers, text, or cell references used by the function to return a value.

Required arguments are needed for the function to return a value. These are displayed in bold.

Optional arguments are not required for the function to return a value.

A relative **reference** is a cell reference that is interpreted in relation to the location of the cell containing the formula. For example, M23 is a relative reference to cell M23.

An absolute **reference** is a cell reference that remains fixed when the cell formula is copied to a new location. It includes a $ in front of the column letter and row number. For example, $M$23 is the absolute reference to cell M23.

Making Workbooks User-Friendly

Every workbook should be accessible to its intended users. When a workbook is user-friendly, anyone who needs to enter data in the workbook or interpret its results can understand the workbook's contents, including any jargon or unusual terms, what is being calculated, and how the equations make those calculations.

Many of the fitness calculations needed for Ken's workbook involve terms and equations that are unfamiliar to people not in the fitness industry. Because both trainers and clients will access this workbook, these terms and equations need to be explained. Ken has already included information about the fitness equations in the workbook. You will open the workbook, and examine its layout and structure.

To open and review the Fitness workbook:

▶ **1.** Open the **Fitness** workbook located in the Excel3 ▶ Tutorial folder included with your Data Files, and then save the workbook as **Fitness Tracker** in the location specified by your instructor.

▶ **2.** In the Documentation sheet, enter your name in cell B3 and the date in cell B4.

▶ **3.** Go to the **Fitness Report** worksheet. See Figure 3-1.

Figure 3-1   **Fitness Tracker workbook**

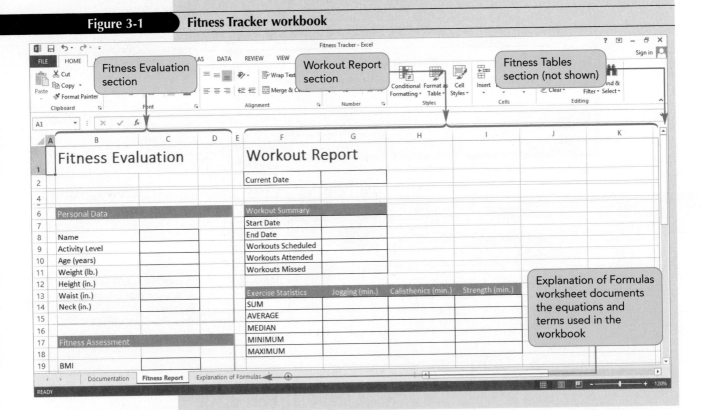

The Fitness Report worksheet is divided into three sections. The Fitness Evaluation in columns B through D will store the client's personal data and calculate his fitness status. The Workout Report in columns F through M will contain monthly reports on the client's workout routine and calculate the results from his workouts. The Fitness Tables in columns O through P contain different fitness values that will be used in the calculations.

The Fitness Evaluation contains a section for personal information on a Fit Fathers client. Ken wants you to enter the personal data for Daniel Pridham, a Fit Fathers client, to help you test the calculations you enter in the workbook.

To enter Daniel's personal data:

▶ **1.** In cell **C8**, enter **Daniel Pridham** as the client's name.

▶ **2.** In cell **C9**, enter **Sedentary** to describe Daniel's activity level.

▶ **3.** In the range **C10:C14**, enter **45** for his age, **193** for his weight in pounds, **70** for his height in inches, **37** for his waist size in inches, and **15.5** for his neck size in inches.

Documenting Formulas

Documenting the contents of a workbook helps to avoid errors and confusion. This type of information can make a workbook easier for other people to understand. For workbooks that include many calculations, as the Fitness Tracker workbook does, it is helpful to explain the formulas and terms used in the calculations. Such documentation also can serve as a check that the equations are accurate. Another way to document formulas and terms is to include notes of explanation within the worksheet where the equations are used.

Ken has included explanations of different fitness terms and equations in the Explanation of Formulas worksheet, and explanatory notes in cells B26 and F46 of the Fitness Report worksheet. Before proceeding, he wants you to review the documentation in these worksheets.

To review the documentation in the Fitness Tracker workbook:

▶ **1.** Click the **Explanation of Formulas** sheet tab to make it the active sheet.

▶ **2.** Read the sheet contents, reviewing the descriptions of common fitness terms and formulas. As you continue developing the Fitness Tracker workbook, you'll learn about these terms and formulas in more detail.

▶ **3.** Click the **Fitness Report** sheet tab to return to the Fitness Report worksheet.

▶ **4.** Read the explanatory notes in cells B26 and F46.

Using Constants in Formulas

The first fitness equation Ken wants you to enter is BMI, or body mass index, which estimates the amount of human body fat. The BMI equation is based on the individual's body weight divided by the square of his or her height. The specific formula is

$$BMI = \frac{703w}{h^2}$$

where w is the body weight in pounds and h is the height in inches. BMI values from 18.5 to 24.9 are considered normal; anything higher is considered overweight.

One common skill you need when creating a workbook is to translate an equation like the BMI equation into an Excel formula. Some equations use constants. A **constant** is a value in a formula that doesn't change. In the BMI equation, 703 is a constant because that value never changes when calculating the body mass index.

INSIGHT

Deciding Where to Place a Constant

Should a constant be entered directly into the formula or placed in a separate worksheet cell and referenced in the formula? The answer depends on the constant being used, the purpose of the workbook, and the intended audience. Placing constants in separate cells that you reference in the formulas can help users better understand the worksheet because no values are hidden within the formulas. Also, when a constant is entered in a cell, you can add explanatory text next to each constant to document how it is being used in the formula. On the other hand, you don't want a user to inadvertently change the value of a constant and throw off all the formula results. You will need to evaluate how important it is for other people to immediately see the constant, and whether the constant requires any explanation for other people to understand the formula. For example, Ken wants you to include the 703 constant in the BMI formula rather than in a separate cell because he doesn't feel that clients need to see this constant to understand BMI.

To convert the BMI equation into a formula, you need to replace *w* and *h* in the equation with Daniel's actual weight and height. Because Daniel's weight is stored in cell C11 and his height is stored in cell C12, you replace the *w* in the formula with the C11 cell reference, and replace the *h* in the formula with the C12 cell reference. The resulting Excel formula is:

```
=703*C11/C12^2
```

Note that the exponent operator ^ is used to square the height value in the denominator of the fraction. Recall that exponentiation raises a value to a power; in this case, the value in cell C12 is raised to the second power, or squared. Following the order of operations, Excel will first square the height value, then multiply the weight value by 703, and finally divide that product by the squared height. You will enter the BMI formula in the Fitness Report worksheet now.

To enter the BMI formula in the Fitness Report worksheet:

▶ 1. In cell **C19**, enter the formula **=703*C11/C12^2**. The formula multiplies the weight in cell C11 by the constant 703, and then divides the resulting value by the square of the height in cell C12. The calculated BMI value that is displayed in cell C19 is 27.68959184.

   Trouble? If your BMI formula results differ from 27.68959184, you probably entered the formula incorrectly. Edit your formula as needed so that the numbers and cell references match those shown in the formula in Step 1.

▶ 2. Select cell **C19**, and then reduce the number of displayed decimals to one. Cell C19 displays 27.7 as the formula results.

The next fitness equation, which calculates the individual's resting basal metabolic rate (BMR), includes four constants. The resting BMR estimates the number of calories a person expends daily (not counting any actual activity). For men, the BMR is calculated with the equation

$$BMR = 6.23w + 12.7h - 6.76a + 66$$

where *w* is the weight in pounds, *h* is the height in inches, and *a* is the age in years. BMR is calculated by multiplying the weight, height, and age by different constants, and then adding the results to another constant. Heavier and taller people require more daily calories to sustain them. As people age, their metabolism slows, resulting in a lower BMR. Daniel's weight, height, and age are stored in cells C11, C12, and C10, respectively, so the BMR equation translates to the following Excel formula:

```
=6.23*C11+12.7*C12-6.76*C10+66
```

You will enter this formula in the Fitness Report worksheet to calculate Daniel's BMR.

To enter the BMR formula in the Fitness Report worksheet:

▶ **1.** In cell **C21**, enter the formula **=6.23*C11+12.7*C12–6.76*C10+66**. Cell C21 displays 1853.19, indicating that Daniel burns about 1853 calories per day before performing any activity.

   Trouble? If your BMR formula results differ from 1853.19, you might have entered the formula incorrectly. Edit the formula as needed so that the numbers and cell references match those shown in the formula in Step 1.

▶ **2.** Select cell **C21**, and then reduce the number of decimals displayed in the cell to zero. The number of calories per day displayed in cell C21 is 1853.

The 1853 calories per day amount assumes no physical activity. However, even the most sedentary person moves a little bit during the day, which increases the BMR value. The table in the range O7:P12 in the Fitness Report worksheet lists the constant multipliers for different activity levels. For example, the BMR of a sedentary man like Daniel is multiplied by 1.2 (shown in cell P8) to account for daily movements. If Daniel were to increase his activities to a moderate level, the multiplier would increase to 1.55 (as shown in cell P10).

You will enter the formula to calculate Daniel's active BMR based on his sedentary lifestyle. Ken wants you to use the constant value stored in the table rather entering it into the formula because he anticipates that Daniel will increase his activity level under the direction of Fit Fathers, and it is easier to update the amount in a cell rather than editing a formula.

To calculate Daniel's active BMR:

▶ **1.** In cell **C22**, enter the formula **=C21*P8** to multiply Daniel's resting BMR by the sedentary activity level. Based on this calculation, Daniel's active BMR is 2223.828 calories per day.

▶ **2.** Select cell **C22**, and then decrease the number of decimal places displayed in the cell to zero. The displayed value changes to 2224. See Figure 3-2.

Figure 3-2   BMI and BMR calculated values

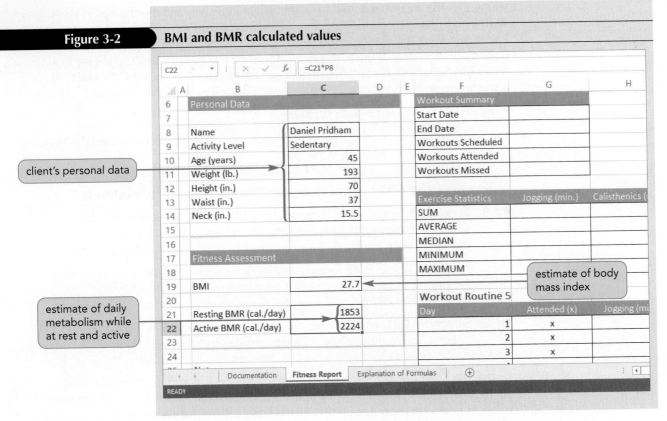

The active BMR shows that Daniel needs about 2224 calories per day to maintain his current weight.

Identifying Notes, Input Values, and Calculated Values

When worksheets involve notes and many calculations, it is useful to distinguish input values that are used in formulas from calculated values that are returned by formulas. Formatting that clearly differentiates input values from calculated values helps others more easily understand the worksheet. Such formatting also helps prevent anyone from entering a value in a cell that contains a formula.

You can use cell styles to identify cells as containing explanatory text, input values, and calculated values. When you use cell styles or other formatting to identify a cell's purpose, you should include a legend in the worksheet describing the purpose of the formatting.

Ken wants to be sure that whenever he and his staff members update a client's workbook, they can easily see where to enter numbers. You will apply cell styles to distinguish between notes, input cells, and formula cells.

To apply cell styles to differentiate cells with notes, input values, and calculated values:

1. Select the merged cell **B26**.

2. On the HOME tab, in the Styles group, click the **Cell Styles** button to open the Cell Styles gallery.

3. Click the **Explanatory Text** cell style located in the Data and Model group. Cell B26 is formatted with the Explanatory Text cell style.

4. Format cell **F46** with the **Explanatory Text** cell style.

▶ **5.** Format the range **C8:C14** with the **Input** cell style. These cells contain the personal information about Daniel that you entered earlier.

▶ **6.** Format the nonadjacent range **C19;C21:C22** containing the calculated BMI and BMR values with the **Calculation** cell style.

▶ **7.** Format the range **G22:J44** with the **Input** cell style. These cells store information about Daniel's workout routine, which Ken enters after each workout.

Next, you'll create a legend to identify which cells are input cells and which cells are calculated cells.

▶ **8.** In cell **C2**, enter **Input Values** as the label, format the cell with the **Explanatory Text** cell style, and then right-align the text in the cell.

▶ **9.** In cell **C4**, enter **Calculated Values** as the label, and then use the Format Painter to copy the formatting in cell C2 and paste it to cell C4.

▶ **10.** Format cell **D2** with the **Input** cell style, and then format cell **D4** with the **Calculation** cell style.

▶ **11.** Select cell **C19**. See Figure 3-3.

Figure 3-3	Input and calculated values formatted with cell styles

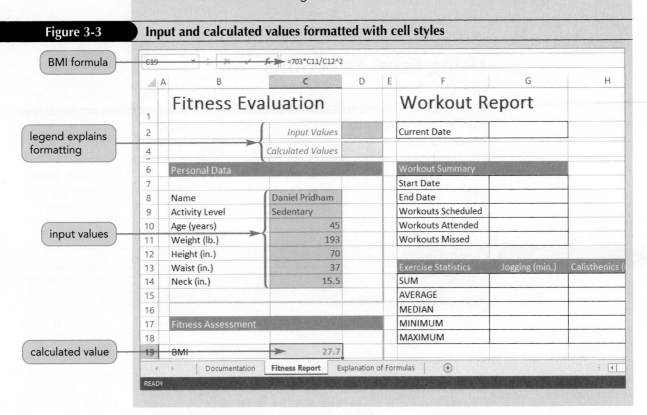

The built-in cell styles are a quick way of marking different types of values in your worksheet. If the formats do not match what you want for your workbook, you can create your own cell styles. However you design your worksheet, your purpose is to make the values easy to interpret.

PROSKILLS

Written Communication: Displaying Significant Digits

Excel stores numbers with up to 15 digits and displays as many digits as will fit into the cell. So even the result of a simple formula such as =10/3 will display 3.33333333333333 if the cell is wide enough.

A number with 15 digits is difficult to read, and calculations rarely need that level of accuracy. Many scientific disciplines, such as chemistry or physics, have rules for specifying exactly how many digits should be displayed with any calculation. These digits are called **significant digits** because they indicate the accuracy of the measured and calculated values. For example, an input value of 19.32 has four significant digits.

The rules are based on several factors and vary from one discipline to another. Generally, a calculated value should display no more digits than are found in any of the input values. For example, because the input value 19.32 has four significant digits, any calculated value based on that input should have no more than four significant digits. Showing more digits would be misleading because it implies a level of accuracy beyond that which was actually measured.

Because Excel displays calculated values with as many digits as can fit into a cell, you need to know the standards for your profession and change the display of your calculated values accordingly.

Using Excel Functions

Functions provide a quick way to calculate summary data such as the total, average, and median values in a collection of values. Ken recorded the amount of time Daniel spent at each workout doing brisk jogging, calisthenics, and strength exercise. Ken wants you to analyze the results from Daniel's workout routine. You will use Excel functions to summarize these results.

Excel supports an extensive library of functions, organized into the 12 categories shown in Figure 3-4. You can use Excel functions to perform statistical analysis, work with financial data, retrieve information from databases, and generate text strings, among many other tasks.

Figure 3-4 **Excel function categories**

Category	Description
Cube	Retrieve data from multidimensional databases involving online analytical processing (OLAP)
Database	Retrieve and analyze data stored in databases
Date & Time	Analyze or create date and time values and time intervals
Engineering	Analyze engineering problems
Financial	Analyze information for business and finance
Information	Return information about the format, location, or contents of worksheet cells
Logical	Return logical (true-false) values
Lookup & Reference	Look up and return data matching a set of specified conditions from a range
Math & Trig	Perform math and trigonometry calculations
Statistical	Provide statistical analyses of data sets
Text	Return text values or evaluate text
Web	Provide information on web-based connections

The Excel Help system provides information on all of the Excel functions.

Exploring Function Syntax

Before you use functions, you should understand the function syntax. Recall that the syntax of an Excel function follows the general pattern

    FUNCTION(argument1,argument2,...)

where FUNCTION is the name of the function, and argument1, argument2, and so forth are arguments used by the function. An argument can be any type of value including text, numbers, cell references, or even other formulas or functions. Not all functions require arguments.

TIP

Optional arguments are always placed last in the argument list.

Some arguments are optional. You can include an optional argument in the function or omit it from the function. Some optional arguments have default values associated with them, so that if you omit the optional argument, Excel will use the default value. These tutorials show optional arguments within square brackets along with the argument's default value (if any), as

    FUNCTION(argument1[, argument2=value2,...])

where argument1 is a required argument, argument2 is optional, and value2 is the default value for argument2. As you work with specific functions, you will learn which arguments are required and which are optional as well as any default values associated with optional arguments.

Figure 3-5 describes some of the more common Math, Trig, and Statistical functions and provides the syntax of those functions.

Figure 3-5   Common Math, Trig, and Statistical functions

Function	Category	Description
AVERAGE(number1[, number2, number3, ...])	Statistical	Calculates the average of a collection of numbers, where number1, number2, and so forth are numbers or cell references; only number1 is required
COUNT(value1[, value2, value3, ...])	Statistical	Counts how many cells in a range contain numbers, where value1, value2, and so forth are text, numbers, or cell references; only value1 is required
COUNTA(value1[, value2, value3, ...])	Statistical	Counts how many cells are not empty in ranges value1, value2, and so forth, or how many numbers are listed within value1, value2, etc.
INT(number)	Math & Trig	Displays the integer portion of number
MAX(number1[, number2, number3, ...])	Statistical	Calculates the maximum value of a collection of numbers, where number1, number2, and so forth are either numbers or cell references
MEDIAN(number1[, number2, number3, ...])	Statistical	Calculates the median, or middle, value of a collection of numbers, where number1, number2, and so forth are either numbers or cell references
MIN(number1[, number2, number3, ...])	Statistical	Calculates the minimum value of a collection of numbers, where number1, number2, and so forth are either numbers or cell references
RAND()	Math & Trig	Returns a random number between 0 and 1
ROUND(number, num_digits)	Math & Trig	Rounds number to the number of digits specified by num_digits
SUM(number1[, number2, number3, ...])	Math & Trig	Adds a collection of numbers, where number1, number2, and so forth are either numbers or cell references

For example, the ROUND function rounds a number to a specified number of decimal places and has the syntax

    ROUND(*number*, *num_digits*)

where *number* is the number to be rounded and *num_digits* is the number of decimal places to which you want to round the *number* argument. The following function rounds 2.718282 to two decimal places, resulting in 2.72:

    ROUND(2.718282, 2)

However, you usually reference data values stored in worksheet cells rather than entering the numbers directly in the function. For example, the following function rounds the number in cell A10 to three decimal places:

    ROUND(A10, 3)

Both arguments in the ROUND function are required. An example of a function that uses optional arguments is the AVERAGE function, which can calculate averages from several ranges or entered values. For example, the function

    AVERAGE(A1:A10)

averages the values in the range A1:A10, while the function

    AVERAGE(A1:A10, C5:C10, E10)

includes two optional arguments and averages the values from the cells in range A1:A10, range C5:C10, and cell E10.

Functions can be included as part of larger formulas. The following formula calculates the average of the values in the range A1:A100, and then squares that result using the $\wedge$ operator:

    =AVERAGE(A1:A100)^2

Functions can also be placed inside another function, or **nested**. If a formula contains several functions, Excel starts with the innermost function and then moves outward. For example, the following formula first calculates the average of the values in the range A1:A100 using the AVERAGE function, and then rounds that value to two decimal places:

    =ROUND(AVERAGE(A1:A100),2)

One challenge of nesting functions is to make sure that you include all of the parentheses. You can check this by counting the number of opening parentheses and making sure that number matches the number of closing parentheses. Excel also displays each level of nested parentheses in different colors to make it easier for you to match the opening and closing parentheses in the formula. If the number of parentheses doesn't match, Excel will not accept the formula and will provide a suggestion for how to rewrite the formula so the number of opening and closing parentheses does match.

There are several ways to enter a function. You have already entered a function by typing directly in a cell and using the AutoSum button. Another way to enter a function is with the Quick Analysis tool.

Entering Functions with the Quick Analysis Tool

The Quick Analysis tool, which you have already used to apply conditional formats that highlight specific data values, can also be used to generate columns and rows of summary statistics that can be used for analyzing data.

Columns F through M in the Fitness Report worksheet will contain the workout report. The range H22:J44 records the number of minutes Daniel spent at each workout jogging, doing calisthenics, and doing strength training. Ken needs to know the total minutes Daniel spent at each exercise to evaluate Daniel's workout effort during the past month. The most efficient way to calculate these totals is with the SUM function. You will use the Quick Analysis tool to enter the SUM function to calculate the total minutes spent at each exercise.

To calculate the total minutes spent on each exercise:

▶ 1. Select the range **H22:J44** containing the minutes spent on each exercise during each workout. The Quick Analysis button 📊 appears in the lower-right corner of the selected range.

▶ 2. Click the **Quick Analysis** button 📊 (or press the **Ctrl+Q** keys) to display the Quick Analysis tool.

▶ 3. Click the **TOTALS** category to display Quick Analysis tools for calculating totals.

▶ 4. Point to the **Sum** button. Live Preview shows the results of Sum. See Figure 3-6.

| Figure 3-6 | Quick Analysis tool to calculate totals |

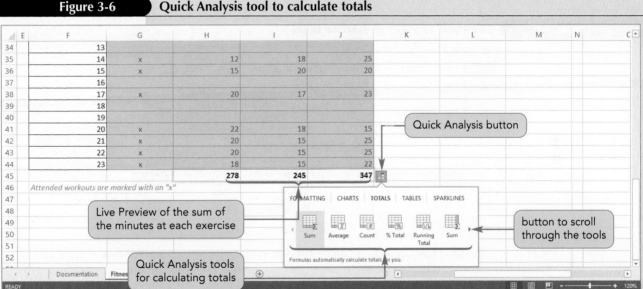

▶ 5. Click **Sum** to enter the SUM function for each cell in the selected range. The results show that Daniel spent 278 minutes jogging, 245 minutes doing calisthenics, and 347 minutes doing strength exercises during the previous month's workouts.

The Quick Analysis tool automatically inserts the formulas containing the SUM function at the bottom of the table. Ken wants you to move this information near the top of the worksheet where it can be viewed first.

▶ 6. Select the range **H45:J45**, and then cut the selected range.

▶ 7. Select cell **G14**, and then paste the formulas with the SUM functions. The totals now appear in the range G14:I14.

The Quick Analysis tool can also be used to quickly calculate averages. An average provides an estimate of the most typical value from a data sample. Ken wants to know the average number of minutes that Daniel spent on each exercise during his sessions.

To calculate the average minutes spent per exercise:

1. Select the range **H22:J44**, and then click the **Quick Analysis** button 📖 that appears in the lower-right corner of the selected range (or press the **Ctrl+Q** keys).

2. Click the **TOTALS** category, and then click **Average** to enter the AVERAGE function in the range H45:J45 and calculate the average minutes per exercise type.

3. Cut the formulas from the range **H45:J45**, and then paste them into the range **G15:I15**.

   Excel displays the averages to eight decimal places, which implies a far greater accuracy in measuring the exercise time than could be recorded.

4. In the range **G15:I15**, decrease the number of decimal places displayed to one. On average, Daniel spent about 16.4 minutes per session jogging, 14.4 minutes on calisthenics, and 20.4 minutes on strength exercises. See Figure 3-7.

Figure 3-7 | **Sums and averages of exercise times**

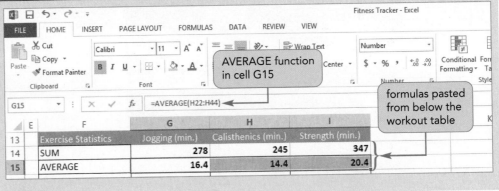

The Quick Analysis tool can be used to summarize values across rows as well as down columns. Ken wants to calculate how long Daniel worked out each day. You will use the Quick Analysis tool to calculate the total exercise minutes per workout.

To calculate the total workout times per session:

1. In cell **K21**, enter **Total Minutes** as the heading.

2. Select the range **H22:J44**, and then open the Quick Analysis tool.

3. Click the **TOTALS** category, and then click the right scroll button to scroll to the right through the list of calculations.

4. Click the **Sum** button for the column of summary statistics. SUM functions are entered in the range K22:K44, calculating the sum of the workout minutes per session.

   The Quick Analysis tool applies its own style to the formulas it generates. Instead of the bold text, you want the formulas to be formatted with the Calculation style.

5. Format the range **K22:K44** with the **Calculation** cell style.

> **6.** In cell **J13**, enter **Total Minutes** as the heading.

> **7.** Copy the formulas in the range **I14:I15**, and then paste them into the range **J14:J15** to calculate the sum and average of the total exercise minutes from all of the workouts. As shown in Figure 3-8, Daniel worked out for 870 minutes during the month with an average of 37.8 minutes per workout.

Figure 3-8   **Total exercise time per workout**

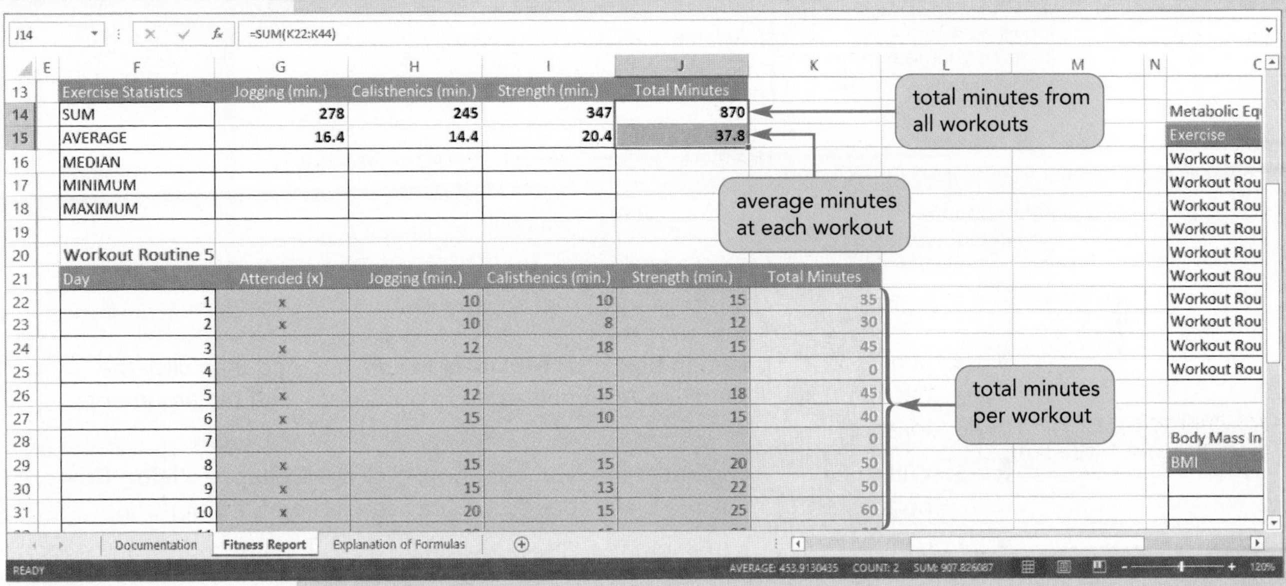

Entering Functions with the Insert Function Dialog Box

Functions are organized in the Function Library group on the FORMULAS tab. In the Function Library, you can select a function from a function category. You can also open the Insert Function dialog box to search for a particular function based on a description you enter. When you select a function, the Function Arguments dialog box opens, listing all of the arguments associated with that function. Required arguments are in bold type; optional arguments are in normal type.

Ken wants his report to include the median exercise times for the three exercise categories. The **median** provides the middle value from a data sample. You can use the MEDIAN function to determine the middle value in a range of numbers. The Quick Analysis tool doesn't include median, so you will use the Insert Function and Function Arguments dialog boxes to help you correctly insert the MEDIAN function.

To calculate the median exercise time:

> **1.** Select cell **G16**. This is the cell in which you will enter the MEDIAN function.

> **2.** Click the **Insert Function** button f_x to the left of the formula bar to open the Insert Function dialog box. From the Insert Function dialog box, you can describe the function you want to search for.

> **3.** In the Search for a function box, type **middle value**, and then click the **Go** button. Functions for finding a middle value appear in the Select a function box. The second entry in the list, MEDIAN, is the one you want to use. See Figure 3-9.

Figure 3-9 **Insert Function dialog box**

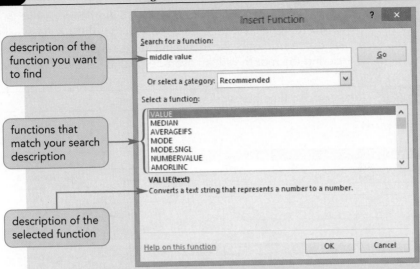

description of the function you want to find

functions that match your search description

description of the selected function

▶ **4.** In the Select a function box, click **MEDIAN** to select it, and then click the **OK** button. The Function Arguments dialog box opens with the arguments for the MEDIAN function.

▶ **5.** With the insertion point in the Number1 box, click the **Collapse Dialog Box** button ▦ to shrink the dialog box so you can see more of the worksheet.

▶ **6.** In the worksheet, select the range **H22:H44**. These cells contain the times Daniel spent jogging.

▶ **7.** In the Function Arguments dialog box, click the **Expand Dialog Box** button ▦ to redisplay the entire dialog box. The dialog box now shows a preview of the MEDIAN function and the value it will return to the formula. See Figure 3-10.

Figure 3-10 **Function Arguments dialog box**

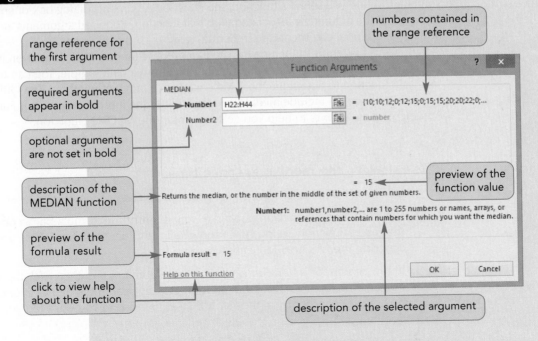

numbers contained in the range reference

range reference for the first argument

required arguments appear in bold

optional arguments are not set in bold

description of the MEDIAN function

preview of the formula result

click to view help about the function

preview of the function value

description of the selected argument

8. Click the **OK** button. The formula =MEDIAN(H22:H44) is entered in cell G16, which displays 15 (the median exercise time for jogging).

9. Copy cell **G16**, and then paste the copied formula into the range **H16:J16** to calculate the median exercise times for calisthenics, strength training, and all exercises. See Figure 3-11.

Figure 3-11	Median exercise times

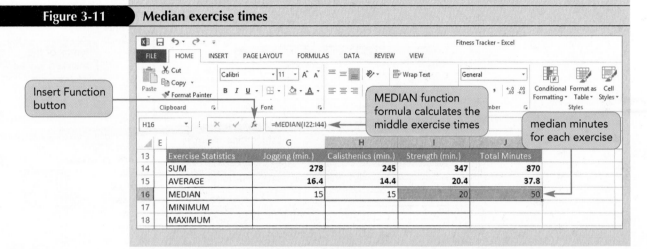

Daniel spent a median time of 15 minutes on calisthenics and 20 minutes on strength training. The median total exercise time was 50 minutes, which is quite a bit higher than the average total exercise time of 37.8 minutes. Why this difference? One reason is that averages are greatly influenced by extremely low or high values. Because Daniel missed several workouts, his exercise time for those days was 0, bringing down the overall average. A median, or middle value, is not as affected by these extreme values, which is why some statisticians advocate medians over averages for analyzing data with widely spaced values.

Ken also wants to know the minimum and maximum minutes Daniel spent exercising during the month. You can access functions by scrolling through the Function Library. You will use this method to enter the functions to calculate the minimum and maximum exercise times.

To calculate the minimum and maximum minutes of exercise:

1. Select cell **G17**, which is where you will calculate the minimum exercise time.

2. On the ribbon, click the **FORMULAS** tab to display the function categories in the Function Library.

3. Click the **More Functions** button to display the rest of the function categories. Calculations involving maximums and minimums are included with the Statistical functions.

4. Click **Statistical** to display the statistical functions, and then scroll down and point to **MIN**. A ScreenTip appears, displaying the MIN function syntax and a description of the function. See Figure 3-12.

Figure 3-12 | **MIN function in the Function Library**

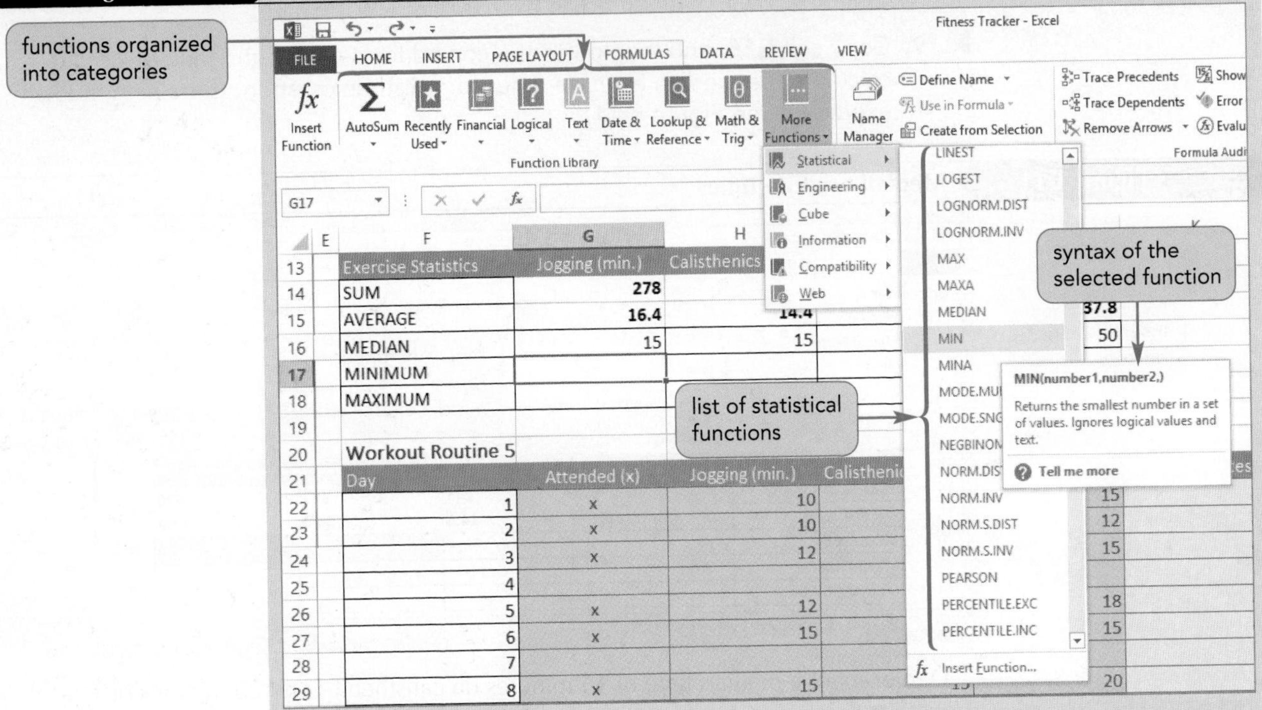

5. Click **MIN** to open the Function Arguments dialog box.

6. With the insertion point in the Number1 box, select the range **H22:H44** in the worksheet. These cells store the amount of time Daniel spent jogging.

7. Click the **OK** button. The dialog box closes, and the formula =MIN(H22:H44) is entered in cell G17, which displays 10, the minimum minutes that Daniel spent jogging during the month.

8. Select cell **G18**, click the **More Functions** button in the Function Library group, click **Statistical**, and then scroll down and click **MAX**. The Function Arguments dialog box opens.

9. With the insertion point in the Number1 box, select the range **H22:H44** in the worksheet, and then click the **OK** button. The formula =MAX(H22:H44) is entered in cell G18, which displays 22, the maximum minutes that Daniel spent jogging.

10. Copy the range **G17:G18**, and then paste the formulas in the range **H17:J18** to calculate the minimum and maximum times for the other exercises and overall.

11. Format the range **G14:J18** with the **Calculation** cell style, and then select cell **F19**. See Figure 3-13.

Figure 3-13   Summary statistics of the exercise times

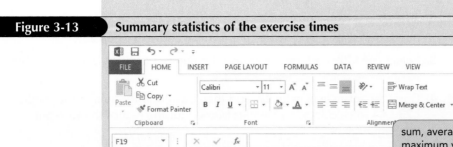

Referencing Function Results in a Formula

The amount of calories burned during exercise is a function of intensity and time. The more intense the exercise or the longer it lasts, the more calories burned. Ken uses the fitness equation

$$Calories = \frac{METS \times w \times t}{125.7143}$$

to calculate how many calories will be used during exercise, where *METS* is a metabolic factor that measures the intensity of the exercise, *w* is the individual's weight in pounds, *t* is the exercise time in minutes, and 125.7143 is a constant that converts the quantity into calories. Ken listed the METS values for the different workout routines he created in the range O15:P25 of the Fitness Report worksheet. For example, the METS for Workout Routine 5 is 7.0 and the METS for Workout Routine 10 is 16.0. Using the METS information and the weight and exercise times, you can calculate the total calories burned during each workout.

The fitness equation that calculates calories burned during the first workout translates into the formula

```
=P20*C11*K22/125.7143
```

where `P20` references the cell with the METS for Workout Routine 5, `C11` references the cell that stores Daniel's weight, and `K22` references the cell that calculates the total exercise time of the first workout.

You will enter this formula in cell L22, and then copy it to the remaining cells in the column to calculate the calories burned during each workout.

To calculate the calories burned during Daniel's first workout:

▶ **1.** In cell **L21**, enter **Calories Burned** as the label.

▶ **2.** In cell **L22**, enter the formula **=P20*C11*K22/125.7143** to calculate the calories Daniel burned at his first workout. Cell P20 stores the METS value, cell C11 contains Daniel's weight, and cell K22 is the total exercise time for Workout Routine 5 on the first day of the month. Cell L22 displays 376.1306391, which is the number of calories burned at the first workout.

Trouble? If your value differs from 376.1306391, edit your formula as needed so it exactly matches the formula shown in Step 2.

3. Select cell **L22**, and then decrease the number of decimal places shown to one. The displayed value is 376.1.

4. Copy the formula in cell **L22**, and then paste the formula to the range **L23:L44** to calculate the calories burned for the rest of the workouts. See Figure 3-14.

Figure 3-14 **Formulas incorrectly calculating the calories burned per workout**

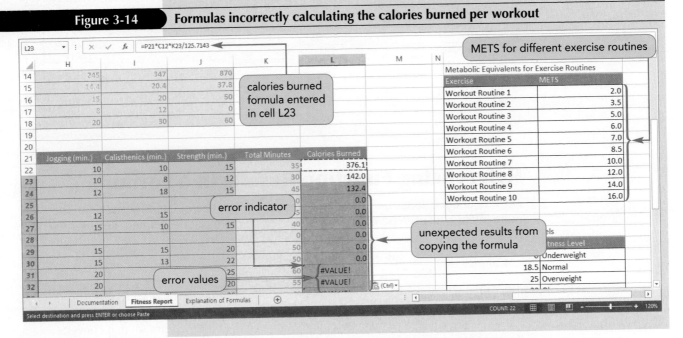

The first few values seem somewhat reasonable, but then several workouts show no calories burned. These are followed by cells displaying #VALUE! rather than a number. Obviously something went wrong when you copied and pasted the formula.

Interpreting Error Values

The #VALUE! that appears in some of the cells in the Fitness Report worksheet is an error value. An **error value** indicates that some part of a formula is preventing Excel from returning a calculated value. An error value begins with a pound sign (#) followed by an error name that indicates the type of error. Figure 3-15 describes common error values that you might see instead of the results from formulas and functions. For example, the error value #VALUE! indicates that the wrong type of value is used in a function or formula. You will need to examine the formulas in the cells with error values to determine exactly what went wrong.

Figure 3-15   **Excel error values**

Error Value	Description
#DIV/0!	The formula or function contains a number divided by 0.
#NAME?	Excel doesn't recognize text in the formula or function, such as when the function name is misspelled.
#N/A	A value is not available to a function or formula, which can occur when a workbook is initially set up prior to entering actual data values.
#NULL!	A formula or function requires two cell ranges to intersect, but they don't.
#NUM!	Invalid numbers are used in a formula or function, such as text entered in a function that requires a number.
#REF!	A cell reference used in a formula or function is no longer valid, which can occur when the cell used by the function was deleted from the worksheet.
#VALUE!	The wrong type of argument is used in a function or formula. This can occur when you reference a text value for an argument that should be strictly numeric.

© 2014 Cengage Learning

The error value messages are not particularly descriptive or helpful. To help you locate the error, an error indicator appears in the upper-left corner of the cell with the error value. When you point to the error indicator, a ScreenTip appears with more information about the source of the error.

Deciding When to Correct an Error Value

An error value does not mean that you must correct the cell's formula or function. Some error values appear simply because you have not yet entered any data into the workbook. For example, if you use the AVERAGE function to find the average value of an empty column, the #DIV/0! error value appears because the formula cannot calculate the average of a collection of empty cells. However, as soon as you begin entering data, the #DIV/0! message will disappear.

Ken wants you to figure out why the #VALUE error value appears in some of the cells where you copied the calories burned formula. To figure this out, you will examine the formula in cell L31, which is the first cell that displays the error value instead of the expected number results.

To view the formula in cell L31 that results in an error value:

▶ **1.** Double-click cell **L31**, which displays the #VALUE! error value. In Edit mode, the cell references used in the formula are color coded to match the corresponding cells, making it easier to see which cells are used in the formula.

▶ **2.** Observe that cell L31 contains the formula =P29*C20*K31/125.7143.

3. Look at the first cell reference in the formula. The first cell reference is to cell P29 containing the text "Fitness Level" instead of cell P20 containing the METS value for Workout Routine 5. The formula is attempting to multiply the text in cell P29, but multiplication can be done only with numbers. This is the problem causing the #VALUE! error value.

4. Look at the second cell reference in the formula. The second cell reference is to cell C20, an empty cell, rather than to cell C11 containing Daniel's weight.

5. Look at the third cell reference in the formula. The third cell reference is to cell K31, which contains the total exercise times for the tenth workout—the correct cell reference.

Exploring Cell References

Most workbooks include data entered in cells that are then referenced in formulas to perform calculations on that data. The formulas can be simple, such as the formulas you entered to add the total minutes of each workout, or they can be more complex, such as the formulas you entered to calculate the calories burned during each workout. Each of these formulas includes one or more cell references.

Understanding Relative References

When a formula includes a cell reference, Excel interprets that cell reference as being located relative to the position of the current cell. For example, Excel interprets the following formula entered in cell A1 to mean "add the value of the cell one column to the right of this cell to the value of the cell one column to the right and one row below this cell":

```
=B1+B2
```

This relative interpretation is retained when the formula is copied to a new location. So, if the formula in cell A1 is copied to cell A3 (two rows down in the worksheet), the relative references in the formula also shift two rows down, resulting in the following formula:

```
=B3+B4
```

Figure 3-16 shows another example of how relative references change when a formula is copied to new cell locations. In this figure, the formula =A4 entered in cell D7 displays 10, which is the number entered in cell A4. When pasted to a new location, each of the pasted formulas contains a reference to a cell that is three rows up and three rows to the left of the current cell's location.

Figure 3-16   Formulas using relative references

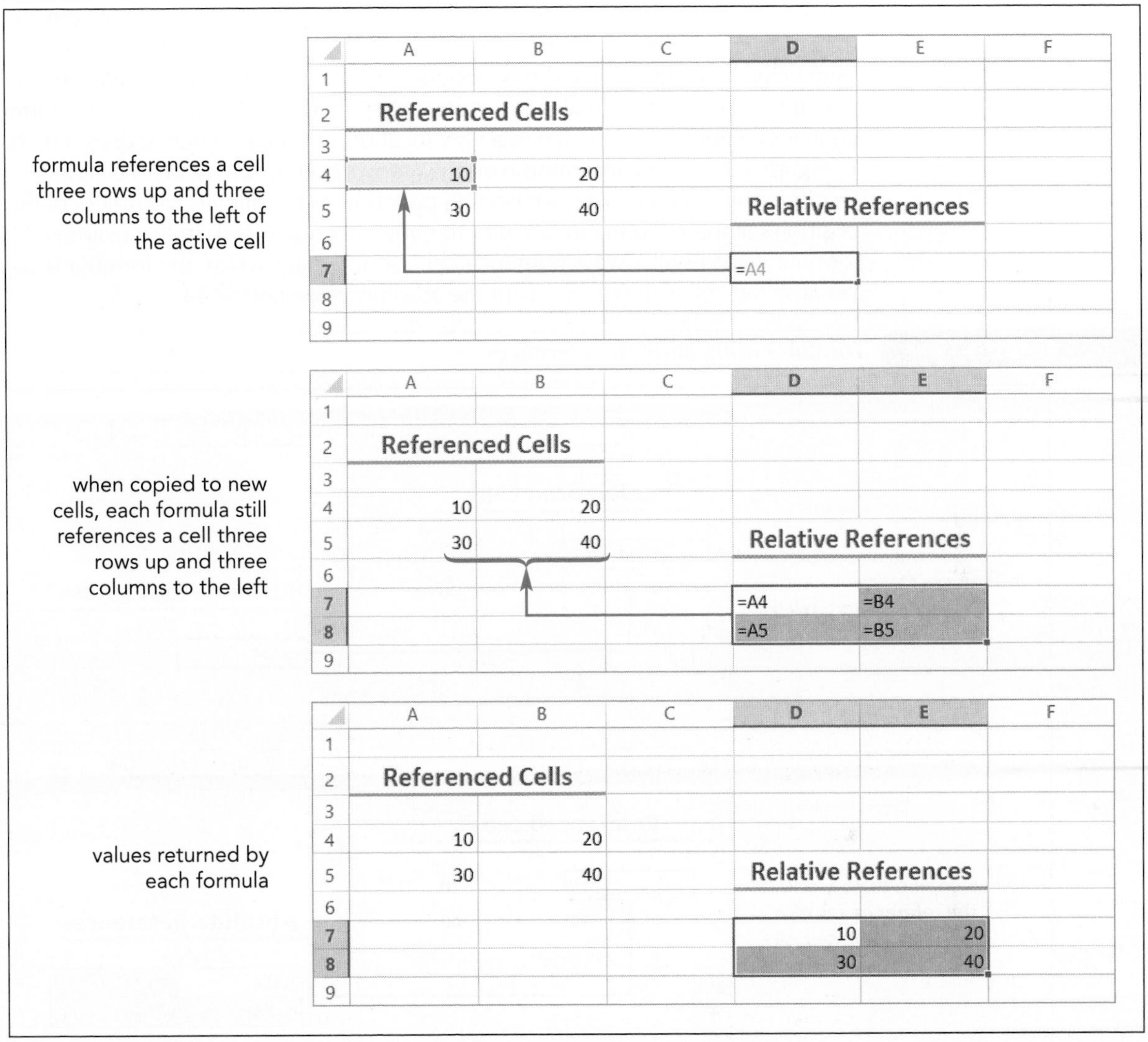

formula references a cell three rows up and three columns to the left of the active cell

when copied to new cells, each formula still references a cell three rows up and three columns to the left

values returned by each formula

© 2014 Cengage Learning

This explains what happened with the relative references you used to calculate calories burned for each workout. When you entered the following formula in cell L22, cell C11 correctly references the client's weight and the other cells correctly reference the METS for Workout Routine 5 and the total exercise time:

`=P20*C11*K22/125.7143`

When you copied the formula down to cell L31, all of the cell references contained in that formula also shifted down nine rows, resulting in the following formula, which accurately references the total exercise time for the corresponding workout but no longer references Daniel's weight or the METS for Workout Routine 5—both of which are necessary for the calculation:

`=P29*C20*K31/125.7143`

What you need is a cell reference that remains fixed when the formula is copied to a new location.

Understanding Absolute References

A fixed reference—one that always references the same cell no matter where it is moved—is called an absolute reference. In Excel, absolute references include a $ (dollar sign) before each column and row designation. For example, B8 is a relative reference to cell B8, and $B$8 is an absolute reference to that cell. When you copy a formula that contains an absolute reference to a new location, that cell reference does not change.

Figure 3-17 shows an example of how copying a formula with an absolute reference results in the same cell reference being pasted in different cells regardless of their position compared to the location of the original copied cell. In this example, the formula =$A$4 will always reference cell A4 no matter where the formula is copied to, because the cell is referenced with the absolute reference $A$4.

Figure 3-17   **Formulas using absolute references**

formula absolutely references the cell located in column A and row 4

when copied to new cells, the reference remains fixed on cell A4

values returned by each formula

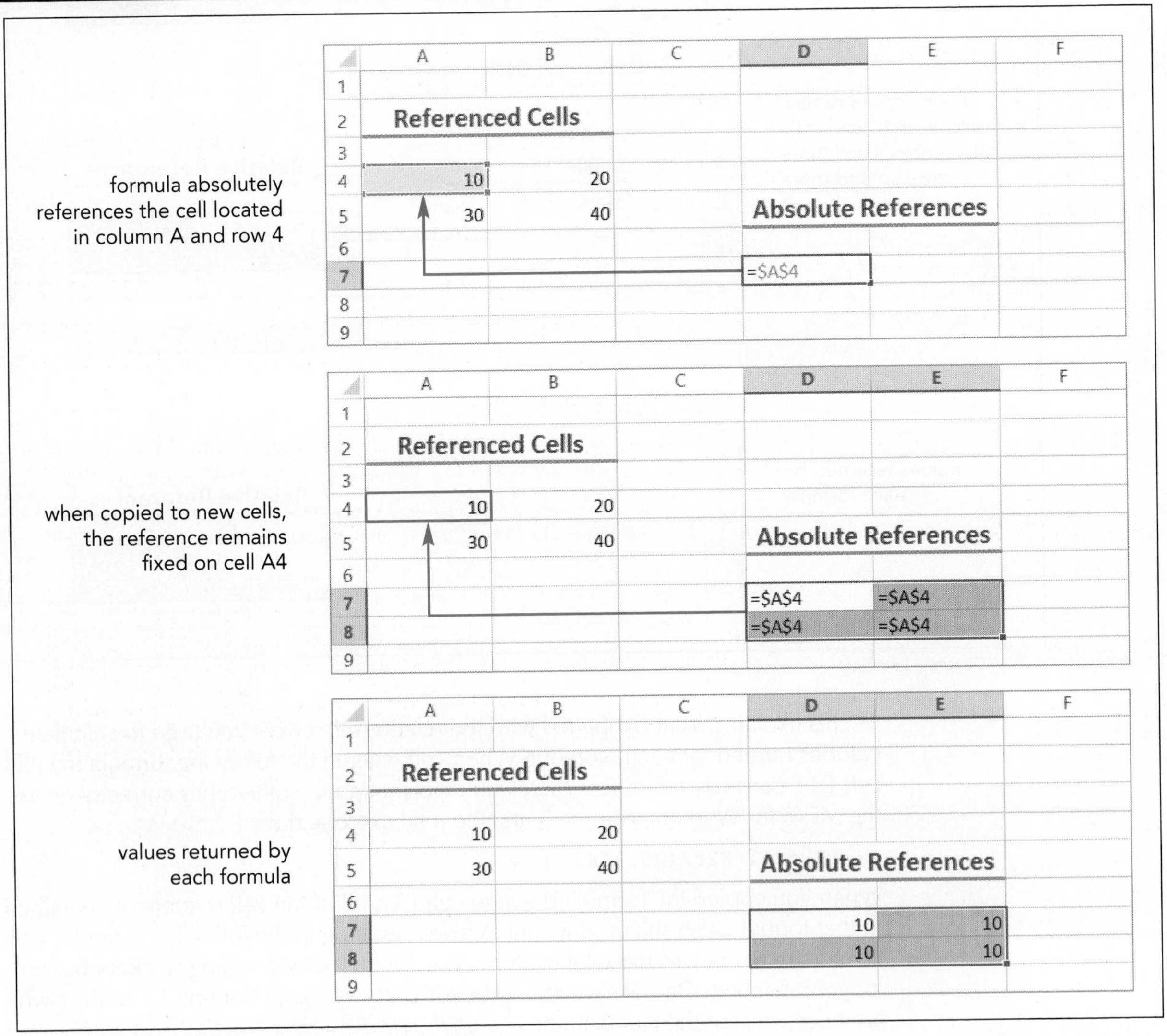

© 2014 Cengage Learning

Understanding Mixed References

A formula can also include cell references that are mixed. A **mixed reference** contains both relative and absolute references. For example, a mixed reference for cell A2 can be either $A2 or A$2. In the mixed reference $A2, the reference to column A is absolute and the reference to row 2 is relative. In the mixed reference A$2, the column reference is relative and the row reference is absolute. A mixed reference "locks" one part of the cell reference while the other part can change. When you copy and paste a cell with a mixed reference to a new location, the absolute portion of the cell reference remains fixed and the relative portion shifts along with the new location of the pasted cell.

Figure 3-18 shows an example of using mixed references to complete a multiplication table. The first cell in the table, cell B3, contains the formula =$A3*B$2, which multiplies the first column entry (A3) by the first row entry (B2), returning 1. When this formula is copied to another cell, the absolute portions of the cell references remain unchanged and the relative portions of the references change. For example, if the formula is copied to cell E6, the first mixed cell reference changes to $A6 because the column reference is absolute and the row reference is relative, and the second cell reference changes to E$2 because the row reference is absolute and the column reference is relative. The result is that cell E6 contains the formula =$A6*E$2 and returns 16. Other cells in the multiplication table are similarly modified so that each entry returns the multiplication of the intersection of the row and column headings.

Figure 3-18   **Formulas using mixed references**

mixed cell reference that fixes the column reference for the first term and the row reference for the second term

when copied to the B3:B7 range, the fixed references remain unchanged and the relative references are shifted

values returned by each formula

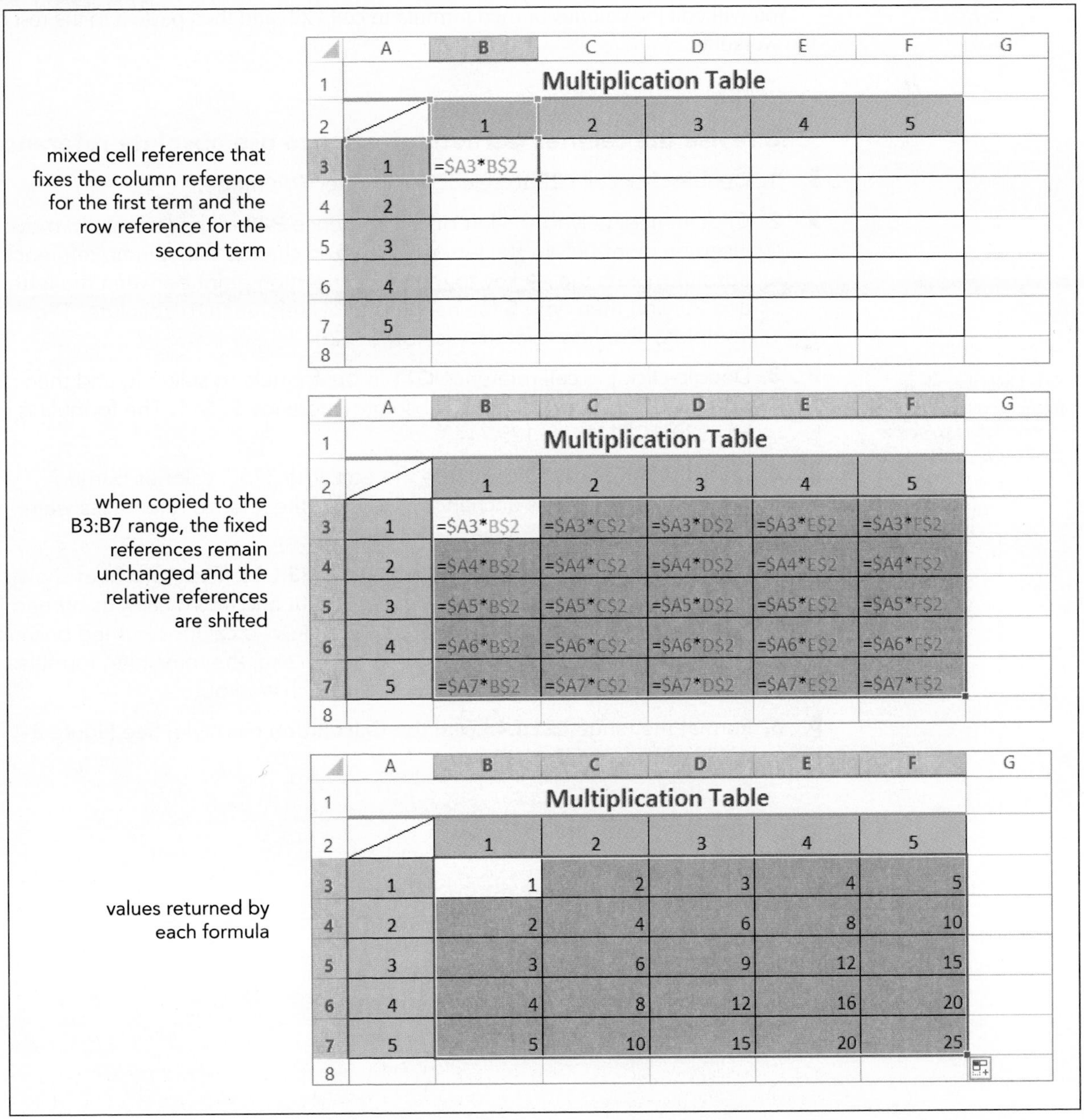

Changing Cell References in a Formula

You can quickly switch a cell reference from relative to absolute or mixed. Rather than retyping the formula, you can select the cell reference in Edit mode and then press the F4 key. As you press the F4 key, Excel cycles through the different reference types—starting with the relative reference, followed by the absolute reference, then to a mixed reference with the row absolute, and finally to a mixed reference with the column absolute.

Ken wants you to fix the problem with the cell references in the calories burned formulas. You need to revise the formula to use absolute references to Daniel's weight and the METS value that will not change when the formula is copied to new locations. You will leave the relative reference to the total exercise time so that the copied formulas will retrieve the exercise times from the corresponding workouts. The revised formula in cell L22 uses an absolute reference to the METS values in $P$20 and an absolute reference to Daniel's weight in $C$11, as follows:

```
=$P$20*$C$11*K22/125.7143
```

You will edit the calories burned formula in cell L22, and then paste it to the rest of the workouts.

To revise the calories burned formulas to use absolute references:

1. Double-click cell **L22** to select it and enter Edit mode.

2. Click immediately to the left of cell reference **P20** in the formula to move the insertion point before the letter P, type **$** to change the column reference to absolute, press the → key to move the insertion point between the letter P and 20, and then type **$** to change the row reference to absolute. The complete absolute reference is now $P$20.

3. Double-click the cell reference **C11** in the formula to select it, and then press the **F4** key to change it to the absolute reference $C$11. The formula is now =$P$20*$C$11*K22/125.7143.

4. Press the **Enter** key to complete the edit. The 376.1 calories burned displayed in the cell is unchanged because the relative references were accurate in this first formula.

5. Copy cell **L22** and paste it into the range **L23:L44**. The worksheet shows 322.4 calories burned for the second workout and 483.6 calories burned for the third workout. The next row in the list shows 0 calories burned because Daniel did not work out that day. As you can see, the remaining formulas now correctly calculate the calories burned at each workout.

6. Format the range **L22:L44** with the **Calculation** cell style. See Figure 3-19.

Select only the cell reference you want to change before you press the F4 key.

Figure 3-19   **Formulas with absolute and relative references**

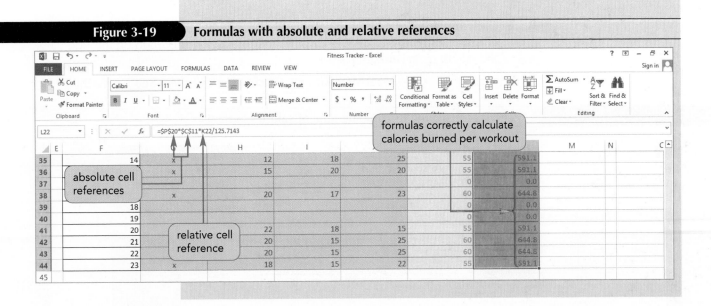

Planning Which Cell Reference to Use in a Formula

You can include the correct type of cell reference in a formula as you create the formula. This requires a little more thought up front, as you consider how each cell in a formula needs to be referenced before you create the formula. Ken wants you to create a running total of the calories burned during each workout. You can use the SUM function with a combination of absolute and relative cell references to add the values in a range. The formula to calculate the total in the first cell is:

```
=SUM($L$22:L22)
```

In this formula, the starting cell of the range is fixed at cell L22, but the ending cell of the range is relative. When you copy this formula down the column, the starting cell remains absolutely referenced to cell L22, but the ending cell changes to include the current row. For example, when the formula is pasted three rows down, the formula changes to add the numbers in cells L22, L23, L24, and L25, as follows:

```
=SUM($L$22:L25)
```

Continuing in this way, the last cell will contain the sum of all of the calories burned totals using the following formula:

```
=SUM($L$22:L44)
```

Instead of entering the formulas yourself, you can use the Quick Analysis tool to calculate the total calories burned up through the end of each workout session.

To calculate the running total of calories burned:

▸ **1.** In cell **M21**, enter **Calories Subtotal** as the label.

▸ **2.** Select the range **L22:L44** containing the calories burned during each workout, and then click the **Quick Analysis** button ▣ (or press the **Ctrl+Q** keys).

▸ **3.** Click the **TOTALS** category, and then scroll right to the end of the TOTALS tools.

4. Click **Running Total** (the last entry in the list, which is the Running Total of a column). The range M22:M44 displays the total calories burned up through the end of each workout session.

5. Format the range **M22:M44** with the **Calculation** cell style. See Figure 3-20.

Figure 3-20	Formulas calculating the running total of calories burned

Daniel burned 698.5 calories during the first two workouts and more than 1180 calories after the first three workouts. The formula used to calculate the running totals for the column includes both absolute and relative references. You will review the formulas in column M to see the formulas calculating the running totals.

To view the formulas for the running totals:

1. Select cell **M22**, and then review the formula, which is =SUM($L$22:L22). Notice the absolute and relative references to cell L22.

2. Select cell **M23**, and then review the formula, which is =SUM($L$22:L23). Notice that the absolute reference to cell L22 remains unchanged, but the relative reference is now cell L23, expanding the range being added with the SUM function.

3. Select each cell in column M and review its formula, noticing that the absolute reference $L$22 always appears as the top cell of the range but the relative reference for the last cell of the range changes.

4. Save the workbook.

You can see that the running total is calculated with the SUM function using a combination of absolute and relative cell references. The top of the range used in the SUM function is locked at cell L22, but the bottom of the range is relative, expanding in size as the formula was copied down column M. Entered this way, with absolute and relative cell references, the SUM function calculates partial sums, providing the total calories burned up through the end of each workout session.

Understanding When to Use Relative, Absolute, and Mixed References

Part of effective workbook design is knowing when to use relative, absolute, and mixed references. Use relative references when you want to apply the same formula with input cells that share a common layout or pattern. Relative references are commonly used when copying a formula that calculates summary statistics across columns or rows of data values. Use absolute references when you want your copied formulas to always refer to the same cell. This usually occurs when a cell contains a constant value, such as a tax rate, that will be referenced in formulas throughout the worksheet. Mixed references are seldom used other than when creating tables of calculated values such as a multiplication table in which the values of the formula or function can be found at the intersection of the rows and columns of the table.

So far, you have entered the fitness formulas and summary statistics in the Fitness Tracker workbook. In the next session, you will explore date and time functions, and then look up values to use in formulas and functions.

Session 3.1 Quick Check

1. What is an optional argument? What does Excel do if you do not include an optional argument?
2. Write the function to return the middle value from the values in the range X1:X10.
3. Write the function to round the value in cell A5 to the fourth decimal place.
4. The range of a set of values is defined as the maximum value minus the minimum value. Write the formula to calculate the range of values in the range Y1:Y10.
5. If cell A11 contains the formula =SUME(A1:A10), what error value will appear in the cell?
6. You need to reference cell Q57 in a formula. What is its relative reference? What is its absolute reference? What are the two mixed references?
7. If cell R10 contains the formula =R1+R2, which is then copied to cell S20, what formula is entered in cell S20?
8. If cell V10 contains the formula = AVERAGE($U1:$U5), which is then copied to cell W20, what formula is entered in cell W20?

Session 3.2 Visual Overview:

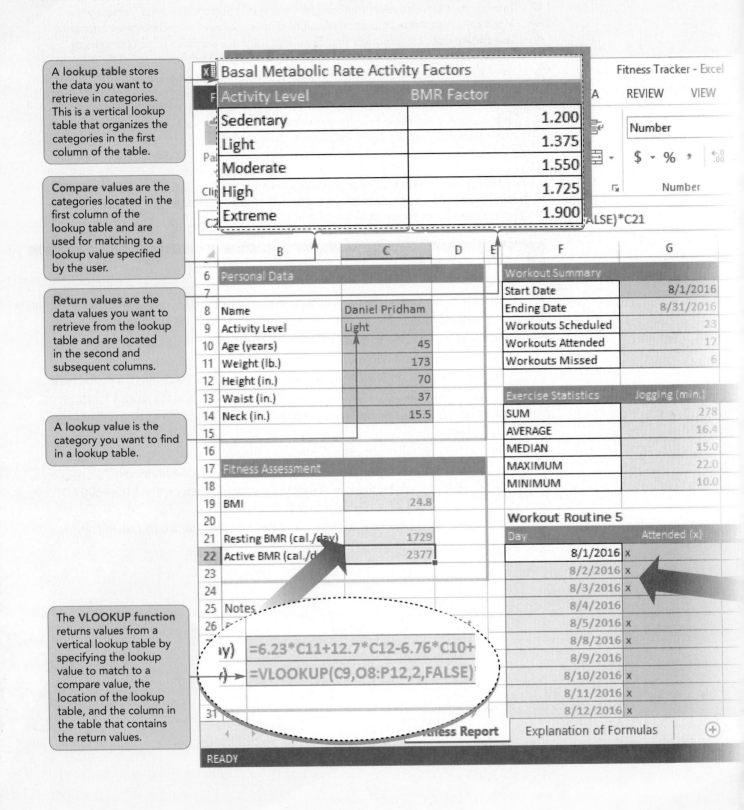

A lookup table stores the data you want to retrieve in categories. This is a vertical lookup table that organizes the categories in the first column of the table.

Compare values are the categories located in the first column of the lookup table and are used for matching to a lookup value specified by the user.

Return values are the data values you want to retrieve from the lookup table and are located in the second and subsequent columns.

A lookup value is the category you want to find in a lookup table.

The VLOOKUP function returns values from a vertical lookup table by specifying the lookup value to match to a compare value, the location of the lookup table, and the column in the table that contains the return values.

Basal Metabolic Rate Activity Factors

Activity Level	BMR Factor
Sedentary	1.200
Light	1.375
Moderate	1.550
High	1.725
Extreme	1.900

Fitness Tracker - Excel

REVIEW   VIEW

Number

$ - % ,

Number

C2   ...LSE)*C21

	B	C	D	E	F	G
6	Personal Data				Workout Summary	
7					Start Date	8/1/2016
8	Name	Daniel Pridham			Ending Date	8/31/2016
9	Activity Level	Light			Workouts Scheduled	23
10	Age (years)	45			Workouts Attended	17
11	Weight (lb.)	173			Workouts Missed	6
12	Height (in.)	70				
13	Waist (in.)	37			Exercise Statistics	Jogging (min.)
14	Neck (in.)	15.5			SUM	278
15					AVERAGE	16.4
16					MEDIAN	15.0
17	Fitness Assessment				MAXIMUM	22.0
18					MINIMUM	10.0
19	BMI	24.8				
20					Workout Routine 5	
21	Resting BMR (cal./day)	1729			Day	Attended (x)
22	Active BMR (cal./d	2377			8/1/2016	x
23					8/2/2016	x
24					8/3/2016	x
25	Notes				8/4/2016	
26					8/5/2016	x
	ay)	=6.23*C11+12.7*C12-6.76*C10+			8/8/2016	x
					8/9/2016	
	)	=VLOOKUP(C9,O8:P12,2,FALSE)			8/10/2016	x
					8/11/2016	x
31					8/12/2016	x

Fitness Report   Explanation of Formulas

READY

Logical and Lookup Functions

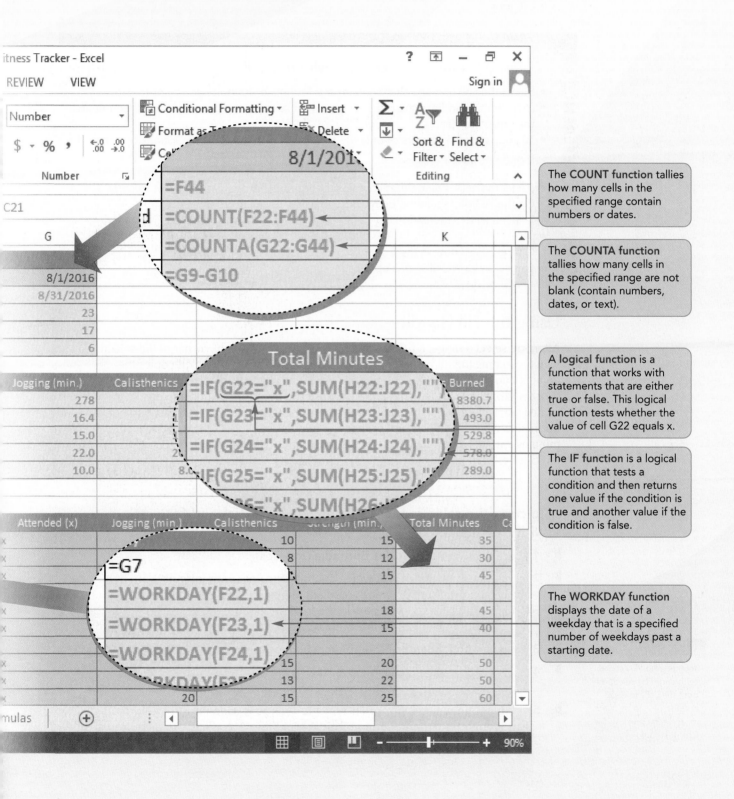

The COUNT function tallies how many cells in the specified range contain numbers or dates.

The COUNTA function tallies how many cells in the specified range are not blank (contain numbers, dates, or text).

A logical function is a function that works with statements that are either true or false. This logical function tests whether the value of cell G22 equals x.

The IF function is a logical function that tests a condition and then returns one value if the condition is true and another value if the condition is false.

The WORKDAY function displays the date of a weekday that is a specified number of weekdays past a starting date.

AutoFilling Formulas and Data

AutoFill provides a quick way to enter content and formatting in cells based on existing entries in adjacent cells. Ken wants you to include summary statistics for calories burned across all of the scheduled workouts. To add these statistics, you'll use the AutoFill tool.

REFERENCE

Copying Formulas and Formats with AutoFill

- Select the cell or range that contains the formula or formulas you want to copy.
- Drag the fill handle in the direction you want to copy the formula(s), and then release the mouse button.
- To copy only the formats or only the formulas, click the Auto Fill Options button and select the appropriate option.

or

- Select the cell or range that contains the formula or formulas you want to copy.
- On the HOME tab, in the Editing group, click the Fill button.
- Select a fill direction and fill type.

or

- On the HOME tab, in the Editing group, click Series.
- Enter the desired fill series options, and then click the OK button.

Using the Fill Handle

After you select a range, a **fill handle** appears in the lower-right corner of the selection. When you drag the fill handle over an adjacent cell or range, AutoFill copies the content and formats from the original cell or range into the adjacent cell or range. This process is often more efficient than the two-step process of copying and pasting.

Ken wants you to calculate the same summary statistics for the calories burned during the workouts as you did for the total minutes of each workout. Because the total minutes formulas use relative references, you can use the fill handle to copy these for the calories burned statistics.

To copy the calories burned summary statistics and formatting with the fill handle:

1. In cell **K13**, enter **Calories Burned** as the label.

2. Select the range **J14:J18**, which contains the cells with formulas for calculating the sum, average, median, minimum, and maximum total minutes. A fill handle appears in the lower-right corner of the selected range, directly above and to the left of the Quick Analysis button.

TIP

You can also fill a series to the right by selecting both the cells to copy and the cells to be filled in, and then pressing the Ctrl+R keys.

3. Point to the **fill handle**. The pointer changes to **+**.

4. Click and drag the fill handle over the range **K14:K18**. A solid outline appears around the selected range as you move the pointer.

5. Release the mouse button. The selected range is filled in with the formulas and formatting from the range J14:J18, and the Auto Fill Options button appears in the lower-right corner of the selected cells. See Figure 3-21.

Figure 3-21   **Formulas and formatting copied with AutoFill**

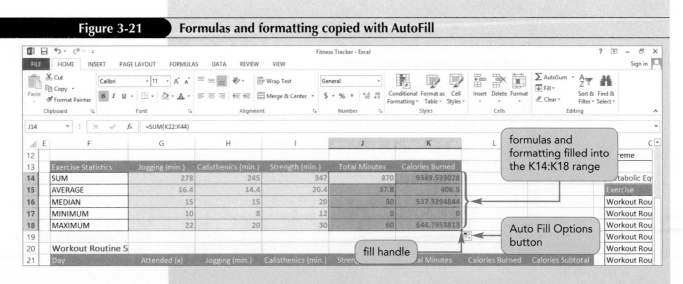

6. Format the range **K14:K18** to display one decimal place.

Based on the summary statistics, Ken can see that Daniel burned 9349.5 calories during the month, burned an average of 406.5 calories per session, burned a median of 537.3 calories per session, and burned a minimum of 0.0 calories and a maximum of 644.8 calories per session during the month.

Using the Auto Fill Options Button

By default, AutoFill copies both the content and the formatting of the original range to the selected range. However, sometimes you might want to copy only the content or only the formatting. The Auto Fill Options button that appears after you release the mouse button lets you specify what is copied. As shown in Figure 3-22, clicking this button provides a menu of AutoFill options. The Copy Cells option, which is the default, copies both the content and the formatting. The Fill Formatting Only option copies the formatting into the selected cells but not any content. The Fill Without Formatting option copies the content but not the formatting.

Figure 3-22   **Auto Fill Options button**

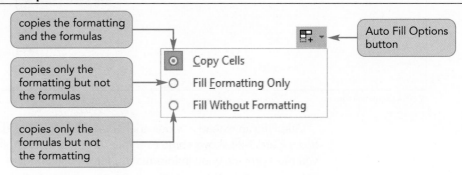

Because you want to copy the content and the formatting of the summary statistics, you don't need to use the Auto Fill Options button.

Filling a Series

AutoFill can also be used to create a series of numbers, dates, or text based on a pattern. To create a series of numbers, you enter the initial values in the series in a selected range and then use AutoFill to complete the series.

REFERENCE

Creating a Series with AutoFill

- Enter the first few values of the series into a range.
- Select the range, and then drag the fill handle of the selected range over the cells you want to fill.

or

- Enter the first few values of the series into a range.
- Select the entire range into which you want to extend the series.
- On the HOME tab, in the Editing group, click the Fill button, and then click Down, Right, Up, Left, Series, or Justify to set the direction in which you want to extend the series.

Figure 3-23 shows how AutoFill can be used to insert the numbers from 1 to 10 in a selected range. You enter the first few numbers in the range A2:A4 to establish the pattern you want AutoFill to use—consecutive positive numbers in this example. Then, you select the range and drag its fill handle over the cells where you want the pattern continued—in this case, the range A5:A11—and Excel fills in the rest of the series.

Figure 3-23 **AutoFill extends a numeric sequence**

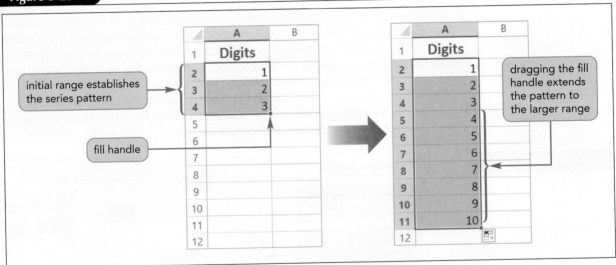

© 2014 Cengage Learning

AutoFill can extend a wide variety of series, including dates and times and patterned text. Figure 3-24 shows some examples of series that AutoFill can generate. In each case, you must provide enough information for AutoFill to identify the pattern. AutoFill can recognize some patterns from only a single entry—such as Jan or January, to create a series of month abbreviations or names, or Mon or Monday, to create a series of the days of the week. A text pattern that includes text and a number such as Region 1, Region 2, and so on can also be automatically extended using AutoFill. You can start the series at any point, such as Weds, June, or Region 10, and AutoFill will complete the next days, months, or text.

Figure 3-24	AutoFill extends numbers, dates and times, and patterned text

Type	Initial Pattern	Extended Series
Numbers	1, 2, 3	4, 5, 6, ..
	2, 4, 6	8, 10, 12, ...
Dates and Times	Jan	Feb, Mar, Apr, ...
	January	February, March, April, ...
	15-Jan, 15-Feb	15-Mar, 15-Apr, 15-May, ...
	12/30/2016	12/31/2016, 1/1/2017, 1/2/2017, ...
	12/31/2016, 1/31/2017	2/29/2017, 3/31/2017, 4/30/2017, ...
	Mon	Tue, Wed, Thu, ...
	Monday	Tuesday, Wednesday, Thursday, ...
	11:00AM	12:00PM, 1:00PM, 2:00PM, ...
Patterned Text	1st period	2nd period, 3rd period, 4th period, ...
	Region 1	Region 2, Region 3, Region 4, ...
	Quarter 3	Quarter 4, Quarter 1, Quarter 2, ...
	Qtr3	Qtr4, Qtr1, Qtr2, ...

© 2014 Cengage Learning

Ken wants you to fill in the dates of the workouts, replacing the numbers in the range F22:F44. You will use AutoFill to insert the calendar dates starting with 8/1/2016.

To use AutoFill to enter the calendar dates:

1. In cell **F22**, enter **8/1/2016**. This is the first date you want to use for the series.

2. Select cell **F22** to select the cell with the first date in the series.

3. Drag the fill handle over the range **F23:F44**.

4. Release the mouse button. AutoFill enters the calendar dates ending with 8/23/2016 in cell F44.

TIP

You can also fill a series down by selecting both the cells to copy and the cells to be filled in, and then pressing the Ctrl+D keys.

For more complex AutoFill patterns, you can use the Series dialog box to specify a linear or growth series for numbers; a date series for dates that increase by day, weekday, month, or year; or an AutoFill series for patterned text. With numbers, you can also specify the step value (how much each number increases over the previous entry) and a stop value (the endpoint for the entire series).

Ken notices that the workout dates are wrong in the Fitness Report worksheet. Fit Fathers meets only Monday through Friday. He asks you to change the fill pattern to include only weekdays. You will use the Series dialog box to set the fill pattern for the rest of the weekdays in the month.

To fill the dates of weekdays in August:

1. Make sure the range **F22:F44** is selected. Cell F22 contains the first value for the series that will be entered in the range F23:F44.

2. On the HOME tab, in the Editing group, click the **Fill** button, and then click **Series**. The Series dialog box opens.

3. In the Type section, make sure that the **Date** option button is selected.

4. In the Date unit section, click the **Weekday** option button so that the series includes only dates for Mondays through Fridays. See Figure 3-25.

Figure 3-25   **Series dialog box**

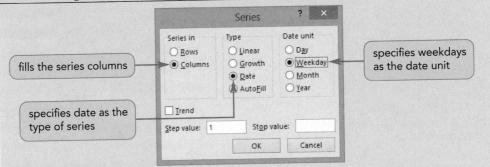

fills the series columns

specifies date as the type of series

specifies weekdays as the date unit

5. Click the **OK** button. The dates of weekdays in August are filled into the selected range ending with 8/31/2016. See Figure 3-26.

Figure 3-26   **Weekday values filled in**

only weekdays are entered in the selected range

	E	F	G	H	I	J	
20		Workout Routine 5					
21		Day	Attended (x)	Jogging (min.)	Calisthenics (min.)	Strength (min.)	Tota
22		8/1/2016	x	10	10	15	
23		8/2/2016	x	10	8	12	
24		8/3/2016	x	12	18	15	
25		8/4/2016					
26		8/5/2016	x	12	15	18	
27		8/8/2016	x	15	10	15	
28		8/9/2016					
29		8/10/2016	x	15	15	20	
30		8/11/2016	x	15	13	22	
31		8/12/2016	x	20	15	25	
32		8/15/2016	x	20	15	20	
33		8/16/2016	x	22	8	30	
34		8/17/2016					
35		8/18/2016	x	12	18	25	
36		8/19/2016	x	15	20	20	
37		8/22/2016					
38		8/23/2016	x	20	17	23	

‹ ›   Documentation   **Fitness Report**   Explanation of Formulas   ⊕

READY   AVERAGE: 8

Working with Date Functions

Excel has several functions that work with dates and times. **Date functions** insert or calculate dates and times. They are particularly useful in business workbooks that involve production schedules and calendar applications. Figure 3-27 describes some of the commonly used Date functions.

| Figure 3-27 | Date functions |

Function	Description
DATE(*year, month, day*)	Creates a date value for the date represented by the *year, month,* and *day* arguments
DAY(*date*)	Extracts the day of the month from *date*
MONTH(*date*)	Extracts the month number from *date* where 1=January, 2=February, and so forth
YEAR(*date*)	Extracts the year number from *date*
NETWORKDAYS(*start, end*[, *holidays*])	Calculates the number of whole working days between *start* and *end*; to exclude holidays, add the optional *holidays* argument containing a list of holiday dates to skip
WEEKDAY(*date*[, *return_type*])	Calculates the weekday from *date*, where 1=Sunday, 2=Monday, and so forth; to choose a different numbering scheme, set *return_type* to 1 (1=Sunday, 2=Monday, ...), 2 (1=Monday, 2=Tuesday, ...), or 3 (0=Monday, 1=Tuesday, ...)
WORKDAY(*start, days*[, *holidays*])	Returns the workday after *days* workdays have passed since the *start* date; to exclude holidays, add the optional *holidays* argument containing a list of holiday dates to skip
NOW( )	Returns the current date and time
TODAY( )	Returns the current date

© 2014 Cengage Learning

Displaying the Current Date with the TODAY function

Many workbooks include the current date. You can use the **TODAY function** to display the current date in a worksheet. The TODAY function has the following syntax:

=TODAY()

TIP

To display the current date and time, which is updated each time the workbook is reopened, use the NOW function.

Note that although the TODAY function doesn't have any arguments, you still must include the parentheses for the function to work. The date displayed by the TODAY function is updated automatically whenever you reopen the workbook or enter a new calculation.

Ken wants the Fitness Report worksheet to show the current date each time it is used or printed. You will use the TODAY function to display the current date in cell G2.

To display the current date with the TODAY function:

1. Select cell **G2**.

2. On the FORMULAS tab, in the Function Library group, click the **Date & Time** button to display the date and time functions.

3. Click **TODAY**. The Function Arguments dialog box opens and indicates that the TODAY function requires no arguments.

4. Click the **OK** button. The formula =TODAY() is entered in cell G2.

5. Verify that the current date is displayed in the cell.

6. Format the cell using the **Calculation** style.

Finding the Next Weekday with the WORKDAY function

Instead of using AutoFill to enter a series of dates in a range, you can use the WORKDAY function to fill in the remaining weekdays based on the start date you specify. The WORKDAY function displays the date of the weekday a specific number of weekdays past a starting date. The syntax of the WORKDAY function is

```
=WORKDAY(start, days[, holiday])
```

TIP

You can enter the dates to skip into worksheet cells, and then reference that range in the *holiday* argument of the WORKDAY function.

where *start* is a start date, *days* is the number of weekdays after *start*, and *holiday* is an optional list of dates to skip. If you do not include anything for the optional *holiday* argument, the WORKDAY function does not skip any days. For example, if cell A1 contains the date 11/4/2016, a Friday, the following formula displays the date 11/9/2016, a Wednesday that is three working days after 11/4/2016:

```
=WORKDAY(A1, 3)
```

Ken wants to automate the process of inserting the exercise dates. You will use the WORKDAY function to do this.

To insert the exercise dates using the WORKDAY function:

1. In cell **G7**, enter **8/1/2016** to specify the date the workouts will begin, and then format the cell using the **Input** cell style.

2. In cell **G8**, enter the formula **=F44** to display the date of the last scheduled workout, which is 8/31/2016 in this instance, and then format the cell using the **Calculation** cell style.

3. In cell **F22**, enter the formula **=G7** to replace the date with a reference to the start date you specified in cell G7. The cell still displays 8/1/2016.

4. Select cell **F23**, if necessary, and then click the **Insert Function** button _fx_ next to the formula bar. The Insert Function dialog box opens.

5. Type **working days** in the Search for a function box, and then click the **Go** button to find all of the functions related to working days.

6. In the Select a function box, click **WORKDAY** to select the function, and then click the **OK** button. The WORKDAY Function Arguments dialog box opens.

7. In the Start_date box, type the cell reference **F22** to specify that cell F22 contains the start date you want to use.

8. In the Days box, type **1** to specify the number of workdays after the date in cell F22 that you want the formula results to show. See Figure 3-28.

Figure 3-28   Function Arguments dialog box for the WORKDAY function

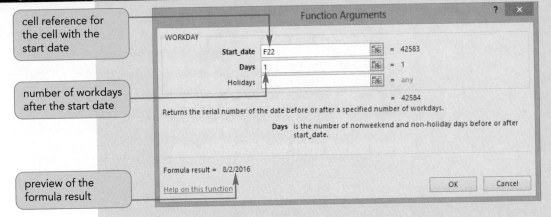

cell reference for the cell with the start date

number of workdays after the start date

preview of the formula result

TIP

To select a working day prior to the start date, enter a negative number rather than a positive number.

9. Click the **OK** button. Cell F23 contains the formula =WORKDAY(F22, 1) and displays the date 8/2/2016, which is the next workday after 8/1/2016.

You want to use the same formula to calculate the rest of the workout dates. You can use AutoFill to quickly repeat the formula.

10. Select cell **F23**, and then drag the fill handle down over the range **F23:F44** to copy the formula and enter the rest of the workdays in the month.

Because the copied formulas use relative references, each cell displays a date that is one workday after the date in the previous cell. The dates should not be different from the dates you entered previously using AutoFill.

11. Format the range **F22:F44** with the **Calculation** cell style to show that these dates are calculated by a formula rather than entered manually.

You will test that the formulas in the range F22:F44 are working correctly by entering a different start date.

12. In cell **G7**, enter **9/1/2016** as the new start date.

13. Review the dates in the range F22:F44, verifying that the workout dates start with 9/2/2016 in cell F23, continue with 9/5/2016 in cell F24, and end with 10/3/2016 in cell F44.

Trouble? If the workout dates do not end with 10/3/2016, compare the formula in cell F23 to the formula shown in Step 9, make any edits needed, and then repeat Step 10.

14. In cell **G7**, enter **8/1/2016** to return to the original start date.

INSIGHT

Selecting the Days in the Work Week

Different countries, regions, and even businesses might have different rules for what constitutes a workday. If you need to create a schedule that doesn't follow the standard U.S. business days (Monday through Friday), you can use the WORKDAY.INTL function to specify the days to use as the work week. The syntax of the WORKDAY.INTL function is:

```
=WORKDAY.INTL(start, days[, weekend=1, holidays])
```

The only difference between the syntax of the WORKDAY.INTL function and the syntax of the WORKDAY function is the optional *weekend* argument, which specifies the days of the week considered to be weekend or nonworking days. If you omit the *weekend* argument, weekends are considered to occur only on Saturday and Sunday. If you include the *weekend* argument, you enter one of the following numbers to specify the two days or the one day to consider as the weekend:

Weekend	Two-Day Weekend	Weekend	One-Day Weekend
1	Saturday, Sunday	11	Sunday
2	Sunday, Monday	12	Monday
3	Monday, Tuesday	13	Tuesday
…		…	
7	Friday, Saturday	17	Saturday

For example, a business that is open every day except Sunday would use a *weekend* value of 11 to indicate that only Sunday is considered a nonworking day, and a business that is closed on Monday and Tuesday would use a *weekend* value of 3 to specify a work week of Wednesday through Sunday. For other working week schedules, you can enter text to specify which days are workdays. See Excel Help for more information.

Counting Cells

Excel has two functions for counting cells—the COUNT function and the COUNTA function. The COUNT function tallies how many cells in a range contain numbers or dates (because they are stored as numeric values). The COUNT function does not count blank cells or cells that contain text. Its syntax is

```
COUNT(value1[, value2, value3, ...])
```

where *value1* is the first item or cell reference containing the numbers you want to count. The remaining *value* arguments are used primarily when you want to count numbers and dates in nonadjacent ranges. For example, the following function counts how many cells in the range A1:A10, the range C1:C5, and cell E5 contain numbers or dates:

```
COUNT(A1:A10, C1:C5, E5)
```

If you want to know how many cells contain entries—whether those entries are numbers, dates, or text—you use the COUNTA function, which tallies the nonblank cells in a range. The following is the syntax of the COUNTA function, which has the same arguments as the COUNT function:

```
COUNTA(value1[, value2, value3, ...])
```

Ken wants the Workout Summary to show the total number of scheduled workouts for the month, the number of attended workouts, and the number of missed workouts. You will use the COUNT function to count the total number of workout dates in the Workout Routine 5 table. Then, you will use the COUNTA function to count the number of workouts actually attended. Each attended workout is marked by an "x" in column G of the Workout Routine 5 table; missing workouts are left blank. Finally, you will enter a formula to calculate the missed workouts.

To count the scheduled, attended, and missed workouts:

▶ 1. In cell **G9**, enter the formula **=COUNT(F22:F44)**. Cell G9 displays 23, indicating that Ken scheduled 23 workouts for the month.

▶ 2. In cell **G10**, enter the formula **=COUNTA(G22:G44)**. Cell G10 displays 17, indicating that Daniel attended 17 of the 23 scheduled workouts.

▶ 3. In cell **G11**, enter the formula **=G9–G10** to calculate the difference between the number of scheduled workouts and the number of attended workouts. Cell G11 displays 6, which is the number of missed workouts.

▶ 4. Format the range **G9:G11** with the **Calculation** cell style.

▶ 5. Select cell **G10**. See Figure 3-29.

Figure 3-29   **Completed Workout Summary**

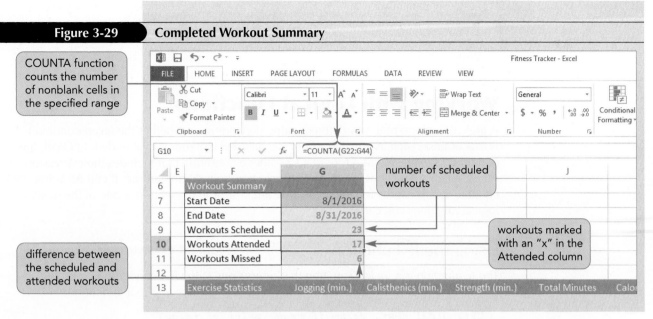

COUNTA function counts the number of nonblank cells in the specified range

number of scheduled workouts

workouts marked with an "x" in the Attended column

difference between the scheduled and attended workouts

It is important to understand the difference between the COUNT and COUNTA functions. For example, if you had used the COUNT function in cell G10 to tally the number of attended workouts, the result would have been 0 because the range G22:G44 contains no entries with numbers.

Like the COUNT function, many of Excel's statistical functions ignore cells that are blank or contain text. This can create unexpected results with calculated values if you are not careful. Figure 3-30 shows how some of the common summary statistics change when blank cells are used in place of zeroes.

Figure 3-30   **Calculations involving blank cells and zeroes**

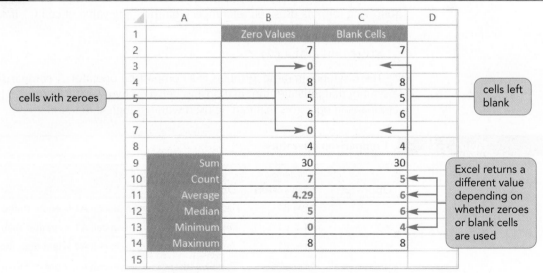

cells with zeroes

cells left blank

Excel returns a different value depending on whether zeroes or blank cells are used

Some of the fitness statistics for total exercise minutes and calories burned include the six workouts that Daniel missed. For example, the minimum exercise minutes and calories burned are both listed as 0 because the calculated values show up as 0 in the worksheet when the workout session was missed. Ken wants the summary statistics based on only the workouts actually attended. One way to exclude missed workouts is to delete the zeroes, leaving blank cells. However, Ken wants the worksheet to be user-friendly and not require anyone to double-check and edit entries for missed workouts. Instead of editing the worksheet, you can use a logical function to automatically replace zeroes with blanks for missed workouts.

Working with Logical Functions

A logical function returns a different value depending on whether the given condition is true or false, such as whether or not a scheduled workout was attended. In Excel, the condition is expressed as a formula. Consider a condition that includes the expression A5=3. If cell A5 is equal to 3, this expression and condition are true; if cell A5 is not equal to 3, this expression and condition are false. The IF function is one of the many logical functions you can use in Excel.

Using the IF Function

The IF function is a logical function that returns one value if a condition is true, and returns a different value if that condition is false. The syntax of the IF function is

    IF(logical_test, value_if_true, value_if_false)

where logical_test is a condition that is either true or false, value_if_true is the value returned by the function if the condition is true, and value_if_false is the value returned if the condition is false. The value can be a number, text, a date, or a cell reference. For example, the following formula tests whether the value in cell A1 is equal to the value in cell B1:

    =IF(A1=B1, 100, 50)

If the value in cell A1 equals the value in cell B1, the formula result is 100; otherwise, the formula result is 50.

In many cases, however, you will not use values directly in the IF function. The following formula uses cell references, returning the value of cell C1 if A1 equals B1; otherwise, it returns the value of cell C2:

    =IF(A1=B1, C1, C2)

The = symbol in these formulas is a comparison operator. A **comparison operator** is a symbol that indicates the relationship between two values. Figure 3-31 describes the comparison operators that can be used within a logical function.

Figure 3-31   **Comparison operators**

Operator	Expression	Description
=	A1 = B1	Tests whether the value in cell A1 is equal to the value in cell B1
>	A1 > B1	Tests whether the value in cell A1 is greater than the value in cell B1
<	A1 < B1	Tests whether the value in cell A1 is less than the value in cell B1
>=	A1 >= B1	Tests whether the value in cell A1 is greater than or equal to the value in cell B1
<=	A1 <= B1	Tests whether the value in cell A1 is less than or equal to the value in cell B1
<>	A1 <> B1	Tests whether the value in cell A1 is not equal to the value in cell B1

The IF function also works with text. For example, the following formula tests whether the value of cell A1 is equal to "yes":

```
=IF(A1="yes", "done", "restart")
```

If true (the value of cell A1 is equal to "yes"), the formula returns the text "done"; otherwise, it returns the text "restart". Notice that the text in the function is enclosed in quotation marks.

In addition, you can nest other functions inside an IF statement. The following formula first tests whether cell A5 is equal to the maximum of values within the range A1:A100:

```
=IF(A5=MAX(A1:A100), "Maximum", "")
```

If it is, the formula returns the text "Maximum"; otherwise, it returns no text.

In the Fitness Report worksheet, you need to rewrite the formulas that calculate the total minutes and total calories from each workout as IF functions that test whether Daniel actually attended the workout. Because every attended workout is marked with an "x" in column G, you can test whether the cell entry in column G is an "x". For example, the following formula in cell K22 is currently being used to calculate the total minutes from the first workout:

```
=SUM(H22:J22)
```

This formula can be revised to the following IF function, which first determines if cell G22 contains an "x" (indicating that the workout was attended), and then uses the SUM function to calculate the total minutes if there is an "x":

```
=IF(G22="x", SUM(H22:J22), "")
```

Otherwise, the formula displays nothing, leaving the cell blank.

You will use relative references in the revised formula so that you can copy it for the other workouts and total columns. You will create the formula with the IF function for the total minutes column now.

TIP

For the formula result to show no text, include opening and closing quotation marks with nothing between them.

To use an IF function to calculate total minutes for attended workouts:

▶ 1. Select cell **K22**, and then press the **Delete** key to clear the original formula from the cell.

▶ 2. Click the **Insert Function** button f_x next to the formula bar to open the Insert Function dialog box.

▶ 3. Type **if function** in the Search for a function box, and then press the **Enter** key. Functions that match your description appear in the Select a function box.

▶ 4. Click **IF** in the Select a function box, and then click the **OK** button to open the Function Arguments dialog box.

▶ 5. In the Logical_test box, type **G22="x"** as the expression that tests whether cell G22 is equal to x.

▶ 6. Press the **Tab** key to move the insertion point to the Value_if_true box, and then type **SUM(H22:J22)**. If cell G22 does contain an x (the logical test is true), the sum of the values in the range H22:J22 will be displayed in cell K22.

▶ 7. Press the **Tab** key to move the insertion point to the Value_if_false box, and then type **""** (opening and closing quotation marks). If cell G22 does not contain an x (the logical test is false), the cell will be left blank. See Figure 3-32.

Figure 3-32   **Function Arguments dialog box for the IF function**

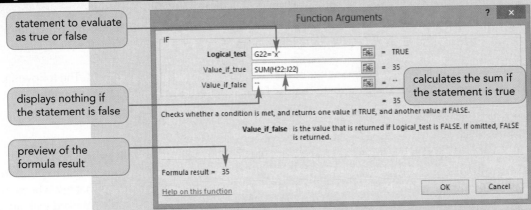

statement to evaluate
as true or false

displays nothing if
the statement is false

preview of the
formula result

calculates the sum if
the statement is true

8. Click the **OK** button. The formula =IF(G22="x", SUM(H22:J22), "") is entered into cell K22. The cell displays 35, which is the number of minutes Daniel spent exercising at that workout session.

You will copy the formula with the IF function to calculate the total minutes for the rest of the workouts.

9. Select cell **K22**, and then drag the fill handle down over the range **K22:K44** to copy the IF formula to the remaining cells in the column. The total number of minutes for each workout is recalculated so that the missed workouts in cells K25, K28, K34, K37, K39, and K40 are now left blank.

10. Select cell **K22**. The #VALUE! error value appears in columns L and M for each of the missed workouts because the current formulas cannot calculate calories burned when no total minutes are provided. See Figure 3-33.

Figure 3-33   **IF function excludes the total minutes for missed workouts**

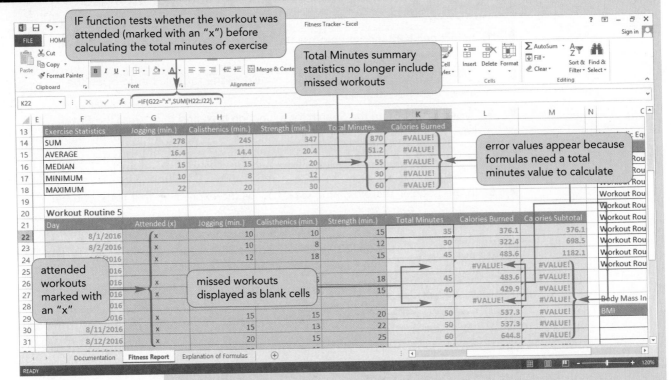

IF function tests whether the workout was attended (marked with an "x") before calculating the total minutes of exercise

Total Minutes summary statistics no longer include missed workouts

error values appear because formulas need a total minutes value to calculate

attended workouts marked with an "x"

missed workouts displayed as blank cells

Next, you will update the calories burned formulas so that they don't display the #VALUE! error value when a workout is missed. This requires another IF statement similar to the one you used to calculate total minutes. As with the total minutes calculation, any missed workout will display a blank cell for the calories burned in place of a 0. Rather than reentering the complete formula for calories burned, you can edit the existing formula, inserting the IF function.

To change the calories burned formulas to IF functions:

▶ **1.** Double-click cell **L22** to enter Edit mode.

▶ **2.** Press the **Home** key to move the insertion point to the beginning of the formula, and then press the → key to move the insertion point one space to the right, directly after = (the equal sign). You will begin the IF function after the equal sign.

▶ **3.** Type **IF(G22="x",** to insert the function name and the expression for the logical test.

▶ **4.** Press the **Ctrl+End** keys to move the insertion point to the end of the formula.

Make sure your formula matches the one shown here.

▶ **5.** Type **, "")** to enter the value if false and complete the IF function. The complete formula is now =IF(G22="x", $P$20*$C$11*K22/125.7143, "").

▶ **6.** Press the **Enter** key to exit Edit mode and make cell L23 active. Cell L22 still displays 376.1 because Ken did not miss the first workout.

You will use AutoFill to copy the IF function to the rest of the cells in the Calories Burned column.

▶ **7.** Select cell **L22**, and then drag the fill handle down over the range **L22:L44**. As shown in Figure 3-34, the missed workouts now display blank cells instead of zeroes, and the attended workouts show the same calculated values as earlier.

Figure 3-34   **IF function excludes the calories burned for missed workouts**

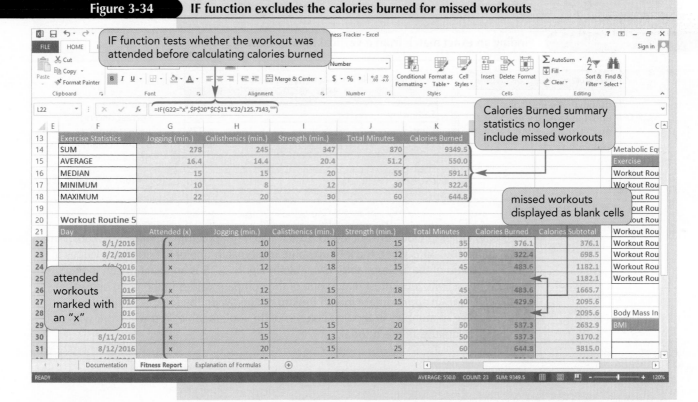

By excluding the missed workouts, Daniel's average exercise time increased from 37.8 minutes to 51.2 minutes, and the average calories burned increased to 550 calories. These averages more closely match the median values because zeroes were removed from the calculations. The minimum values for Total Minutes and Calories Burned now also reflect only attended workouts, changing from 0 (when they were based on a missed workout) to 30 minutes and 322.4 calories, respectively. These measures reflect the true results of the workouts Daniel attended.

Using a Lookup Function

Lookup functions find values in tables of data and insert them in another location in the worksheet such as cells or in formulas. For example, consider the active BMR calculated in cell C22, which adjusts the calculation of Daniel's metabolic rate to account for his activity level. The more active Daniel is, the more calories he can consume without gaining weight. The multiplying factors for each activity level (Sedentary, Light, Moderate, High, or Extreme) are stored in a table in the range O8:P12; you used the value in cell P8 to adjust Daniel's BMR value for his sedentary lifestyle. Instead of including a direct reference to one of the multiplying factors in the table, you can use a function to have Excel choose the multiplying factor that corresponds to the specified activity level.

The table that stores the data you want to retrieve is called a lookup table. A lookup table organizes numbers or text into categories. This particular lookup table organizes the BMR factors by activity levels, as shown in Figure 3-35. Every activity level category in the first column of the lookup table has a corresponding BMR factor in the second column of the table. This table is a vertical lookup table because the categories are arranged vertically. The entries in the first column of a vertical lookup table are referred to as the compare values because they are compared to the category you want to find (called the lookup value). When a match is found, the corresponding value in one of the subsequent columns is returned. For example, to find the return value for the Moderate lookup value, you look down the first column of the lookup table until you find the Moderate entry. Then, you move to the second column to locate the corresponding return value, which is 1.550, in this case.

Figure 3-35	Finding an exact match from a vertical lookup table

© 2014 Cengage Learning

Lookup tables can be constructed for exact match or approximate match lookups. An **exact match lookup** is when the lookup value must match one of the compare values in the first column of the lookup table. The table in Figure 3-35 is an exact match lookup because the activity level must match one of the compare values in the table or a value is not returned. An **approximate match lookup** occurs when the lookup value falls within a range of numbers in the first column of the lookup table. You will work with exact match lookups in this tutorial.

Finding an Exact Match with the VLOOKUP Function

To retrieve the return value from a vertical lookup table, you use the VLOOKUP function. The syntax of the VLOOKUP function is

```
VLOOKUP(lookup_value, table_array, col_index_num[, range_lookup=TRUE])
```

where *lookup_value* is the compare value to find in the first column of the lookup table, *table_array* is the range reference to the lookup table, and *col_index_num* is the number of the column in the lookup table that contains the return value. Keep in mind that *col_index_num* refers to the number of the column within the lookup table, not the worksheet column. For example, *col_index_num* 2 refers to the second column of the table, *col_index_num* 3 refers to the third column of the table, and so forth. Finally, *range_lookup* is an optional argument that specifies whether the compare values are an exact match or a range of values (for an approximate match). For an exact match, you set the *range_lookup* value to FALSE. For approximate match lookups, you set the *range_lookup* value to TRUE or you can omit it because its default value is TRUE.

For example, the following formula performs an exact match lookup to find the BMR factor for an Extreme activity level based on the values from the lookup table in the range O8:P12 (shown earlier in Figure 3-35):

```
=VLOOKUP("Extreme", O8:P12, 2, FALSE)
```

The *col_index_num* is 2 because the BMR factors are in the second column of the table. The *range_lookup* is FALSE because this is an exact match. The function looks through the compare values in the first column of the table to locate the "Extreme" entry. When the exact entry is found, the function returns the corresponding value in the second column of the table, which in this case is 1.900.

Daniel's activity level in cell C9 is entered as Sedentary, which has a BMR factor of 1.2. The following active BMR formula you entered earlier calculated that Daniel can consume about 2224 calories per day and maintain his current weight:

```
=P8*C21
```

In this formula, P8 references the Sedentary BMR value in cell P8 and C21 references Daniel's base or resting metabolic rate. To have Excel look up the BMR value, you need to replace the P8 cell reference with a VLOOKUP function, as follows:

```
=VLOOKUP(C9, O8:P12, 2, FALSE)*C21
```

In this formula, C9 contains Daniel's activity level (Sedentary), O8:P12 references the lookup table, 2 specifies the table column to find the BMR factors, and FALSE indicates that this is an exact match lookup. You will enter this formula into the worksheet now.

To use the VLOOKUP function to calculate Daniel's active BMR:

1. Select cell **C22**, and then press the **Delete** key to clear the formula currently in the cell.

2. On the ribbon, click the **FORMULAS** tab. Because VLOOKUP has several arguments to manage, you will enter the function using the Function Arguments dialog box.

3. In the Function Library group, click **Lookup & Reference** to display a list of functions, and then click **VLOOKUP**. The Function Arguments dialog box opens.

4. With the insertion point in the Lookup_value box, click cell **C9** in the worksheet to enter that cell reference as the location containing the value to look up in the first column of the lookup table.

5. Press the **Tab** key to move the insertion point into the Table_array box, and then select the range **O8:P12**, which contains the vertical lookup table in the worksheet.

6. Press the **Tab** key to move the insertion point to the Col_index_num box, and then type **2** to return a value from the second column of the lookup table.

7. Press the **Tab** key to move the insertion point to the Range_lookup box, and then type **FALSE** to specify an exact match lookup. The dialog box shows the resulting value of the function with these arguments, which in this case is 1.2. See Figure 3-36.

Figure 3-36   Function Arguments dialog box for the VLOOKUP function

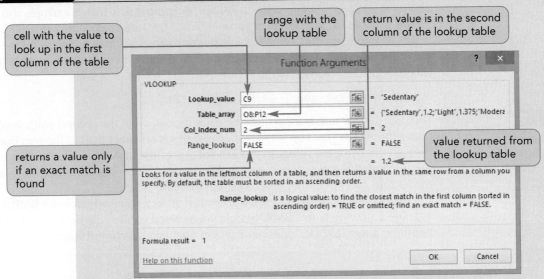

cell with the value to look up in the first column of the table

range with the lookup table

return value is in the second column of the lookup table

returns a value only if an exact match is found

value returned from the lookup table

8. Click the **OK** button to close the dialog box.

9. Double-click cell **C22** to enter Edit mode, press the **Ctrl+End** keys to move the insertion point to the end of the formula, type ***C21** to complete the formula, and then press the **Enter** key. The completed formula in cell C22 is =VLOOKUP(C9,O8:P12,2,FALSE)*C21, resulting in an active BMR of 2224 calories per day for a Sedentary activity level.

You will change the activity level to ensure that the formula works correctly.

10. In cell **C9**, enter **Moderate** to change the activity level from Sedentary. The active BMR value changes to 2872 because the VLOOKUP function returns a 1.55 BMR factor from the lookup table.

Ken decides that Light is a more accurate description of Daniel's activity level.

11. In cell **C9**, enter **Light** as the activity level. At that activity level, the active BMR changes to 2548. With a Light activity level, Daniel can consume about 2548 calories per day and maintain his current weight.

12. Select cell **C22** to view the formula. See Figure 3-37.

TIP

Exact matches are not case sensitive, so the lookup values Light, light, and LIGHT are considered to be the same.

| Figure 3-37 | VLOOKUP function calculates the active BMR |

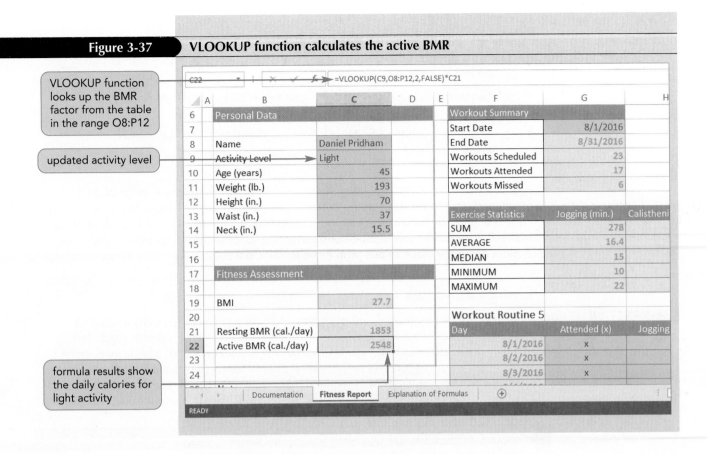

VLOOKUP function looks up the BMR factor from the table in the range O8:P12

updated activity level

formula results show the daily calories for light activity

Performing What-If Analysis

A **what-if analysis** lets you explore the impact that changing input values has on the calculated values in the workbook. For example, Ken could perform a what-if analysis to determine how many pounds Daniel needs to lose to reach a more healthy weight. Current fitness standards suggest that a body mass index between 18.5 and 24.9 is considered to be within the "normal" classification. Daniel's body mass index is 27.7, which is rated as overweight. So Ken wants to know how many pounds Daniel needs to lose to reduce his body mass index to 24.9.

Using Trial and Error

One way to perform a what-if analysis is by changing one or more of the input values to see how they affect the calculated results. This **trial-and-error method** requires some guesswork as you estimate which values to change and by how much. In this case, Ken wants you to find out the weight at which Daniel would reach a BMI of 24.9. You'll start by checking the resulting body mass index if Daniel were to lose 10 pounds, reducing his weight to 183 pounds.

To perform a what-if analysis by trial and error:

▶ 1. In cell **C11**, change the weight from 193 pounds to **183** pounds. Daniel's body mass index decreases from 27.7 to 26.3, as shown in cell C19. At this weight, he is still considered overweight.

2. In cell **C11**, enter **163** pounds. At this weight, Daniel's BMI shown in cell C19 is 23.4. So losing 30 pounds is more than enough to classify Daniel's body weight as normal.

Ken wants to know if Daniel can lose fewer than 30 pounds to reach that classification.

3. In cell **C11**, enter **168** pounds. At this weight, Daniel's BMI value is 24.1, which is still within the normal classification, but not exactly equal to 24.9.

If you want to find the exact weight that will result in a body mass index of 24.9, you would have to continue trying different weight values as you close in on the correct weight. This is why the method is called "trial and error." For some calculations, trial and error can be a very time-consuming way to locate the exact input value. A more direct approach to this problem is to use Goal Seek.

Using Goal Seek

Goal Seek automates the trial-and-error process by allowing you to specify a value for a calculated item, which Excel uses to determine the input value needed to reach that goal. In this case, because Ken wants to know how Daniel can reach a body mass index of exactly 24.9 (the upper level of the normal classification), the question that Goal Seek answers is: "What weight value is required to reach that goal?" Goal Seek starts by setting the calculated value and works backward to determine the correct input value.

REFERENCE

Performing What-If Analysis and Goal Seek

To perform a what-if analysis by trial and error:
- Change the value of a worksheet cell (the input cell).
- Observe its impact on one or more calculated cells (the result cells).
- Repeat until the desired results are achieved.

To perform a what-if analysis using Goal Seek:
- On the DATA tab, in the Data Tools group, click the What-If Analysis button, and then click Goal Seek.
- Select the result cell in the Set cell box, and then specify its value (goal) in the To value box.
- In the By changing cell box, specify the input cell.
- Click the OK button. The value of the input cell changes to set the value of the result cell.

You will use Goal Seek to find the weight that will result in Daniel's BMI reaching exactly 24.9.

To use Goal Seek to find a weight resulting in a 24.9 BMI:

1. On the ribbon, click the **DATA** tab.

2. In the Data Tools group, click the **What-If Analysis** button, and then click **Goal Seek**. The Goal Seek dialog box opens.

3. Make sure the value in the Set cell box is selected, and then click cell **C19** in the Fitness Report worksheet. The absolute cell reference $C$19 appears in the Set cell box. The set cell is the calculated value you want Goal Seek to change to meet your goal.

4. Press the **Tab** key to move the insertion point to the To value box, and then type **24.9**. This indicates that you want Goal Seek to set this value to 24.9 (the highest body mass index in the normal classification).

5. Press the **Tab** key to move the insertion point to the By changing cell box. There are often various input values you can change to meet a goal. In this case, you want to change the weight value in cell C11.

6. Click cell **C11**. The absolute reference $C$11 appears in the By changing cell box. See Figure 3-38.

Figure 3-38   **Goal Seek dialog box**

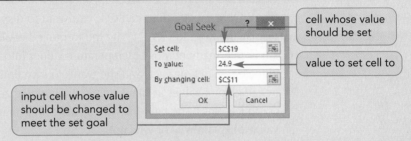

- cell whose value should be set
- value to set cell to
- input cell whose value should be changed to meet the set goal

7. Click the **OK** button. The Goal Seek dialog box closes, and the Goal Seek Status dialog box opens, indicating that Goal Seek found a solution.

8. Click the **OK** button. A weight value of about 173 pounds is displayed in cell C11. Daniel would need to lose roughly 20 pounds, reducing his weight to 173 pounds to reach a weight within the normal classification for BMI. See Figure 3-39.

Figure 3-39   **Target weight determined by Goal Seek**

	A	B	C	D	E	F	G	H
6		Personal Data				Workout Summary		
7						Start Date	8/1/2016	
8		Name	Daniel Pridham			End Date	8/31/2016	
9		Activity Level	Light			Workouts Scheduled	23	
10		Age (years)	45			Workouts Attended	17	
11		Weight (lb.)	173.5561878			Workouts Missed	6	
12		Height (in.)	70					
13		Waist (in.)	37			Exercise Statistics	Jogging (min.)	Calistheni
14		Neck (in.)	15.5			SUM	278	
15						AVERAGE	16.4	
16						MEDIAN	15	
17		Fitness Assessment				MINIMUM	10	
18						MAXIMUM	22	
19		BMI	24.9					
20						Workout Routine 5		
21		Resting BMR (cal./day)	1732			Day	Attended (x)	Jogging
22		Active BMR (cal./day)	2382			8/1/2016	x	
23						8/2/2016	x	
24						8/3/2016	x	

- solution weight
- desired BMI

Documentation   **Fitness Report**   Explanation of Formulas   (+)

READY

9. Save and close the workbook.

Ken appreciates all of the work you have done in developing the Fitness Tracker workbook. He will use this workbook as a model for all of his other clients at Fit Fathers.

Session 3.2 Quick Check

1. The first three values in a selected series are 3, 6, and 9. What are the next three values that will be inserted by AutoFill?
2. Write a formula to display the current date.
3. Write a formula to find the date four workdays after the date value stored in cell B10. There are no holidays.
4. Explain the difference between the COUNT function and the COUNTA function.
5. If cell Q3 is greater than cell Q4, you want to display the text "OK"; otherwise, display the text "RETRY". Write the formula that accomplishes this.
6. Jan is entering hundreds of temperature values into an Excel worksheet for a climate research project, and she wants to save time on data entry by leaving freezing point values as blanks rather than typing zeroes. Will this cause complications if she later tries to calculate an average temperature from her data values? Explain why or why not.
7. Provide the formula to perform an exact match lookup with the lookup value from cell G5 using a lookup table located in the range A1:F50. Return the value from the third column of the table.
8. What is the difference between a what-if analysis by trial and error and by Goal Seek?

ASSESS

PRACTICE

Review Assignments

Data File needed for the Review Assignments: Mothers.xlsx

Ken and his wife, Sally, are expanding the business, changing its name to Fit Fathers and Mothers Inc., and adding fitness classes for mothers with a special emphasis on pregnant women. The fitness equations for women are different from those for men. Ken and Sally want you to create a workbook similar to the one you created for fathers, but focused on the fitness needs of women. Sally also wants you to calculate the total fat burned in the course of completing the workout schedule. She has already designed much of the workbook's contents, but she needs you to add the formulas and functions. Complete the following:

1. Open the **Mothers** workbook located in the Excel3 ▸ Review folder included with your Data Files, and then save the workbook as **Mothers Fitness** in the location specified by your instructor.

2. In the Documentation sheet, enter your name and the date.

3. Go to the Fitness Analysis worksheet. In the range C8:C15, enter the personal data for **Dorothy Young**. Her activity level is **Moderate**, she is **38** years old, **152** pounds, **64** inches tall, with a **33**-inch waist, **35**-inch hips, and a **14**-inch neck.

4. In cell C20, enter a formula to calculate Dorothy's body mass index based on the equation

    $BMI = 703w/h^2$

    where w is the weight in pounds and h is the height in inches. Display the formula results with one decimal place.

5. In cell C22, enter a formula to calculate the resting metabolism rate for women based on the equation

    $BMR = 4.338w + 4.698h - 4.68a + 655$

    where w is the weight in pounds, h is the height in inches, and a is the age in years. Display the formula results with no decimal places.

6. In cell C23, enter a formula using the VLOOKUP function to calculate the active BMR based on the equation

    Active BMR = *Activity Factor* × *BMR*

    where *Activity Factor* is an exact match lookup for the value in the range O8:Q12 that corresponds to the activity level entered in cell C9, and *BMR* is the value in cell C22. Display the formula results with no decimal places.

7. In cell K22, enter a formula using an IF function to calculate the total minutes for the first workout that displays a blank cell if Dorothy did not attend a workout that day.

8. Use AuotFill to copy the formula you entered in cell K22 to the range K23:K44 to calculate the total minutes for each workout.

9. In cell L22, enter a formula to calculate the calories burned at the first workout based on the equation

    $$Calories = \frac{METS \times w \times t}{125.7143}$$

    where *METS* is the metabolic factor for the exercise, w is the client's weight, and t is the exercise time. Use the METS value located in cell P19, the weight value located in cell C11, and the time value located in the corresponding cell in column K. Be sure to use an absolute reference for both weight and METS.

10. Edit the formula you entered in cell L22 to be included as part of an IF function that returns a blank cell if Dorothy did not attend the workout that day. Display the formula results with one decimal place.

11. Use AutoFill to copy the formula you entered in cell L22 to the range L23:L44 to calculate the calories burned at each workout.

12. In the range M22:M44, use the Quick Analysis tool to calculate a column running total of the calories burned in the range L22:L44. Display the formula results with two decimal places.

13. Complete the exercise statistics in the range G14:K18 by entering formulas calculating the sum, average, median, maximum, and minimum values of the exercise times, and calories burned values from the workout log. Display the averages and the calories burned statistics with one decimal place.

14. In cell G2, use a function to display the current date whenever the workbook is opened.

15. In cell F22, enter a formula to reference the start date entered in cell G7.

16. In the range F23:F44, use a function to increase the value of the date in the previous row by 1 workday. Format the formula results with the Short Date format.

17. In cell G8, enter a formula to display the ending date entered in cell F44.

18. In cell G9, enter a formula to count the number of days included in the range F22:F44.

19. In cell G10, enter a formula to count the number of attended workouts as indicated in the range G22:G44.

20. In cell G11, enter a formula to calculate the difference between the number of scheduled workouts and the number of attended workouts. Save the workbook.

21. Use Goal Seek to determine the weight Dorothy must attain to reach a body mass index of 22.

22. Save the revised workbook as **Mothers Fitness Goal**, and then close the workbook.

Case Problem 1

APPLY

Data File needed for this Case Problem: Hernandez.xlsx

Hernandez Family Juan and Olivia Hernandez are a recently married couple in Fort Wayne, Indiana. Juan is currently in graduate school and Olivia is the manager at a local bakery. They want to use Excel to help manage their family budget, but they need help setting up the formulas and functions to project their monthly expenses and help them meet their financial goals. Complete the following:

1. Open the **Hernandez** workbook located in the Excel3 ▶ Case1 folder included with your Data Files, and then save the workbook as **Hernandez Budget** in the location specified by your instructor.

2. In the Documentation sheet, enter your name and the date.

3. Go to the Budget worksheet. In cell B7, calculate the couple's total monthly income.

4. In row 23, use AutoFill to replace the numbers 1 through 12 with the month abbreviations **Jan** through **Dec**.

5. In rows 24 and 25, enter the couple's monthly income by referencing the monthly income estimates in cells B5 and B6. Use an absolute cell reference.

6. In row 26, calculate the couple's monthly income.

7. In row 37, enter formulas to calculate the total estimated expenses for each month.

8. In row 38, calculate each month's net cash flow, which is equal to the total income minus the total expenses.

9. In row 39, calculate the running total of the net cash flow so that Olivia and Juan can see how their net cash flow changes as the year progresses.

10. In the range B10:B19, calculate the average monthly expenses by category based on the values previously entered in rows 27 through 36.

11. In cell B20, calculate the total average monthly expenses.

12. The couple currently has $7,350 in their savings account. Each month the couple will either take money out of their savings account or deposit money. In row 41, calculate the end-of-month balance in their savings account by adding the value in cell E5 to the running total values of the net cash flow in row 39. Use an absolute cell reference for cell E5.

13. In cell E6, enter a formula to display the value of the savings balance at the end of December.

14. Juan and Olivia would like to have $15,000 in their savings account by the end of the year. Olivia is planning to ask for a raise at her job. Use Goal Seek to determine the value of cell B6 that will achieve a final savings balance of $15,000.

15. Save and close the workbook.

CHALLENGE

Case Problem 2

Data File needed for this Case Problem: Econ.xlsx

Introduction to Economics 102   Alice Keyes teaches Introduction to Economics 102 at Mountain View Business School in Huntington, West Virginia. She wants to use Excel to track the grades from her class. Alice has already entered the homework, quiz, and final exam scores for all of her students in a workbook, and she has asked you to set up the formulas and functions for her.

You will calculate each student's final average based on his or her homework score, quiz scores, and final exam. Homework counts for 20 percent of the student's final grade. The first two quizzes count for 10 percent each. The second two quizzes count for 15 percent each. The final exam counts for 30 percent of the final grade.

You will also calculate each student's rank in the class. The rank will display which student placed first in terms of his or her overall score, which student placed second, and so forth. Ranks are calculated using the function

```
RANK(number, ref, [order=0])
```

where *number* is the value to be ranked, *ref* is a reference to the cell range containing the values against which the ranking is done, and *order* is an optional argument that specifies whether to rank in descending order or ascending order. The default *order* value is 0 to rank the values in descending order.

Finally, you will create formulas that will look up information on a particular student based on that student's ID so Alice doesn't have to scroll through the complete class roster to find a particular student. Complete the following:

1. Open the **Econ** workbook located in the Excel3 ▶ Case2 folder included with your Data Files, and then save the workbook as **Econ Grades** in the location specified by your instructor.

2. In the Documentation sheet, enter your name and the date.

3. Go to the Grade Book worksheet. In cell B5, count the number of student IDs in the range A22:A57.

⊕ **Explore** 4. Cells C15 through H15 contain the weights assigned to each assignment, quiz, or exam. In cell J22, calculate the weighted average of the first student's scores by entering a formula that multiplies each score by its corresponding weight and adds the resulting products.

5. Edit the formula in cell J22, changing the references to the weights in cells C15 through H15 from relative references to absolute references.

6. Use AutoFill to copy the formula from cell J22 into the range J23:J57.

⊕ **Explore** 7. In cell K22, use the RANK function to calculate how the first student compares to the other students in the class. Use the weighted average from cell J22 for the *number* argument and the range of weighted averages in the cell range $J$22:$J$57 for the *ref* argument. You do not need to specify a value for the *order* argument.

8. Use AutoFill to copy the formula you entered in cell K22 into the range K23:K57.

9. In the range C16:H18, calculate the class average, minimum, and maximum for each of the six grading components (homework, quizzes, and final exam).

10. In cell B8, enter the student ID **14858**.

⊕ **Explore** 11. Using the VLOOKUP function with an exact match and the student data table in the range A22:K57, retrieve the first name, last name, weighted average, and class rank for student 14858 in the range B9:B12. Use an absolute reference to the lookup table. Note that the first name is found in the third column of the student data table, the last name is found in the second column, the weighted average is found in the tenth column, and the class rank is found in the eleventh column.

12. Brenda Dunford missed the final exam and will be taking a make-up exam. She wants to know what score she would need on the final exam to achieve an overall weighted average of 90. Use Goal Seek to calculate what final exam score Brenda needs to result in a weighted average of 90.

13. Save and close the workbook.

Case Problem 3

Data File needed for this Case Problem: Homes.xlsx

Homes of Dreams Larry Helt is a carpenter and a woodcrafter in Coventry, Rhode Island, who loves to design and build custom dollhouses. He started his business, Homes of Dreams, a few years ago and it has expanded into a very profitable sideline to his ongoing carpentry work. Larry wants to create a shipping form that will calculate the cost for the purchased items, including taxes, shipping, and handling. Larry already designed the worksheet, which includes a table of shipping rates, shipping surcharges, and items sold by Homes of Dreams. He asks you to complete the worksheet. Complete the following:

1. Open the **Homes** workbook located in the Excel3 ▸ Case3 folder included with your Data Files, and then save the workbook as **Homes of Dreams** in the location specified by your instructor.

2. In the Documentation sheet, enter your name and the date.

3. Go to the Order Form worksheet.

4. In cell B21, enter the Item ID **DH007**.

5. In cell C21, enter the VLOOKUP function with an exact match to return the name of the item referenced in cell B21. Reference the lookup table in the range M4:O50 using an absolute cell reference. Return the value from the second column of the table.

6. In cell E21, enter the VLOOKUP function with an exact match to return the price of the item referenced in cell B21. Use an absolute reference to the lookup table in the range M4:O50. Return the value from the third column of the table.

7. In cell F21, enter **1** as the quantity of the item ordered.

8. In cell G21, calculate the price of the item multiplied by the quantity ordered.

⊕ **Explore** 9. Revise your formulas in cells C21, E21, and G21, nesting them within an IF formula. For each cell, test whether the value of cell B21 is not equal to "" (a blank). If it is not, return the value of the VLOOKUP function in cells C21 and E21 and the calculated value in cell G21. Otherwise, those cells should return a blank ("") value.

10. Use AutoFill to copy the formulas in cells C21, E21, and G21 through row 30 in the order items table.

11. In row 22, enter **BD002** as the Item ID and **3** as the quantity of items ordered. Verify that the formulas you created automatically enter the name, price, and charge for the item.

12. In rows 23 through 25, enter **1** order for item **BH003**, **1** order for item **DR002**, and **1** order for item **KR009**.

13. In cell G32, calculate the sum of the item charges from all possible orders.

14. In cell G33, calculate the sales tax on the order, which is equal to the subtotal multiplied by the tax rate (entered in cell J9).

15. In cell C15, enter a function to insert the current date whenever the workbook is opened.

16. In cell C16, enter **3 Day** as the type of delivery for this order.

17. In cell C17, calculate the number of working days it will take to ship the order by inserting a VLOOKUP function using an exact match lookup. Use the delivery type in cell C16 as the lookup value, and use the shipping data in the range I4:K7 as the lookup table. Return the value from the third column of the table.

✛ **Explore** 18. In cell C18, estimate the date of delivery. Use cell C15 as the start date and cell C17 as the number of working days after the start date.

✛ **Explore** 19. The shipping and handling fee is based on the delivery method (Standard, 3 Day, 2 Day, or Overnight). In cell G34, calculate the shipping and handling fee for the order using an exact match lookup with the data in the range I4:J7. Use the delivery method specified in cell C16 to find the corresponding shipping and handling fee in the Delivery table.

20. In cell G36, calculate the sum of the merchandise subtotal, sales tax, and shipping and handling fee.

21. Save the workbook, and then delete the item IDs and quantities from the order table.

22. Save the workbook as **Homes of Dreams 2**, calculate the cost of ordering 1 of item BD001 using overnight delivery, and then save the workbook.

23. Save the workbook as **Homes of Dreams 3**, and then delete the item IDs and quantities from the order table. Calculate the cost of ordering 1 of item KR001, 2 of item BH004, and 1 of item DR001 using standard delivery. Save and close the workbook.

Case Problem 4

TROUBLESHOOT

Data File needed for this Case Problem: Quality.xlsx

Karleton Manufacturing Carmen Garza is a quality control manager at Karleton Manufacturing, a manufacturing plant located in Trotwood, Ohio. One project that Carmen oversees is the manufacture of tin cans for a major food company. The can widths must be consistent. To compensate for the fact that metal working tools tend to wear down during the day, the pressure behind the tools is increased as the blades become worn. Quality control technicians monitor the process to check that it remains "in control" creating cans whose widths are neither too narrow nor too wide. Carmen has recorded the widths of four cans from 39 batches in an Excel workbook that she wants to use to determine whether the process is "in control." One standard for determining whether a process is "in control" is whether the average value from a process batch falls within the lower and upper control limits. The workbook itself is in need of quality control as some of the formulas are not calculating correctly. You will fix these and then enter the remainder of the formulas needed in the worksheet. Complete the following:

1. Open the **Quality** workbook located in the Excel3 ▸ Case4 folder included with your Data Files, and then save the workbook as **Quality Control Analysis** in the location specified by your instructor.

2. In the Documentation sheet, enter your name and the date.

3. In the Quality Control worksheet, use AutoFill with the value in cell A7 and fill the series of batch numbers from B-1 to B-39 into the range A7:A45.

⚙ **Troubleshoot** 4. In the Quality Control worksheet, cells M3 and M4 display the #NAME? error value instead of the averages. Make the necessary changes to correct the formulas.

⚙ **Troubleshoot** 5. The formulas in the range H7:H45 are supposed to calculate the range of values (maximum minus minimum) within each batch. However, the formula results display 6.2 for every batch. Make the necessary changes in the formulas to fix the problem.

⚙ **Troubleshoot** 6. The formulas in the range I7:I45 are supposed to calculate the average width of the four cans tested in each batch. Unfortunately, the formulas' results don't equal the average widths. Make the necessary changes in the formulas to fix the problem.

7. In cell J7, calculate the lower control limit for the first batch based on the equation

$LCL = XBAR - A2 \times RBAR$

where LCL is the lower and upper control limits, $XBAR$ is the average value from all batches, $RBAR$ is the average range from all batches, and $A2$ is a correction factor that depends on the sample size of the batch. In this case, use the $XBAR$ value from cell M3 and the $RBAR$ value from cell M4. Determine the $A2$ value using an exact match lookup with the sample size in cell G7 as the reference value, and the second column from the table in the range O7:P30 as the return value.

8. AutoFill the lower control limit formula from cell J7 into the rest of the LCL column in the Control Limits table. Check to make sure your formulas were properly copied and that they still reference the correct cells.

9. In cell K7, calculate the upper control limit for the first batch based on the equation

   $UCL=XBAR+A2 \times RBAR$

   where UCL is the upper control limit. Copy your formula into the rest of the UCL column in the Control Limits table.

10. In cell L7, indicate whether the B-1 batch process is "in control low" by testing whether the batch's average is less than its LCL value. If it is, display "NO"; otherwise, display a blank cell.

11. In cell M7, indicate whether the B-1 batch process is "in control high" by testing whether the batch's average is greater than its UCL value. If it is, display "NO"; otherwise, display a blank cell.

12. Fill the in control low and in control high formulas for the rest of the batches.

13. Add conditional formatting to the range L7:M45 so that cells displaying "NO" are formatted in dark red text on a light red background.

⚙ **Troubleshoot** 14. The computer program that recorded the width values entered a missing width value as a 0 instead of leaving the cells blank. This affects the calculations about sample size and which batches are in control. Fix this in the data set and any formulas so that the worksheet accurately indicates which batches are not in control on the low side or not in control on the high side.

15. Save and close the workbook.

OBJECTIVES

Session 4.1
- Use the PMT function to calculate a loan payment
- Create an embedded pie chart
- Apply styles to a chart
- Add data labels to a pie chart
- Format a chart legend
- Create a clustered column chart
- Create a stacked column chart

Session 4.2
- Create a line chart
- Create a combination chart
- Format chart elements
- Modify the chart's data source
- Add sparklines to a worksheet
- Format cells with data bars
- Insert a watermark

EXCEL

Analyzing and Charting Financial Data

Presenting Data for a Business Plan

Case | *Levitt Winery*

Bob and Carol Levitt want to establish a new winery in Northern Michigan near the town of Traverse City. After many years of working as a winemaker for other wineries, Bob is eager to strike out on his own. Carol will handle the business and finances side of the business, building on her experience managing other companies.

To establish Levitt Winery, Bob and Carol need to borrow money to supplement their personal funds. Bob and Carol are in the process of applying for a business loan. They plan to use this money to help cover the startup costs for their winery. As part of the business loan application, Bob and Carol need to develop a 10-year business plan. They have analyzed the market and made reasonable projections for future production, expenses, and revenue. This information is compiled in an Excel workbook.

Because they are providing a lot of detailed information, Bob and Carol want to include charts in their Excel workbook to make this information easy to read and interpret. Before you create the financial charts that Bob and Carol need for their workbook, you will complete the contents of this worksheet by calculating the cost of the business loan they will need to get started.

STARTING DATA FILES

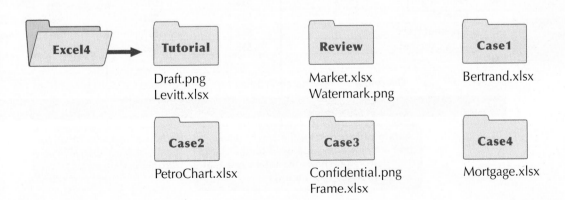

Excel4 → Tutorial
Draft.png
Levitt.xlsx

Review
Market.xlsx
Watermark.png

Case1
Bertrand.xlsx

Case2
PetroChart.xlsx

Case3
Confidential.png
Frame.xlsx

Case4
Mortgage.xlsx

Session 4.1 Visual Overview:

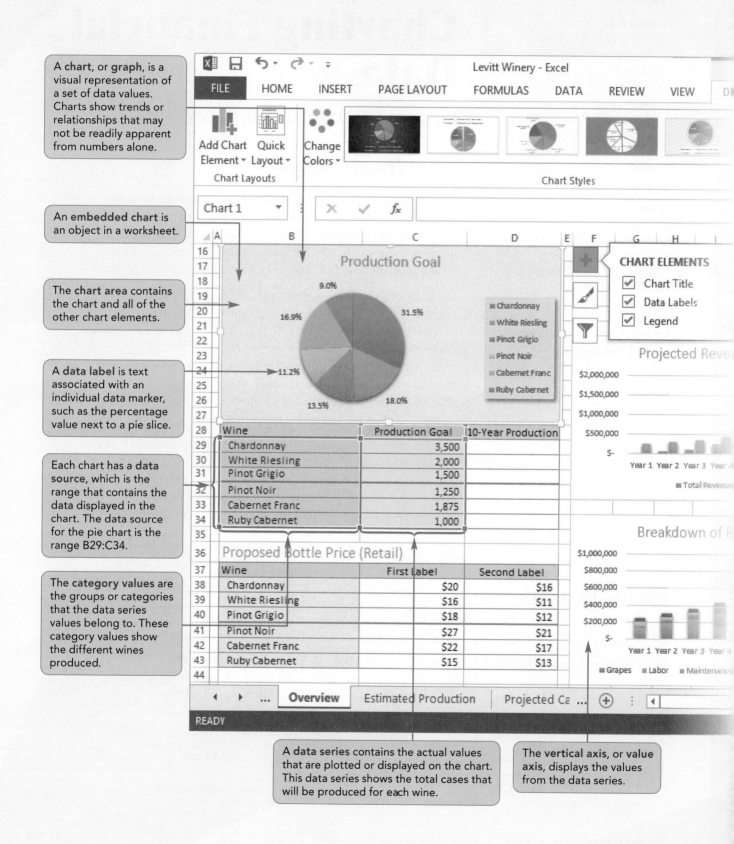

A **chart**, or **graph**, is a visual representation of a set of data values. Charts show trends or relationships that may not be readily apparent from numbers alone.

An **embedded chart** is an object in a worksheet.

The **chart area** contains the chart and all of the other chart elements.

A **data label** is text associated with an individual data marker, such as the percentage value next to a pie slice.

Each chart has a **data source**, which is the range that contains the data displayed in the chart. The data source for the pie chart is the range B29:C34.

The **category values** are the groups or categories that the data series values belong to. These category values show the different wines produced.

A **data series** contains the actual values that are plotted or displayed on the chart. This data series shows the total cases that will be produced for each wine.

The **vertical axis**, or **value axis**, displays the values from the data series.

Levitt Winery - Excel

FILE   HOME   INSERT   PAGE LAYOUT   FORMULAS   DATA   REVIEW   VIEW

Add Chart Element ▾   Quick Layout ▾   Change Colors ▾

Chart Layouts

Chart Styles

Chart 1

Production Goal

9.0%
31.5%
16.9%
11.2%
13.5%   18.0%

CHART ELEMENTS
☑ Chart Title
☑ Data Labels
☑ Legend

■ Chardonnay
■ White Riesling
■ Pinot Grigio
■ Pinot Noir
■ Cabernet Franc
■ Ruby Cabernet

Projected Reven

Wine	Production Goal	10-Year Production
Chardonnay	3,500	
White Riesling	2,000	
Pinot Grigio	1,500	
Pinot Noir	1,250	
Cabernet Franc	1,875	
Ruby Cabernet	1,000	

Proposed Bottle Price (Retail)

Wine	First Label	Second Label
Chardonnay	$20	$16
White Riesling	$16	$11
Pinot Grigio	$18	$12
Pinot Noir	$27	$21
Cabernet Franc	$22	$17
Ruby Cabernet	$15	$13

$2,000,000
$1,500,000
$1,000,000
$500,000
$-

Year 1 Year 2 Year 3 Year 4

■ Total Revenue

Breakdown of B

$1,000,000
$800,000
$600,000
$400,000
$200,000
$-

Year 1 Year 2 Year 3 Year 4

■ Grapes ■ Labor ■ Maintenance

◀ ▶ ... Overview   Estimated Production   Projected Ca ... ⊕

READY

Chart Elements

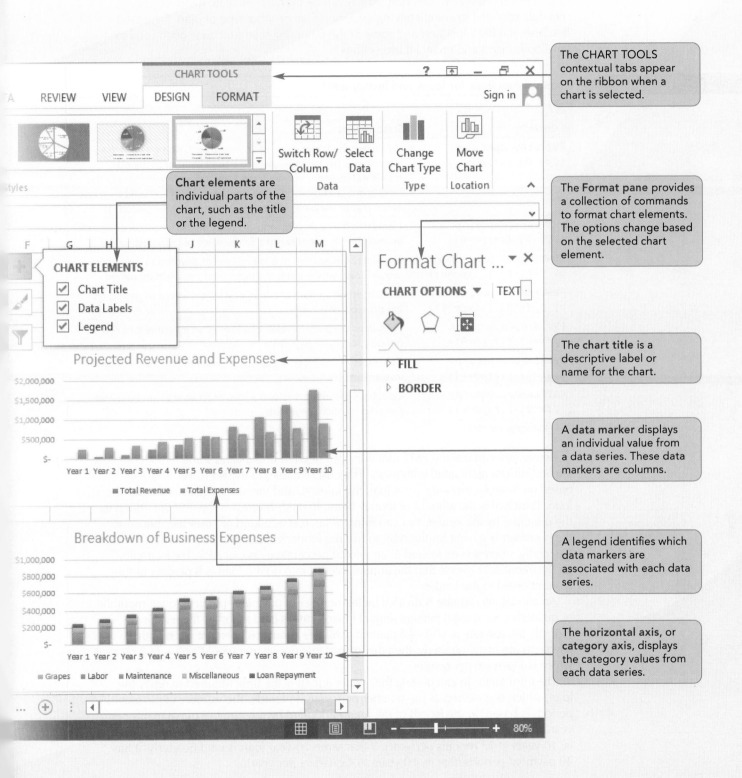

The CHART TOOLS contextual tabs appear on the ribbon when a chart is selected.

Chart elements are individual parts of the chart, such as the title or the legend.

The Format pane provides a collection of commands to format chart elements. The options change based on the selected chart element.

The chart title is a descriptive label or name for the chart.

A data marker displays an individual value from a data series. These data markers are columns.

A legend identifies which data markers are associated with each data series.

The horizontal axis, or category axis, displays the category values from each data series.

Introduction to Financial Functions

Excel provides a wide range of financial functions related to loans and investments. One of these is the **PMT function**, which can be used to calculate the payment schedule required to completely repay a mortgage or other type of loan. Figure 4-1 describes the PMT function and some of the other financial functions often used to develop budgets and financial projections.

| Figure 4-1 | Financial functions for loans and investments |

Function	Description
FV(rate, nper, pmt [,pv=0] [,type=0])	Calculates the future value of an investment, where *rate* is the interest rate per period, *nper* is the total number of periods, *pmt* is the payment in each period, *pv* is the present value of the investment, and *type* indicates whether payments should be made at the end of the period (0) or the beginning of the period (1)
PMT(rate, nper, pv [,fv=0] [,type=0])	Calculates the payments required each period on a loan or an investment, where *fv* is the future value of the investment
IPMT(rate, per, nper, pv [,fv=0] [,type=0])	Calculates the amount of a loan payment devoted to paying the loan interest, where *per* is the number of the payment period
PPMT(rate, per, nper, pv [,fv=0] [,type=0])	Calculates the amount of a loan payment devoted to paying off the principal of a loan
PV(rate, nper, pmt [,fv=0] [,type=0])	Calculates the present value of a loan or an investment based on periodic, constant payments
NPER(rate, pmt, pv [,fv=0] [,type=0])	Calculates the number of periods required to pay off a loan or an investment
RATE(nper, pmt, pv [,fv=0] [,type=0])	Calculates the interest rate of a loan or an investment based on periodic, constant payments

© 2014 Cengage Learning

Before you can use the PMT function, you need to understand some of the concepts and definitions associated with loans. The cost of a loan to the borrower is largely based on three factors—the principal, the interest, and the time required to repay the loan. **Principal** is the amount of money being loaned. **Interest** is the amount added to the principal by the lender. You can think of interest as a kind of "user fee" because the borrower is paying for the right to use the lender's money for an interval of time. Generally, interest is expressed at an annual percentage rate, or APR. For example, an 8 percent APR means that the annual interest rate on the loan is 8 percent of the amount owed to the lender.

An annual interest rate is divided by the number of payments per year (often monthly or quarterly). So, if the 8 percent annual interest rate is paid monthly, the resulting monthly interest rate is 1/12 of 8 percent, which is about 0.67 percent per month. If payments are made quarterly, then the interest rate per quarter would be 1/4 of 8 percent, which is 2 percent per quarter.

The third factor in calculating the cost of a loan is the time required to repay the loan, which is specified as the number of payment periods. The number of payment periods is based on the length of the loan multiplied by the number of payments per year. For example, a 10-year loan that is paid monthly has 120 payment periods (that is, 10 years × 12 months per year). If that same 10-year loan is paid quarterly, it has 40 payment periods (that is, 10 years × 4 quarters per year).

Using the PMT Function

To calculate the costs associated with a loan, such as the one that Bob and Carol need to start their winery, you must have the following information:

- The annual interest rate
- The number of payment periods per year
- The length of the loan in terms of the total number of payment periods
- The amount being borrowed
- When loan payments are due

The PMT function uses this information to calculate the payment required in each period to pay back the loan. The syntax of the PMT function is

$$PMT(rate, nper, pv [, fv=0] [, type=0])$$

where $rate$ is the interest rate for each payment period, $nper$ is the total number of payment periods required to repay the loan, and pv is the present value of the loan or the amount that needs to be borrowed. The PMT function has two optional arguments—fv and $type$. The fv argument is the future value of the loan. Because the intent with most loans is to repay them completely, the future value is equal to 0 by default. The $type$ argument specifies when the interest is charged on the loan, either at the end of the payment period ($type=0$), which is the default, or at the beginning of the payment period ($type=1$).

For example, you can use the PMT function to calculate the monthly payments required to repay a car loan of $10,000 over a 5-year period at an annual interest rate of 9 percent. The $rate$ or interest rate per period argument is equal to 9 percent divided by 12 monthly payments, which is 0.75 percent per month. The $nper$ or total number of payments argument is equal to 12 × 5 (12 monthly payments over 5 years), which is 60. The pv or present value of the loan is 10,000. In this case, because the loan will be repaid completely and payments will be made at the end of the month, you can accept the default values for the fv and $type$ arguments. The resulting PMT function

$$PMT(0.09/12, 5*12, 10000)$$

returns the value −207.58, or a monthly loan payment of $207.58. The PMT function results in a negative value because that value represents an expense to the borrower. Essentially, the loan is money you subtract from your funds to repay the loan.

Rather than entering the argument values directly in the PMT function, you should include the loan terms in worksheet cells that are referenced in the function. This makes it clear what values are being used in the loan calculation. It also makes it easier to perform a what-if analysis exploring other loan options.

Bob and Carol want to borrow $310,000 for their winery at an 8 percent annual interest rate. They plan to repay the loan in 10 years with monthly payments. You will enter these loan terms in the Overview worksheet.

To enter the loan information in the Overview worksheet:

1. Open the **Levitt** workbook located in the Excel4 ▸ Tutorial folder included with your Data Files, and then save the workbook as **Levitt Winery**.

2. In the Documentation sheet, enter your name in cell B4 and the date in cell B5.

3. Go to the **Overview** worksheet. The Overview worksheet provides a summary of Bob and Carol's business plan, including their loan request and business forecasts.

4. In cell **C5**, enter **310,000** as the loan amount.

5. In cell **C6**, enter **8%** as the annual interest rate.

6. In cell **C7**, enter **12** as the number of payments per year. Twelve payments indicate monthly payments.

7. In cell **C8**, enter the formula **=C6/C7** to calculate the interest rate per period. In this case, the 8 percent interest rate is divided by 12 payments per year, calculating the monthly interest rate of 0.67 percent.

8. In cell **C9**, enter **10** as the number of years in the loan.

9. In cell **C10**, enter **=C7*C9** to multiply the number of payments per year by the number of years in the loan, calculating the total number of payments on the loan, which is 120.

The Overview worksheet includes all the data you need to calculate the monthly payment required to repay the $310,000 loan in 10 years at an 8 percent annual interest rate paid monthly. Next, you will use the PMT function to calculate the monthly payment needed to repay the loan.

To use the PMT function to calculate Bob and Carol's monthly payment:

1. Select cell **C12** to make it the active cell. You will enter the PMT function in this cell.

2. On the ribbon, click the **FORMULAS** tab to display the function library.

3. In the Function Library group, click the **Financial** button, and then scroll down and click **PMT** in the list of financial functions. The Function Arguments dialog box opens.

4. With the insertion point in the Rate box, click cell **C8** in the worksheet to enter the reference to the cell with the interest rate per month.

5. Click in the **Nper** box, and then click cell **C10** in the worksheet to enter the reference to the cell with the total number of monthly payments required to repay the loan.

6. Click in the **Pv** box, and then click cell **C5** in the worksheet to enter the reference to the cell with the present value of the loan. See Figure 4-2.

TIP

Be sure to enter the interest rate per month (not per year) for the Rate argument for any loan or investment that has monthly payments.

Figure 4-2   **Function Arguments dialog box for the PMT function**

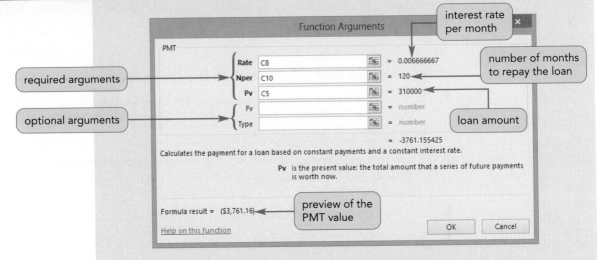

7. Click the **OK** button. The monthly payment amount ($3,761.16) appears in cell C12. The number is displayed in parentheses to indicate a negative amount, specifying the amount to be paid.

8. In cell **C13**, enter the formula **=C7*C12** to multiply the number of payments per year by the monthly payment amount, calculating the total payments for the entire year. The annual payments would be ($45,133.87), shown as a negative number to indicate money being paid out.

9. Select cell **C12**. See Figure 4-3.

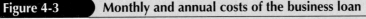

| Figure 4-3 | Monthly and annual costs of the business loan |

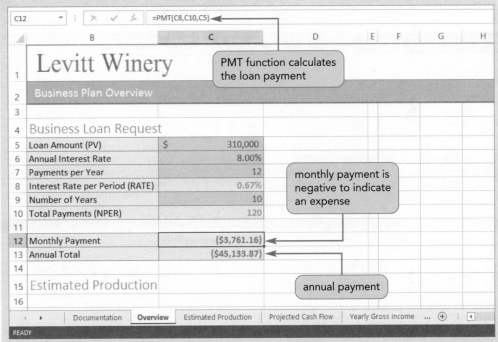

Carol wants to see the financial impact of taking out a smaller loan.

10. In cell **C5**, change the loan amount to **250,000**. With a loan of that size, the monthly payment drops to $3,033 and the annual total decreases to $36,398.

Although the lower loan amount will save money, Bob feels that the winery cannot get off the ground with less than a $310,000 loan.

11. In cell **C5**, return the loan amount to **310,000**.

Based on your analysis, the Levitts would spend about $45,000 a year repaying the $310,000 business loan. Carol and Bob want this information included in the Projected Cash Flow worksheet, which estimates Levitt Winery's annual revenue, expenses, and cash flow for the first 10 years. You will enter that amount as an expense for each year, completing the projected cash flow calculations.

To enter the loan repayment amount in the Projected Cash Flow worksheet:

▶ 1. Go to the **Projected Cash Flow** worksheet and review the estimated annual revenue, expenses, and cash flow for the next decade.

▶ 2. In cell **C17**, enter **45,000** as the projected yearly amount of the loan repayment. Because the projected cash flow is a rough estimate of the projected income and expenses, it is not necessary to include the exact dollar-and-cents cost of the loan.

▶ 3. Copy the annual loan payment in cell **C17** into the range **D17:L17** to enter the projected annual loan payment in each year of the cash flow projections. See Figure 4-4.

| Figure 4-4 | Completed Projected Cash Flow worksheet |

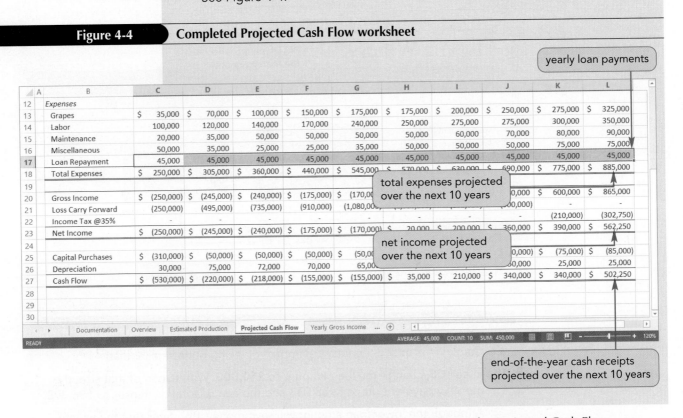

yearly loan payments

total expenses projected over the next 10 years

net income projected over the next 10 years

end-of-the-year cash receipts projected over the next 10 years

After including the projected annual loan payments, the Projected Cash Flow worksheet shows that the winery's projected net income at the end of the tenth year would be about $560,000, assuming all of the other projections are accurate. Based on these figures, the winery should have about $500,000 in cash at that time as well.

Using Functions to Manage Personal Finances

Excel has many financial functions to manage personal finances. The following list can help you determine which function to use for the most common personal finance calculations:

- To determine how much an investment will be worth after a series of monthly payments at some future time, use the FV (future value) function.
- To determine how much you have to spend each month to repay a loan or mortgage within a set period of time, use the PMT (payment) function.
- To determine how much of your monthly loan payment is used to pay the interest, use the IPMT (interest payment) function.
- To determine how much of your monthly loan payment is used for repaying the principal, use the PPMT (principal payment) function.
- To determine the largest loan or mortgage you can afford given a set monthly payment, use the PV (present value) function.
- To determine how long it will take to pay off a loan with constant monthly payments, use the NPER (number of periods) function.

For most loan and investment calculations, you need to enter the annual interest rate divided by the number of times the interest is compounded during the year. If interest is compounded monthly, divide the annual interest rate by 12; if interest is compounded quarterly, divide the annual rate by 4. You must also convert the length of the loan or investment to the number of payments per year. If you will make payments monthly, multiply the number of years of the loan or investment by 12.

Now that you have completed the cash flow projections for the winery, you can begin displaying this information in charts.

Creating a Chart

Charts show trends or relationships in data that are easier to see than by looking at the actual numbers. Creating a chart is a several-step process that involves selecting the data to display in the chart, choosing the chart type, moving the chart to a specific location in the workbook, sizing the chart so that it matches the layout of the worksheet, and formatting the chart's appearance. When creating a chart, remember that your goal is to convey important information that would be more difficult to interpret from columns of data in a worksheet.

Creating a Chart

- Select the range containing the data you want to chart.
- On the INSERT tab, in the Charts group, click the Recommended Chart button or a chart type button, and then click the chart you want to create (or click the Quick Analysis button, click the CHARTS category, and then click the chart you want to create).
- On the CHART TOOLS DESIGN tab, in the Location group, click the Move Chart button, select whether to embed the chart in a worksheet or place it in a chart sheet, and then click the OK button.

Selecting a Chart's Data Source

The data displayed in a chart comes from the chart's data source. A data source includes one or more data series and a series of category values. A data series contains the actual values that are plotted on the chart, whereas the category values provide descriptive labels for each data series or data value. Category values are usually located in the first column or first row of the data source. The data series are usually placed in subsequent columns or rows. However, you can select category and data values from anywhere within a workbook.

Bob and Carol want a chart to display information about the winery's estimated production in 10 years. The data source for this chart is located in the range B28:C34 of the Overview worksheet. You will select this range now as the data source for the chart.

To select the data source for a chart showing the projected production:

▶ 1. Go to the **Overview** worksheet. The production projections are included in this worksheet.

▶ 2. Select the range **B28:C34** containing the production estimates as the data source for the chart. See Figure 4-5.

Figure 4-5   Selected chart data source

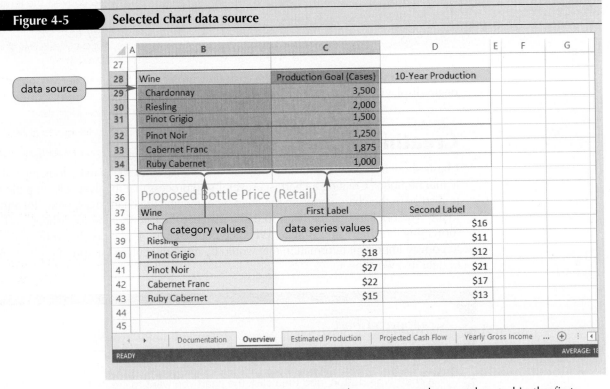

This data source includes two columns. The category values are located in the first column, and the one and only data series is located in the second column. When the selected range is taller than it is wide, Excel assumes that the category values and data series are laid out in columns. Conversely, a data source that is wider than it is tall is assumed to have the category values and data series laid out in rows. Note that the first row in this selected data source contains labels that identify the category values (Wine) and the data series (Production Goal).

Now that you've selected the data source for the chart, you want to consider the type of chart to create.

Exploring Chart Types and Subtypes

Excel provides 53 types of charts organized into the 10 categories described in Figure 4-6. Each category includes variations of the same chart type, which are called **chart subtypes**. You can also design your own custom chart types to meet the specific needs of your reports and projects.

Figure 4-6   Excel chart types

Chart Type	Description
Column	Compares values from different categories. Values are indicated by the height of the columns.
Line	Compares values from different categories. Values are indicated by the height of the lines. Often used to show trends and changes over time.
Pie	Compares relative values of different categories to the whole. Values are indicated by the areas of the pie slices.
Bar	Compares values from different categories. Values are indicated by the length of the bars.
Area	Compares values from different categories. Similar to the line chart except that areas under the lines contain a fill color.
X Y (Scatter)	Shows the patterns or relationship between two or more sets of values. Often used in scientific studies and statistical analyses.
Stock	Displays stock market data, including the high, low, opening, and closing prices of a stock.
Surface	Compares three sets of values in a three-dimensional chart.
Radar	Compares a collection of values from several different data sets.
Combo	Combines two or more chart types to make the data easy to visualize, especially when the data is widely varied.

© 2014 Cengage Learning

For example, Figure 4-7 presents the same labor cost data displayed as a line chart, a bar chart, and column charts. The column charts are shown with both a 2-D subtype that has two-dimensional or flat columns and a 3-D subtype that gives the illusion of three-dimensional columns. The various charts and chart subtypes are better suited for different data. You should choose the one that makes the data easiest to interpret.

Figure 4-7 Chart types and subtypes

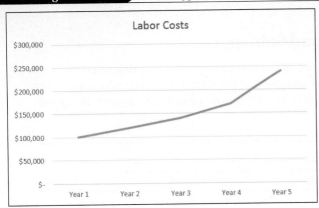

Line chart

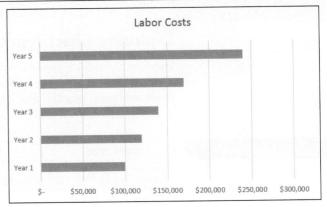

Bar chart

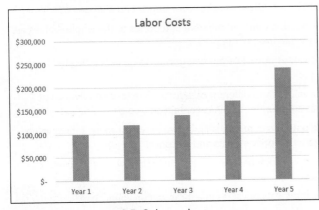

2-D Column chart

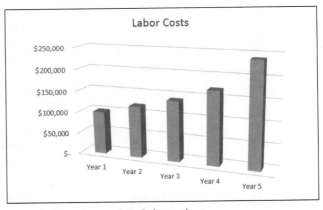

3-D Column chart

TIP

Most charts should include only the category labels and data values and not row or column totals because Excel will treat those totals as another category to be graphed.

The first chart you will create is a pie chart. A **pie chart** is a chart in the shape of a circle divided into slices like a pie. Each slice represents a single value from a data series. Larger data values are represented with bigger pie slices. The relative sizes of the slices let you visually compare the data values and see how much each contributes to the whole. Pie charts are most effective with six or fewer slices, and when each slice is large enough to view easily.

Inserting a Pie Chart with the Quick Analysis Tool

After you select an adjacent range to use as a chart's data source, the Quick Analysis tool appears. It includes a category for creating charts. The CHART category lists recommended chart types, which are the charts that are most appropriate for the data source you selected.

For the wine production data, a pie chart provides the best way to compare the production levels for the six wines Levitt Winery plans to produce. You will use the Quick Analysis tool to create a pie chart of the projected wine production data that you selected.

TIP

You can also insert a chart by selecting a chart type in the Charts group on the INSERT tab.

To create a pie chart with the Quick Analysis tool:

1. Make sure the range **B28:C34** is selected.

2. Click the **Quick Analysis** button in the lower-right corner of the selected range (or press the **Ctrl+Q** keys) to open the Quick Analysis tool.

3. Click the **CHARTS** category. The chart types you will most likely want to use with the selected data source are listed. See Figure 4-8.

Figure 4-8   **CHARTS category of the Quick Analysis tool**

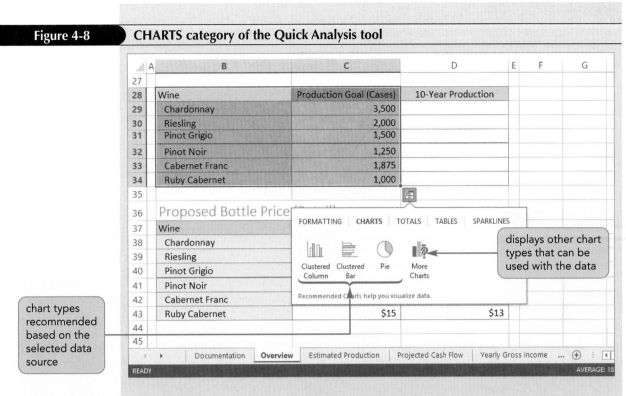

chart types recommended based on the selected data source

displays other chart types that can be used with the data

4. Click **Pie**. A pie chart appears in the Overview worksheet. Each slice is a different size based on its value in the data series. The biggest slice represents the 3500 cases of Chardonnay that the Levitts estimate they will produce. The smallest slice of the pie represents 1000 cases of Ruby Cabernet. See Figure 4-9.

Figure 4-9   **Pie chart in the Overview worksheet**

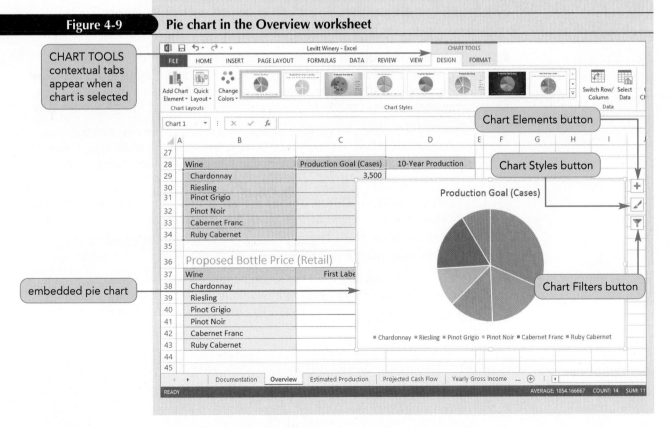

CHART TOOLS contextual tabs appear when a chart is selected

Chart Elements button

Chart Styles button

embedded pie chart

Chart Filters button

When you create or select a chart, two CHART TOOLS contextual tabs appear on the ribbon. The DESIGN tab provides commands to specify the chart's overall design. The FORMAT tab supplies the tools needed to format the graphic shapes found in the chart, such as the chart's border or the slices from a pie chart. When you select a worksheet cell or another object that is not a chart, the CHART TOOLS contextual tabs disappear until you reselect the chart.

Three buttons appear to the right of the selected chart. The Chart Elements button ⊞ is used for adding, removing, or changing elements displayed in the chart. The Chart Styles button ✐ sets the style and color scheme of the chart. The Chart Filters button ▼ enables you to edit the data points and names displayed on the chart.

Moving and Resizing a Chart

TIP

You can print an embedded chart with the rest of the worksheet, or you can select the embedded chart and print only the chart without the rest of the worksheet.

Excel charts are either placed in their own chart sheets or embedded in a worksheet. When you create a chart, it is embedded in the worksheet that contains the data source. For example, the chart shown in Figure 4-9 is embedded in the Overview worksheet. The advantage of an embedded chart is that you can display the chart alongside its data source and any text that describes the chart's meaning and purpose. Because an embedded chart covers worksheet cells, you might have to move or resize the chart so that important information is not hidden.

Before you can move or resize a chart, it must be selected. When a chart is selected, a **selection box** appears around the selected chart that is used to move or resize the chart. **Sizing handles** appear along the edges of the selection box and are used to change the chart's width and height.

Bob and Carol want the wine production chart to appear above its data source in the Overview worksheet. You will move and resize the chart to fit this location.

To move and resize the wine production pie chart:

Be sure to drag the chart from an empty part of the chart area so the entire chart moves, not just chart elements within the chart.

1. Move the pointer over an empty area of the selected chart until the pointer changes to ⬧ and "Chart Area" appears in a ScreenTip.

2. Hold down the **Alt** key, drag the chart up and to the left until its upper-left corner snaps to the upper-left corner of cell B16, and then release the mouse button and the **Alt** key. The upper-left corner of the chart is aligned with the upper-left corner of cell B16.

   Trouble? If the pie chart resizes or does not move to the new location, you probably didn't drag the chart from an empty part of the chart area. Press the Ctrl+Z keys to undo your last action, and then repeat Steps 1 and 2, being sure to drag the pie chart from the chart area.

   The chart moves to a new location, but it still covers some data and needs to be resized.

3. Move the pointer over the sizing handle in the lower-right corner of the selection box until the pointer changes to ⬂.

4. Hold down the **Alt** key, drag the sizing handle up to the lower-right corner of cell D27, and then release the mouse button and the **Alt** key. The chart resizes to cover the range B16:D27 and remains selected. See Figure 4-10.

Figure 4-10   **Moved and resized chart**

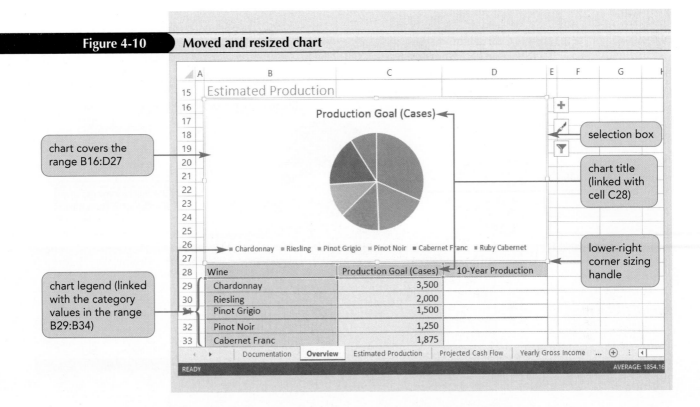

chart covers the range B16:D27

selection box

chart title (linked with cell C28)

lower-right corner sizing handle

chart legend (linked with the category values in the range B29:B34)

Working with Chart Elements

Every chart contains elements that can be formatted, added to the chart, or removed from the chart. For example, a pie chart has three elements—the chart title, the chart legend identifying each pie slice, and data labels that can be displayed next to each slice providing the data value or percentage associated with that slice. The Chart Elements button that appears next to a selected chart lists the elements associated with that chart. You can use this button to add, remove, and format individual elements. When you add or remove a chart element, the other elements resize to fit in the space. Live Preview shows how changing an element will affect the chart's appearance.

Carol doesn't want the pie chart to include a title because the text in cell B15 and the data in the range B28:D34 sufficiently explain the chart's purpose. However, she does want to display the data values next to the pie slices. You will remove the chart title element and add the data labels element.

TIP

To add and remove chart elements, you can also use the Add Chart Element button in the Chart Layouts group on the CHART TOOLS DESIGN tab.

To remove the pie chart title and add data labels to the slices:

1. Click the **pie chart** to select it. The selection box appears around the chart.

2. To the right of the selected chart, click the **Chart Elements** button ➕. A menu of chart elements that are available for the pie chart opens. As the checkmarks indicate, only the chart title and the chart legend are displayed in the pie chart.

3. Click the **Chart Title** check box to deselect it. The chart title is removed from the pie chart and the chart elements resize to fill the space.

4. Point to the **Data Labels** check box. Live Preview shows how the chart will look when the data labels showing the production goal for each wine are added to the pie slices.

5. Click the **Data Labels** check box to select it. The data labels are added to the chart. See Figure 4-11.

Figure 4-11   Chart elements

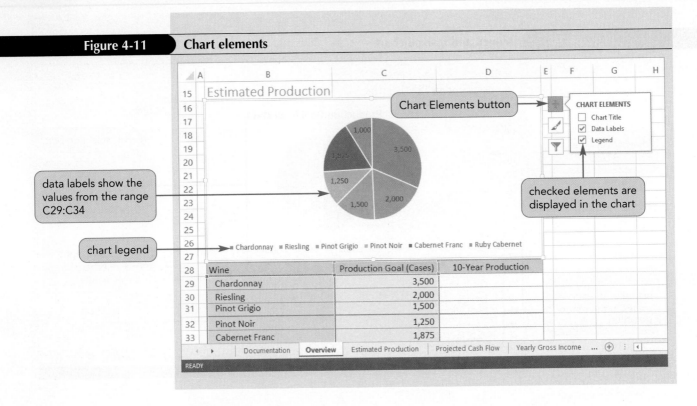

Choosing a Chart Style

When you create a chart, the chart is formatted with a style. Recall that a style is a collection of formats that are saved with a name and can then be applied at one time. In the pie chart you just created, the format of the chart title, the location of the legend, and the colors of the pie slices are all part of the default pie chart style. You can quickly change the appearance of a chart by selecting a different style from the Chart Styles gallery. Live Preview shows how a chart style will affect the chart.

Carol wants the pie slices to have a raised, three-dimensional look. You will explore different chart styles to find a style that best fulfills her request.

TIP

You can also select a chart style from the Chart Styles gallery in the Chart Styles group on the CHART TOOLS DESIGN tab.

To choose a different chart style for the wine production pie chart:

1. Click the **Chart Styles** button next to the selected pie chart. The Chart Styles gallery opens.

2. Point to different styles in the gallery. Live Preview shows the impact of each chart style on the pie chart's appearance.

3. Scroll to the bottom of the gallery, and then click the **Style 12** chart style. The chart style is applied to the pie chart. See Figure 4-12.

Figure 4-12   Chart Styles gallery

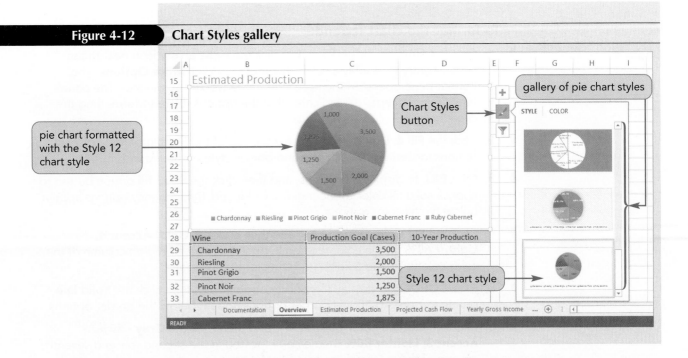

pie chart formatted with the Style 12 chart style

Chart Styles button

gallery of pie chart styles

Style 12 chart style

Formatting the Pie Chart Legend

You can fine-tune a chart style by formatting individual chart elements. From the Chart Elements button, you can open a submenu for each element that includes formatting options, such as the element's location within the chart. You can also open a Format pane, which has more options for formatting the selected chart element.

The default location for the pie chart legend is alongside the chart's bottom edge. Carol thinks the chart would look better if the legend were aligned with the right edge of the chart.

To reposition the pie chart legend:

▶ 1. Click the **Chart Elements** button ⊞ next to the selected pie chart.

▶ 2. Point to **Legend** in the CHART ELEMENTS menu to display a right arrow icon, and then click the **right arrow** icon ▶. A submenu opens with formatting options available for the selected chart element. For a chart legend, the submenu offers placement options.

▶ 3. Point to **Left** to see a Live Preview of that formatting. The legend is aligned along the left side of the chart area, and the pie moves to the right to occupy the remaining space.

▶ 4. Click **Right** to place the legend along the right side of the chart area. The pie shifts to the left to make room for the legend.

The Chart Elements button also provides access to the Format pane, which has more design options. Carol wants you to add a drop shadow to the legend similar to the pie chart's drop shadow, change the fill color to a light gold, and add a light gray border. You'll use the Format pane to make these changes.

To format the chart legend:

TIP

You can also open the Format pane by double-clicking any chart element.

1. On the CHART ELEMENTS menu, click the **right arrow** icon next to the Legend entry to display a submenu, and then click **More Options**. The Format pane opens on the right side of the workbook window. The pane's title, "Format Legend," indicates that the options relate to formatting the chart legend.

2. Click the **Fill & Line** button near the top of the Format pane to display options for setting the fill color and border style of the legend.

3. Click **FILL** to display fill options, and then click the **Solid fill** option button to apply a solid fill color to the legend. Color and Transparency options appear below the fill color options.

4. Click the **Fill Color** button, and then click the **Gold, Accent 4, Lighter 60%** theme color located in the third row and eighth column of the color palette to add a light gold fill color to the legend.

5. Click **BORDER** to display the border options, and then click the **Solid line** option button. Additional border options appear below the border options.

6. Click the **Outline color** button, and then click the **Gray - 50%, Accent 3, Lighter 80%** theme color located in the second row and seventh column of the color palette to add a light gray border around the legend.

7. At the top of the Format Legend pane, click the **Effects** button to display options for special visual effects.

8. Click **Shadow** to display the shadow options, and then next to the Presets label, click the **Shadow** button to display a gallery of shadow effects.

9. Click the **Offset Diagonal Button Right** button in the first row and first column to apply the drop shadow effect to the legend. See Figure 4-13.

Figure 4-13   Formatted chart legend

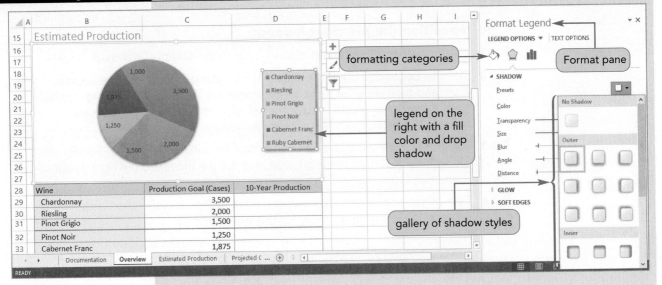

Formatting Pie Chart Data Labels

You can modify the content and appearance of data labels, selecting what the labels contain as well as where the labels are positioned. By default, data labels are placed where they will keep the chart nicely proportioned, but you can specify a different location. For pie chart labels, you can move the labels to the center of the pie slices or place them outside of the slices. Another option is to set the labels as data callouts, with each label placed within a text bubble and connected to the slice with a callout line. Likewise, you can change the text and number styles used in the data labels as well. These options are all available in the Format pane. You can also drag and drop individual data labels, placing them anywhere within the chart. When a data label is placed far from its pie slice, a **leader line** is added to connect the data label to its pie slice.

The pie chart data labels display the production goal values for the different wines, but this information also appears on the worksheet directly below the chart. The Levitts want to include data labels that add new information to the chart—in this case, the percentage that each wine varietal adds to the whole. You will make this change.

To display percentages in the wine production pie chart:

TIP

You can also format chart elements using the formatting buttons on the HOME tab or on the CHART TOOLS FORMAT tab.

1. At the top of the Format pane, click the **Legend Options** arrow to display a menu of chart elements, and then click **Series "Production Goal (Cases)" Data Labels** to display the formatting options for data labels. The title of the Format pane changes to "Format Data Labels" and includes formatting options for data labels. Selection boxes appear around every data label in the pie chart.

2. Click the **Label Options** button 📊 near the top of the pane to display the options for the label contents and position. Data labels can contain series names, category names, values, and percentages.

3. Click the **Percentage** check box to display the percentage associated with each data label in the pie chart next to its value.

4. Click the **Value** check box to deselect it, removing the data series values from the data labels. The pie chart shows that Chardonnay accounts for 31.5 percent of the estimated wine production.

5. Click the **Outside End** option button to move the labels outside of the pie slices. The labels are easier to read in this location.

   The percentages are displayed with no decimal places, but Carol wants them to show one decimal place to provide a bit more accuracy in the chart.

6. Scroll down the Format pane, and then click **NUMBER** to show the formatting options for numbers.

7. Scroll down the Format pane, click the **Category** box to display the number formats, and then click **Percentage**. The percentages in the data labels include two decimal places.

8. In the Decimal places box, replace the value 2 with **1**, and then press the **Enter** key. The percentages display one decimal place. See Figure 4-14.

Figure 4-14   **Formatted data labels**

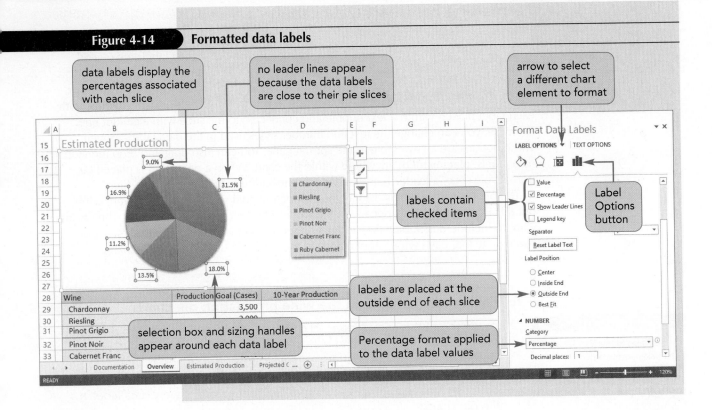

data labels display the percentages associated with each slice

no leader lines appear because the data labels are close to their pie slices

arrow to select a different chart element to format

labels contain checked items

Label Options button

labels are placed at the outside end of each slice

selection box and sizing handles appear around each data label

Percentage format applied to the data label values

Setting the Pie Slice Colors

A pie slice is an example of a data marker that represents a single data value from a data series. You can format the appearance of individual data markers to make them stand out from the others. Pie slice colors should be as distinct as possible to avoid confusion. Depending on the printer quality or the monitor resolution, it might be difficult to distinguish between similarly colored slices. If data labels are displayed within the slice, you also need enough contrast between the slice color and the data label color to make the text readable.

The Levitts are concerned that the blue color of the Cabernet Franc slice will appear too dark when printed, and they want you to change it to a light shade of green.

To change the color of the Cabernet Franc pie slice:

1. Click any pie slice to select all of the slices in the pie chart.

2. Click the **Cabernet Franc** slice, which is the darker blue slice that represents 16.9 percent of the pie. Only that slice is selected, as you can see from the handles that appear at each corner of the slice.

3. Click the **HOME** tab, click the **Fill Color button arrow** in the Font group, and then click the **Green, Accent 6, Lighter 40%** theme color in the fourth row and last column of the gallery. The Cabernet Franc pie slice changes to a light green and the chart legend automatically updates to reflect that change.

You can also change the colors of all the pie slices by clicking the Chart Styles button next to the selected chart, clicking the COLOR heading, and then selecting a color scheme.

Exploding a Pie Chart

Pie slices do not need to be fixed within the pie. An **exploded pie chart** moves one slice away from the others as if someone were taking the piece away from the pie. Exploded pie charts are useful for emphasizing one category above all of the others. For example, to emphasize the fact that Levitt Winery will be producing more Chardonnay than any other wine, you could explode that single slice, moving it away from the other slices.

To explode a pie slice, first click the pie to select all of the slices, and then click the single slide you want to move. Make sure that a selection box appears around only that slice. Drag the slice away from the pie to offset it from the others. You can explode multiple slices by selecting each slice in turn and dragging them away. To explode all of the slices, select the entire pie and drag the pointer away from the pie's center. Each slice will be exploded and separated from the others. Although you can explode more than one slice, the resulting pie chart is rarely effective as a visual aid to the reader.

Formatting the Chart Area

The chart's background, which is called the chart area, can also be formatted using fill colors, border styles, and special effects such as drop shadows and blurred edges. The chart area fill color used in the pie chart is white, which blends in with the worksheet background. Carol wants you to change the fill color to a light gold to match the worksheet's color scheme, and to make the chart stand out better.

TIP

You can select any chart element using the Chart Elements box in the Current Selection group on the CHART TOOLS FORMAT tab.

To change the chart area of the pie chart to light gold:

1. Click a blank area within the chart, not containing either a pie slice or the chart legend. The chart area is selected, which you can verify because the Format pane title changes to "Format Chart Area."

2. On the HOME tab, in the Font group, click the **Fill Color button arrow** , and then click the **Gold, Accent 4, Lighter 80%** theme color in the second row and eighth column. The chart area fill color is now light gold. See Figure 4-15.

Figure 4-15 **Chart area fill color**

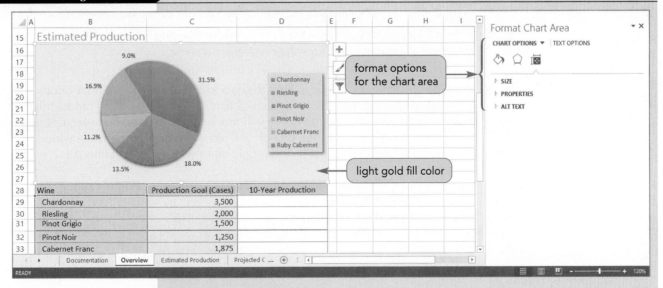

You are done formatting the pie chart, so you will close the Format pane to keep the window uncluttered.

▶ **3.** Click the **Close** button X on the title bar of the Format pane. The pane closes, leaving more space for viewing the worksheet contents.

Performing What-If Analyses with Charts

A chart is linked to its data source. For the wine production pie chart, the chart title is linked to the text of cell C28, the size of the pie slices is based on the production goals in the range C29:C34, and the category names are linked to the category values in the range B29:B34. Any changes to these cells affect the chart's content and appearance. This makes charts a powerful tool for data exploration and what-if analysis. Excel uses **chart animation** to slow down the effect of changing data source values, making it easier to see how changing one value affects the chart.

Bob and Carol want to see how the pie chart would change if they were to alter some of their production goals. You will edit the data source to see how the changes affect the chart.

To apply a what-if analysis to the pie chart:

▶ **1.** In cell **C29,** enter **5500** to increase the production goal for Chardonnay by 2000 cases. The pie slice associated with Chardonnay becomes larger, slowly changing from 31.5 percent to 41.9 percent because of the chart animation. The size of the remaining slices and their percentages are reduced to compensate.

▶ **2.** In cell **C29**, restore the value to **3,500**. The pie slices return to their initial sizes and the percentages return to their initial values.

▶ **3.** In cell **C30**, change the production goal for Riesling from 2,000 to **4,000**. The orange slice representing Riesling is now the largest slice in the pie, comprising 30.5 percent of the projected production.

▶ **4.** In cell **C30**, restore the value to **2,000**.

Bob points out that the legend entry "Riesling" should be changed to "White Riesling" to distinguish it from other Riesling varietals.

▶ **5.** In cells **B30** and **B39**, change the text to **White Riesling**. The chart legend automatically updates to show the revised wine name.

Another type of what-if analysis is to limit the data to a subset of the original values in a process called **filtering**. For example, the pie chart shows the estimated production for all six varietals of wine that Levitt Winery will produce. Sometimes, however, Carol and Bob might want to see information on only the red wines or only the white wines. Rather than creating a new chart that includes only those wines, you can filter an existing chart.

Levitt Winery plans to produce three white wines—Chardonnay, White Riesling, and Pinot Grigio. Carol and Bob want to see the different percentages of white wine. You will use the Chart Filters button to limit the pie chart to those three wines.

To filter the pie chart to show only white wines:

▶ **1.** Click the pie chart to select it.

▶ **2.** Click the **Chart Filters** button next to the chart to open a menu listing the categories in the chart. In this case, the categories are the different types of wines.

▶ **3.** Click the **Pinot Noir**, **Cabernet Franc**, and **Ruby Cabernet** check boxes to deselect them, leaving only the Chardonnay, White Riesling, and Pinot Grigio check boxes selected.

▶ **4.** At the bottom of the Chart Filters menu, click the **Apply** button. Excel filters the chart, showing only the white wines. After filtering the data, the chart shows that 50 percent of the white wines produced will be Chardonnay. See Figure 4-16.

| Figure 4-16 | Filtered pie chart |

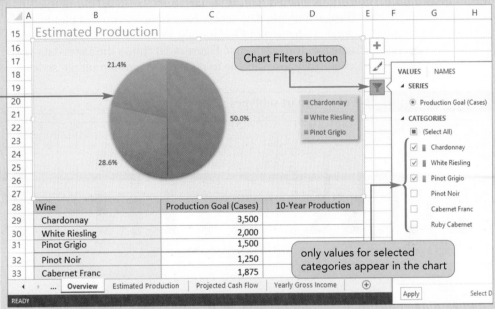

pie chart shows only the white wines

Chart Filters button

only values for selected categories appear in the chart

Wine	Production Goal (Cases)	10-Year Production
Chardonnay	3,500	
White Riesling	2,000	
Pinot Grigio	1,500	
Pinot Noir	1,250	
Cabernet Franc	1,875	

▶ **5.** In the CATEGORIES section of the Chart Filters menu, double-click the **Select All** check box to reselect all six wines.

▶ **6.** Click the **Apply** button to update the chart's appearance.

▶ **7.** Press the **Esc** key to close the menu, leaving the chart selected.

The pie chart that displays the winery's projected level of production for different wines is complete. Next, you'll use column charts to examine the winery's financial projections for the next 10 years.

Creating a Column Chart

A **column chart** displays data values as columns with the height of each column based on the data value. A column chart turned on its side is called a **bar chart**, with the length of the bar determined by the data value. It is better to use column and bar charts than pie charts when the number of categories is large or the data values are close in value. For example, Figure 4-17 displays the same data as a pie chart and a column chart. As you can see, it's difficult to determine which pie slice is biggest and by how much. It is much simpler to see the differences in a column or bar chart.

Figure 4-17 Data displayed as a pie chart and a column chart

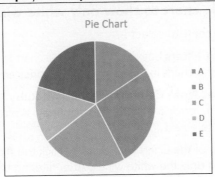
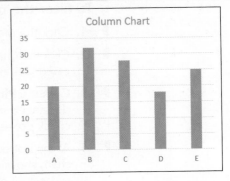

Comparing Column Chart Subtypes

Unlike pie charts, which can show only one data series, column and bar charts can display multiple data series. For example, you can plot three data series (such as the wine production of Chardonnay, White Riesling, and Cabernet Franc) against one category (such as Years). Figure 4-18 shows the same data charted on the three column chart subtypes available to display data from multiple series.

Figure 4-18 Column chart subtypes

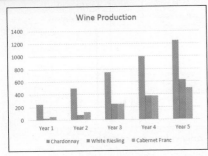
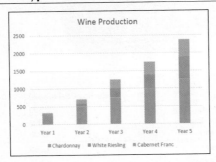
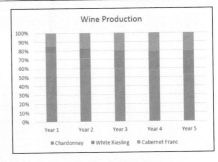

Clustered Column   Stacked Column   100% Stacked Column

The **clustered column chart** displays the data series in separate columns side-by-side so that you can compare the relative heights of the columns in the three series. The clustered column chart in Figure 4-18 compares the number of cases of each wine produced in Year 1 through Year 5. Note that the winery produces mostly Chardonnay with the other varietals increasing in volume in the later years.

The **stacked column chart** places the data series values within combined columns showing how much is contributed by each series. The stacked column chart in Figure 4-18 gives information on the total number of wine cases produced each year, and how each year's production is split among the three wine varietals.

Finally, the **100% stacked column chart** makes the same comparison as the stacked column chart except that the stacked sections are expressed as percentages. As you can see from the 100% stacked column chart in Figure 4-18, Chardonnay accounts for about 75 percent of the wine produced in Year 1, and that percentage steadily declines to about 50 percent in Year 5 as more cases of White Riesling and Cabernet Franc are produced.

The chart subtype you use depends on what you want to highlight with your data.

Creating a Clustered Column Chart

The process for creating a column chart is the same as for creating a pie chart. First, you select the data source. Then, you select the type of chart you want to create. After the chart is embedded in the worksheet, you can move and resize the chart as well as change the chart's design, layout, and format.

Bob and Carol want to show the projected revenue and expenses for each of the next 10 years. Because this requires comparing the data series values, you will create a clustered column chart.

To create a column chart for the revenue and expenses data:

1. Go to the **Projected Cash Flow** worksheet.

2. Select the nonadjacent range **B4:L4;B10:L10;B18:L18** containing the Year categories in row 4, the Total Revenue data series in row 10, and the Total Expenses data series in row 18. Because you selected a nonadjacent range, the Quick Analysis tool is not available.

3. On the ribbon, click the **INSERT** tab. The Charts group contains buttons for inserting different types of charts.

TIP

You can also open the Insert Chart dialog box to see the chart types recommended for the selected data source.

4. In the Charts group, click the **Recommended Charts** button. The Insert Chart dialog box opens with the Recommended Charts tab displayed. The charts show how the selected data would appear in that chart type. See Figure 4-19.

Figure 4-19   **Clustered column chart being created**

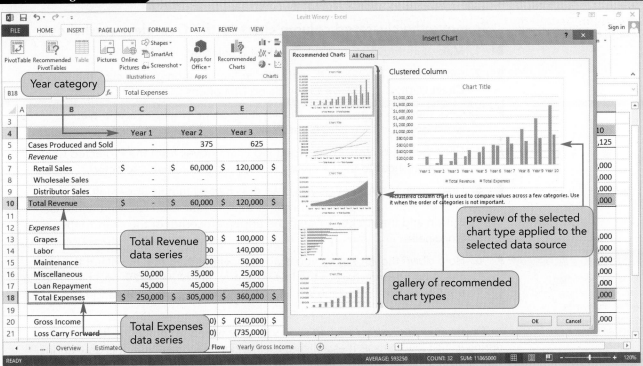

5. Make sure the **Clustered Column** chart is selected, and then click the **OK** button. The clustered column chart is embedded in the Projected Cash Flow worksheet.

6. Click the **Chart Styles** button next to the selected column chart.

7. In the STYLE gallery, scroll down and click the **Style 14** chart style to format the columns with drop shadows.

8. Click the **Chart Styles** button to close the STYLE gallery.

INSIGHT

Changing a Chart Type

After creating a chart, you can easily switch the chart to a different chart type without having to recreate the chart from scratch. For example, if the data in a column chart would be more effective presented as a line chart, you can change its chart type rather than creating a new chart. Clicking the Change Chart Type button in the Type group on the CHART TOOLS DESIGN tab opens a dialog box similar to the Insert Chart dialog box, from which you can select a new chart type.

Moving a Chart to a Different Worksheet

You can move a chart from one worksheet to another, or you can place the chart in its own chart sheet. In a chart sheet, the chart is enlarged to fill the entire workspace. The Move Chart dialog box provides options for moving charts between worksheets and chart sheets. You can also cut and paste a chart between workbooks.

Bob and Carol want all of the charts to be displayed in the Overview worksheet. You will move the clustered column chart to the Overview worksheet, and then resize it.

To move the clustered column chart to the Overview worksheet:

1. Make sure the clustered column chart is selected.

2. On the CHART TOOLS DESIGN tab, in the Location group, click the **Move Chart** button. The Move Chart dialog box opens.

3. Click the **Object in** arrow to display a list of the worksheets in the active workbook, and then click **Overview**.

4. Click the **OK** button. The embedded chart moves from the Projected Cash Flow worksheet to the Overview worksheet, and remains selected.

5. Hold down the **Alt** key as you drag the chart so that its upper-left corner is aligned with the upper-left corner of cell F16, and then release the mouse button and the **Alt** key to snap the upper-left corner of the chart to the worksheet.

6. Hold down the **Alt** key as you drag the lower-right sizing handle of the clustered column chart to the lower-right corner of cell **M29**, and then release the mouse button and the **Alt** key. The chart now covers the range F16:M29.

TIP

To set an exact chart size, enter the height and width values in the Size group on the CHART TOOLS FORMAT tab.

The revenue and expenses chart shows that the winery will produce little revenue during its first few years as it establishes itself and its customer base. It is only during Year 6 that the revenue will outpace the expenses. After that, Bob and Carol hope that the winery's revenue will increase rapidly while expenses grow at a more moderate pace.

Changing and Formatting a Chart Title

When a chart has a single data series, the name of the data series is used for the chart title. When a chart has more than one data series, the "Chart Title" placeholder appears as the temporary title of the chart. You can then replace the placeholder text with a more descriptive title.

The clustered column chart includes the Chart Title placeholder. Bob and Carol want you to replace this with a more descriptive title.

To change the title of the column chart:

1. At the top of the column chart, click **Chart Title** to select the placeholder text.

2. Type **Projected Revenue and Expenses** as the new title, and then press the **Enter** key. The new title is entered into the chart, and the chart title element remains selected.

3. Click the **HOME** tab, and then use the buttons in the Font group to remove the bold from the chart title, change the font to **Calibri Light**, and change the font color to the **Blue, Accent 1** theme color. See Figure 4-20.

Figure 4-20	Column chart

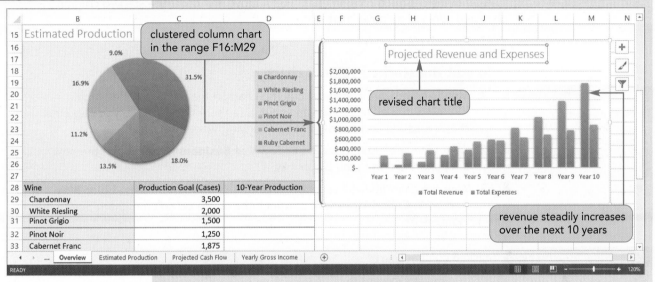

Creating a Stacked Column Chart

The next chart that the Levitts want added to the Overview worksheet is a chart that projects the expenses incurred by the winery over the next 10 years broken down by category. Because this chart looks at how different parts of the whole vary across time, it would be better to display that information in a stacked column chart. You will create this chart based on the data located in the Projected Cash Flow worksheet.

To create a stacked column chart:

1. Go to the **Projected Cash Flow** worksheet, and then select the nonadjacent range **B4:L4;B13:L17** containing the year categories and five data series for different types of expenses.

2. Click the **INSERT** tab, and then click the **Insert Column Chart** button in the Charts group. A list of column chart subtypes appears.

3. Click the **Stacked Column** icon (the second icon in the 2-D Column section). The stacked column chart is embedded in the Projected Cash Flow worksheet.

4. With the chart still selected, click the **Chart Styles** button ⟨⟩, and then apply the **Style 11** chart style located at the bottom of the style gallery.

You'll place this stacked column chart on the Overview worksheet.

5. On the CHART TOOLS DESIGN tab, in the Location group, click the **Move Chart** button to open the Move Chart dialog box.

6. Click the **Object in** arrow, and then click the **Overview** worksheet.

7. Click the **OK** button. The stacked column chart is moved to the Overview worksheet.

As with the clustered column chart, you'll move and resize the stacked column chart and add a descriptive chart title.

To edit the stacked column chart:

TIP

To retain the chart's proportions as you resize it, hold down the Shift key as you drag the sizing handle.

1. Move and resize the stacked column chart so that it covers the range **F31:M43** in the Overview worksheet. Use the Alt key to help you align the chart's location and size with the underlying worksheet grid.

2. Select the chart title, type **Breakdown of Business Expenses** as the new title, and then press the **Enter** key.

3. With the chart title still selected, change the font style to **non-bold**; **Blue, Accent 1**; **Calibri Light** font to match the clustered column chart. See Figure 4-21.

Figure 4-21 Stacked column chart

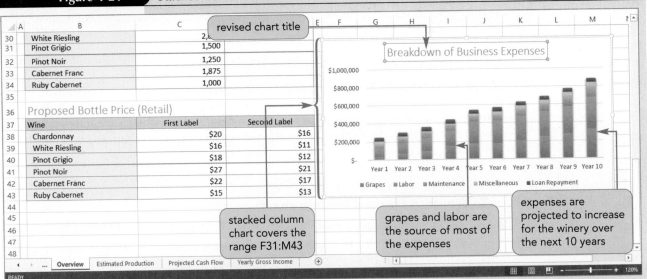

4. Save the workbook.

The chart clearly shows that the winery's main expenses over the next 10 years will come from the purchase of grapes and labor costs. General maintenance, miscellaneous, and the business loan repayment constitute a smaller portion of the company's projected expenses. The overall yearly expense of running the winery is expected to increase from about $250,000 in Year 1 to almost $900,000 by Year 10.

PROSKILLS

Aa

Written Communication: Communicating Effectively with Charts

Studies show that people more easily interpret information when it is presented as a graphic rather than in a table. As a result, charts can help communicate the real story underlying the facts and figures you present to colleagues and clients. A well-designed chart can illuminate the bigger picture that might be hidden by viewing only the numbers. However, poorly designed charts can mislead readers and make it more difficult to interpret data.

To create effective and useful charts, keep in mind the following tips as you design charts:

- **Keep it simple.** Do not clutter a chart with too many graphical elements. Focus attention on the data rather than on decorative elements that do not inform.
- **Focus on the message.** Design the chart to highlight the points you want to convey to readers.
- **Limit the number of data series.** Most charts should display no more than four or five data series. Pie charts should have no more than six slices.
- **Choose colors carefully.** Display different data series in contrasting colors to make it easier to distinguish one series from another. Modify the default colors as needed to make them distinct on the screen and in the printed copy.
- **Limit your chart to a few text styles.** Use a maximum of two or three different text styles in the same chart. Having too many text styles in one chart can distract attention from the data.

The goal of written communication is always to inform the reader in the simplest, most accurate, and most direct way possible. When creating worksheets and charts, everything in the workbook should be directed toward that end.

So far, you have determined monthly payments by using the PMT function, and created and formatted a pie chart and two column charts. In the next session, you'll continue your work on the winery's business plan by creating line charts, combination charts, sparklines, and data bars.

REVIEW

Session 4.1 Quick Check

1. You want to take out a loan for $130,000. The annual interest on the loan is 5 percent with payments due monthly. You plan to repay the loan in 15 years. Write the formula to calculate the monthly payment required to completely repay the loan under those conditions.
2. What function do you use to determine how many payment periods are required to repay a loan?
3. What three chart elements are included in a pie chart?
4. A data series contains values grouped into 10 categories. Would this data be better displayed as a pie chart or a column chart? Explain why.
5. A research firm wants to create a chart that displays the total population growth of a county over a 10-year period broken down by five ethnicities. Which chart type best displays this information? Explain why.
6. If the research firm wants to display the changing ethnic profile of the county over time as a percentage of the county population, which chart type should it use? Explain why.
7. If the research firm is interested in comparing the numeric sizes of different ethnic groups over time, which chart should it use? Explain why.
8. If the research firm wants to display the ethnic profile of the county only for the current year, which chart should it use? Explain why.
9. How does chart animation help you perform a what-if analysis?

Session 4.2 Visual Overview:

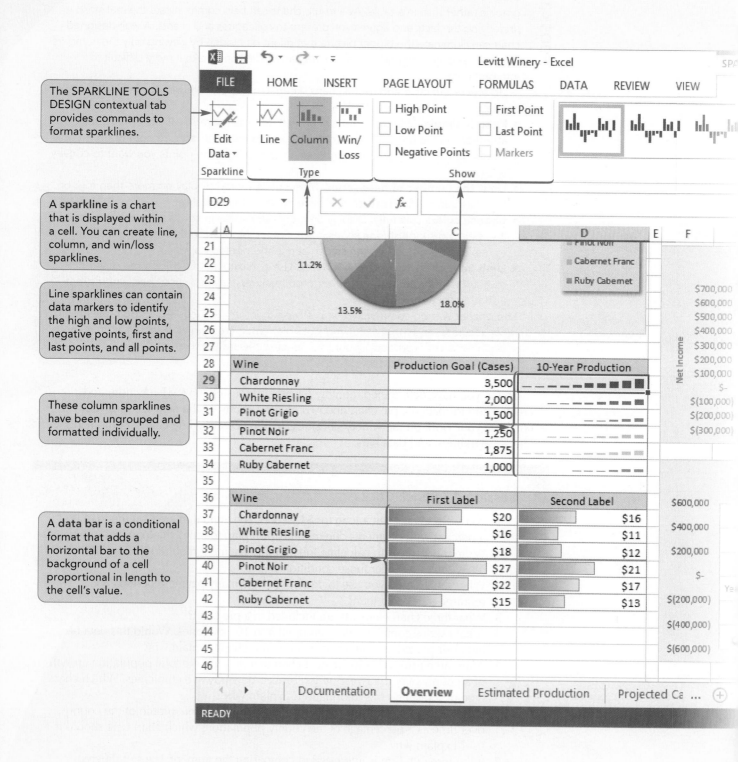

The SPARKLINE TOOLS DESIGN contextual tab provides commands to format sparklines.

A sparkline is a chart that is displayed within a cell. You can create line, column, and win/loss sparklines.

Line sparklines can contain data markers to identify the high and low points, negative points, first and last points, and all points.

These column sparklines have been ungrouped and formatted individually.

A data bar is a conditional format that adds a horizontal bar to the background of a cell proportional in length to the cell's value.

Levitt Winery - Excel

FILE   HOME   INSERT   PAGE LAYOUT   FORMULAS   DATA   REVIEW   VIEW

Edit Data   Line   Column   Win/Loss

☐ High Point   ☐ First Point
☐ Low Point   ☐ Last Point
☐ Negative Points   ☐ Markers

Sparkline   Type   Show

D29   ✕ ✓ fx

	Wine	Production Goal (Cases)	10-Year Production
29	Chardonnay	3,500	
30	White Riesling	2,000	
31	Pinot Grigio	1,500	
32	Pinot Noir	1,250	
33	Cabernet Franc	1,875	
34	Ruby Cabernet	1,000	

	Wine	First Label	Second Label
37	Chardonnay	$20	$16
38	White Riesling	$16	$11
39	Pinot Grigio	$18	$12
40	Pinot Noir	$27	$21
41	Cabernet Franc	$22	$17
42	Ruby Cabernet	$15	$13

11.2%   18.0%   13.5%

Pinot Noir
Cabernet Franc
Ruby Cabernet

$700,000
$600,000
$500,000
$400,000
$300,000
$200,000
$100,000
$-
$(100,000)
$(200,000)
$(300,000)

Net Income

$600,000
$400,000
$200,000
$-
$(200,000)
$(400,000)
$(600,000)

◄ ►   Documentation   **Overview**   Estimated Production   Projected Ca ...   ⊕

READY

Charts, Sparklines, and Data Bars

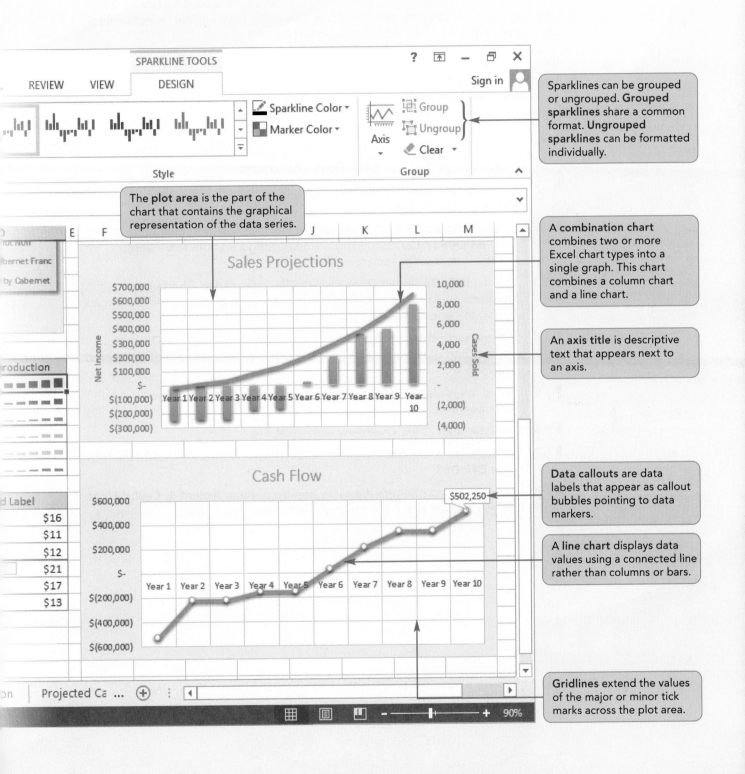

Sparklines can be grouped or ungrouped. **Grouped sparklines** share a common format. **Ungrouped sparklines** can be formatted individually.

The **plot area** is the part of the chart that contains the graphical representation of the data series.

A **combination chart** combines two or more Excel chart types into a single graph. This chart combines a column chart and a line chart.

An **axis title** is descriptive text that appears next to an axis.

Data callouts are data labels that appear as callout bubbles pointing to data markers.

A **line chart** displays data values using a connected line rather than columns or bars.

Gridlines extend the values of the major or minor tick marks across the plot area.

Creating a Line Chart

Line charts are typically used when the data consists of values drawn from categories that follow a sequential order at evenly spaced intervals, such as historical data that is recorded monthly, quarterly, or yearly. Like column charts, a line chart can be used with one or more data series. When multiple data series are included, the data values are plotted on different lines with varying line colors.

Bob and Carol want to use a line chart to show the winery's potential cash flow over the next decade. Cash flow measures the amount of cash flowing into and out of a business annually; it is one measure of a business's financial health and ability to make its payments. Because the cash flow values are the only data series, only one line will appear on the chart. You will create the line chart now.

When charting table values, do not include the summary totals because they will be treated as another category.

To create the projected cash flow line chart:

1. If you took a break at the end of the previous session, make sure the Levitt Winery workbook is open.

2. Go to the **Projected Cash Flow** worksheet, and then select the nonadjacent range **B4:L4;B27:L27** containing the Year categories from row 4 and the Cash Flow data series from row 27.

3. Click the **INSERT** tab, and then click the **Recommended Charts** button in the Charts group. The Insert Chart dialog box opens, showing different ways to chart the selected data.

4. Click the second chart listed (the Line chart), and then click the **OK** button. The line chart of the year-end cash flow values is embedded in the Projected Cash Flow worksheet.

5. Format the line chart with the **Style 15** chart style to give the line a raised 3-D appearance.

6. Move the chart to the **Overview** worksheet.

7. Move and resize the line chart in the Overview worksheet so that it covers the range **B45:D58**.

8. Format the chart title with the same **non-bold**; **Blue, Accent 1**; **Calibri Light** font you applied to the two column charts. See Figure 4-22.

Figure 4-22   **Line chart of the projected cash flow**

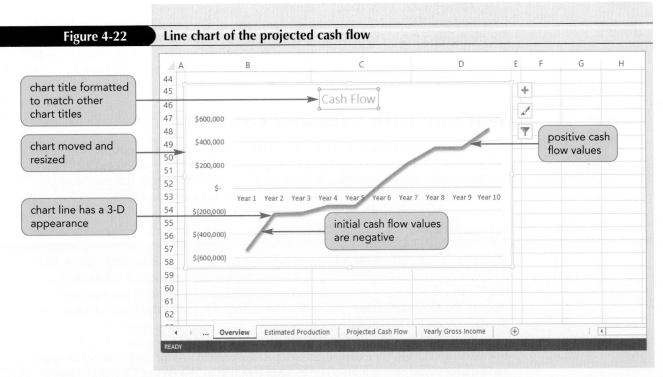

chart title formatted to match other chart titles

chart moved and resized

chart line has a 3-D appearance

positive cash flow values

initial cash flow values are negative

The line chart shows that Levitt Winery will have a negative cash flow in its early years and that the annual cash flow will increase throughout the decade, showing a positive cash flow starting in its sixth year.

INSIGHT

Line Charts and Scatter Charts

Line charts can sometimes be confused with XY (Scatter) charts; but they are very different chart types. A line chart is more like a column chart that uses lines instead of columns. In a line chart, the data series are plotted against category values. These categories are assumed to have some sequential order. If the categories represent dates or times, they must be evenly spaced in time. For example, the Cash Flow line chart plotted the cash flow values against categories that ranged sequentially from Year 1 to Year 10.

A scatter chart has no category values. Instead, one series of data values is plotted against another. For example, if you were analyzing the relationship between height and weight among high school students, you would use a scatter chart because both weight and height are data values. On the other hand, if you charted height measures against weight categories (Underweight, Normal, Overweight), a line chart would be more appropriate.

Scatter charts are more often used in statistical analysis and scientific studies in which the researcher is attempting to find a relationship between one variable and another. For that purpose, Excel includes several statistical tools to augment scatter charts, such as trendlines that provide the best fitting line or curve to the data. You can add a trendline by right-clicking the data series in the chart, and then clicking Add Trendline on the shortcut menu. From the Format Trendline pane that opens you can select different types of trendlines, including exponential and logarithmic lines as well as linear (straight) lines.

You have created three charts that provide a visual picture of the Levitt Winery business plan. Bob and Carol anticipate lean years as the winery becomes established; but they expect that by the end of 10 years, the winery will be profitable and stable. Next, you'll look at other tools to fine-tune the formatting of these charts. You'll start by looking at the scale applied to the chart values.

Working with Axes and Gridlines

A chart's vertical and horizontal axes are based on the values in the data series and the category values. In many cases, the axes display the data in the most visually effective and informative way. Sometimes, however, you will want to modify the axes' scale, add gridlines, and make other changes to better highlight the chart data.

Editing the Scale of the Vertical Axis

The range of values, or **scale**, of an axis is based on the values in the data source. The default scale usually ranges from 0 (if the data source has no negative values) to the maximum value. If the scale includes negative values, it ranges from the minimum value to the maximum value. The vertical, or value, axis shows the range of values in the data series; the horizontal, or category, axis shows the category values.

Excel divides the scale into regular intervals, which are marked on the axis with **tick marks** and labels. For example, the scale of the vertical axis for the Projected Revenue and Expenses chart ranges from $0 up to $2,000,000 in increments of $200,000. Having more tick marks at smaller intervals could make the chart difficult to read because the tick mark labels might start to overlap. Likewise, having fewer tick marks at larger intervals could make the chart less informative. **Major tick marks** identify the main units on the chart axis while **minor tick marks** identify the smaller intervals between the major tick marks.

Some charts involve multiple data series that have vastly different values. In those instances, you can create dual axis charts. You can plot one data series against a **primary axis**, which usually appears along the left side of the chart, and the other against a **secondary axis**, which is usually placed on the right side of the chart. The two axes can be based on entirely different scales.

By default, no titles appear next to the value and category axes. This is fine when the axis labels are self-explanatory. Otherwise, you can add descriptive axis titles. In general, you should avoid cluttering a chart with extra elements such as axis titles when that information is easily understood from other parts of the chart.

The Levitts think that the value axis scale for the Projected Revenue and Expenses chart is too crowded, and they want tick marks placed at intervals of $250,000 ranging from $0 to $1,750,000. You will modify the scale of the value axis.

To change the scale of the vertical axis:

1. Double-click the vertical axis of the Projected Revenue and Expenses chart to open the Format pane.

   The Format Axis pane has options to modify the value axis. The Bounds section provides the minimum and maximum boundaries of the axis, which in this case are set from 0.0 to 2.0E6 (which stands for 2,000,000). Note that minimum and maximum values are set to Auto, which means that Excel automatically set these boundaries based on the data values.

TIP

To return a scale value to Auto, click the Reset button next to the value in the Format pane.

2. In the Bounds section of the AXIS OPTIONS, click in the **Maximum** box, delete the current value, type **1750000** as the new value, and then press the **Enter** key. Excel changes the maximum value of the vertical axis to $1,750,000.

The Units section provides the intervals between the major tick marks and between minor tick marks. These intervals are also set automatically by Excel.

3. In the Units section, click in the **Major** box, delete the current value, type **250000** as the new interval between major tick marks, and then press the **Enter** key. The scale of the value axis has been changed. See Figure 4-23.

Figure 4-23   **Formatted value axis**

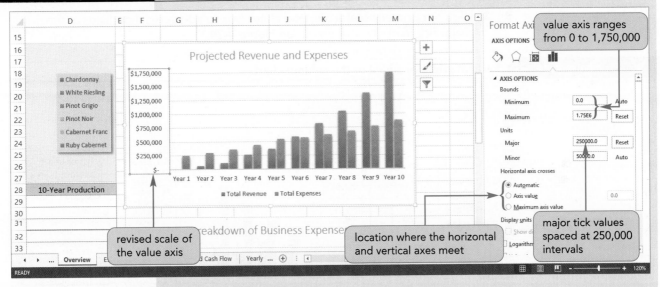

The revised axis scale makes the values easier to read and interpret.

INSIGHT

Displaying Unit Labels

When a chart involves large numbers, the axis labels can take up a lot of the available chart area and be difficult to read. You can simplify the chart's appearance by displaying units of measure more appropriate to the data values. For example, you can display the value 20 to represent 20,000 or 20,000,000. This is particularly useful when space is at a premium, such as in an embedded chart confined to a small area of the worksheet.

To display a units label, you double-click the axis to open the Format pane displaying options to format the axis. Select the units type from the Display units box. You can choose unit labels to represent values measured in the hundreds up to the trillions. Excel will modify the numbers on the selected axis and add a label so that readers will know what the axis values represent.

Adding Gridlines

Gridlines are horizontal and vertical lines that help you compare data and category values. Depending on the chart style, gridlines may or may not appear in a chart, though you can add or remove them separately. Gridlines are placed at the major tick marks on the axes, or you can set them to appear at the minor tick marks.

The chart style used for the two column charts and the line chart includes horizontal gridlines. Carol and Bob want you to add vertical gridlines to help further separate one set of year values from another. You'll add major vertical gridlines to the Projected Revenue and Expenses chart.

To add vertical gridlines to the Projected Revenue and Expenses chart:

▶ **1.** With the Projected Revenue and Expenses chart still selected, click the **Chart Elements** button ⊞ next to the selected column chart. The menu of chart elements appears.

▶ **2.** Point to **Gridlines**, and then click the **right arrow** that appears to open a submenu of gridline options.

▶ **3.** Click the **Primary Major Vertical** check box to add vertical gridlines at the major tick marks on the chart. See Figure 4-24.

Figure 4-24	Vertical gridlines added to the column chart

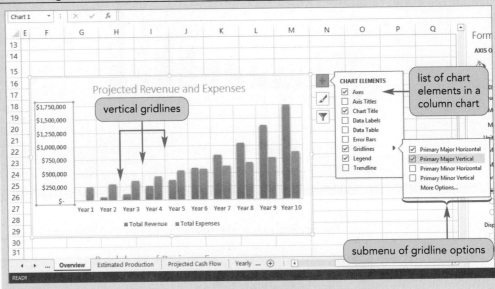

▶ **4.** Press the **Esc** key to close the Chart Elements menu.

Working with Column Widths

Category values do not have the scale options used with data values. However, you can set the spacing between one column and another in your column charts. You can also define the width of the columns. As with the vertical axis, the default spacing and width are set automatically by Excel. A column chart with several categories will naturally make those columns thinner and more tightly packed.

The Levitts think that the columns in the Projected Revenue and Expenses chart are spaced too closely, making it difficult to distinguish one year's values from another. They want you to increase the gap between the columns.

To format the chart columns:

▶ **1.** Make sure the Projected Revenue and Expenses chart is still selected and the Format pane is still open.

▶ **2.** In the Format pane, click the **AXIS OPTIONS arrow**, and then click **Series "Total Revenue"** from the list of chart elements. The Format pane title changes to "Format Data Series" and all of the columns that show total revenue values are selected.

TIP

You can use the up and down spin arrows in the Gap Width box to fine-tune the gap width in 1 percent increments.

3. In the Format pane, click **SERIES OPTIONS** to display the list of options, if necessary. Series Overlap sets the amount of overlap between columns of different data series. Gap Width sets the amount of space between one group of columns and the next.

4. Drag the **Gap Width** slider until **150%** appears in the Gap Width box. The gap between groups of columns increases and the individual column widths decrease to make room for the larger gap. See Figure 4-25.

Figure 4-25   Gap width between columns

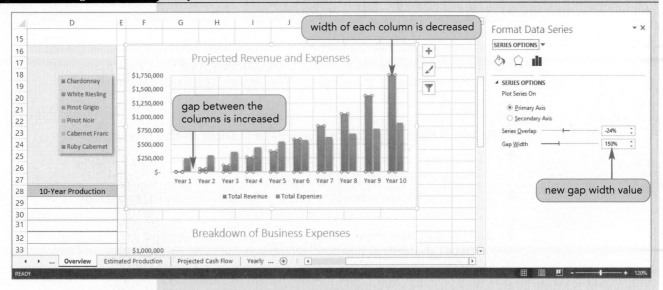

Formatting Data Markers

Each value from a data series is represented by a data marker. In pie charts, the data markers are the individual pie slices. In column charts, the columns are the data markers. In a line chart, the data markers are the points connected by the line. Depending on the line chart style, these data marker points can be displayed or hidden.

In the Cash Flow line chart, the data marker points are hidden and only the line connecting them is visible. Carol wants you to display these data markers and change their fill color to white so that they stand out, making the chart easier to understand.

To display and format the line chart data markers:

1. Scroll down the worksheet to display the Cash Flow line chart, and then double-click the line to change the Format pane to the Format Data Series pane.

2. Click the **Fill & Line** button ⬙. You can choose to display the format options for lines or data markers.

3. Click **MARKER**, if necessary, and then click **MARKER OPTIONS** to display a list of options for the line chart data markers. Currently, the None option button is selected to hide the data markers.

4. Click the **Automatic** option button to automatically display the markers. The data markers are now visible in the line chart, but they have a blue fill color. You will change this fill color to white.

▶ **5.** Click **FILL**, if necessary, to expand the fill options.

▶ **6.** Click the **Solid fill** option button, click the **Fill Color** button, and then click the **White, Background 1** theme color. The fill color for the data markers in the line chart changes to white.

▶ **7.** Press the **Esc** key to deselect the data markers in the line chart.

In many charts, you will want to highlight an important data point. Data labels provide a way to identify the different values in a chart. Whether you include data labels depends on the chart, the complexity of the data and presentation, and the chart's purpose. You can include data labels for every data marker, or you can include data labels for individual data points.

Carol and Bob want to highlight that at the end of the tenth year, the winery should have an annual cash flow that exceeds $500,000. They want you to add a data label that displays the value of the last data marker in the chart at that data point.

To add a data label to the last data marker in the line chart:

▶ **1.** Click the line in the line chart to select the entire data series, including all of the data markers.

▶ **2.** Click the last data marker to select it. Selection handles appear around this data marker, but not any of the others.

▶ **3.** Click the **Chart Elements** button ⊞ next to the line chart, and then click the **Data Labels** check box to insert a checkmark. The data label appears above only the selected data marker.

▶ **4.** Click the **Data Labels arrow** to display a menu of data label positions and options, and then click **Data Callout**. The data label is changed to a data callout box that includes both the category value and the data value, displaying "Year 10, $502,250." You will modify this callout to display only the data value.

▶ **5.** Double-click the data callout to select it. The Format pane is titled "Format Data Labels."

▶ **6.** Click the **Label Options** button ▥, and then click **LABEL OPTIONS**, if necessary, to display those options.

▶ **7.** Click the **Category Name** check box to deselect it.

▶ **8.** Press the **Esc** key to deselect the data label. The data callout now displays only $502,250. See Figure 4-26.

Figure 4-26	Formatted data markers and data label

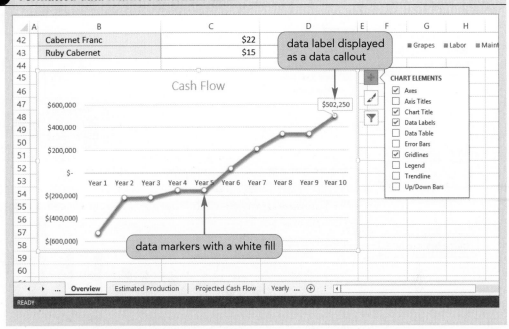

Formatting the Plot Area

The chart area covers the entire background of the chart, whereas the plot area includes only that portion of the chart in which the data markers, such as the columns in a column chart, have been placed or plotted. You can format the plot area by changing its fill and borders, and by adding visual effects. Changes to the plot area are often made in conjunction with the chart area.

Carol and Bob want you to format the chart area and plot area of the Projected Revenue and Expenses chart. You'll set the chart area fill color to a light gold to match the pie chart, and the plot area fill color to white.

To change the fill colors of the chart and plot areas:

1. Scroll the worksheet up and select the Projected Revenue and Expenses chart.

2. On the ribbon, click the **CHART TOOLS FORMAT** tab.

3. In the Current Selection group, click the **Chart Elements** arrow to display a list of chart elements in the current chart, and then click **Chart Area**. The chart area is selected in the chart.

4. In the Shape Styles group, click the **Shape Fill** button, and then click the **Gold, Accent 4, Lighter 80%** theme color in the second row and eighth column. The entire background of the chart changes to light gold.

5. In the Current Selection group, click the **Chart Elements** arrow, and then click **Plot Area** to select that chart element.

6. Change the fill color of the plot area to **white**. See Figure 4-27.

Figure 4-27   **Final Projected Revenue and Expenses chart**

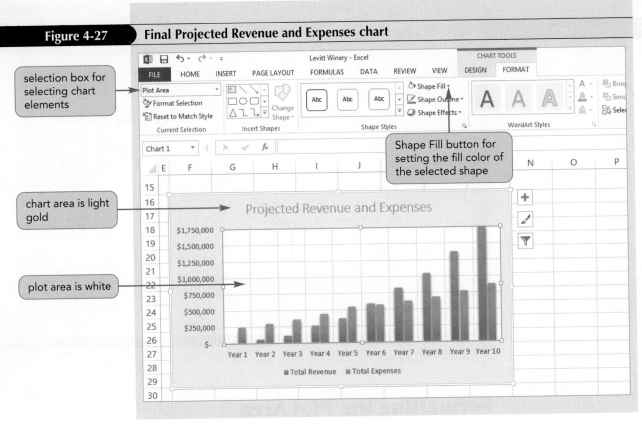

Bob and Carol like the appearance of the Projected Revenue and Expenses chart, and they want the same general design applied to the Breakdown of Business Expenses column chart and the Cash Flow line chart. You will add vertical gridlines to each chart, and then change the chart area fill color to light gold and the plot area fill color to white.

To format the Breakdown of Business Expenses column chart and the Cash Flow line chart:

1. Select the **Breakdown of Business Expenses** column chart.

2. Select the **chart area**, and then set the fill color of the chart area to the **Gold, Accent 4, Lighter 80%** theme color.

3. Select the **plot area**, and then change the fill color to **white**.

   Next, you'll add vertical gridlines to the chart. You can also use the CHART TOOLS DESIGN tab to add chart elements such as gridlines.

4. On the ribbon, click the **CHART TOOLS DESIGN** tab.

5. In the Chart Layouts group, click the **Add Chart Element** button, scroll down the chart elements, point to **Gridlines**, and then click **Primary Major Vertical** on the submenu. Vertical gridlines are added to the chart. See Figure 4-28.

Figure 4-28   Final Breakdown of Business Expenses chart

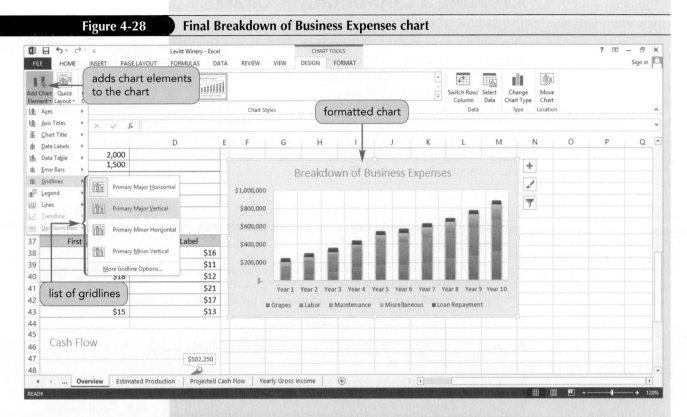

6. Scroll down the worksheet, select the **Cash Flow** line chart, and then repeat Steps 2 through 5 to set the chart area fill color to light gold, set the plot area fill color to white, and add major gridlines to the chart's primary axis.

The Breakdown of Business Expenses column chart and the Cash Flow line chart are now formatted with the same design.

Overlaying Chart Elements

An embedded chart takes up less space than a chart sheet. However, it can be challenging to fit all of the chart elements into that smaller space. One solution is to overlay one element on top of another. The most commonly overlaid elements are the chart title and the chart legend. To overlay the chart title, click the Chart Title arrow from the list of Chart Elements and select Centered Overlay from the list of position options. Excel will place the chart title on top of the plot area, freeing up more space for other chart elements. Chart legends can also be overlaid by opening the Format pane for the legend and deselecting the Show the legend without overlapping the chart check box in the LEGEND OPTIONS section. Other chart elements can be overlaid by dragging them to new locations in the chart area and then resizing the plot area to recover the empty space.

Don't overuse the technique of overlaying chart elements. Too much overlaying of chart elements can make your chart difficult to read.

Creating a Combination Chart

A combination chart combines two chart types, such as a column chart and a line chart, within a single chart. Combination charts enable you to show two sets of data using the chart type that is best for each data set. Combination charts can have data series with vastly different values. In those instances, you can create dual axis charts, using primary and secondary axes.

Bob and Carol want to include a chart that projects the net income and cases sold by Levitt Winery over the next 10 years. Because these two data series are measuring different things (dollars and wine cases), the chart might be better understood if the Net Income data series was displayed as a column chart and the Cases Produced and Sold data series was displayed as a line chart.

To create a combination chart that shows net income and sales data:

▶ 1. Go to the **Projected Cash Flow** worksheet, and then select the nonadjacent range **B4:L5;B23:L23** containing the Year category values, the data series for Cases Produced and Sold, and the data series for Net Income.

▶ 2. On the ribbon, click the **INSERT** tab.

▶ 3. In the Charts group, click the **Recommended Charts** button. The Insert Chart dialog box opens.

▶ 4. Click the **All Charts** tab to view a list of all chart types and subtypes.

▶ 5. Click **Combo** in the list of chart types, and then click the **Custom Combination** icon (the fourth subtype). At the bottom of the dialog box, you choose the chart type for each data series and whether that data series is plotted on the primary or secondary axis.

▶ 6. For the Cases Produced and Sold data series, click the **Chart Type** arrow, and then click **Line**.

▶ 7. Click the **Secondary Axis** check box to display the values for that series on a secondary axis.

▶ 8. For the Net Income data series, click the **Chart Type** arrow, and then click **Clustered Column**. See Figure 4-29.

Figure 4-29   Combo chart type

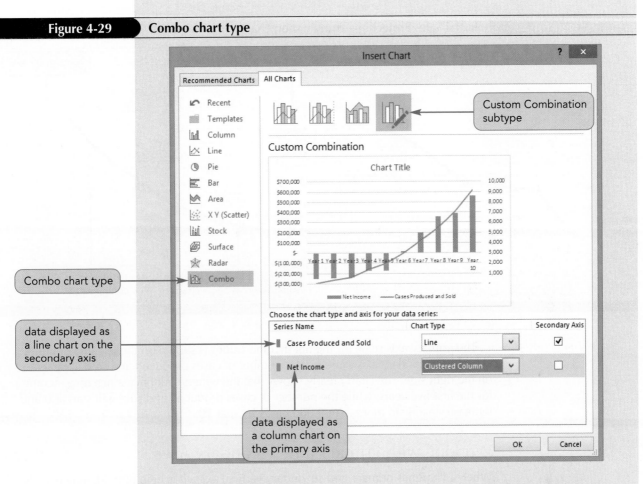

9. Click the **OK** button. The combination chart is embedded in the Projected Cash Flow worksheet.

10. Format the combination chart with the **Style 8** chart style to give both the line and the columns a raised 3-D effect.

Bob and Carol want the combination chart to appear in the Overview worksheet and be formatted to resemble the other charts. You will make those changes now.

To move and format the combination chart:

1. Move the combination chart to the **Overview** worksheet.

2. Position and resize the combination chart so that it covers the range **F45:M58**.

3. Change the title of the combination chart to **Sales Projections**, and then format the title in the same **non-bold**; **Blue, Accent 1**; **Calibri Light** font you used with the other chart titles.

4. Remove the **Legend** chart element from the combination chart.

5. Add **Primary Major Vertical** gridlines to the combination chart.

6. Change the fill color of the plot area to **white**, and then change the fill color of the chart area to the same light gold (**Gold, Accent 4, Lighter 80%**) as the other charts. See Figure 4-30.

Figure 4-30   **Initial Sales Projections combination chart**

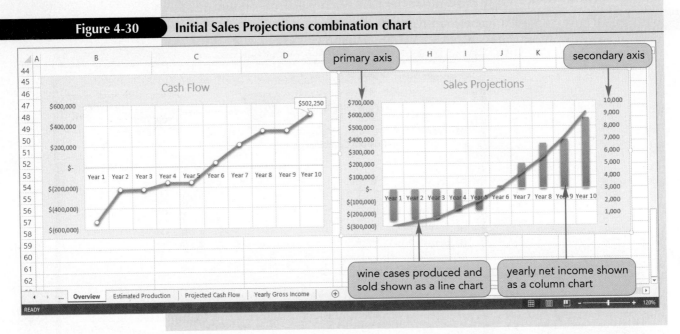

The primary axis scale for the net income values is shown on the left side of the chart; the secondary axis scale for the number of cases produced and sold appears on the right side. The chart clearly shows that the winery will have a negative income for the first five years, while the number of cases produced and sold will start at 0 and increase steadily to more than 9,000 cases by Year 10.

Working with Primary and Secondary Axes

When a chart has primary and secondary vertical axes, it is helpful to identify exactly what each axis is measuring. You can do this by adding an axis title to the chart. An axis title is descriptive text that appears next to the axis. As with other chart elements, you can add, remove, and format axis titles.

Bob and Carol want the Sales Projections chart to include labels describing what is being measured by the primary and secondary axes. You will add descriptive axis titles to the primary and secondary vertical axes.

To add axis titles to the primary and secondary vertical axes:

1. Click the **Chart Elements** button ⊞ next to the combination chart, and then click the **Axis Title** check box to select it. Titles with the placeholders "Axis Title" are added to the primary and secondary axes.

2. Click the left axis title to select it, type **Net Income** as the descriptive title, and then press the **Enter** key.

3. With the left axis title selected, change the font color to the **Orange, Accent 2, Darker 25%** theme color to match the color of the columns in the chart.

4. Select the numbers on the left axis scale, and then change the font color to the **Orange, Accent 2, Darker 25%** theme color. The left axis title and scale are now the same color as the columns that reference that axis.

5. Select the right axis title, type **Cases Sold** as the descriptive title, and then press the **Enter** key.

6. With the right axis title still selected, change the font color to the **Blue, Accent 1, Darker 25%** theme color to match the color of the line in the chart.

7. Change the orientation of the right axis title to **Rotate Text Down**. The text is easier to read in this orientation.

8. Select the numbers on the right axis scale, and then change the font color to the **Blue, Accent 1, Darker 25%** theme color. The right axis title and scale are now the same color as the line that references that axis.

Excel added the "Axis Title" placeholder to the horizontal category values axis. You can remove this title, freeing up more space for other chart elements.

9. Click the horizontal axis title to select it, and then press the **Delete** key to remove it from the chart. See Figure 4-31.

Figure 4-31   **Combination chart with axis titles**

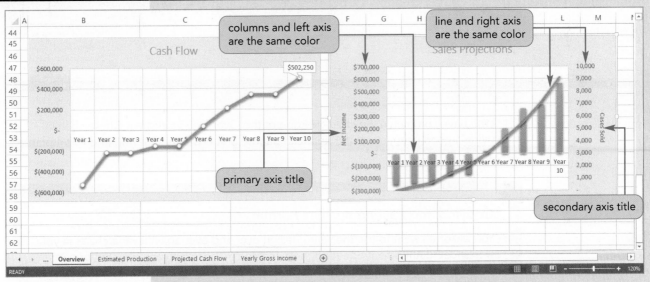

The Levitts are concerned that the line chart portion of the graph makes it look as if the number of cases produced and sold was negative for the first five years. This is because the secondary axis scale, which is automatically generated by Excel, goes from a minimum of 0 to a maximum of 10,000. You will change the scale so that the 0 tick mark for Cases Sold better aligns with the $0 for Net Income.

To modify the secondary axis scale:

1. Double-click the secondary axis scale to select it and open the Format pane.

2. Verify that the **AXIS OPTIONS** list of commands is displayed.

3. Click the **Minimum** box, change the value from 0.0 to **–4000**, and then press the **Enter** key. The secondary axis scale is modified. The Cases Sold scale is now better aligned with the Net Income scale, providing a more realistic picture of the data.

> **4.** Close the Format pane, and then press the **Esc** key to deselect the secondary axis. See Figure 4-32.

Figure 4-32   **Final combination chart**

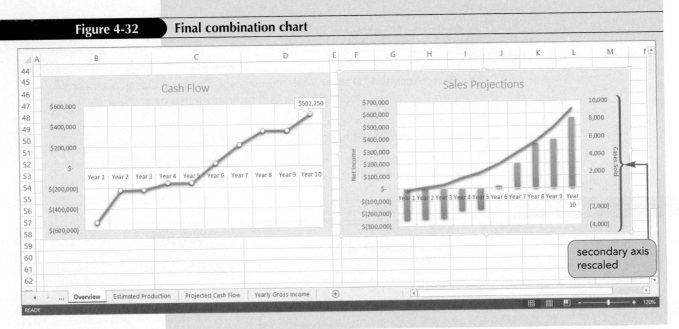

You have completed the charts portion of the Overview worksheet. These charts provide a good overview of the financial picture of the winery that Bob and Carol plan to open.

INSIGHT

Copying and Pasting a Chart Format

You will often want to use the same design over and over again for the charts in your worksheet. Rather than repeating the same commands, you can copy the formatting from one chart to another. To copy a chart format, first select the chart with the existing design that you want to replicate, and then click the Copy button in the Clipboard group on the HOME tab (or press the Ctrl+C keys). Next, select the chart that you want to format, click the Paste button arrow in the Clipboard group, and then click Paste Special to open the Paste Special dialog box. In the Paste Special dialog box, select the Formats option button, and then click the OK button. All of the copied formats from the original chart—including fill colors, font styles, axis scales, and chart types—are then pasted into the new chart. Be aware that the pasted formats will overwrite any formats previously used in the new chart.

Editing a Chart Data Source

Excel automates most of the process of creating and formatting a chart. However, sometimes the rendered chart does not appear the way you expected. One situation where this happens is when the selected cells contain numbers you want to treat as categories, but Excel treats them as a data series. When this happens, you can modify the data source to specify exactly which ranges should be treated as category values and which ranges should be treated as data values.

Modifying a Chart's Data Source

- Click the chart to select it.
- On the CHART TOOLS DESIGN tab, in the Data group, click the Select Data button.
- In the Legend Entries (Series) section of the Select Data Source dialog box, click the Add button to add another data series to the chart, or click the Remove button to remove a data series from the chart.
- Click the Edit button in the Horizontal (Category) Axis Labels section to select the category values for the chart.

The Yearly Gross Income worksheet contains a table that projects the winery's gross income for 2015 through 2024. Carol wants to see a simple line chart of this data.

To create the line chart:

1. Go to the **Yearly Gross Income** worksheet, and then select the range **B4:C14**.

2. On the ribbon, click the **INSERT** tab.

3. In the Charts group, click the **Insert Line Chart** button 📈.

4. In the 2-D Line charts section, click the **Line with Markers** subtype (the first subtype in the second row). The 2-D line chart is created. See Figure 4-33.

Figure 4-33   Line chart with Year treated as a data series

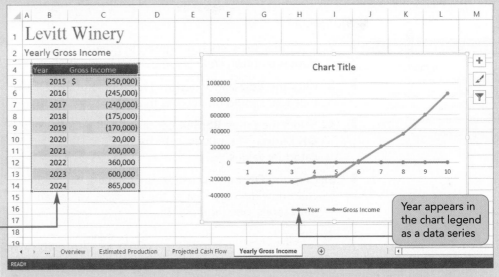

The line chart is incorrect because the Year values from the range B5:B14 are treated as another data series rather than category values. The line chart actually doesn't even have category values; the values are charted sequentially from the first value to the tenth. You can correct this problem from the Select Data dialog box by identifying the data series and category values to use in the chart.

To edit the chart's data source:

1. On the CHART TOOLS DESIGN tab, in the Data group, click the **Select Data** button. The Select Data Source dialog box opens. Note that Year is selected as a legend entry and the category values are simply the numbers 1 through 10. See Figure 4-34.

Figure 4-34 **Select Data Source dialog box**

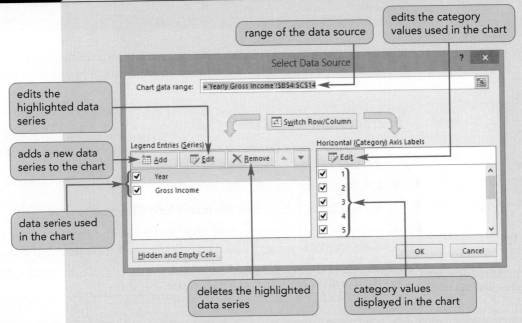

- range of the data source
- edits the category values used in the chart
- edits the highlighted data series
- adds a new data series to the chart
- data series used in the chart
- deletes the highlighted data series
- category values displayed in the chart

TIP

You can organize your data series in rows rather than columns by clicking the Switch Row/Column button in the Select Data Source dialog box.

2. With Year selected (highlighted in gray) in the list of legend entries, click the **Remove** button. Year is removed from the line chart.

3. Click the **Edit** button for the Horizontal (Category) Axis Labels. You'll specify that Year should be used as the category values.

4. Select the range **B5:B14** containing the Year values, and then click the **OK** button. The values 2015 through 2024 now appear in the list of category values.

5. Click the **OK** button to close the Select Data Source dialog box. The line chart now displays Year as the category values and Gross Income as the only data series. See Figure 4-35.

| Figure 4-35 | Revised Gross Income line chart |

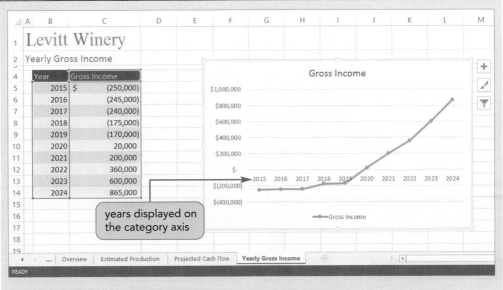

The Select Data Source dialog box is also useful when you want to add more data series to a chart. For example, if Bob and Carol wanted to include other financial estimates in an existing chart, they could add the data series to the existing chart rather than creating a new chart. To add a data series to a chart, select the chart, click the Select Data button in the Data group on the CHART TOOLS DESIGN tab to open the Select Data Source dialog box, click the Add button, and then select the range for the data series.

PROSKILLS

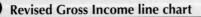

Decision Making: Choosing the Right Chart

Excel supports a wide variety of charts and chart styles. To decide which type of chart to use, you must evaluate your data and determine the ultimate purpose or goal of the chart. Consider how your data will appear in each type of chart before making a final decision.

- In general, pie charts should be used only when the number of categories is small and the relative sizes of the different slices can be easily distinguished. If you have several categories, use a column or bar chart.
- Line charts are best for categories that follow a sequential order. Be aware, however, that the time intervals must be a constant length if used in a line chart. Line charts will distort data that occurs at irregular time intervals, making it appear that the data values occurred at regular intervals when they did not.
- Pie, column, bar, and line charts assume that numbers are plotted against categories. In science and engineering applications, you will often want to plot two numeric values against one another. For that data, use **XY scatter charts**, which show the patterns or relationship between two or more sets of values. XY scatter charts are also useful for data recorded at irregular time intervals.
- If you still can't find the right chart to meet your needs, you can create a custom chart based on the built-in chart types. Third-party vendors also sell software to allow Excel to create chart types that are not built into the software.

Choosing the right chart and chart style can make your presentation more effective and informative.

Creating Sparklines

A sparkline is a chart that is displayed entirely within a worksheet cell. Because sparklines are compact in size, they don't include chart elements such as legends, titles, or gridlines. The goal of a sparkline is to convey the maximum amount of information within a very small space. As a result, sparklines are useful when you don't want charts to overwhelm the rest of your worksheet or take up valuable page space.

You can create the following three types of sparklines:

- A line sparkline for highlighting trends
- A column sparkline for column charts
- A win/loss sparkline for highlighting positive and negative values

Figure 4-36 shows examples of each sparkline type. The line sparklines show the sales history from each department and across all four departments of a computer manufacturer. The sparklines provide enough information for you to examine the sales trend within and across departments. Notice that although total sales rose steadily during the year, some departments, such as Printers, showed a sales decline midway through the year.

Figure 4-36   Types of sparklines

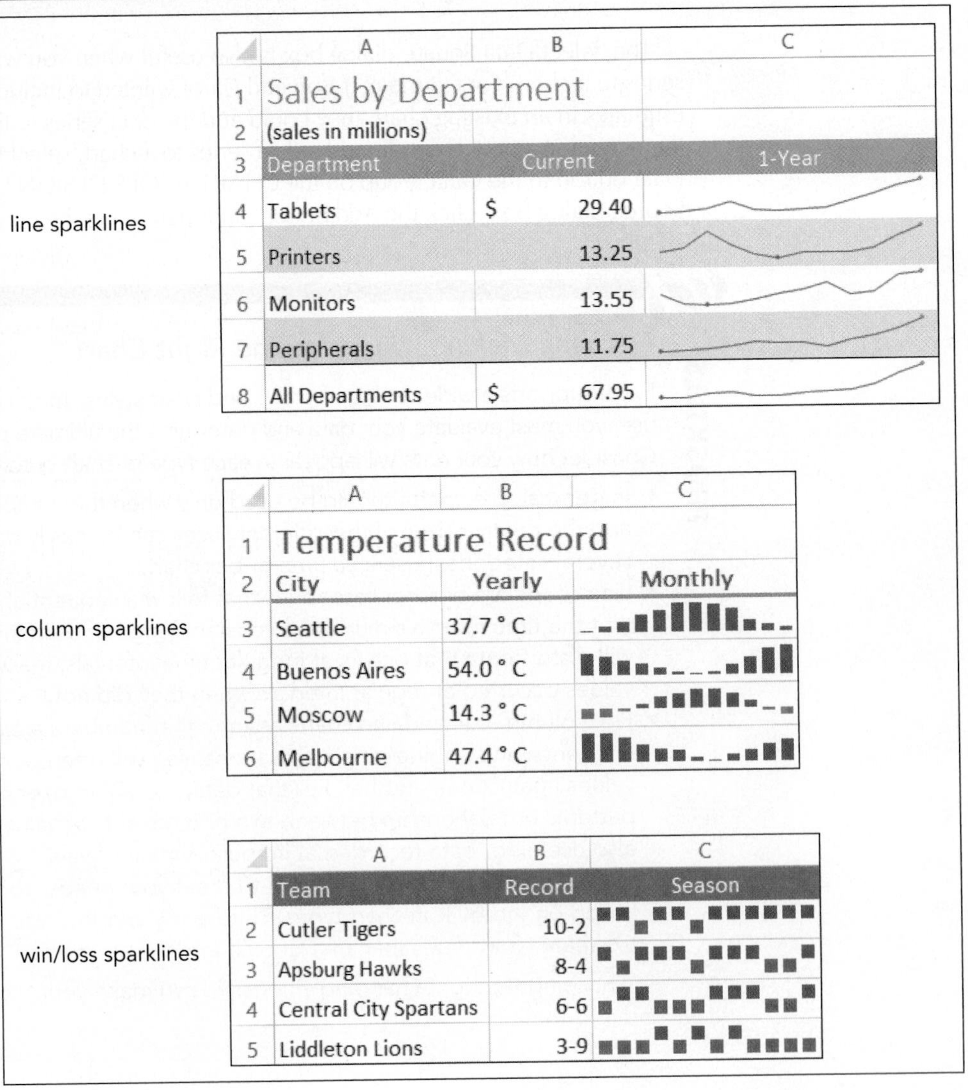

line sparklines

column sparklines

win/loss sparklines

The column sparklines present a record of monthly temperature averages for four cities. Temperatures above 0 degrees Celsius are presented in blue columns; temperatures below 0 degrees Celsius are presented in red columns that extend downward. The height of each column is related to the magnitude of the value it represents.

Finally, the win/loss sparklines reveal a snapshot of the season results for four sports teams. Wins are displayed in blue; losses are in red. From the sparklines, you can quickly see that the Cutler Tigers finished their 10–2 season with six straight wins and the Liddleton Lions finished their 3–9 season with four straight losses.

To create a set of sparklines, you first select the data you want to graph, and then select the location range where you want the sparklines to appear. Note that the cells in which you insert the sparklines do not need to be blank. Sparklines are added as part of the cell background and do not replace any cell content.

REFERENCE

Creating and Editing Sparklines

- On the INSERT tab, in the Sparklines group, click the Line, Column, or Win/Loss button.
- In the Data Range box, enter the range for the data source of the sparkline.
- In the Location Range box, enter the range into which to place the sparkline.
- Click the OK button.
- To edit a sparkline's appearance, click the SPARKLINE TOOLS DESIGN tab.
- In the Show group, click the appropriate check boxes to specify which markers to display on the sparkline.
- In the Group group, click the Axis button, and then click Show Axis to add an axis to the sparkline.

The Levitts' business plan involves rolling out the different wine types gradually, starting with Chardonnay and Cabernet Franc and then adding more varietals over the first five years. They won't start producing all six wines until Year 6. They want you to add a column sparkline to the Overview worksheet that displays this 10-year production plan.

To insert column sparklines showing the 10-year production plan in the Overview worksheet:

1. Go to the **Overview** worksheet, and then select the range **D29:D34**. This is the location range into which you will insert the sparklines.

2. On the INSERT tab, in the Sparklines group, click the **Column** button. The Create Sparklines dialog box opens. The location range is already entered because you selected it before opening the dialog box.

3. With the insertion point in the Data Range box, click the **Estimated Production** sheet tab, and then select the data in the range **C6:L11**. This is the range that contains the data you want to chart in the sparklines.

4. Click the **OK** button. The Create Sparklines dialog box closes and the column sparklines are added to the location range in the Overview worksheet. See Figure 4-37.

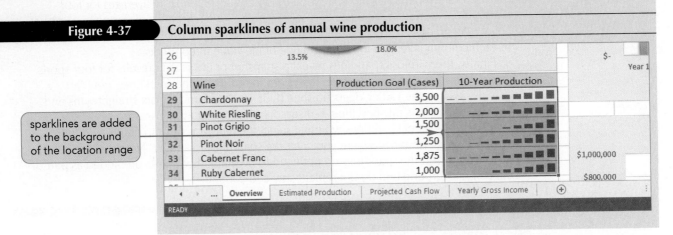

Figure 4-37   Column sparklines of annual wine production

sparklines are added to the background of the location range

The column sparklines make it clear how the wines are placed into production at different times—Chardonnay and Cabernet Franc first, and Pinot Grigio in Year 6. Each wine, once it is introduced, is steadily produced in greater quantities as the decade progresses.

Formatting the Sparkline Axis

Because of their compact size, you have few formatting options with sparklines. One thing you can change is the scale of the vertical axis. The vertical axis will range from the minimum value to the maximum value. By default, this range is defined differently for each cell to maximize the available space. But this can be misleading. For example, the column sparklines in Figure 4-37 seem to show that Levitt Winery will be producing the same amount of each wine by the end of Year 10 because the heights of the last columns are all the same. You can change the vertical axis scale to be the same for the related sparklines.

Carol and Bob want to use the same vertical axis range for each sparkline showing the 10-year production. You will set the scale of the vertical axis to range from 0 cases to 3500 cases.

To set the scale of the vertical axis of the column sparklines:

1. If necessary, select the range **D29:D34**. Because you have selected the sparklines, the SPARKLINE TOOLS DESIGN tab appears on the ribbon.

2. On the SPARKLINE TOOLS DESIGN tab, in the Group group, click the **Axis** button, and then click **Custom Value** in the Vertical Axis Maximum Value Options section. The Sparkline Vertical Axis Setting dialog box opens.

3. Replace the value in the box with **3500**, and then click the **OK** button. You do not have to set the vertical axis minimum value because Excel assumes this to be 0 for all of the column sparklines. The column sparklines are now based on the same vertical scale, and the height of each column is based on the number of cases produced per year.

Working with Sparkline Groups

The sparklines in the location range are part of a single group. Clicking any cell in the location range selects all of the sparklines in the group. Any formatting you apply to one sparkline affects all of the sparklines in the group, as you saw when you set the range of the vertical axis. This ensures that the sparklines for related data are formatted consistently. To format each sparkline differently, you must first ungroup them.

Carol and Bob think that the column sparklines would look better if they used the same colors as the pie chart for the different wines. You will first ungroup the sparklines so you can format them separately, and then you will apply a different fill color to each sparkline.

To ungroup and format the column sparklines:

▶ **1.** Make sure the range **D29:D34** is still selected.

▶ **2.** On the DESIGN tab, in the Group group, click the **Ungroup** button. The sparklines are ungrouped, and selecting any one of the sparklines will no longer select the entire group.

▶ **3.** Click cell **D30** to select it and its sparkline.

▶ **4.** On the DESIGN tab, in the Style group, click the **Sparkline Color** button, and then click the **Orange, Accent 2, Darker 25%** theme color in the sixth row and fifth column. The fill color of the column sparkline changes to a medium orange.

▶ **5.** Click cell **D31**, click the **Sparkline Color** button, and then click the **Gray-50%, Accent 3** theme color.

▶ **6.** Set the color of the sparkline in cell **D32** to **Gold, Accent 4**, set the color of the sparkline in cell **D33** to **Green, Accent 6, Lighter 60%**, and then set the color of the sparkline in cell D34 to **Green, Accent 6**.

▶ **7.** Select cell **B35** to deselect the sparklines. See Figure 4-38.

Figure 4-38   **Formatted sparklines**

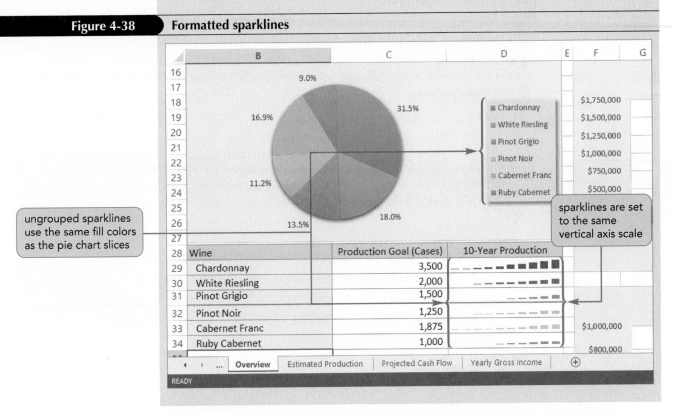

ungrouped sparklines use the same fill colors as the pie chart slices

sparklines are set to the same vertical axis scale

To regroup sparklines, you select all of the cells in the location range containing the sparklines, and then click the Group button in the Group group on the SPARKLINE TOOLS DESIGN tab. Be aware that regrouping sparklines causes them to share a common format, so you will lose any formatting applied to individual sparklines.

The Sparkline Color button applied a single color to the entire sparkline. You can also apply colors to individual markers within a sparkline by clicking the Marker Color button. Using this button, you can set a distinct color for negative values, maximum values, minimum values, first values, and last values. This is useful with line sparklines that track data across a time range in which you might want to identify the maximum value within that range or the minimum value.

Creating Data Bars

A data bar is a conditional format that adds a horizontal bar to the background of a cell containing a number. When applied to a range of cells, the data bars have the same appearance as a bar chart, with each cell containing one bar. The lengths of data bars are based on the value of each cell in the selected range. Cells with larger values have longer bars; cells with smaller values have shorter bars. Data bars are dynamic, which means that if one cell's value changes, the lengths of the data bars in the selected range are automatically updated.

Data bars differ from sparklines in that the bars are always placed in the cells containing the value they represent, and each cell represents only a single bar from the bar chart. By contrast, a column sparkline can be inserted anywhere within the workbook and can represent data from several rows or columns. However, like sparklines, data bars can be used to create compact graphs that can be easily integrated alongside the text and values stored in worksheet cells.

REFERENCE

Creating Data Bars

- Select the range containing the data you want to chart.
- On the HOME tab, in the Styles group, click the Conditional Formatting button, point to Data Bars, and then click the data bar style you want to use.
- To modify the data bar rules, click the Conditional Formatting button, and then click Manage Rules.

As part of their business plan, Bob and Carol have added a table with the proposed bottle prices for their six wines under the designation First Label (highest quality) and Second Label (average quality). They want these bottle prices to be displayed graphically. You will do this using data bars.

To add data bars to the proposed bottle prices:

1. In the Overview worksheet, select the range **C38:D43**.

2. On the HOME tab, in the Styles group, click the **Conditional Formatting** button, and then click **Data Bars**. A gallery of data bar styles opens.

3. Click the **Blue Data Bar** style in the Gradient Fill section. Blue data bars are added to each of the bottle price cells.

4. Select cell **B44** to deselect the range. See Figure 4-39.

| Figure 4-39 | Data bars added to the Overview worksheet |

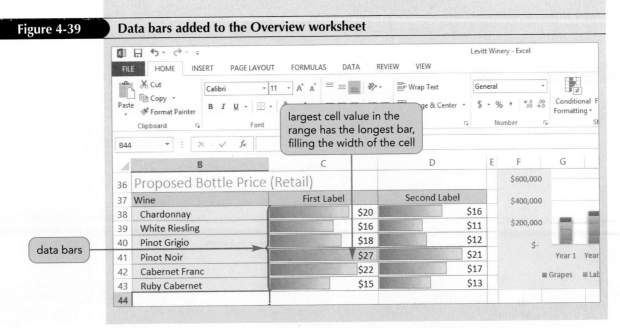

The data bars make it easy to visually compare the proposed prices of the different wines. Pinot Noir will be the most expensive wine sold by the Levitts; White Riesling and Ruby Cabernet will be the least expensive.

Modifying a Data Bar Rule

The lengths of the data bars are determined based on the values in the selected range. The cell with the largest value contains a data bar that extends across the entire width of the cell, and the lengths of the other bars in the selected range are determined relative to that bar. In some cases, this will result in the longest data bar overlapping its cell's data value, making it difficult to read. You can modify the length of the data bars by altering the rules of the conditional format.

The first label price for Pinot Noir in cell C41 contains the largest value ($27) in the range C38:D43 and has the longest data bar. The data bar for the second label price for Ruby Cabernet ($13) fills only half the cell width by comparison. The Levitts don't want data bars to overlap the cell values. You will change the data bar rule that sets the maximum length of the data bars to 35 so that the longest bar no longer fills the entire cell.

TIP

When data bars are used with negative values, the data bars originate from the center of the cell—negative bars extend to the left, and positive bars extend to the right.

To modify the data bar rule:

▶ **1.** Select the range **C38:D43** containing the data bars.

▶ **2.** On the HOME tab, in the Styles group, click the **Conditional Formatting** button, and then click **Manage Rules**. The Conditional Formatting Rules Manager dialog box opens, displaying all the rules applied to any conditional format in the workbook.

▶ **3.** Make sure **Current Selection** appears in the Show formatting rules for box. You'll edit the rule applied to the current selection—the data bars in the Sectors worksheet.

▶ **4.** Click the **Edit Rule** button. The Edit Formatting Rule dialog box opens. You want to modify this rule so that the maximum value for the data bar is set to 35. All data bar lengths will then be defined relative to this value.

▶ **5.** In the Type row, click the **Maximum** arrow, and then click **Number**.

6. Press the **Tab** key to move the insertion point to the Maximum box in the Value row, and then type **35**. See Figure 4-40.

Figure 4-40 Edit Formatting Rule dialog box

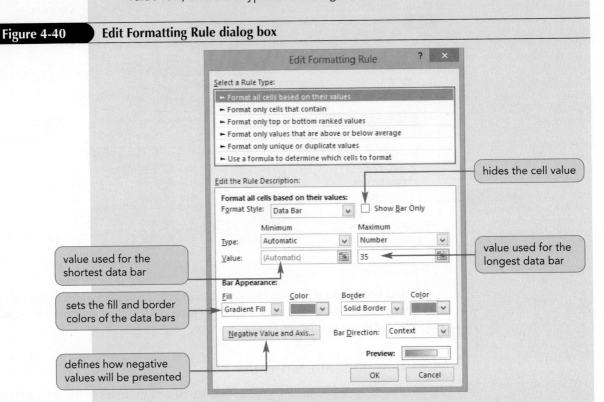

7. Click the **OK** button in each dialog box, and then select cell **B44**. The lengths of the data bars are reduced so that the longest bar covers about three-fourths of the cell width. See Figure 4-41.

Figure 4-41 Revised data bars

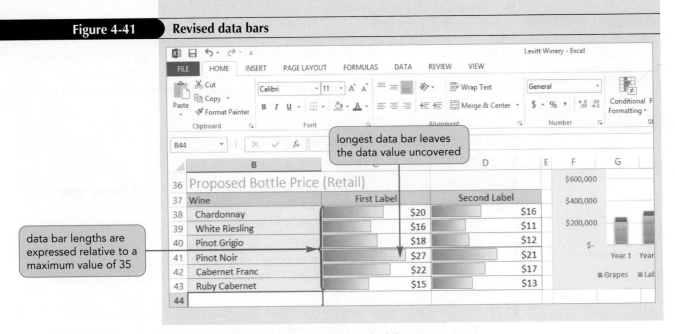

The data bars provide a good visual of the wine prices.

INSIGHT

Edward Tufte and Chart Design Theory

Any serious study of charts will include the works of Edward Tufte, who pioneered the field of information design. One of Tufte's most important works is *The Visual Display of Quantitative Information*, in which he laid out several principles for the design of charts and graphics.

Tufte was concerned with what he termed as "chart junk," in which a proliferation of chart elements—chosen because they look "nice"—confuse and distract the reader. One measure of chart junk is Tufte's data-ink ratio, which is the amount of "ink" used to display quantitative information compared to the total ink required by the chart. Tufte advocated limiting the use of non-data ink. Non-data ink is any part of the chart that does not convey information about the data. One way of measuring the data-ink ratio is to determine how much of the chart you can erase without affecting the user's ability to interpret the chart. Tufte would argue for high data-ink ratios with a minimum of extraneous elements and graphics.

To this end, Tufte helped develop sparklines, which convey information with a high data-ink ratio within a compact space. Tufte believed that charts that can be viewed and comprehended at a glance have a greater impact on the reader than large and cluttered graphs, no matter how attractive they might be.

Inserting a Watermark

TIP

Fill colors hide a watermark. So if a sheet has a watermark, don't use a fill color for the worksheet background.

Many businesses distinguish works in progress from final versions by including the word "Draft" as a watermark on each page. A **watermark** is text or an image that appears in the background behind other content. You insert a watermark into the header or footer of a worksheet. Even though the watermark is inserted into the header or footer, a large watermark will overflow those sections and appear on the entire sheet. Generally, watermarks are given a "washed-out" appearance and are placed behind text or charts on the sheet so that they don't obscure any of the other content on the sheet. Because the watermark is included in the header/footer section, it is visible in Page Layout view and Page Break Preview but not in Normal view.

Because the current business plan for Levitt Winery will change as Bob and Carol continue to explore their financial options and the status of the wine market, they want to include a watermark with the word "Draft" on the Overview worksheet.

To insert a watermark into the worksheet:

1. On the ribbon, click the **PAGE LAYOUT** tab.

2. In the Page Setup group, click the **Dialog Box Launcher** to open the Page Setup dialog box.

3. Click the **Header/Footer** tab to display options for the header or footer of the current worksheet.

4. Click the **Custom Header** button to open the Header dialog box.

5. Click the **Center section** box. You want to insert the watermark in the center section of the header.

6. Click the **Insert Picture** button 🖻 to open the Insert Pictures dialog box.

7. Click the **From a file**, navigate to the **Excel4 ▸ Tutorial** folder included with your Data Files, click the **Draft.png** file, and then click the **Insert** button. Code for the inserted picture is added to the center section of the header. See Figure 4-42.

Figure 4-42   **Inserting a watermark graphic image**

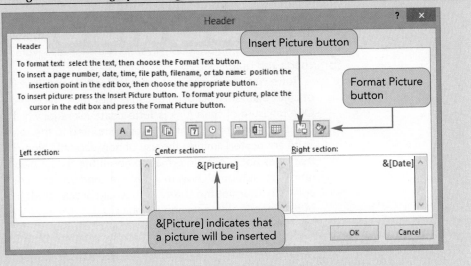

Generally, watermarks are lighter or washed out so that they don't obscure or distract from the sheet content. You can format the appearance of the watermark from the Header dialog box.

To format the appearance of the watermark:

1. In the Header dialog box, click the **Format Picture** button to open the Format Picture dialog box.

2. Click the **Picture** tab, click the **Color** box, and then click **Washout** from the color options.

3. Click the **OK** button in each dialog box to return to the Page Setup dialog box.

4. Click the **Print Preview** button to preview the printed worksheet in Backstage view. As shown in Figure 4-43, the Draft graphic image appears in the background, faded out so as to not obscure the sheet contents.

| Figure 4-43 | Print preview of the worksheet with the watermark |

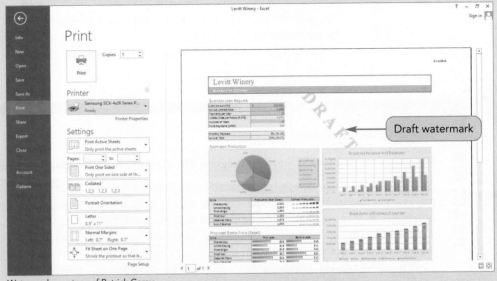

Watermark courtesy of Patrick Carey

▶ **5.** Click the **Back** button ⬅ to return to the workbook.

▶ **6.** Save and close the workbook.

The Levitts are pleased with the charts and graphics you have created. They provide useful visuals for anyone who is studying the Levitts' proposal.

Session 4.2 Quick Check

REVIEW

1. What is the difference between a line chart and a scatter chart?
2. A researcher wants to plot weight versus blood pressure. Should the researcher use a line chart or a scatter chart? Explain why.
3. What are major tick marks, minor tick marks, and gridlines?
4. How do you change the scale of a chart axis?
5. What is the difference between the chart area and the plot area?
6. What are sparklines? Describe the three types of sparklines.
7. What are data bars? How do data bars differ from sparklines?
8. What is a watermark?

ASSESS

SAM Projects

Put your skills into practice with SAM Projects! SAM Projects for this tutorial can be found online. If you have a SAM account, go to www.cengage.com/sam2013 to download the most recent Project Instructions and Start Files.

PRACTICE

Review Assignments

Data Files needed for the Review Assignments: Market.xlsx, Watermark.png

Another part of Carol and Bob Levitt's business plan for the new Levitt Winery is to analyze current market conditions. The Levitts have created a workbook that explores customer preferences and sales of wine in the United States. The workbook also explores the current wineries in Michigan against which the Levitt Winery will be competing. Bob and Carol asked you to complete their workbook by presenting this data in graphic form using Excel charts. Complete the following:

1. Open the **Market** workbook located in the Excel4 ▸ Review folder included with your Data Files, and then save the workbook as **Market Analysis** in the location specified by your instructor.

2. In the Documentation sheet, enter your name in cell B3 and the date in cell B4.

3. In the Loan Analysis sheet, enter the data values and formulas required to calculate the monthly payment on a business loan of **$225,000** at **8.2** percent annual interest to be repaid in **15** years.

4. In the Market Summary worksheet, use the data in the range E21:F27 showing the types of grapes cultivated by Michigan wineries to create a pie chart comparing production rates. Embed the pie chart in the Market Summary worksheet covering the range B5:G18.

5. Format the pie chart by removing the chart title, applying the Style 11 chart style, and aligning the legend with the right edge of the chart area.

6. In the Michigan Wineries worksheet, create a line chart based on the data in the nonadjacent range B4:B16;F4:F16 showing the increase in the number of wineries in Michigan over the past 12 years. Embed the line chart in the Market Summary worksheet covering the range I5:O16.

7. Format the line chart by making the following changes:
   a. Format the chart with the Style 14 chart style.
   b. Change the chart title to **Michigan Wineries**.
   c. Change the fill color of the chart area to light blue and the plot area to white.
   d. Add primary major vertical gridlines to the plot area.
   e. Change the scale of the primary axis to range from **50** to **140** in steps of **10** units.

8. In the Michigan Wineries worksheet, create a clustered column chart using the data in the range B4:E16 showing the growth of Michigan wineries by region. Embed the chart in the Market Summary worksheet over the range I18:O28.

9. Format the column chart by making the following changes:
   a. Format the chart with the Style 13 chart style.
   b. Change the chart title to **Michigan Wineries** and reduce its font size to 14 points.
   c. Set the fill color of the chart area to light blue and the plot area to white.
   d. Add primary major vertical gridlines to the plot area.

10. In the U.S. Wine Sales worksheet, create a stacked column chart using the data in the range B3:E15 showing the breakout of the wine market into table wines, dessert wines, and sparkling wines or champagne. Embed the stacked column chart in the range B30:G43 of the Market Summary worksheet.

11. Format the stacked column chart by making the following changes:

    a. Format the chart with the Style 6 chart style.

    b. Change the chart title to **U.S. Wine Sales** and set its font size to 14 points.

    c. Add a primary vertical axis title with the text **Millions of Cases** and remove the primary horizontal axis title.

    d. Add primary major vertical gridlines.

    e. Set the fill color of the chart area to light blue and the plot area to white.

12. In the U.S. Wine Consumption worksheet, create a combination chart based on the data in the range B3:D15 showing how much wine Americans consume annually. Display the Gallons (millions) data series as a clustered column chart on the primary axis, and then display the Gallons (per Capita) data series as a line chart on the secondary axis.

13. Move the combination chart to the Market Summary worksheet; embed it over the range I30:O43.

14. Format the combination chart by making the following changes:

    a. Format the chart with the Style 4 chart style.

    b. Change the chart title to **U.S. Wine Consumption** and set its font size to 14 points.

    c. Add the primary axis title **Gallons (millions)** and the secondary axis title **Gallons (per Capita)**. Change the font color of the axis titles and scales to match the column and line markers.

    d. Remove the horizontal axis title and chart legend.

    e. Change the rotation of the secondary axis title to Rotate Text Down.

    f. Change the primary axis scale to range from **650** to **950** in intervals of **50**. Change the scale of the secondary axis to range from **2.2** to **3.0** in steps of **0.1** units.

    g. Change the fill color of the chart area to light blue and the plot area to white.

    h. Add primary major vertical gridlines to the chart.

15. Insert column sparklines in the range G21:G27 of the Market Summary worksheet based on the data in the range C5:N11 of the Michigan Grapes worksheet to show whether the number of wineries growing their own grapes has increased over the past 12 years.

16. Set the axis of the sparklines so that the column heights range from **0** to a maximum of **26** for each sparkline. Ungroup the sparklines and set the color of each to match the color of the corresponding grape in the pie chart.

17. Because the Levitts plan to grow their own grapes rather than purchasing them from out-of-state vendors, they are interested in knowing how many wineries in Michigan also grow their own grapes. The results of their survey are shown in the range B20:C22 in the Market Summary worksheet. Add data bars to the values in the range C20:C22 using the blue gradient fill. Define a rule that sets the maximum length of the data bars in those cells to a value of **100**.

18. Insert the **Watermark.png** graphic file located in the Excel4 ▶ Review folder as a washed-out watermark in the center section of the header of the Market Summary worksheet.

19. Save the workbook, and then close it.

Case Problem 1

Data File needed for this Case Problem: Bertrand.xlsx

Bertrand Family Budget   Andrew and Maria Bertrand of Santa Fe, New Mexico, are hoping to purchase their first home and they are using Excel to help manage their family budget. The couple needs to estimate the monthly payments required for a $275,000 mortgage. They want to track their income and expenses using tables, charts, data bars, and sparklines. You will help them do all of these tasks. Complete the following:

1. Open the **Bertrand** workbook located in the Excel4 ▶ Case1 folder included with your Data Files, and then save the workbook as **Bertrand Budget** in the location specified by your instructor.

2. In the Documentation sheet, enter your name in cell B3 and the date in cell B4.

3. In the Budget worksheet, in the range O4:O6, enter the parameters of a **$275,000** loan that is repaid at an annual interest rate of **4.35** percent over **30** years.

4. In the range O8:O9, calculate the total number of months to repay the loan and the interest rate per month.

5. In cell O11, use the PMT function to calculate the monthly payment. Multiply the PMT function by −1 so that the result appears as a positive currency value rather than a negative value.

6. In the range D25:O25, enter the value of the monthly mortgage payment by creating an absolute reference to the value in cell O11.

7. In the range D18:O18, calculate the total income per month. In the range D27:O27, calculate the total expenses incurred each month. In the range D28:O28, calculate the couple's net income (total income minus total expenses) each month.

8. In the range C4:C11, calculate the average monthly value of each expense category.

9. Add green gradient data bars to the values in the range C4:C11. Set the maximum length of the data bars to a value of **2500**.

✦ **Explore** 10. Insert line sparklines in the range D4:D11 using the expense values in the range D19:O26. On the SPARKLINE TOOLS DESIGN tab, in the Show group, click the High Point check box to mark the high point of each sparkline.

11. Create a clustered column chart of the income, expenses, and net income for each month of the year based on the data in the nonadjacent range D15:O15;D18:O18;D27:O28. Place the chart within the range E2:K13.

12. Format the clustered column chart by making the following changes:

   a. Format the chart with the Style 8 chart style.

   b. Change the chart title to **Income and Expenses** and format it in a Calibri, non-bold 12-point font.

   c. Change the vertical scale of the chart to range from **−1000** to **6500** in steps of **1000**.

   d. Change the series overlap of the columns to **0%** and the gap width to **200%**.

13. Save the workbook.

14. Perform a what-if analysis by changing the length of the loan from 30 years to **15** years. Determine the monthly payments under this new mortgage plan, and then analyze its impact on the couple's projected income and expenses.

15. Save the workbook as **Bertrand Budget 2**, and then close it.

Case Problem 2

APPLY

Data File needed for this Case Problem: PetroChart.xlsx

PetroChart Reports   William Rawlings runs a blog called *PetroChart Reports* that deals with the energy market with special emphasis on crude oil production and consumption. William likes to augment his writing with informative charts and graphics. He has an Excel workbook with some historic data on the crude oil market. He has asked you to create charts from that data that he can use in an article that reviews the history of oil production and consumption, and their impact on the size of the proven world oil reserves. Complete the following:

1. Open the **PetroChart** workbook located in the Excel4 ▶ Case2 folder included with your Data Files, and then save the workbook as **PetroChart Reports**.

2. In the Documentation sheet, enter your name in cell B3 and the date in cell B4.

3. In the World Oil Production worksheet, create a line chart of world oil production from 1980 to 2010 using the data from the range A6:G37. Move the chart to the Summary worksheet covering the range B4:H19.

4. Format the chart with the Style 9 chart style, and then change the chart title to **Oil Production Historic Trends**.

5. Change the line color for the North America data series to white, which is easier to read against the black backdrop.

✛ **Explore** 6. Revise the vertical axis scale so that the display unit is expressed in terms of thousands (most oil production reports are quoted in terms of thousands of barrels per day). Change the text of the display unit from Thousands to **Thousands of Barrels per Day**.

7. In the World Oil Production worksheet, create a pie chart that displays the relative size of the oil production values for different regions in 2010 based on the data in the nonadjacent range B6:G6;B37:G37. Move the pie chart to the Summary worksheet covering the range J4:P19.

8. Make the following changes to the pie chart:

   a. Format the chart with the Style 7 chart style.

   b. Change the chart title to **2010 Oil Production** and reduce its font size to 14 points.

   c. Move the chart legend to the left edge of the chart area.

   d. Add data labels outside of the pie slices showing the percentage associated with each region.

   e. Change the color of the pie slice for the North America region to white.

9. In the World Oil Consumption worksheet, create a line chart that shows how oil consumption changed from 1980 to 2010 based on the data in the range A6:G37. Move the chart to the Summary worksheet covering the range B21:H36.

10. Change the chart title to **Oil Consumption Historic Trends**.

✛ **Explore** 11. Copy the Oil Production Historic Trends line chart. Use Paste Special to paste the format of that chart into the Oil Consumption Historic Trends line chart.

12. In the World Oil Consumption worksheet, create a pie chart showing the 2010 regional breakdown of oil consumption based on the data in the range B6:G6;B37:G37. Move the chart to the Summary worksheet covering the range J21:P36.

✛ **Explore** 13. Change the chart title to **2010 Oil Consumption**. Use Paste Special to copy the 2010 Oil Production pie chart and paste its format into the 2010 Oil Consumption pie chart.

14. There was a fear that with increased oil production and consumption from 1980 to 2010, there would be decreasing amounts of proven reserves. Was this the case? In the Proven Reserves worksheet, create a combination chart based on the data in the range A5:D36. Display the Oil Production and Oil Consumption data series as line charts on the primary axis. Display the Proven Reserves data series as an area chart on the secondary axis. Move the chart to the Summary worksheet covering the range E38:M53.

15. Make the following changes to the combination chart:

   a. Format the chart with the Style 6 chart style.

   b. Change the chart title to **Historic Trends in Proven Oil Reserves**; reduce the font size to 12 points.

   c. Change the primary axis scale to range from **50,000** to **90,000** in steps of **5,000**.

   d. Change the line color of the Oil Production data series to white.

16. Save the workbook, and then close it.

Case Problem 3

Data Files needed for this Case Problem: Frame.xlsx, Confidential.png

CHALLENGE

Frame Financial   Jeri Carbone is the owner of Frame Financial, a small financial consulting firm in Marion, Iowa. Among her many tasks is to maintain Excel workbooks with information on companies and their stock market activity. One of her workbooks contains information on Harriman Scientific, a company traded on the stock exchange. She wants you to complete the workbook by adding charts that describe the company's financial status and stock charts to display recent values of the company's stock. The stock chart should display the stock's daily opening, high, low, and closing values, and the number of shares traded for each day of the past few weeks. The volume of shares traded should be expressed in terms of millions of shares. Complete the following:

1. Open the **Frame** workbook located in the Excel4 ▶ Case3 folder included with your Data Files, and then save the workbook as **Frame Financial** in the location specified by your instructor.

2. In the Documentation sheet, enter your name in cell B3 and the date in cell B4.

3. Insert the **Confidential.png** graphics file located in the Excel4 ► Case3 folder as a washed-out watermark in the center section of the header of the Documentation worksheet.

4. In the Overview worksheet, create a 3-D pie chart describing the company's shareholders based on the data source values in the range K4:L6.

5. Remove the chart title and chart legend, and then resize the chart so that it is contained within the range M3:O7.

6. Change the fill colors of the ranges K4:L4, K5:L5, and K6:L6 to match their corresponding pie slice colors. Change the font color in those ranges to white.

7. Add pink gradient-colored data bars to the values in the range L10:O14. Edit the data bar rules so that the maximum data bar length corresponds to a value of **15,000**, and the bar direction goes from right to left.

8. In the Income Statement worksheet, create a 3-D clustered column chart of the company's net revenue and operating expenses using the data values in the nonadjacent range B4:F4;B6:F6;B12:F12. Move the chart to the Overview worksheet.

⊕ **Explore** 9. On the CHART TOOLS FORMAT tab, use the Size group to set the height of the chart to 2.44" and the width to 3.51". Move the chart so that its upper-left corner is aligned with the upper-left corner of cell B17.

10. Format the chart with the Style 11 chart style, change the chart title to **Revenue and Expenses**, and then reduce the font size of the chart title to 11 points.

11. In the Balance Sheet worksheet, create a 3-D clustered column chart of the company's assets and liabilities using the data in the range B4:F4;B18:F18;B26:F26. Move the chart to the Overview worksheet. Set its size to 2.44" high by 3.51" wide and place the chart so that it is directly to the right of the Revenue and Expenses chart.

⊕ **Explore** 12. Change the chart title to **Assets and Liabilities**. Copy and paste the format used with the Revenue and Expenses chart into this chart.

13. In the Cash Flow Statement worksheet, create a 2-D line chart of the data in the range C4:F4;C28:F28. Move the chart to the Overview worksheet. Resize the chart to 2.44" high by 3.51" wide and place the chart directly to the right of the Assets and Liabilities chart.

14. In the line chart, apply the Style 15 chart style, change the chart title to **Net Cash Flow**, and then reduce the font size of the chart title to 11 points.

15. In the Income Statement, Balance Sheet, and Cash Flow Statement worksheets, add line sparklines in the Trend column based on the financial values for 2012 through 2015.

⊕ **Explore** 16. In the Stock Values worksheet, select the range A4:F34, and then insert a Volume-Open-High-Low-Close stock chart.

⊕ **Explore** 17. Move the chart to a new chart sheet named **Stock History**.

18. Make the following changes to the stock chart:

   a. Change the chart title to **Recent Stock History** and increase the font size to 24 points.

   b. Set the font size of the horizontal and vertical axes to 12 points.

   c. Add Axis titles to the chart. Set the primary vertical axis title to **Volume of Shares Traded**, the secondary vertical axis title to **Stock Value**, and the horizontal axis title to **Date**.

   d. Set the font size of the axis titles to 16 points and rotate the text of the secondary axis title down.

   e. Remove the chart legend.

   f. Change the scale of the primary vertical axis to range from **200,000** to **2,000,000**, and then change the display unit of the primary vertical axis to Thousands.

   g. Change the scale of the secondary vertical axis to range from **10** to **35**.

   h. Add primary major horizontal and vertical gridlines, and remove any secondary gridlines.

   i. Set the gap width of the columns in the stock chart to **20%**.

19. Save the workbook, and then close it.

TROUBLESHOOT

Case Problem 4

Data File needed for this Case Problem: Mortgage.xlsx

The Mortgage White Paper Kyle Lewis of Rockford, Illinois, runs a newsletter and blog called *The Mortgage White Paper* containing valuable financial information for investors, entrepreneurs, and homeowners. Kyle's emphasis is on tracking the world of home mortgages and home equity loans. Kyle's assistant has been creating an Excel workbook with an updated listing of the 15-year and 30-year interest rates on home loans. Now, his assistant reports that the formulas and charts in the workbook aren't working correctly. Kyle has asked you to fix the problems and finish the workbook. Complete the following:

1. Open the **Mortgage** workbook located in the Excel4 ▶ Case4 folder included with your Data Files, and then save the workbook as **Mortgage Report**.

2. In the Documentation sheet, enter your name in cell B3 and the date in cell B4.

3. In the Mortgage Calculator worksheet, calculate the monthly payments required to repay loans of different amounts, which are listed in the range A9:A24. The annual interest rate and length of the loan in years are provided in the range B5:C6 for 15-year and 30-year fixed loans.

⚙ **Troubleshoot** 4. The formulas used to calculate the monthly payments are displaying error values. Kyle is sure that the value in cell B9 is correct, but something happened when the formula was copied to the range B9:C24. Make the necessary changes so that the formula results are shown instead of the error values.

⚙ **Troubleshoot** 5. The line chart that displays the monthly payments for the 15-year and 30-year fixed rate loans is showing the loan amounts plotted as a third data series rather than as category values. Find the problem and fix it.

6. Format the line chart with the chart style and design you think is most appropriate for the data. Make sure the finished chart is easy to read and interpret.

⚙ **Troubleshoot** 7. In the Mortgage Trends worksheet, the data bars that were added to the Mortgage Application Index values in the range D7:D56 all have the same length. Fix the data bars so that reasonable bar lengths are displayed in the cells.

8. Create a combination chart that displays the 15-year and 30-year fixed rates in a line chart on the primary axis, and the Mortgage Application Index in an area chart on the secondary axis. Move and resize the chart to cover the range F6:M22.

9. Make the following changes to the chart:

   a. Format the chart with the Style 1 chart style.

   b. Change the chart title to **Interest Rates vs. Mortgage Applications** and reduce the font size of the title text to 14 points.

   c. Move the legend to the bottom of the chart area.

   d. Add the axis title **Interest Rate** to the primary vertical axis, and then add the axis title **Application Index** to the secondary vertical axis.

   e. Rotate the text of the secondary vertical axis title down.

   f. Change the scale of the primary vertical axis to range from 2 percent to 4.5 percent in increments of 0.5 percent, and then change the scale of the secondary vertical axis to range from 500 to 1000 in increments of 50.

   g. Add primary major vertical gridlines to the plot area.

   h. Set the fill color of the plot area to white and the fill color of the chart area to Brown, Accent 3, Lighter 80%.

10. Save the workbook.

11. Return to the Mortgage Calculator worksheet. One of Kyle's clients wants to take out a $200,000 mortgage but can afford only an $850 monthly payment. Use Goal Seek to determine how low the 30-year fixed rate needs to be to meet that goal.

12. Save the workbook as **Mortgage Report 2**, and then close it.

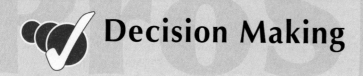

Decision Making

Creating a Budget Worksheet to Make Financial Decisions

Decision making is the process of choosing between alternative courses of action, usually in response to a problem that needs to be solved. Having an understanding of decision-making processes will lead to better decisions and greater confidence in carrying out those decisions. This is especially important when making financial decisions.

Gather Relevant Information

Begin by collecting data and information related to the decision you need to make. This information can include data expressed as currency or numbers, as well as data that cannot be measured numerically. For example, when creating a budget, numerical data includes your income and expenses, current savings, future savings and purchases, and so on. Other data might include the amount of savings you need in order to feel comfortable before making a large purchase, such as buying a car or paying tuition.

Evaluate the Gathered Information and Develop Alternatives

Evaluate the data you collected and determine possible alternatives. Excel workbooks are well suited to evaluating numerical data. You can also use workbooks to evaluate potential outcomes based on other data by assigning numerical weights to them. For example, you can enter your monthly income and fixed expenses into a worksheet along with variable expenses to determine your cash flow. You can then consider this information along with your current savings to determine how much money to contribute to savings or earmark for a purchase. Based on these results, you can develop alternatives for how to distribute your available money among variable expenses (such as entertainment), savings, and a large purchase.

Select the Best Alternative

Carefully evaluate the alternatives you developed based on your analysis. Before making a decision, be sure to take into account all factors. Consider such questions as:

- Does this alternative make sense for the long term? For example, does this budget allow you to achieve all your financial goals?
- Can you realistically carry out this alternative? For example, does this budget provide enough for necessities such as food and housing as well as for luxuries such as entertainment?
- Will this alternative be acceptable even if its outcome is not perfect or some unconsidered factors emerge? For example, will this budget cover unforeseen expenses such as car repairs or an unexpected trip?
- How comfortable are you with this decision? For example, does this budget relieve or add stress about managing your finances?

After analyzing all the factors, one alternative should begin to emerge as the best alternative. If it doesn't, you might need to develop additional alternatives.

Prepare an Action Plan

After making a decision, you need to plan how to implement that decision. Consider what steps you need to take to achieve the final outcome. For example, do you need to open a bank account or change services to reduce expenses (such as switching to a less expensive cell phone plan)? Determine a reasonable time table. When do you want to start? How long will each task take? What tasks must be completed before others start? Can tasks be performed at the same time? Develop milestones to track the success of your plan. For example, one milestone might be to increase your savings by 10 percent in three months. Finally, identify what resources you need to be successful. For example, do you need to talk to a financial advisor at your bank?

Take Action and Monitor the Results

After you develop the action plan, the actual plan begins. For example, you can open bank accounts, change telephone services, and so forth as outlined in your action plan. Be sure to check off completed tasks and assess how well those actions produce the desired outcome. For example, is the budget achieving the financial goals you set? If so, then continue to follow the established plan. If not, you may need to modify the action plan or reevaluate your decision.

PROSKILLS

Develop a Budget Worksheet

Excel is valuable to a wide audience of users: from accountants of Fortune 500 companies to homeowners managing their budgets. An Excel workbook can be a complex document, recording data from thousands of financial transactions, or it can track a few monthly household expenses. Anyone who has to balance a budget, track expenses, or project future income can use the financial tools in Excel to help them make good financial decisions about their financing and future expenditures.

In this exercise, you will use Excel to create a sample budget workbook that will contain information of your choice, using the Excel skills and features presented in Tutorials 1 through 4. Use the following steps as a guide to completing your workbook.

Note: Please be sure *not* to include any personal information of a sensitive nature in any workbooks you create to be submitted to your instructor for this exercise. Later, you can update the workbooks with such information for your personal use.

1. Gather the data related to your monthly cash inflows and outflows. For example, how much do you take home in your paychecks each month? What other sources of income do you have? What expenses do you have—rent, utilities, gas, insurance, groceries, entertainment, car payments, and so on?

2. Create a new workbook for the sample financial data. Use the first worksheet as a documentation sheet that includes your name, the date on which you start creating the workbook, and a brief description of the workbook's purpose.

3. Plan the structure of the second worksheet, which will contain the budget. Include a section to enter values that remain consistent from month to month, such as monthly income and expenses. As you develop the budget worksheet, reference these cells in formulas that require those values. Later, you can update any of these values and see the changes immediately reflected throughout the budget.

4. In the budget worksheet, enter realistic monthly earnings for each month of the year. Use formulas to calculate the total earnings each month, the average monthly earnings, and the total earnings for the entire year.

5. In the budget worksheet, enter realistic personal expenses for each month. Divide the expenses into at least three categories, providing subtotals for each category and a grand total of all the monthly expenses. Calculate the average monthly expenses and total expenses for the year.

6. Calculate the monthly net cash flow (the value of total income minus total expenses).

7. Use the cash flow values to track the savings throughout the year. Use a realistic amount for savings at the beginning of the year. Use the monthly net cash flow values to add or subtract from this value. Project the end-of-year balance in the savings account under your proposed budget.

8. Format the worksheet's contents using appropriate text and number formats. Add colors and borders to make the content easier to read and interpret. Use cell styles and themes to provide your worksheet with a uniform appearance.

9. Use conditional formatting to automatically highlight negative net cash flow months.

10. Insert a pie chart that compares the monthly expenses for the categories.

11. Insert a column chart that charts all of the monthly expenses regardless of the category.

12. Insert a line chart or sparkline that shows the change in the savings balance throughout the 12 months of the year.

13. Insert new rows at the top of the worksheet and enter titles that describe the worksheet's contents.

14. Examine your assumptions. How likely are certain events to occur? Perform several what-if analyses on your budget, providing the impact of (a) reducing income with expenses remaining constant; (b) increasing expenses with income remaining constant; (c) reducing income and expenses; and (d) increasing income and expenses. Discuss the different scenarios you explored. How much cushion does your projected income give you if expenses increase? What are some things you can do in your budget to accommodate this scenario?

15. Think of a major purchase you might want to make—for example, a car or a house. Determine the amount of the purchase and the current annual interest rate charged by your local bank. Provide a reasonable length of time to repay the loan, such as five years for a car loan or 20 to 30 years for a home loan. Use the PMT function to determine how much you would have to spend each month on the payments for your purchase. You can do these calculations in a separate worksheet.

16. Add the loan information to your monthly budget and evaluate the purchase of this item on your budget. Is it affordable? Examine other possible loans you might pursue and evaluate their impact on your budget. Come up with the most realistic way of paying off the loan while still maintaining a reasonable monthly cash flow and a cushion against unexpected expenses. If the payment exceeds your budget, reduce the estimated price of the item you're thinking of purchasing until you determine the monthly payment you can afford under the conditions of the loan.

17. After settling on a budget and the terms of a loan that you can afford, develop an action plan for putting your budget into place. What are some potential pitfalls that will prohibit you from following through on your proposed budget? How can you increase the likelihood that you will follow the budget? Be specific, and write down a list of goals and benchmarks that you'll use to monitor your progress in following your financial plan.

18. With the worksheet set up and your budget in place, you can take action and monitor your results. You will want to update your worksheet each month as income or expense items change to be sure you remain on track to meet your goals. You will also want to confirm that you made a good decision. If not, evaluate your budget and determine what new action you need to take to get yourself back on track.

19. Format the worksheets for your printer. Include headers and footers that display the workbook filename, the workbook's author, and the date on which the report is printed. If the report extends across several pages, repeat appropriate print titles on all of the pages, and include page numbers and the total number of pages on every printed page.

20. Save and close the workbook.

GLOSSARY/INDEX

TASK REFERENCE

TASK	PAGE #	RECOMMENDED METHOD
Absolute reference, create	EX 154	Type a $ before both the row and column references
Action, undo or redo	EX 19	Click ↺ or ↻ on the Quick Access Toolbar
AutoSum feature, enter function with	EX 37	Click a cell, click Σ AutoSum ▾ in the Editing group on the HOME tab, click a function, verify the range, press Enter
Border, add to cells	EX 50	Select a range, click ▦ ▾ in the Font group on the HOME tab, click a border
Cell, change fill color	EX 76	Click ⬥ ▾ in the Font group on the HOME tab, click a color
Cell, clear contents of	EX 58	Select a cell, press Delete
Cell, delete	EX 46	Select a cell, range, column, or row; click Delete button in the Cells group on the HOME tab
Cell, edit	EX 19	Double-click a cell, enter changes
Cell, go to	EX 10	Click Find & Select button in the Editing group on the HOME tab, click Go To
Cell contents, align within a cell	EX 87	Click ≡, ≡, or ≡ in the Alignment group on the HOME tab
Cell contents, change indent of	EX 88	Click ▤ or ▤ in the Alignment group on the HOME tab
Cell contents, rotate	EX 91	Click ⬧ ▾ in the Alignment group on the HOME tab, click angle
Cells, merge and center	EX 90	Select adjacent cells, click ▦ in the Alignment group on the HOME tab
Chart, choose style	EX 204	Select the chart, click ✎, select a chart style
Chart, create	EX 197	See Reference box: Creating a Chart
Chart, resize	EX 202	Select the chart, drag the sizing handle
Chart element, format	EX 205	Double-click the chart element, make changes in the Format pane
Chart type, change	EX 214	Select the chart, click the Change Chart Type button in the Type group on the CHART TOOLS DESIGN tab, click a new chart type
Column, change width	EX 25	Drag the right border of the column heading left or right
Column, select	EX 26	Click the column heading
Compressed folder, extract all files and folders from	FM 27	Click the compressed folder, click the Compressed Folder Tools Extract tab, click the Extract all button
Compressed folder, open	FM 27	Double-click the compressed folder
Conditional format, apply	EX 108	See Reference box: Highlighting a Cell with a Conditional Format
Data bars, create	EX 242	See Reference Box: Creating Data Bars
Date, enter into a cell	EX 23	Click a cell, type the date, press Enter or Tab
Date, insert the current	EX 167	Enter TODAY() or NOW() function in cell
Documents library, open	FM 10	In File Explorer, click ▷ next to Libraries, click ▷ next to Documents
Excel, start	EX 4	Click the Excel 2013 title on the Start screen
File Explorer, open	FM 10	Click 🗀 on the taskbar
File Explorer, return to a previous location	FM 14	Click ⬅

TASK	PAGE #	RECOMMENDED METHOD
File list, sort	FM 14	Click the column heading button
File, copy	FM 24	Right-click the file, click Copy, right-click destination, click Paste
File, delete	FM 25	Right-click the file, click Delete
File, move	FM 21	Drag the file to the folder
File, open from File Explorer	FM 15	Right-click the file, point to Open with, click an application
File, rename	FM 26	Right-click the file, click Rename, type the new filename, press Enter
File, save with new name in WordPad	FM 18	Click the File tab, click Save as, enter the filename, click Save
Files and folders, compress	FM 27	Select the files to compress, click the Share tab, click the Zip button in the Send group
Files, select multiple	FM 24	Press and hold the Ctrl key and click the files
Files, view in Large Icons view	FM 13	Click the View tab, click in the Layout group
Fill handle, use	EX 162	See Reference box: Copying Formulas and Formats with AutoFill
Find and replace, text or format	EX 104	Click Find & Select in the Editing group on the HOME tab, click Replace
Flash Fill, apply	EX 49	Type a few entries in a column to establish a pattern, Flash Fill adds the remaining entries
Folder, create	FM 19	Click the New folder button in the New group on the Home tab
Font, change color	EX 73	Click in the Font group on the HOME tab, click a color
Font, change size	EX 71	Click the Font Size arrow in the Font group on the HOME tab, click a point size
Font, change style	EX 71	Click B, I, or U in the Font group on the HOME tab
Font, change typeface	EX 71	Click the Font arrow in the Font group on the HOME tab, click a font
Formula, enter	EX 32	Click the cell, type = and then a formula, press Enter or Tab
Formulas, display in a worksheet	EX 56	Press Ctrl+`
Function, insert	EX 145	Click a function category in the Function Library group on the FORMULAS tab, click a function, enter arguments, click OK
Goal seek, perform	EX 180	See Reference box: Performing What-if Analysis and Goal Seek
Margins, set	EX 121	Click the Margins button in the Page Setup group on the PAGE LAYOUT tab, select a margin size
Mixed reference, create	EX 154	Type $ before either the row or column reference
My Documents folder, open	FM 10	In File Explorer, click next to Libraries, click next to Documents, click My Documents
Number, enter as text	EX 21	Type ' and then type the number
Number format, apply	EX 82	Click $, %, ', or the Number Format arrow in the Number group on the HOME tab
Page break, insert or remove	EX 116	See Reference box: Inserting and Removing Page Breaks
Print area, set	EX 115	Select range, click the Print Area button in the Page Setup group on PAGE LAYOUT tab, click Set Print Area
Print titles, add	EX 117	Click the Print Titles button in the Page Setup group on the PAGE LAYOUT tab, click Rows to repeat at top, select a range, click OK
Range, select adjacent	EX 11	Click a cell, drag the pointer from the selected cell to the cell in the lower-right corner of the range

TASK	PAGE #	RECOMMENDED METHOD
Range, select nonadjacent	EX 12	Select a cell or an adjacent range, press the Ctrl key as you select additional cells or adjacent ranges
Relative reference, create	EX 150	Type the cell reference as it appears in the worksheet
Ribbon, expand in File Explorer	FM 13	Click ⌄
Row, change height	EX 29	Drag the bottom border of the row heading up or down
Row, select	EX 26	Click the row heading
Rows, repeat in printout	EX 118	Click the Print Titles button in the Page Setup group on the PAGE LAYOUT tab, click Rows to repeat at top, select range, click OK
Series, create with AutoFill	EX 162	Enter the first few entries in a series, drag the fill handle over the adjacent range
Sparklines, create	EX 239	*See Reference box: Creating and Editing Sparklines*
Text, enter into a cell	EX 18	Click cell, type entry, press Enter or Tab
Text, enter multiple lines in a cell	EX 28	Type the first line of the entry, press Alt+Enter, type the next line
Text, wrap within a cell	EX 28	Select the cell, click 🖼 in the Alignment group on the HOME tab
Theme, change for workbook	EX 107	Click the Themes button in the Themes group on the PAGE LAYOUT tab, click a theme
View, change in File Explorer	FM 12	*See Reference box: Changing the View in File Explorer*
Workbook, close	EX 13	Click the FILE tab, click Close
Workbook, create a new	EX 15	Click the FILE tab, click New
Workbook, open an existing	EX 4	Click the FILE tab, click Open, select the workbook file
Workbook, preview and print	EX 55	Click the FILE tab, click Print
Workbook, save	EX 17	Click 💾 on the Quick Access Toolbar
Worksheet, change orientation	EX 53	Click the Orientation button in the Page Setup group on the PAGE LAYOUT tab, click Landscape or Portrait
Worksheet, change view	EX 52	Click 🔲, 🔳, or 🔲 on the status bar
Worksheet, copy	EX 16	Hold down Ctrl and drag a sheet tab to a new location
Worksheet, delete	EX 17	Right-click a sheet tab, click Delete
Worksheet, insert	EX 16	Click ⊕
Worksheet, move	EX 16	Drag the sheet tab to a new location
Worksheet, rename	EX 16	Double-click the sheet tab, type a new name, press Enter
Worksheet, scale for printing	EX 54	Set the width and height in the Scale to Fit group on the PAGE LAYOUT tab
Worksheets, move between	EX 8	Click a sheet tab or click a tab scrolling button and then click a sheet tab